CIVIL WAR GOATS AND SCAPEGOATS

H. DONALD WINKLER

CUMBERLAND HOUSE
NASHVILLE, TENNESSEE

CIVIL WAR GOATS AND SCAPEGOATS
PUBLISHED BY CUMBERLAND HOUSE PUBLISHING INC.
431 Harding Industrial Drive
Nashville, Tennessee 37211

Cover design by Gore Studio Inc., Nashville, Tennessee

Library of Congress Cataloging-in-Publication Data

Winkler, H. Donald, 1932–
    Civil War goats and scapegoats / H. Donald Winkler.
        p.   cm.
    Includes bibliographical references and index.
    ISBN-13: 978-1-58182-631-9 (pbk. : alk. paper)
    ISBN-10: 1-58182-631-1 (pbk. : alk. paper)
    1. Generals—United States—Biography—Anecdotes. 2. Generals—Confederate States of America—Biography—Anecdotes. 3. Failure (Psychology)—Case studies. 4. Scapegoat—Case studies. 5. United States—History—Civil War, 1861–1865—Biography. 6. United States—History—Civil War, 1861–1865—Campaigns. 7. United States—History—Civil War, 1861–1865—Anecdotes. I. Title.
E467.W53 2008
973.7092'2—dc22
[B]   2007049219

Printed in the United States of America

1 2 3 4 5 6 7 8 9 10—10 09 08

To all veterans,
especially my brothers, Ralph and Dwight,
and in memory of
our great-great-grandfather,
Cpl. Robert Wallace
of the
Sixtieth Illinois Volunteer Infantry Regiment,
who was killed in action during
a skirmish at Smyrna, Georgia,
July 4, 1864

Soldiers are averse
to seeing their comrades killed
without compensating results,
and none realize more quickly than they
the blundering that often takes place
on the field of battle.

—*Union Gen. Philip H. Sheridan*

CONTENTS

ACKNOWLEDGMENTS

I AM indebted to numerous Civil War historians, living and deceased, whose books and articles have affected my thinking and inspired my writing, especially Victor Brooks, Edwin B. Coddington, Benjamin Franklin Cooling, William C. Davis, Douglas Southall Freeman, Gary W. Gallagher, Webb Garrison, James Lee McDonough, James M. McPherson, Mark Nesbitt, Edwin F. Roberts, James I. Robertson Jr., Richard A. Sauers, Stephen W. Sears, Edward J. Stackpole, Wiley Sword, Glenn Tucker, and T. Harry Williams. Of course, the final product is my own, and none of the above should be faulted for any shortcomings in the text.

Several individuals have contributed time, knowledge, or materials in their possession. Listed in alphabetical order, they are: Carol Garrison Bates, Atlanta; Jacquelyn Clark, American Studies Department, Skidmore College; James A. Morgan III, Ball's Bluff historian and author; Brenda Morgan, Pigeon Forge, Tennessee; and George E. Tabb Jr., park superintendent, Northern Virginia Regional Park Authority, Fairfax Station.

Special thanks go to Autumn Davis and Betty Webb of the Anna Porter Public Library in Gatlinburg, Tennessee. They provided countless books through the interlibrary loan program, including a number of difficult-to-find oldies but goodies.

My editor at Cumberland House, Ed Curtis, is one of the best in the publishing world. I am indebted to him not only for making this project a reality but also for making this book better than it otherwise would have been.

Last, but never least, I thank my wife, Azile, for her patience, support, and understanding during nine months of research and writing.

INTRODUCTION

Goats: *Persons notorious for colossal failures.*

Scapegoats: *Persons unfairly blamed for the failures of others.*

AT ONE time or another we've all been scapegoats or goats. As children and adults we have been blamed for things we did not do. Is there anything more insulting than to have someone point a finger at you and falsely say, "He did it!" Usually the one doing the pointing is guilty, but he or she seeks out a scapegoat on whom to pin the dirty deed. Such is life. And such was life in the Civil War. Generals who lost battles needed scapegoats to salvage their reputation and honor. Usually, when they failed to successfully stick the label on other officers, they ended up with a new label on their own heads—the label of "goat."

Identifying goats and scapegoats isn't as easy as it might seem. It requires considerable research and analysis. You can't just depend on the words of the accuser or the accused. Battles must be studied in detail, from strategies to execution. Still, it comes down to the eyes and mind of the beholder. Historians see things differently and often disagree. Some change their minds over time and transform goats into heroes and scapegoats into goats.

Confederate cavalry leader James Ewell Brown "Jeb" Stuart, for example, was once considered a goat by nearly all Gettysburg scholars for his alleged "joy ride" around the Union army. He's still very controversial, but recent research casts him in a new light. I devote a chapter to it.

Some generals were goats in one battle and heroes in others. Ulysses S. Grant made terrible mistakes at Shiloh and Cold Harbor but proved himself a great field commander in other battles. Robert E. Lee started off badly in West Virginia and committed a deadly error in ordering Pickett's Charge at Gettysburg, but no one questions his greatness as a general.

Judging generals is kind of like playing baseball. Babe Ruth struck out more times than he hit home runs, but nobody remembers the strikeouts. Thomas J. "Stonewall" Jackson, the greatest of Lee's lieutenants, disgraced himself by striking out five times during Lee's battles of the Seven Days (see chapter 4) but otherwise performed superbly.

Some generals, such as the Confederacy's Braxton Bragg, were goats in every major battle they fought, even when winning. Despised by subordinates and disliked by the army, Bragg remained in command throughout the war. He's a dominant character in this book.

Another Confederate general, John Bell Hood, was a superb combat leader of brigades and divisions but a disaster as commander of the Army of Tennessee. Tactics he applied with great skill at the head of a brigade were inappropriate at the corps and army levels, as will be seen in the chapter on the battles at Spring Hill, Franklin, and Nashville. He simply lacked the right stuff to lead a large force.

Many generals were skilled in the science of war but weak in the art of war—the ability to creatively apply principles to real situations in order to baffle and conquer the enemy. Lee was a master of doing so. Confederates Bragg, Hood, and Albert Sidney Johnston were not. The same could be said of George B. McClellan, Irvin McDowell, Ambrose E. Burnside, and John Pope, among others. That the Union survived these goats was something of a miracle. That Abraham Lincoln survived is equally amazing. After Burnside lost more than 12,600 men at Fredericksburg—the worst defeat of any American army up to that time—Lincoln was convinced that "the Almighty is against us" and "we are on the brink of destruction." He appeared broken, dispirited, and ghostlike. He replaced lots of goats before finding a lion.

Leo Tolstoy, in his novel *War and Peace*, made an observation that could be applied to the men who fought the American Civil War. He wrote:

A commander-in-chief is never dealing with the beginning of any event—the position from which we always contemplate it. The commander-in-chief is always in the midst of a series of shifting events and so he never can at any moment consider the whole import of an event that is occurring. Moment by moment the event is imperceptibly shaping itself, and at every moment of this continuous, uninterrupted shaping of events, the commander-in-chief is in the midst of a most complex play of intrigues, worries, contingencies, authorities, projects, counsels, threats, and deceptions, and is continually obliged to reply to innumerable questions addressed to him, which constantly conflict with one another.

Generals who met these challenges often became heroes.

In the early years of the war, scapegoating occurred frequently among Union generals who needed excuses for losing battles. It was also devilishly popular among the Radical Republicans in Congress who regarded all Republican generals as good and all Democratic generals as bad. They plotted against the latter, even to the point of trying to handicap them so they couldn't win. The chapter on their devious plotting describes their efforts to prevent McClellan from winning the war in his Peninsula campaign—even though he really didn't need their help for him to fail. But it's a little known story that should raise eyebrows.

Poor Charles P. Stone had great potential as a general, but he became caught in a political trap and was crucified and scapegoated because a political commander blundered into defeat and death. No Union general was more unfairly and maliciously maligned than was Stone. One chapter tells his story.

The politically motivated Committee on the Conduct of the War was sometimes the personification of evil. Mired deep in political mud, it destroyed reputations and interfered where it ought not to have trod.

Political generals were another problem. They usually were powerful politicians with little or no military experience. For them the war was an opportunity to fulfill dreams of glory and boost their political careers. For Lincoln their appointment was often a political necessity. He had to build and hold together a precarious wartime coalition, which meant appointing influential Democrats and Republicans from the key Border States and major metropolitan areas. Many of these political generals became battlefield goats, but a few were surprising successes.

Confederate president Jefferson Davis liked to appoint generals who were his buddies at West Point, even though they had little military experience. Episcopal Bishop Leonidas Polk is an example. He had no business wearing a military uniform at any rank, certainly not as a general. Prior to the Civil War his military career consisted of only six months of service after he was graduated from the U.S. Military Academy. He became a military goat not once but many times.

Strengthening the Confederate armies at the beginning of the war were many U.S. Army officers who joined the Southern cause. Among them were Robert E. Lee, Thomas J. Jackson, James Longstreet, Joseph E. Johnston, and Jeb Stuart. Other good officers came from Southern military colleges. Still others came out of nowhere. A Little Rock druggist from Ireland—Patrick R. Cleburne—became famous as the "Stonewall Jackson of the West." A onetime farm laborer who amassed great wealth as a plantation owner, but had no military experience, was one of the best cavalry raiders of the war. His name was Nathan Bedford Forrest. His secret for success was to "get thar fust with the mostest [men]."

This book examines in some detail the good, the bad, and the ugly among numerous politicians and generals in the Civil War. The chapters run chronologically in the eastern and western theaters of the war. Battles fought in the Trans-Mississippi theater (the area west of the Mississippi) are not included. While any chapter may be read apart from the others, I recommend reading them in their present order for better continuity.

For readers who are not familiar with Civil War military organizations, the following information may be helpful. The building blocks of an army, from bottom to top are:

company: led by a captain who commands up to a hundred privates and noncommissioned officers

battalion: five companies (five hundred men) led by a major

regiment: two battalions (ten companies, one thousand soldiers) commanded by a colonel

brigade: four regiments (four thousand soldiers) commanded by a colonel or a brigadier general

division: three brigades (twelve thousand soldiers) under a brigadier general or major general

corps: usually three divisions (thirty-six thousand soldiers) under a major general

army: three or more corps under a major general or general

Cavalry companies are called "troops." A cavalry regiment has twelve troops. Union cavalrymen were provided with horses by the government; Confederate cavalrymen had to bring their own. For much of the war, Southern cavalry were more effective because Southerners had ridden horses most of their lives, while Northerners had not.

Most of the sixteen Union armies constituted during the war bore the names of rivers. The Army of the Potomac and the Army of the Tennessee were among the most prominent of these. Nearly all of the twenty-three Confederate armies, such as the Army of Northern Virginia, were named for states or regions. Often confused with the North's Army of the Tennessee was the South's Army of Tennessee.

Generals, from the lowest to the highest, are:

For the Union: brigadier general (called brigadiers, one star), major general (two stars), and lieutenant general (three stars). For most of the war, only the first two ranks were used. In 1864 the rank of lieutenant general was reactivated and given to Ulysses S. Grant.

For the Confederacy: brigadier general, major general, lieutenant general, general. All wore the same insignia; it was impossible to determine their ranks by the appearance of their uniforms.

Other military terms worth noting are:

battery: a cluster of six cannon of the same caliber (Union); a cluster of four of the same kind (Confederate). Batteries were usually posted on the flanks or behind the infantry on higher areas of the battlefield.

bridgehead: an advanced position in enemy-held country

eastern theater: the battle area east of the Appalachians: Virginia, West Virginia, Maryland, Pennsylvania, the District of Columbia, and coastal North Carolina.

feint: a movement of troops to deceive the opponent as to the location or time of an actual offensive action.

infantry: soldiers trained, armed, and equipped to fight on foot.

reconnaissance: an attempt to gather information about an opponent's position, size, and movements. Cavalry normally scouted in advance of an army in regions where terrain made this feasible.

siege: a partial or complete isolation of a city, port, or fortress designed to compel its surrender.

siege guns: Heavy and cumbersome cannon, mortars, and rifles that were effective but difficult to maneuver from one position to another. These commonly included 12-, 18-, and 24-pounders and 8-inch howitzers.

western theater: the battle area west of the Appalachians to the Mississippi River, as well as the noncoastal areas of the Carolinas

Researching and writing this book has reinforced my belief in the old adage that war is hell and should always be a last resort in conflict resolution. More than 2.5 million men fought in the Civil War. Nearly half of them were casualties. Some 500,000 survived wounds and amputations that left many of them disabled and in pain for the rest of their lives. Another 620,000 died in battle or from disease. One wonders what contributions those 620,000 might have made in science, medicine, engineering, architecture, literature, and so on.

A Northern black woman, Frances Ellen Watkins Harper, born free but subjected to discrimination and injustice, gave speeches and wrote pointed poetry during the war. She sought to build up "true men and women" who would "make every gift, whether gold or talent, fortune or genius, subserve the cause of crushed humanity and carry out the greatest idea of the present age, the glorious idea of human brotherhood." It was an idea regrettably trumped by political considerations in the Civil War and in wars to come.

On Christmas Day 1862, after defeating the Federals at Fredericksburg, Robert E. Lee wrote to his wife, Mary: "What a cruel thing is war; to separate and destroy families and friends, and mar the purest joys and happiness God has granted us in this world; to fill our hearts with hatred instead of love for our neighbors, and to devastate the fair face of this beautiful world. I pray that, on this day, when only peace and goodwill are preached to mankind, better thoughts may fill the hearts of our enemies and turn them to peace." While well said, it would have been better said if his closing line had ended with "better thoughts may fill *all* hearts and turn them to peace." Such a message would be as relevant for the twenty-first century as it should have been for the nineteenth and twentieth.

Hopefully, we will learn from the past so that better thoughts may fill not only the hearts of our enemies but the hearts we ourselves control. Perhaps General Lee would agree if he were alive today.

—*H. Donald Winkler*

THE EASTERN THEATER

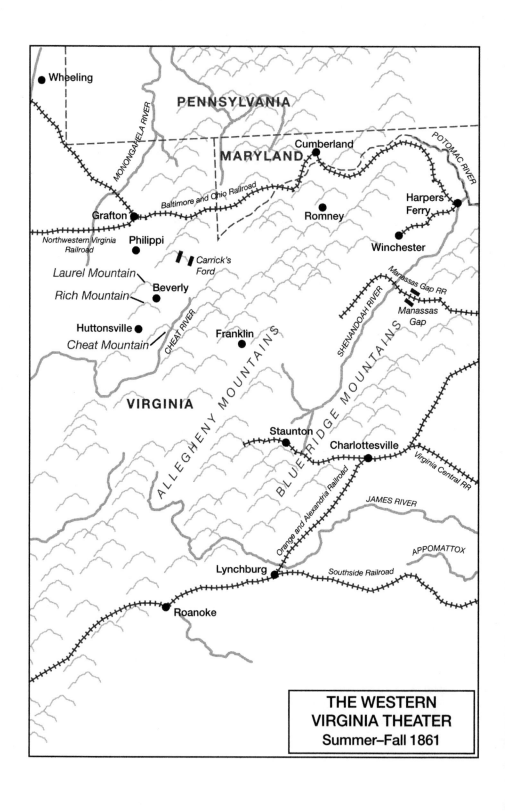

THE WESTERN
VIRGINIA THEATER
Summer–Fall 1861

1

LEE'S "UTTER FIASCO"

HE WAS THE VERY best soldier I ever saw in the field." That's how Lincoln's first general in chief, Winfield Scott, described Robert E. Lee's service in the Mexican War in the 1840s. Lee rose quickly in the peacetime army, became superintendent of West Point, and was so highly regarded that Lincoln offered him command of the Union armies. Loyal more to Virginia than to the Union, Lee turned down Lincoln and accepted Jefferson Davis's offer to become his personal military adviser.

On July 28, 1861, Lee left Richmond to perform his first field duty for the Confederacy. He was accompanied only by two staff officers, a cook, and a servant. Davis had ordered Lee to go to the far western counties of Virginia (known today as West Virginia) where small, separate commands were struggling to prevent a Federal advance. Two in particular were headed by former Virginia governors, Henry A. Wise and John B. Floyd. They were brigadier generals and intense rivals more interested in seeking personal military glory than in working together. Part of Lee's job was to suppress the rivalries and secure a united effort against the enemy.

A complicating factor was the makeup of the people who settled this mountainous region. Many of them were tenant farmers who had migrated from Northern states and were opposed to slavery. For decades they had lived peaceably with pro-slavery neighbors whose ancestors had moved westward from eastern Virginia. Then the war came. Their loyalties clashed. Even families became divided in their sympathies. Brother would fight brother.

The Richmond government had long neglected these western counties. That neglect combined with the widespread opposition to secession and slavery led to the formation of a new government independent of Richmond and loyal to the Union. They called themselves the state of Kanawha. Wheeling was the capitol and Francis H. Pierpont the governor. Lincoln encouraged them because he wanted the Union to maintain control of vital transportation links that crossed the region, especially the Baltimore and Ohio Railroad that brought men and supplies from the Midwest states to serve the Union cause.

The Confederate government was not willing to give up the region without a fight. Thus, they sent Col. George A. Porterfield to recruit and organize Rebel forces. He gathered only a few companies—about a thousand raw volunteers—and moved them into Grafton, a vital B&O Railroad junction. It was less than thirty miles from the Pennsylvania border and about sixty miles from Ohio. Porterfield's mission was to protect the Staunton-Parkersburg Turnpike. It provided access from the upper Shenandoah Valley of Virginia to the Ohio River. An engineering marvel, the road crossed high mountains and deep rivers and opened large sections of western Virginia to settlement and commerce.

The forthcoming mountain campaign would be fought for control of this turnpike and the access it provided to the B&O Railroad and the Chesapeake and Ohio Canal, which paralleled the Potomac River. A lifeline for communities along the river, the 184-mile-long canal carried coal and supplies from Shepherdstown through parts of Maryland to Washington, D.C. The Confederates hoped to cut these supply lines.

For both the Federals and the Confederates, the mountains of western Virginia were viewed as launching points for attacking each other and gaining control of the region. If the Confederates were successful, they would have an ideal jumping-off place for an advance that could divide the North in half. If the Federals retained control, they could threaten the South's valuable breadbasket—the Shenandoah Valley—and perhaps trap Gen. Joseph E. Johnston at Harpers Ferry. Maj. Gen. George B. McClellan, commander of the Federal Department of the Ohio, was charged with keeping these mountains in Union hands.

On June 3, 1861, Union Brig. Gen. Thomas A. Morris with thirty-four hundred troops occupied the heights above the village of Philippi, where Porterfield had positioned his troops near a two-lane covered bridge. Morris surprised the outnumbered Rebels, and they fled in a confused mass—a rout known as the "Philippi Races." Porterfield subsequently lost his command.

Lee, still in Richmond and commanding Virginia's forces, dispatched a few thousand reinforcements and sent them to an encampment at Beverly, twenty-five miles south of Philippi. They were under the command of Brig. Gen. Robert S. Garnett, a forty-one-year-old Virginian. He had served as commandant of cadets at West Point and, while a major in the U.S. Army, had designed California's great seal. Garnett's troops, though "in a most miserable condition as to arms, clothing, equipment, and discipline," fortified the mountain passes through which ran the main roads from the Shenandoah Valley to Wheeling and Parkersburg.

With Union forces massed north of Beverly, Garnett placed the bulk of his troops near them at Laurel Hill and set his headquarters there. A smaller force at Rich Mountain guarded the Stanton-Parkersburg Turnpike.

McClellan was determined to destroy Garnett's little army. Dividing his troops, the Union commander sent several thousand to make a feint against the Rebel force at Laurel Hill while brigades under Brig. Gen. William S.

After a Federal force routed outnumbered Rebels at Philippi and Rich Mountain in western Virginia in the summer of 1861, Jefferson Davis dispatched Robert E. Lee to the area to strengthen Confederate defenses.

When he began his western Virginia campaign, Robert E. Lee looked much like this photograph. Upon his return to Richmond, he had a beard. When a lady commented about it, Lee responded: "Why, you would not have a soldier in the field not to look rough, would you? There is little time there for shaving and personal adornment."

Rosecrans launched the main attack at Rich Mountain. "Old Rosy," as Rosecrans was called, was a West Pointer, a former philosophy and engineering professor there, and a successful businessman in coal mining and oil refining. On July 11 this dashing forty-two-year-old commander led his brigades over a narrow mountain track to flank the Confederate position. His surprise attack rolled up the Rebel flank, captured more than half of the defenders, and sent the remainder into a pell-mell retreat.

Garnett now feared being encircled. Falsely informed that the road to Beverly was blocked, he withdrew his main force of three thousand along the ridges and valleys that flowed into the Cheat River, hoping to cross it and head to his base. Union brigades pursued them over primitive muddy roads and on July 13 attacked Garnett's rear guard. Garnett was shot and killed—the first Civil War general killed in action.

Farther south on July 11 Ohioans under Brig. Gen. Jacob D. Cox, a Canadian-born Ohio lawyer, maneuvered Wise's brigade up the Kanawha River to White Sulphur Springs, a hundred miles southeast of Charleston. Wise's political enemy, Floyd, reinforced him, but the former governors spent so much time feuding that they failed to counterattack, and Cox occupied Charleston.

The campaign ended with three-quarters of western Virginia under Union control. McClellan took the credit; Rosecrans and Cox did the work.

The victories enabled Union supporters to proceed with efforts to separate the region from Virginia and form a new state. The Confederates would make a last-ditch effort to prevent that from happening. They would try to recapture western Virginia.

By August 1861 the Confederates had twenty thousand men in western Virginia, more men than did the Union. Although numerically stronger, the

Southerners were militarily weaker—untrained and poorly armed and a third of them on the sick list. Their major maladies were measles and mumps, which rapidly spread among the farm boys who had never been exposed to these diseases.

About five thousand served in the commands of Wise and Floyd. The other fifteen thousand were farther north—near Cheat Mountain—under the command of either Brig. Gen. William W. Loring, a professional soldier known as "Old Blizzards," or Brig. Gen. Henry R. Jackson, a scholarly former diplomat.

Meanwhile, in eastern Virginia, the Federals were routed at First Manassas, and Lincoln promoted McClellan and summoned him to Washington to command the Army of the Potomac. Rosecrans took over the Federal forces in western Virginia.

Both armies built fortifications guarding major roads—the Rebels at the top of Allegheny Mountain and above Traveller's Repose; the Federals at the summit of Cheat Mountain and at Elkwater, to the west of the summit. A large Union encampment at the western base of the mountain provided supplies. Cheat, a huge mass of a mountain, was more than fifty miles long and five miles wide. The Federal fort at Cheat Summit was 4,848 feet above sea level.

Such was the situation when Robert E. Lee arrived in the area. Besides seeking harmony in the ranks, he was to help reorganize Garnett's shattered forces, strengthen the Rebel positions, and recapture critical roads. Yet he was not in command; he was only an adviser. The difference was significant and would hamper his relationships with the generals in charge.

At Monterey, a little village thirty miles northwest of Stanton and ten miles east of the principal ridge of the Alleghenies, Lee called on Georgian Henry Jackson at his headquarters. Jackson was a Yale graduate, a judge, a poet, and former U.S. minister to Austria. Unusually modest for a general, he

Union Brig. Gens. Jacob D. Cox (pictured) and William S. Rosecrans secured three-quarters of western Virginia for the Union. Maj. Gen. George McClellan took the credit, however.

had urged Lee to come in person to western Virginia and suggested that a person of greater military experience than himself be placed in direct command.

Jackson's report to Lee was discouraging. Only the troops that had not participated in Garnett's campaign—two regiments—were in good condition, he reported. Garnett's survivors were in a pitiable plight, "without tents . . . and with but clothing on their backs." The horses of the artillery and cavalry were "jaded and galled." Morale was bad. And to make matters worse, there was an epidemic of measles. Soldiers who had escaped the malady were wet and dejected. Rain had fallen steadily for days. On the brighter side, reinforcements were expected from Staunton any day.

Most officers Lee met disappointed him. Everything had to be explained in detail to them, and then they took their time in following instructions. "It is so difficult," Lee wrote his wife, Mary, "to get our untrained people to comprehend and promptly execute the measures required for the occasion."

On the northern part of the front, where Lee then was, the terrain was divided, from east to west, into four principal mountain chains: the Alleghenies, Greenbrier Mountain, Cheat Mountain, and Rich Mountain, all of which were traversed by the Staunton-Parkersburg Turnpike. The strongest of the passes through which the road ran was on Cheat Mountain, where there was a long crossing at an elevation of thirty-five hundred feet—a crossing controlled by Union artillery on the summit. The Federals held Cheat and Rich mountains. The Confederates under Jackson held the pass over the Alleghenies. Greenbrier was also available to the Rebels, but only because the Federals didn't want it. They didn't need it as long as they held Cheat. The Union had by far the strongest positions.

Besides the turnpike, other roads of potential strategic significance meandered through the mountains. Control of them could lead to military advantages beyond western Virginia. For example, a route up the Kanawha Valley and New River would take the Federals to the Virginia and Tennessee Railroad, the only direct line of communication between these two states. Another good road ran south from the village of Huttonsville (near Cheat Summit) to a Confederate base at Huntersville. From there a difficult but passable road led over the Alleghenies to a point close to the Virginia Central Railroad and the Confederate supply base at Staunton. Jackson, who seemed more militarily savvy than his counterparts, recognized the importance of this little-used road and divided his small force to protect it. Jackson also had discovered another narrow, rugged road running north from Huntersville to the rear of Cheat Mountain. He had ordered troops at Huntersville to seize a position that commanded this route.

Three facts stood out. First, any advance of the Federals to the Virginia Central Railroad and/or the Virginia and Tennessee Railroad would probably result in a major Confederate disaster. Second, any advance of the Rebels past Cheat Mountain would enable them to continue to the B&O Railroad and sever one of the main railways linking the East to the West. Third, if the Rebels could advance down the Kanawha and reach the Ohio River, they could free the greater part of western Virginia from Federal control.

Lee's first concern was to keep the Federals from reaching the Virginia Central Railroad. That required strong fortifications in the mountains. Offensively, the critical position was the high ground dominating the road at the rear of Cheat Mountain. This was north of Huntersville. Strategically, if the troops Jackson had sent forward were well positioned, then a quick advance might turn Cheat Mountain before the Federals were aware of danger from that direction.

To be sure of his assumptions, Lee left Jackson's headquarters on the morning of August 3 and set out for Huntersville with a few companions. Rain was still falling, and the roads were bad. Damp gloom concealed the majestic scenery. At Huntersville, the gloom could not conceal a wretched and filthy town crowded with ten thousand sick, wet, and hungry Confederate soldiers.

The road coming from the north had its forks here. One branch was the important route over the Alleghenies toward the railroad and Staunton. The other ran southward to the valley of the Kanawha. Lee supported Jackson's decision to protect these roads.

At Huntersville, Lee's first and most important stop was at Loring's headquarters. Coordination and cooperation for the coming campaign were critical to its success. Whatever optimism Lee may have had when he entered "Old Blizzards" office, he lost it before he sat down. Loring did not want to see him. He resented Lee's being there. His reception was "icy" at best.

Only two weeks earlier Lee had given Loring discretionary orders in Richmond and had sent him forward. Now, before Loring had had time to prepare to execute his plans, here was Lee to see what those plans were. Loring felt no need for Lee's advice or supervision. Though he was eleven years younger than Lee, he had seen far more military service, and he had a distinguished record of gallantry in Mexico, Oregon, and New Mexico. He was jealous of Lee's advancement and jealous of Lee's authority to advise him. This petty jealousy would jeopardize the Confederate campaign in western Virginia.

Meanwhile, Col. William Gilham, whom Jackson had ordered to advance from Huntersville, had come to a ridge known as Valley Mountain, across which the Huttonsville–Huntersville Road passed at an elevation of 3,460 feet. Northward, the road descended into a valley to the rear of the Federal position in Cheat Mountain Pass. If Gilham had had a strong enough force and had moved quickly, he could have swept forward and trapped the Federals on Cheat Mountain. But he didn't, and the Federals soon discovered his presence. Sensing a possible Confederate advance, they fortified a position farther down the valley to prevent it.

Lee's best solution for removing the Federals from Cheat Mountain was for Loring to advance with all his troops and to do so immediately. But Loring wouldn't budge. He assured Lee he would do so eventually, after he had stocked the base at Huntersville with enough supplies for a long offensive. Lee had told him to plan only for a short offensive, but Loring chose to be cautious and independent-minded. He could have seized the key Federal positions with a brief advance. His existing personnel and supplies were more than adequate for the mission.

Lee, with his superior military rank, should have ordered the troops forward. But he refused to impose his will on Loring. Lee did not want a controversy. He preferred to try to pacify Loring and win his confidence. He even announced that Loring was "commanding the whole force of the Northwest Army." He sought to abate Loring's jealousy by magnifying his authority. So Lee and Loring passed up an opportunity the Federals carelessly presented to them. Both generals were equally negligent.

Lee's failure was a product of his excessive consideration for the feelings of others. From the slaveholding aristocracy he had not yet learned to command his peers or even his subordinates. He was also too deferential to politicians. Lee's biographer, Douglas Southall Freeman, from whom much of the information in this chapter is drawn, explained this weakness in Lee:

> All his life Lee had lived with gentle people, where kindly sentiments and consideration for the feelings of others were part of *noblesse oblige*. In that at-

mosphere he was expansive, cheerful, buoyant even, no matter what happened. . . . Now that he encountered surliness and jealousy, it repelled him, embarrassed him, and well-nigh bewildered him. Detesting a quarrel as undignified and unworthy of a gentleman, he showed himself willing, in this new state of affairs, to go to almost any length, within the bounds of honor, to avoid a clash. In others this might have been a virtue; in him it was a [definite] weakness, the first serious weakness he had ever displayed as a soldier. It was a weakness that was to be apparent more than once and had to be combated, deliberately or subconsciously. . . . From those days at Huntersville until [General] Longstreet was wounded in the Wilderness on May 6, 1864, there always was a question whether Lee, in any given situation, would conquer his inordinate amiability or would permit his campaigns to be marred or his battles to be lost by it. . . . Of Lee it became necessary to ask, for two years and more, whether his judgment as a soldier or his consideration as a gentleman dominated his acts.

While Loring waited for his wagon train of supplies, Lee rode to Valley Mountain, where Jackson's men were encamped.

Lee looked for an alternative to the plan Loring had scotched. He suspected that there had to be an obscure, unguarded trail to the rear of Cheat Mountain, and he was determined to find it. That required a cautious reconnoiter, and he chose to do it himself. Every morning he went out, in the endless rain, to search for a usable path.

By August 10, it had rained twenty consecutive days, and the roads were deep in mud. Supply wagons were scraping the roadbeds, and it was feared that the army could not be fed where it was. No more than two or three days of food were ever at hand. The measles epidemic was still spreading through the various commands along with intestinal ailments.

Despite these complications, Lee continued his reconnoitering, and Loring finally, but slowly, brought the rest of his troops to Valley Mountain. The Rebels then fulfilled one of Lee's objectives by closing the road leading to the Virginia Central Railroad and Staunton.

Rosecrans, McClellan's successor, placed Brig. Gen. Joseph J. Reynolds in direct command of the Union forces in the Cheat Mountain sector. Lee referred to Reynolds as "our old friend" in a letter to Mary. Reynolds had been an assistant professor of philosophy at West Point when Lee was superintendent there.

Lee was handicapped by the lack of information about the size and movements of Reynolds's force. Reynolds, on the other hand, was kept well informed about Confederate activities.

The bad weather became worse. Ice formed on the night of August 14–15, and the sickly, shivering Confederates hovered around large fires. "It rains here all the time, literally," Lee wrote his wife. "There has not been sunshine enough since my arrival to dry my clothes." The torrential rains and the search for a new line of advance held all operations at a standstill. Better days were ahead, but not very many of them.

Lee learned on August 31 that he was confirmed as a full general and that Davis approved of his conduct of operations and wished him to return to his former duties as soon as he felt he could leave western Virginia. Aware of Lee's promotion, Loring began to show him more respect. Loring raised no objections as Lee gradually took over the strategy of operations.

Then Lee found not one but two ways to get behind Cheat Mountain. The first he discovered himself. It was a route by which a courageous column could make its way along the western ridges of Cheat Mountain to a position two miles west of its crest. That point was directly on the road by which the enemy's force on top of the mountain was being supplied.

The second route was discovered by an anonymous civilian engineer. The man had set out from the Greenbrier River and, after days of scrambling through thickets and across ravines, had reached a point south of the summit, where the enemy had some trenches and a blockhouse. From this lofty position, the engineer believed that the Federals on the mountaintop could be routed. To get a second opinion, he had taken Col. Albert Rust of the Third Arkansas Infantry with him on a second scouting of the position. Rust agreed with the engineer's assessment. They reported their findings to Jackson, who sent them to Loring, who forwarded them to Lee.

Rust insisted that the enemy's flank was exposed and that a surprise attack from the height would surely carry Cheat Mountain and open the way to a general advance against the Federals. He spoke enthusiastically about the opportunity and asked Lee for the privilege of leading the assault on the crest. Lee, without giving sufficient thought to the request, approved it. It was a critical mistake.

Before quickly agreeing to such an attack, Lee should have weighed many considerations: the steep abysses, the absence of roads, the dense

Lee's worst mistake at Cheat Mountain was allowing Col. Albert Rust (pictured) to lead the assault. Rust, a former congressman, had never been in action. Although his forces outnumbered those of the Federals, he was tricked into believing otherwise and withdrew without firing a shot.

growth of almost impenetrable laurel in Rust's path, and the enemy's strength. Instead, he gave a quick "yes."

Lee assumed that Reynolds's force on Cheat Mountain numbered about two thousand and that his total force in the area at least equaled that of Loring and Jackson combined. The Confederates totaled about fifteen thousand, of whom half were sick.

Lee's available forces were separated by Cheat Mountain. They would have no way to communicate with each other. A surprise attack was possible on the crest and the western side of the crest, but every contingency had to be planned for, and the attack would have to be delivered simultaneously on the peak and from both sides of the mountain.

Rust had no military experience before 1861. He had never been in action. He was a politician, a former member of Congress. He knew nothing about reconnaissance. He was the wrong person to trust with the most crucial element of the operation. He could guide the troops there, but he had no business commanding them.

Nevertheless, Lee prepared a complicated plan for a convergence of five separate columns against two Union positions of unknown size. Two columns would focus on Cheat Mountain. Two others were to assail the Federals at nearby Elkwater. The fifth was to be ready to isolate the rear of either Federal position.

Rust was to secretly take two thousand men to the position he had selected. At the same time, Brig. Gen. S. R. Anderson was to move along the route Lee had reconnoitered, occupy the western crest, and block the road. Two other units, led by Brig. Gen. Daniel S. Donelson and Col. Jesse S. Burks, were to advance down either side of Tygart's River toward Elkwater. Jackson, on the eastern side, was to march up the Staunton-Parkersburg Turnpike when Rust had cleared it. William Gilham's men were to remain in reserve.

Rust was to initiate the action by opening fire on the flank of the Union line at Cheat Mountain. That would be the signal for all others to proceed. Jackson would advance, and Anderson would prevent reinforcements from reaching the fort on Cheat Mountain, supporting Jackson if necessary. The cavalry would cover the extreme left. Action was to commence as soon as Rust was in position at daylight on September 12.

Anderson's brigade, which had the most difficult journey to make, began its movement on September 10. With no road, they marched in single file through muddy fields and over steep ridges in weather unusually cold for that time of the year. "It was no uncommon thing," a surgeon wrote, "for a mule to slide twenty feet down a slope, and I could see strong men sink exhausted trying to get up the mountain side." Their all-day march continued until 10 p.m., halted by a driving rainstorm. The other Confederate forces went forward as scheduled, with Lee himself setting out on September 11.

By dawn on September 12, all columns were in their assigned positions, undetected and ready for action, though wet, hungry, and weary. It

Confederate Brig. Gen. John B. Floyd's division withdrew across the Gauley River forty-five miles east of what later became Charleston, West Virginia. The retreat, on September 10, 1861, followed an attack by Union Brig. Gen. William S. Rosecrans.

BATTLES AND LEADERS

was a remarkable feat for green troops led by several inexperienced officers. They waited, as planned, for the sound of a volley from the crest that would announce that Rust was storming the blockhouse and trenches. By 8 a.m. it was long past due. Lee wondered if Rust had gotten lost.

Meanwhile, Anderson's men had crossed Cheat Mountain Road, driven in the Federal pickets, and cut communication between the summit and the Huntersville-Huttonsville Road. Soon, every Union regiment in the valley would be aware of the Rebel movements. Rust's signal was urgently needed.

Instead, the silence was broken by random firing. But the noise came from the wrong direction. It wasn't from Cheat Mountain. Lee rode down the ridge to find the source. Just before he reached the main road from a wooded area, he heard horses in full gallop and watched as Federal cavalry dashed toward the firing. After shouts and bugle calls and more firing, the Union horsemen rode back the way they had come. They had run into Donelson's pickets and were scurrying back with news of the advance. When the Federals were out of sight, Lee went into Donelson's lines. To his disgust, he learned that impatient soldiers had fired their guns as a way to clean them quickly! Now the Federals were on the alert.

It was ten o'clock. Still, no word or sound from Rust. Lee's only viable option was to strike with the troops west of Cheat Mountain. He issued new orders to the generals and rode from regiment to regiment to urge colonels to get their men in hand. Nearly all of the officers balked. There were too many excuses, too little enthusiasm. Loring said he couldn't get into position without crossing the river, and it was too high for fording. Morale was horrible.

There would be no assault on Cheat Mountain. Lee's plan unraveled. The execution was an utter fiasco. He called off the operation. The day passed with no word from Rust. So did the next morning.

On September 16 Lee finally learned, through Loring, what had happened to Rust. His column had reached its position unobserved and had captured several Federal pickets. The pickets, being ingenious Yankees, told Rust there were about five thousand strongly fortified men on Cheat Mountain and that they had known of his approach and had telegraphed for reinforcements. All were lies, but Rust was suckered. He believed them and later said, "The enemy had four times my force." He waited, without firing a gun, and then withdrew after he had carelessly made the enemy aware of his presence. He actually faced only about three hundred

Federals outside the Union fortifications and only eighteen hundred at Cheat Summit—less than half the number in Rust's and Anderson's combined forces.

All Lee could do was order the columns back to Jackson's original encampment at Valley Head. "Well," said one Tennessean, "at the end of seven days' marching and starvation, we got back to Valley Mountain, the whole affair having proved a failure—in the opinion of our brigade, chiefly from the old fogyism and want of pluck among the Virginians. Never were men more sick of Virginia and Virginians than we are."

The Southern people had expected great things of Lee, but he had accomplished nothing. From Valley Mountain, Lee wrote to Virginia governor John Letcher on September 17. He made it plain that he was not responsible for the failure, but he refused to blame others or name any scapegoats:

> I had considered the subject well. With great effort the troops intended for the surprise had reached their destination having traversed twenty miles of steep, rugged mountain paths; and the last day a terrible storm, which lasted all night, and in which they had to stand drenched to the skin in cold rain. Still, their spirits were good. When morning broke, I could see the enemy's tents on Valley River, at the point on the Huttonsville Road just below me. It was a tempting sight. We waited for the attack on Cheat Mountain, which was to be the signal. Till 10 a.m., the men were cleaning their unserviceable arms. But the signal did not come. All chance for a surprise was gone. The provisions of the men had been destroyed the previous day by the storm. They had nothing to eat that morning, could not hold out another day, and were obliged to be withdrawn. The party sent to Cheat Mountain [from the] rear had also to be withdrawn. The attack to come off from the east side failed from the difficulties in the way; the opportunity was lost, and our plan discovered. It is a grievous disappointment to me, I assure you. But for the rainstorm, I have no doubt it would have succeeded. . . . It has been raining in these mountains for about six weeks. It is impossible to get along. It is that which has paralyzed all our efforts.

A few days later—on September 20—Lee struck his tent and ordered Loring and most of his troops to follow him south to the Kanawha Valley to reinforce the two political generals—Floyd and Wise. They had been squabbling for weeks over tactics and the strength and movements of the

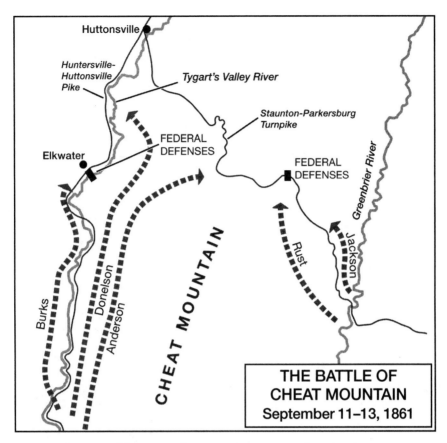

THE BATTLE OF
CHEAT MOUNTAIN
September 11–13, 1861

enemy. They would meet and agree on a course of action, but as soon as Wise returned to his command, Floyd would send word of a change in plans. Wise was totally frustrated with Floyd. Lee hoped he could motivate them to work together amicably and strike at Rosecrans.

At the time of Lee's arrival, they were arguing over which of them held the stronger position—Wise at Sewell Mountain or Floyd at Meadow Bluff. Lee looked at both positions and determined that Floyd was in no immediate danger. He withdrew part of Floyd's force to Wise's position and ordered Floyd to follow him. He refused. Lee was right, and Floyd was wrong. Scouts reported on September 23 that Rosecrans appeared to be preparing to attack Wise on Sewell Mountain.

There were skirmishes for several days but no major assault. A Confederate soldier recalled, "It was nothing but an Indian fight—Virginians behind trees fighting Ohioans behind trees."

During the days of skirmishing, a dispatch from Confederate secretary of war Judah Benjamin ordered Wise to relinquish his command to Floyd and report "with the least delay" to the adjutant general in Richmond. This ended the unseemly controversy between the two commanders.

When Loring's nine thousand troops showed up on September 29, the Confederates had more men than Rosecrans and were in a position to trap him. With floods threatening his supply lines on one side, and Loring and Floyd on the other, Rosecrans pulled back to a more defensible position.

For two weeks Lee considered his options. By October 7, he believed he could accomplish nothing by assuming the offensive against Rosecrans or Reynolds. Brig. Gen. William Starke, however, thought differently and reminded Lee, "Your reputation [is] suffering, the press [is] denouncing you, your own state [is] losing confidence in you, and the army needed a victory to add to its enthusiasm." Lee sadly replied, "I could not afford to sacrifice the lives of five or six hundred of my people to silence public clamor."

A Rebel detachment from Brig. Gen. John B. Floyd's command prepares to shell the camp of Brig. Gen. William S. Rosecrans. Floyd and Brig. Gen. William W. Loring were in a position to trap Rosecrans, but they failed to do so.

BATTLES AND LEADERS

His Kanawha campaign ended as ingloriously as had his efforts to attack Cheat Mountain. By the end of October, as the leaves lost their crimson and yellow shades and dropped to the ground, Lee's hair had turned from dark brown to completely gray, and his chin was sprouting its first beard. Recalled to Richmond, he left the day before Halloween, with no treats, a face disguised from its appearance three months earlier and a bearing transformed from hope to near despair.

Less than two years later—on June 20, 1863—the new state of West Virginia would enter the Union. West Virginia and the B&O Railroad—the Union's vital link to the West—were lost to the Confederacy and to the Old Dominion.

As for the battle of Cheat Mountain, while Lee placed the blame for his failure on the weather, clearly Loring and Rust were major goats in this campaign. Loring's jealousy and slowness to cooperate with Lee, as well as Rust's failure to launch the attack, were inexcusable. They had cost Lee (and the South) a possible victory. But Lee's own performance was equally bad. He should have ordered Loring forward and not have allowed him to procrastinate. Further, he should never have allowed Rust to lead the attack; he should have chosen a skilled military officer from those available to him.

The Richmond newspapers were among his harshest critics. The *Examiner* accused Lee of being "outwitted, outmaneuvered, and outgeneraled"; the *Dispatch* advised Lee that "in mountain warfare the learning of the books and of the strategists is of little value. . . . In a country where it is impossible to find enough level land to muster a company of militia, there is very little scope for ingeniously studied military evolutions or consummately arranged plans of campaign on paper."

Cynics began to mock him as "Granny Lee" and "Evacuating Lee." They claimed that his reputation had been based on his historic name and not on his ability as a field commander. At age fifty-four, Lee was only a "desk soldier," they asserted, adding that he wouldn't have much value on a battlefield.

E. A. Pollard wrote about the West Virginia operations in his *First Year of the War*. He contemptuously declared: "The most remarkable circumstance of this campaign was that it was conducted by a general who had never fought a battle, who had a pious horror of guerrillas, and whose extreme tenderness of blood induced him to depend exclusively upon the resources of strategy to essay the achievement of victory without the cost of life."

Lee had failed miserably, and he was justifiably written down as one of the disappointments of the war's first year. Here was a general who could rightfully cast blame on others, but he refused to do so because he did not want to stir up strife where unity was essential to the successful conduct of the war.

Jefferson Davis may have been the only person who didn't lose confidence in Lee. When Lee did not present any report on his western Virginia campaign, Davis pressed him for details. Lee was reluctant. He said he'd discuss them only if Davis promised that nothing would be said publicly in censure of those who had failed. Davis agreed, and Lee reviewed the campaign verbally, not in writing. Historian Douglas Southall Freeman noted, "The interview ended with the President as convinced as ever both of the high character and of the high ability of the man at whom the people already were sneering."

Very soon Lee would turn from deplorable to adorable. Of the notable generals who fought in western Virginia, Lee would be the one to achieve the greatest fame. He would become the South's greatest hero of the war.

2

CRIMINAL MINDS IN THE CAPITAL

CHARLES POMEROY STONE STOOD proudly as President Grover Cleveland dedicated the Statue of Liberty on October 28, 1886. Stone was the chief engineer in charge of constructing the base and pedestal and overseeing the statue's assembly. Now, as grand marshal of the dedication, he looked up at the symbol of freedom and democracy and then instinctively looked beyond, toward the narrows of New York Bay. There, in the military prison at Fort Lafayette, Stone had endured six months of solitary confinement twenty-four years earlier. He had been the innocent victim of vicious and near criminal conduct within the federal government—by a congressional committee, Secretary of War Edwin M. Stanton, and a cadre of conspiratorial subordinates. In 1886, all that was a far cry from Miss Liberty's raised torch welcoming those "yearning to breathe free."

The firestorm that engulfed Stone was accidentally ignited in another October, twenty-five years earlier, in the first year of the Civil War. He was then a thirty-seven-year-old brigadier general. The place was Ball's Bluff, standing above the Potomac on the Virginia side of the river thirty-five miles upriver from Washington, near Leesburg. The town was the anchor of the Confederate line on the upper Potomac. Nearby river crossings could enable a Rebel army to smash into Washington.

At the time, three months after the embarrassment at Bull Run, Maj. Gen. George B. McClellan wasn't ready to lead the Army of the Potomac in open combat at Leesburg or anywhere else. The troops weren't adequately trained, he said. So he had no intention of attacking Leesburg. But after he received word that the Confederate brigade in Leesburg was observed moving south, he instead planned a reconnaissance. He would investigate. Were they really evacuating or were they baiting him? If they were still in Leesburg, he'd try to nudge them into leaving.

He ordered Brig. Gen. George A. McCall to move his division from its recently established camp at Langley, Virginia, to Dranesville, Virginia, ten miles from Leesburg. McCall's mission was "to obtain topographical information of the country" and, hopefully, "to shake the enemy out of Leesburg." At the very least, McCall was to find out what the Rebels were planning. McClellan's objective was to take Leesburg without a fight.

The Rebel force at Leesburg was a twenty-eight-hundred-man brigade under the command of Col. Nathan "Shanks" Evans. When he learned that the Yankees had established a base at Langley, Virginia, within striking distance of Leesburg and with a division four times the size of his brigade, he became very concerned. On his own initiative he withdrew from Leesburg on October 16 and formed a new line of defense about eight miles to the south. When news of this development came to the attention of Evans's superior, Gen. P. G. T. Beauregard, he objected and ordered him back to Leesburg. Evans did so on the night of October 19.

McCall's forces arrived in Dranesville the same day, and he met with McClellan that night. McCall's scouts had seen Evans's movement back toward Leesburg, and McClellan suspected they were returning permanently. Being cautious, McClellan changed his mind about the reconnaissance. He ordered McCall to return to Langley the next morning, Sunday, October 20. McCall requested an extra day to finish mapping roads, and McClellan consented.

Evans's unauthorized withdrawal from Leesburg and McCall's need for an extra day to map the area were two links in a chain of peculiar circumstances that would lead to tragic consequences for Charles Stone. During the extra day McCall requested, McClellan devised another maneuver and sent the following message to Stone via his adjutant:

> General McCall occupied Dranesville yesterday, and is still there. Will send out heavy reconnaissances today in all directions from that point. The general desires that you keep a good lookout upon Leesburg, to see if this movement

has the effect to drive them away. Perhaps a slight demonstration on your part would have the effect to move them.

McClellan, however, neglected to tell Stone that McCall was taking his division back to Langley on October 21. Thus, Stone assumed that McCall could support him if necessary.

McClellan chose Stone because his division was already posted along the upper Potomac. It was the extreme right portion of the Union line guarding Washington.

Carrying out his assigned duties, Stone conducted his "slight demonstration" on the afternoon of October 20. In clear view of the enemy on the Virginia side, Stone moved troops to Edwards Ferry, about twenty-seven miles upstream from Washington. Then to create the impression that he was about to cross the Potomac and attack, Stone ordered three flatboats to be passed from the canal to the river. In addition, he ordered his artillery to fire on the woods where the enemy was concealed. These actions "caused the rapid retiring of the [enemy]," Stone reported.

To determine if the demonstration had any effect, Stone sent the Fifteenth Massachusetts Infantry three miles farther upstream to Harrison's Island, a two-mile-long, narrow strip of land in the middle of the Potomac. From there a patrol of twenty men was assigned to "explore by a little-used

Hoping to encourage Confederates to abandon Leesburg, Virginia, Union Brig. Gen. Charles P. Stone conducted "a slight demonstration" by firing shells from the Maryland side of the Potomac into the woods across the river where the Rebels were concealed.

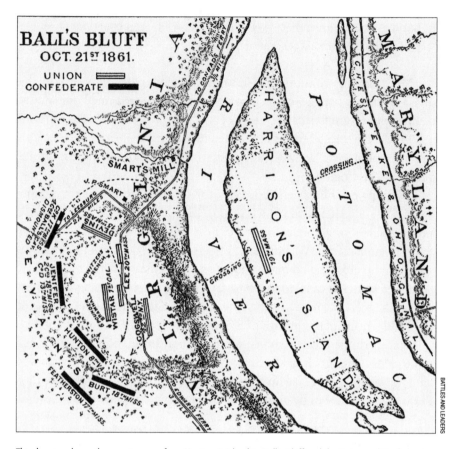

This drawing shows the crossing area from Harrison's Island to Ball's Bluff and the Union and Confederate positions on October 21, 1861.

path through the woods in the direction of Leesburg" to see if they could find anything "concerning the enemy's position" and to report what they found.

The patrol, led by Capt. Chase Philbrick, crossed the stream in small boats and landed at the base of a rocky cliff known as Ball's Bluff. It was more than a hundred feet high. The Federals followed a steep, meandering cow path to the top of the bluff and moved inland about a mile. In the twilight of October 20, Philbrick spotted what he thought was a Confederate camp of about thirty tents. Hurrying back to Harrison's Island that night, he reported this discovery to his superior, Col. Charles Devens, who passed the information by messenger to his commanding officer, Charles Stone, back at Edwards Ferry.

Stone then ordered Devens to cross half of his regiment over the river. "March silently," he said, "under cover of night to the position of the camp [and] attack and destroy it at daybreak . . . and return rapidly to the island."

When the three-hundred-man raiding party arrived at the site, they found nothing. The evening shadows had likely tricked the scouts into mistaking a row of trees for a row of tents. With nothing to raid, Devens sent a messenger to Stone, asking for further instructions. Stone responded with an order to reconnoiter closer to Leesburg. To expand the recon, Stone reinforced Devens with the rest of the Fifteenth Massachusetts and gave command of the operation to one of his brigade leaders, Col. Edward D. Baker.

Baker's orders were to "ascertain the exact position and force of the enemy in our front" and to either withdraw the troops from the Virginia shore or to pass over reinforcements "if he found the position on the other side strong and favorable." Do what the situation dictates, Stone asserted.

Fifty-year-old Baker was a Washington VIP: a charismatic, handsome U.S. senator, and a former Illinois lawyer. Of greater importance, he was a close friend to Lincoln and the president's family—so close that the Lincolns named their second son after him. And on inauguration day in 1861, Baker was one of only two Senate escorts for the president-elect.

Unknown to Stone and Baker, Devens's original raiding party had pushed ahead and glimpsed a few real tents before encountering and exchanging shots with forty pickets from the Seventeenth Mississippi. This occurred at 8 a.m. just as Stone was told there was no camp to raid and all was quiet. About 10 a.m., as Baker was on his way to take command of the mission, he learned of the skirmishing from a messenger on his way to inform Stone. Baker then realized that his task was going to be much greater than just scouting.

After the surrender of Fort Sumter back in April, Senator Baker had urged "bold, forward, and determined war." At Ball's Bluff, he was going to put his own words into action. Stone had given him that option, and he was determined to exercise it. Here was an opportunity for him to become a war hero.

Soon after arriving at Harrison's Island, Baker began the long process of shuttling his whole force across the river. During these hours, the Confederate commander, Evans, moved his troops up to meet the Federals. After the eight o'clock encounter, the two forces clashed two more times before Devens pulled his men back to the bluff at around 2 p.m., just as Baker was arriving on the field. "I congratulate you, sir, on the prospects of a battle," Baker announced to Devens as he assumed command.

In the midst of the fighting, though, Baker was uncertain or confused about what action he should take. He conferred with Col. Milton Cogswell of the Forty-second New York. Baker, a romantic who loved poetry, greeted Cogswell by quoting from Sir Walter Scott's *The Lady of the Lake*: "One blast upon your bugle horn is worth a thousand men."

Cogswell advised moving their entire force forward, but Baker, being cautious, ordered only a couple of California regiments to advance and investigate, while he arranged the remainder of his troops at one end of the clearing atop the bluff. Now mostly in the open, the Federals' backs were to the bluff. Their ability to maneuver was limited by the wooded ravines and ridges around the clearing. In this position they were trapped and easy targets for Rebel snipers in the woods.

Cogswell wanted to advance up the open slope where they would have more room to maneuver. The top of the slope was like the mouth of a bottle: it was the only way in or out. But Baker said no. Had he done as Cogswell advised, he would have minimized the risk of being trapped. By not advancing, he enabled Rebel units to deploy there and move to good positions to fire on and attack the Federals.

Baker also erred by placing his three cannon in front of his force, without sufficient infantry support. The gun crews were quickly killed by sharpshooters.

Confederate reinforcements—Virginians and Mississippians—came up to challenge the Federals. The opposing numbers were almost equal, with slightly more than seventeen hundred on each side. The fighting became fierce and continuous after 3:30 p.m. and was often hand-to-hand. The slugfest raged back and forth across the clearing. To inspire his men, Baker went in front of them to lead by example, shouting, "Stand firm! Stand firm!"

Around 5 p.m., Baker was hit by four bullets, including one to the brain. He fell dead—the only U.S. senator ever killed in battle. A group of soldiers carried his body to the rear.

Cogswell took over and attempted a breakout that would have allowed the Federals to move downriver toward Edwards Ferry. The attempt failed.

The Rebels then moved in on three sides while keeping up a galling fire. They pushed the Federals to the rim of the bluff. The bluecoats panicked.

A Union raiding party crossed over the Potomac to Ball's Bluff to destroy what was mistakenly identified as a Confederate camp. The raid became a skirmish and then a battle.

The only way left to retreat was down the cliff. But in the commotion they couldn't wait to take the cow path. Many lunged and stumbled down the steep terrain and over jagged rocks. Others behind them jumped from the rim and tumbled over the heads of the men below, some skewering themselves on the bayonets of those who had leaped first. An onlooking Confederate soldier later wrote: "The side of the bluff was worn smooth by the number sliding down."

Only those men at the scene knew the situation; Baker had failed to send messengers with reports of what was going on during the fighting. Thus, Stone assumed that all was well.

Those fleeing Federals who made it to the river overloaded the only large boat there. The smaller boats had disappeared; no one knew where. Baker apparently left no one in charge of them. The large boat capsized fifteen feet from the shore. These soldiers had only three options: surrender, be killed, or try to escape by swimming the swift-moving river.

Deadly gunfire rained down on those in the river, on the bank, and still on the bluff. Some soldiers floated on logs while paddling out of range. Others concealed themselves in bushes to make their way up or down the riverbank to a safe place for crossing. Several hundred took cover at the base of the bluff until the shooting stopped and then surrendered.

Fewer than half of the seventeen hundred Federals returned safely to the Maryland shore. One of them looked back and muttered "that cursed Ball's Bluff." Forty-nine were killed, 158 wounded, 553 captured. More than a hundred had drowned. Bodies floating downriver to Washington brought the shocking reality of war to the public's attention.

Among the Union casualties was a grandson of Revolutionary War hero Paul Revere, who was captured, and a son of poet Oliver Wendell Holmes, who was wounded.

Confederate casualties were minimal—36 killed, 117 wounded, 2 captured.

McClellan expressed surprise and shock when he learned of the battle. No chain of communication existed after Baker took command. McClellan had heard nothing because Baker had relayed nothing to Stone.

In Washington, Lincoln was at the War Department when the telegraph reported the disaster and the death of his friend Baker. The president sat stunned for several minutes and then walked away, tears streaming down his face. Ten-year-old Willie Lincoln, who had inherited his father's literary talent, poured out his grief in a poem published in a Washington newspaper. The public regarded Baker as a hero, a brave officer who had led his men into battle and made the ultimate sacrifice.

Ball's Bluff was a minor action by Civil War standards, but the humiliating affair aroused the Radical Republicans in Congress to savage anger. They had lost one of their bright stars. Someone had blundered. They would investigate the matter and identify the culprit. They would not blame their martyred colleague. They would seek revenge. They would find a scapegoat. Very soon it became apparent that their scapegoat would be Charles P. Stone.

Clearly, Baker, not Stone, was at fault.

LIBRARY OF CONGRESS

Col. Edward D. Baker, a U.S. senator and close friend of Abraham Lincoln, was ordered to determine the exact position and size of the enemy force. By the time he arrived at Ball's Bluff, a battle was already underway.

Baker failed to appraise the situation before committing to fight. He was unprepared. He managed his troops poorly, placing them in a trapped position. He did not keep his superiors informed. He did not take into account the shortage of boats. And he did not protect the ones he had. Stone wrongly gave discretionary authority to Baker, who lacked the needed military skills and experience, but that was a minor mistake compared to Baker's actions. Baker's poor discretion was not Stone's fault.

McClellan himself made two major mistakes: ordering an operation that had no valid purpose and failing to tell Stone that he had withdrawn McCall's division. But to his credit he did not blame Stone. McClellan wrote to his wife: "The man directly to blame for the affair was Colonel Baker. . . . He was in command. [He] disregarded entirely the instructions he had received from Stone, and [he] violated all military rules and precautions." McClellan officially cleared Stone of any wrongdoing, stating on October 24: "The disaster was caused by errors committed by the immediate Commander—not General Stone."

War Department officials meanwhile silenced any criticism of Baker and kept secret Stone's official report of the battle. A copy, however, somehow came into the hands of a *New York Tribune* reporter and was published. In his report, Stone blamed Baker for bungling generalship while praising his courage. The Radicals immediately damned the report and defended Baker. Stone reacted with a supplemental report even more critical of the president's friend. Then, the politics turned nasty, and the Radicals began to point their fingers at Stone.

Capitalizing on the "era of suspicion" and the "Rebel scare," individuals stepped forward to accuse Stone of having Southern sympathies. The fact that Stone's wife had Southern relatives didn't help. Rumors circulated that the Stones associated with slaveholders in Maryland and that the general had assigned troops to protect their property. These were unforgivable actions, if true—the kind of things a traitor would do.

Stone's command was based in Maryland. It was a slave state that would have seceded had it not been for the strong-arm tactics of the Lincoln administration. Slaves running from their Maryland owners frequently sought sanctuary in the Union camps, including those under Stone's command. Both Maryland and Federal laws required runaways to be returned to their owners, who technically were U.S. citizens. Stone, however, took a further step. He issued a general order admonishing his men "not to incite and encourage insubordination among the colored servants in the neighborhood of the camps."

The policy and Stone's order especially infuriated the New England soldiers in Stone's regiments. Intense abolitionists, they wanted to assist runaway slaves, and they angrily resented doing anything for slaveholders. Many of these soldiers were outraged when two runaway Maryland slaves appeared in the camp of the Twentieth Massachusetts on November 24 and were promptly returned under guard to their owner. This prompted one of the unit's officers to complain to Massachusetts governor John Andrew that Stone had used his soldiers as "slave-catchers." The governor responded with letters to the secretary of war and various military officers.

At about the same time, Stone arranged for the return of two slaves who had crossed the river with the Union troops during the retreat. In fact, they wanted to go back to their families in Virginia. Their return was voluntary, but Stone's critics overlooked that.

Governor Andrew then sought the support of Senator Charles Sumner, a staunch Massachusetts abolitionist. In a December 18 speech on the Senate floor, Sumner said: "[Gen. Charles] Stone is now . . . engaging ably and actively in the work of surrendering fugitive slaves. He does this, sir, most successfully. He is victorious when the simple question is whether a fugitive slave shall be surrendered to a Rebel." Sumner called Stone's action "vile and unconstitutional" even though Stone was actually enforcing the laws.

Stone responded by writing Sumner a letter that came close to challenging him to a duel. The general also chided Governor Andrew for "unwarrantable and dangerous interference" in military affairs. Then, on December 23, Stone accused Sumner of uttering "a slander and a falsehood" and called him "a well-known coward."

Those accusations drew Sumner's rage, and he set out to destroy Stone's career. He began by convincing political ally Benjamin Wade of Ohio to target Stone. Wade was chairman of the newly constituted Joint Committee on the Conduct of the War (JCCW). The committee, controlled by the Radical Republicans, first met on December 10. It was focused on the cause of defeats at First Bull Run and Ball's Bluff, but it would soon use Ball's Bluff as the excuse to unleash forces to stampede and destroy Stone for his alleged lack of leniency toward runaway slaves.

Stone, although a Massachusetts native, was not an abolitionist. He enforced the federal government's policy regarding fugitive slaves as he was expected to do, regardless of what Senator Sumner, the Radicals, or his New England soldiers thought. In his testimony before the committee, he said:

> I have tried to obey every order of the War Department I have ever received . . . and I have insisted upon my troops obeying every law of the State of Maryland. I do not allow them to harbor the slaves . . . of the farmers in that neighborhood. [But] the slaves that run away from the enemy [Confederates] and come over are got to my headquarters as quickly as possible. . . . They are made as comfortable as they can be. . . . If they have needed assistance, they have been fed and clothed and put to work by the quartermaster or commissary. I am not aware of any slaves coming over from the enemy's line having been given up to any claimant.

While leading and inspiring his men, Col. Edward Baker was pierced by bullets in the brain, body, arm, and side. He died instantly. He was the only U.S. senator ever killed in battle.

LESLIE'S

Both sides tried to claim Baker's body, but Baker's sword-wielding adjutant allowed Union soldiers finally to remove the colonel from the field of battle.

That didn't satisfy the abolitionist-minded Radical Republicans, however. The committee was established to investigate every aspect of military policy, and (in the words of Sen. Henry Wilson) to "teach men in civil and in military authority that the people expect that they will not make mistakes, and that we shall not be easy with their errors."

Wade, the JCCW chairman, was an all-out abolitionist with jet black eyes and a bulldog countenance. He reveled in browbeating witnesses and using flimsy evidence to relieve generals (who happened to be Democrats) of their commands. After securing testimony in secret sessions against military officials they did not like or did not trust, the JCCW then summoned the accused to answer charges against them without facing their accusers or even knowing who their accusers were. That's how the JCCW approached Stone's case.

First came the accusers. Ten of the thirty-nine witnesses were from the Second New York Militia. Their regiment had not even participated in the Ball's Bluff battle. Stone did not think much of them. They lacked discipline and the right stuff to be good soldiers. And they did not like Stone. Their ringleader was Col. George W. B. Tomkins—an officer Stone had charged with cowardice and filing a false muster to gain the pay of nonexistent soldiers. For Tomkins and the other witnesses it was payback time at any price and by any means necessary.

Tomkins claimed that Stone was well liked by secessionist-minded Marylanders, that he communicated with the enemy under flags of truce, and that sealed packages were exchanged on such occasions. He said that he had witnessed strange bonfires and mysterious messengers passing between the lines. The colonel insisted that no one in the regiment wanted to fight under the general.

"Do they doubt Stone's ability or loyalty?" asked Wade.

"Both," replied Tomkins.

The other witnesses from this New York militia unit supported these allegations, but none could offer any direct evidence of disloyalty, just rumors of suspicious goings-on with the Rebels. Interestingly, two of these witnesses had to be released from prison to testify. One was a quartermaster Stone had charged with fraud for falsifying accounts; the other had been charged by Stone with filing a false muster. The similarity of their statements and their obvious desire for revenge suggested a concerted conspiracy to destroy Stone—a conspiracy the JCCW seemed all too eager to join. The JCCW, for example, ignored witnesses who explained that flags of truce were not unusual, that the only exchanges that took place were packages of letters from prisoners of war.

Building upon Tomkins's allegation, the JCCW asked leading questions designed to make Stone the scapegoat. For example: "So far as you know, is not there such a general suspicion of General Stone among officers and men that they would be unwilling to go into battle under him?" Those who hesitated were bullied into answering yes.

When Stone was called before the JCCW, the senators and representatives had already decided he was a sinister plotter against his country—a pro-slavery Southern sympathizer who had sent soldiers across the river at Ball's Bluff to get them killed, probably in collaboration with the enemy.

Prior to Stone's testimony, McClellan instructed him *not* to reveal anything "regarding his [McClellan's] plans, his orders for the movement of troops, or his orders concerning the position of troops." McClellan was concerned about saving his own job. He suspected he was the real target of the JCCW inquiry. This gag order, however, placed a tremendous burden upon Stone. It made it difficult for him to present facts explaining his situation at Ball's Bluff. It also kept McClellan out of the inquiry.

Stone was not allowed to examine the testimony given by those who had already appeared before the JCCW and was not informed of the specific charges against him. Wade, however, did cite Stone's failure to reinforce Baker during the battle.

Stone explained that he was unaware of Baker's crisis, but he could not have assisted him even if he had known about it. Being four miles away from Baker, and with the battle brief but brutal, there wasn't time, and he lacked the manpower. He emphasized he had given Baker wide discretionary power, and that Baker's actions reflected his own rashness.

Stanton had informed Stone that earlier testimony before the JCCW had impugned his loyalty and suggested treason. That devastated Stone. He stated: "That is one humiliation I had hoped I never should be subjected to. . . . That one I should have supposed that you personally, Mr. Chairman, would have rejected at once."

Stone was right. He was the first soldier to answer his country's call during the secession crisis. In January 1861 he was commissioned to take command of the District of Columbia volunteers and organize them to defend the capital. On inauguration day, amid multiple threats to kill Lincoln, Stone included himself in the cavalry detachment that accompanied the Lincoln carriage. Later, after Virginia seceded from the Union, he led troops across the river to secure Alexandria, a major southern approach to the capital. He was a West Point graduate and the recipient of two brevets for gallantry in the Mexican War. No one had displayed his loyalty more conspicuously and with greater success than had Stone.

He reminded the committee of his services in organizing the defenses of Washington in the early weeks of the war. "I could have surrendered Washington [if I had been disloyal]. I have, so help me Heaven, but one object in all this, and that is to see the United States successful. . . . I have been as faithful as I can be. And I am exceedingly sore at this outrageous charge."

The JCCW was not persuaded. The members had already made up their minds. Wade forwarded the committee's evidence to Stanton, and Stanton ordered McClellan to relieve Stone of his command and place him "in close custody until further orders." McClellan was reluctant to follow the committee's directives. He knew that Stone was innocent of all charges. He later told a group of officers at a dinner that he ignored Stanton's order for days because he believed "the Committee's evidence was flimsy and based on hearsay."

A conversation between an officer and McClellan is revealing. McClellan said: "They want a victim." The officer replied, "Yes—and when they have once tasted blood, got one victim, no one can tell who will be the next." Attorney General Edward Bates, who recorded these comments in his diary, added: "Thereupon the General colored up, and the conversation ceased."

McClellan showed some courage by going to the JCCW to ask that Stone be allowed to respond to the specific charges against him. It was allowed, but to no avail. More hearsay evidence against Stone came from McClellan's military intelligence detective, Allan Pinkerton, who reported comments from Leesburg refugees who supposedly overheard Confederate officers referring to Stone as "a very fine man" and "a brave man and a gentleman." Pinkerton's report was placed in Stanton's files and marked "Full account of Gen. Stone's treachery." With the "new" evidence, Stanton pressured McClellan to act immediately and arrest and imprison Stone.

Sometime near midnight on February 8, 1862, a detail of eighteen guardsmen under Brig. Gen. George Sykes went to Stone's residence in Washington. Not finding him at home, they waited on the street until he approached the house.

Sykes said to Stone: "I have now the most disagreeable duty to perform that I ever had—it is to arrest you."

"Arrest me!" shouted Stone. "For what?"

"I don't know," said Sykes. "It's by order of Maj. Gen. George B. McClellan, general-in-chief of the army. . . . I may as well tell you that you are to be sent to Fort Lafayette."

Shocked and bewildered, Stone responded: "That's where they send secessionists! [But] I have been as true a soldier to the Government as any in service."

Early that morning Stone wrote McClellan's adjutant general and demanded a copy of "whatever charges may have been preferred against me, and the opportunity of promptly meeting them." He did not get a response.

That night, with three escorts, he was put on a train to New York after being required to pay for his own ticket. A few hours later he found himself in solitary confinement in a small room in the military prison at Fort Lafayette.

Under the articles of war, an officer ordering an arrest must file charges within eight days. McClellan didn't. Stone and his attorney requested copies of the charges from McClellan, Stanton, and the army's adjutant general.

"They would be filed in good season," Stanton stated.

"The matter is still under investigation," replied McClellan's staff.

The adjutant general did not reply.

Thus Stone was never charged with any crime by anyone.

When those responsible for enforcing the articles of war do nothing, the victim (or scapegoat in this case) is helpless.

Stanton publicly declared that the case involved disloyalty. Pinkerton spoke of Stone's treachery. Wade said, "If people are shut up in dungeons, and restrained of their liberties, it is that the Constitution may live!"

The public regarded Stone as the Benedict Arnold of the Civil War.

Lincoln would say only that Stone had been arrested under his "general authority," but it would not serve the public interest "to make a more particular statement of the evidence."

After fifty days in the dungeon at Fort Lafayette, Stone's health deteriorated. His physician protested the conditions, and Stanton, in a rare moment of compassion, ordered Stone transferred to Fort Hamilton, where he was allowed to exercise under guard.

Stone might have remained at Fort Hamilton throughout the war had it not been for Senator James A. McDougall of California. On his initiative, a section was placed in a pending military bill stating that officers under arrest must be told of the charges against them within eight days of arrest and must be entitled to a trial within thirty days. The legislation applied to all persons now under arrest and awaiting trial. The bill passed both houses and was signed by Lincoln on July 17, 1862.

Stanton, back to his vindictive self, waited the full thirty days before releasing Stone from prison. As a well-versed attorney, Stanton realized he had no case against Stone. Hearsay would never stand up in a court-martial. And a trial would bring out information embarrassing to the War Department and the army. But keeping Stone locked up would be an example to others whom Stanton regarded as soft on the South. Now Stanton had no choice but to let him go. After serving 189 days, Stone was freed.

Stone, however, wanted more than freedom. He wanted to clear his name and to restore his reputation. Again he demanded to know the charges against him so he could respond to them. He appealed to Lincoln, Stanton, and General in Chief Henry W. Halleck. The president responded, according to Stone, "that if he told me all he knew about the matter he should not tell me much."

Brig. Gen. Charles P. Stone, the scapegoat of Ball's Bluff, was falsely blamed for the Union defeat and confined in prison for more than six months without ever being officially charged with any crime. His career was destroyed by a flagrantly unfair congressional committee and Secretary of War Edwin M. Stanton.

In the ensuing months Stanton refused several requests for Stone's services. McClellan wanted him to command a division, and later, Maj. Gen. Joseph Hooker asked for him to serve as his chief of staff. Lt. Gen. Ulysses S. Grant also requested that Stone be given responsible duties. Maj. Gen. Philip Kearny, who seldom praised anyone, called Stone "the ablest man in the army." But Stanton remained adamant. He said that the requests were "not considered in the interests of the service."

Finally, on February 27, 1863—a few days after the death of Stone's wife—the general was allowed to appear before the JCCW. With McClellan no longer in command, his gag order was lifted, and Stone could speak freely about the orders governing his actions. He heard their specific charges, answered and demolished each accusation, and discredited each witness.

Wade expressed shock and astonishment. He asked, "Why did you not give us these explanations when you were here before?" Stone replied, "Because . . . the Committee did not state to me the particular cases . . . I gave general answers to general allegations."

A few weeks later the JCCW published the entire Ball's Bluff investigation. This time, they got it right. Stone had been the scapegoat. Justice finally triumphed over injustice, suspicion, and conspiracy.

The *New York Times* editorialized: "General Stone has sustained a most flagrant wrong—a wrong which will probably stand as the very worst blot on the National side in the history of the war."

With extreme reluctance, Stanton allowed Stone to resume his military service. He was assigned to report to Maj. Gen. Nathaniel P. Banks in New Orleans and later became his chief of staff. Serving creditably for nearly a year, problems arose when Stone, a Catholic, was lenient in granting passes to Catholic priests, one of whom turned out to be a spy. Then Stone raised eyebrows when he married a New Orleans lady whose brother was serving in the Confederate army. Malicious gossip linked the marriage to the dismal

Union failure of Banks's troops to defeat heavily outnumbered Confederates in a series of battles fought along the Red River in Louisiana from March 10 to May 22, 1864. The Federal debacle was due to Banks's poor planning and mismanagement, not to anything Stone had done. Nevertheless, a diarist wrote of "another Ball's Bluff at the hands of General Stone—who married a secesh wife six months after losing his first one."

Banks, needing a scapegoat, relieved Stone immediately. Charles Sumner then used his influence to strip Stone of his volunteer brigadier's commission and revert him to his regular army rank of colonel. Grant, who liked Stone, gave him a brigade in the Fifth Corps, but Stone had had enough. He resigned from the army in September 1864.

After his career had been destroyed, he went to Egypt after the war and for thirteen years served as chief of staff in the army of the Khedive of Egypt. When he returned to the United States he pursued a career in engineering. His success in that field earned him supervision of the construction of the Statue of Liberty. Ironically, he caught a chill during the dedication and died of pneumonia on January 24, 1887, at age sixty-two. He is buried at West Point.

3

DEVIOUS RADICAL PLOTTERS

IF THE POLITICIANS HAD left Maj. Gen. George B. McClellan alone, he might have won the Civil War in 1862. Instead, history records him as a brilliant failure on the battlefield.

Lincoln called him to Washington on the day after Brig. Gen. Irvin McDowell's army suffered an embarrassing defeat at Bull Run on July 21, 1861. That was supposed to have been an easy victory, but it became a rout. The army fled back to the capital. Lincoln turned to McClellan to repair the damage.

There was an indefinable air of success about the young general. He was a cultured gentleman with the look of a warrior: handsome, dignified, and Napoleonic—possessing an extreme ego and posing like Napoleon by standing with folded arms. As the only Union general who won any battles in 1861, he had reason to crow. These were minor battles; the opposing forces were small. But by driving the Confederates out of western Virginia he caught Lincoln's attention as well as that of the public. People were crazy about him. Wherever he went on his sleek black stallion, crowds rallied around him. His troops loved him. They dubbed their short, muscular general "Little Mac."

Although only thirty-four, McClellan's background was impressive: the best private schools, second in his class at West Point, an officer in the

Maj. Gen. George B. McClellan, commander of the Army of the
Potomac, performed superbly on defense but was weak on
offense even when winning.

Mexican War, an expert for the War Department on the organization and meth-
ods of Continental armies, an observer for
the army in the Crimean War, a successful
executive of railroad companies, and then,
with the outbreak of the Civil War, a commission as major general, commanding the
Department of the Ohio.

NATIONAL ARCHIVES

What he lacked were lessons of adversity learned
from the despair of defeat. The possibility of failure haunted him. The risk
of heavy losses in battle frightened him. These fears made him overly cautious. They made him a perfectionist. He could not fight until every *i* was
dotted and every *t* crossed. This attitude—fine for an executive but bad for
a general—gave him what Lincoln called "a case of the slows."

He wasn't slow, however, in remaking and reshaping McDowell's demoralized army and strengthening the Washington defenses. With a calm
confidence he worked with nonstop energy, sleeping hardly at all. He
rounded up stragglers and drunken soldiers and yanked their officers out of
the capital's saloons. A superb organizer and a fine trainer of troops, McClellan instilled discipline and pride in them. By early fall 1861 he had forged
the Army of the Potomac into one of the finest fighting machines in the history of warfare. Then he resisted efforts to make him use it. He claimed he
was too outnumbered to launch an offensive or to defend Washington if he
was attacked.

McClellan believed that the Confederates in northern Virginia numbered 150,000 and could attack him at any time. He insisted that he needed
huge numbers of reinforcements. He was wrong on both counts. There
were only 45,000 Confederates in or near Manassas, while he had 120,000
men in the Army of the Potomac.

Never doubting his false estimates of the enemy's strength and regarding himself as the only man who could preserve the Union, he wrote to his
wife: "The people call on me to save the country. I must save it, and cannot
respect anything that is in the way." The person in the way, he asserted, was

the country's foremost living soldier: General in Chief Winfield Scott. McClellan blamed Scott for not meeting his demands and for holding up his plans to expand and prepare the army for an early offensive. McClellan complained to his wife that he could do nothing as long as the "old Gen'l" controlled the army and threw obstacles in his way. He tried to make Scott the scapegoat for his own fears and frustrations. "I am leaving nothing undone to increase our force," he wrote to his wife, "but that confounded old Gen'l always comes in my way. . . . He understands nothing, appreciates nothing."

McClellan began to go around Scott and communicate directly with Lincoln. Scott, infuriated, asked to be retired. At age seventy-five, "Old Fuss and Feathers" was sick and tired and willing to step down. But Lincoln supported Scott, and McClellan backed off.

Part of the squabble stemmed from Scott's opposition to McClellan's appointment to command the Army of the Potomac. McClellan's resentment spurred his determination to get Scott's job.

By October nearly everyone in the capital wondered why McClellan hadn't moved his army on Richmond. Leading Republicans urged Lincoln to order McClellan to fight. McClellan said he needed more time to train the troops. He meant to fight soon, he said, and if he failed, nobody would see him again. At a meeting with senators that same day, McClellan emphasized that he wanted to fight and "to crush the Rebels in one campaign" but was held back by Scott's defensive policy. It was McClellan's way of freeing himself from Scott and placing the blame on Scott for the inaction of the eastern army. It worked. Senators pushed successfully for Scott's retirement. On November 1, Lincoln named McClellan "to command the whole army." It ended Scott's public career of nearly fifty years. The old general would live five more years and die at West Point.

During November, Lincoln and McClellan conferred every day. The president emphasized, "In addition to your present command, the supreme command of the Army will entail a vast labor upon you." McClellan responded, "I can do it all." In the process he would become perhaps the biggest political scapegoat of the war.

McClellan was a Democrat, and he was opposed to wartime emancipation of the slaves. Those two factors would get him into serious trouble with the Joint Committee on the Conduct of the War—a committee controlled by Radical Republicans who were abolitionists determined to eradicate the great evil, slavery. Secretary of War Edwin M. Stanton sided with them and worked with them.

Stanton and the JCCW were wrong to allow either factor to influence their actions against McClellan. Up to the fall of 1862, it was official government policy that the war was fought solely to restore the Union. Generals, in fact, were instructed not to campaign against slavery. McClellan supported these policies. Yet by doing so, he angered the Radicals.

With pressure from the Radicals for McClellan to strike a blow, Lincoln issued two orders. One called for "a general movement of the land and naval forces" on February 22, 1862. The other directed McClellan to provide for the safety of Washington and then to move his army southward to seize the railroad supplying the Southern forces at Manassas, twenty-five miles from the Union capital.

McClellan didn't like the plan and had no intention of carrying it out. His own plan was to take Richmond from the east, approaching it by marching up the Virginia Peninsula and using the York River as a line of supply, with naval units guarding the rear. Lincoln objected to this elaborate plan. He feared that Washington would be in danger if the main Union army was on the far side of Richmond. He wanted McClellan to keep his army between the Confederates and Washington by moving south toward Richmond.

McClellan asked for permission to submit his objections in writing. Lincoln agreed and sent questions to McClellan requiring "satisfactory answers." The key points in McClellan's response were: (1) the Peninsula plan offered the shortest land route to Richmond; (2) he could retreat safely if necessary, because the fleet would protect the army's flanks; and (3) the Rebels wouldn't dare attack Washington because they would have their hands full defending Richmond. Further, asserted McClellan, he would capture Richmond and the war would be over. This time Lincoln approved McClellan's plan and informally withdrew his earlier order to move all Union forces on February 22.

The Radicals, however, objected, displeased with McClellan's influence over Lincoln. They also expressed concern that McClellan had allowed the Rebels to erect batteries on the Potomac, thus blockading the river to Union forces. Ohio senator Benjamin Wade, chairman of the JCCW, met secretly with Stanton to press "the importance and necessity of at once wiping out that disgrace to the nation—the blockade of the Potomac and the siege of our capital." Stanton agreed and said "that he did not go to his bed at night without his cheek burning with shame at this disgrace upon the nation."

Stanton and Wade shared these concerns with Lincoln, knowing that the Rebel blockade would alarm him. "Force McClellan to fight or remove him," they demanded. Wade threatened congressional action to direct Lincoln to do so. Fearful of splitting the party, Lincoln promised to talk to McClellan.

At a very early hour on the morning of March 7, Lincoln summoned McClellan and told him that he had changed his mind about the Peninsula plan. He was now opposed to it. Washington would be exposed, he said. The president added that he had heard ugly things about McClellan, specifically that he wanted to strip the capital of defenses so the Rebels could seize it. Drive the Confederates away from Manassas before you attempt anything else, Lincoln ordered.

McClellan, feeling threatened, noted that he and his officers would that day be discussing the coming campaign. Lincoln, always interested in the advice of military experts, made a tactical mistake. He suggested that McClellan submit the two rival plans to these generals for a decision. "I will accept the opinion of the majority," Lincoln said. He seemed to have been unaware of the army politics guaranteed to endorse McClellan's plan.

McClellan's army had twelve division commanders, most of whom were West Point graduates. They were split into two factions that hated each other. In one group were five senior generals who had been in military service many years. They despised McClellan and resented his rapid rise to power. He, in turn, seldom asked them for advice or opinions. They were Republicans and abolitionists who socialized with the Radicals in Congress. These brigadiers were forty-seven-year-old John G. Barnard, a career army engineer who later published many books on engineering and science; forty-four-year-old Irvin McDowell, whose army had been routed at Bull Run; fifty-seven-year-old Samuel P. Heintzelman, whose Michigan infantry was responsible for the ransacking and

General in Chief Winfield Scott was America's foremost living soldier at the start of the Civil War. He retired after Maj. Gen. George McClellan, wanting his job, engaged in political shenanigans.

destruction of historic Pohick Church in Lorton, Virginia, in 1861, causing the loss of many irreplaceable artifacts associated with George Washington, George Mason, and Francis Scott Key; fifty-two-year-old Erasmus D. Keyes, a veteran of frontier and Indian fighting; and sixty-five-year-old Edwin "Bull Head" Sumner, whose nickname came from a legend that a musket ball once bounced off his head, and whose daughter was a Richmond socialite and dear friend of the Confederate first lady, Varina Davis.

The opposing group was made up of seven brigadiers who agreed with McClellan on nearly everything. All of them were conservatives, and most of them were from his home state of Pennsylvania. They believed that the Radical Republicans had no business interfering with the conduct of the war. Stanton scornfully called them "McClellan's pets." Several had fought in the Mexican War with distinction. This group included: fifty-year-old Louis Blenker, a native of Germany who led a division of German brigades in the Army of the Potomac; thirty-nine-year-old William B. Franklin, who had ranked first in his West Point class, served as a professor at the academy, and was the supervising engineer for construction of the U.S. Capitol dome; sixty-year-old George A. McCall, who was one of the oldest West Point graduates to serve in the Civil War; thirty-six-year-old James S. Negley, a horticulturist who had raised a brigade of Pennsylvania volunteers and later commanded a division in the Department of the Ohio; forty-two-year-old Andrew Porter, who had commanded a brigade at Bull Run and was a second cousin of Mary Todd Lincoln; forty-year-old Fitz John Porter, a career army officer who came from a family prominent in naval service; and thirty-eight-year-old William F. "Baldy" Smith, a civil engineer and former mathematics professor at West Point.

Being in the majority, the latter group controlled the vote and favored McClellan's plan over Lincoln's. One Republican, Keyes, sided with them to make the vote eight to four.

During a cabinet meeting, Secretary of War Edwin M. Stanton denounced McClellan as "a traitor and a force for evil" and then wrote to the general to declare that McClellan had no firmer friend in Washington than the secretary of war.

Lincoln kept his promise and told McClellan to proceed. The president, however, decreed a few qualifiers: McClellan must leave an adequate force to defend Washington; he must either silence the Rebel batteries on the Potomac or take only half of the army on the campaign; and he must commence the campaign by March 18.

Stanton and the JCCW were outraged by these developments and became even more determined to manipulate military politics. They regarded the conservative generals (all of whom were Democrats) to be as traitorous as McClellan—too slow to fight, too soft on slavery, and too uncommitted to the South's defeat. So they crafted a plan to remove them from positions of power. After a series of secret meetings at Stanton's home, they proposed to Lincoln the consolidation of McClellan's twelve divisions into five corps, with the commands going to the senior generals—all of whom were part of the Republican faction.

Lincoln saw the light after his proposal had been shot down by "McClellan's pets." On March 8, the president, without consulting McClellan, endorsed the Stanton-JCCW position and ordered the army to be reorganized into five corps. He even designated the generals to command them. Four were from the group of senior Republican generals (all except Barnard), and the fifth was Maj. Gen. Nathaniel P. Banks, a Republican politician from Massachusetts. With this arrangement McClellan would be obligated to consult and work with men who did not trust him and did not like his Peninsula plan. Thus McClellan suspected his generals would be watching his every move and reporting any mistakes to Stanton or Wade. He was right.

Historian T. Harry Williams wrote that "plots and counterplots boiled beneath the troubled surface" in March 1862 as both sides struggled feverishly to control the hesitant Lincoln, who wanted to do the right thing. Williams details these political shenanigans in his book *Lincoln and the Radicals*.

McClellan openly opposed the corps arrangement and the choice of commanders. He complained to Lincoln that some of the generals were incompetent and unlikely to be of any help to him. He requested the authority to either appoint new commanders or to revert to the division organization.

Lincoln did not want to place obstacles in McClellan's path, but he resented the general's stubborn opposition to the corps plan. He asked McClellan rhetorically, "Are you strong enough—are you strong enough even with my help—to set your foot upon the necks of Sumner, Heintzelman, and

Keyes all at once?" Lincoln added that such a move would appear as "an effort to pamper one or two pets and to persecute and degrade their supposed rivals."

Lincoln and McClellan compromised, keeping those three generals as corps commanders but allowing McClellan to name his most trusted friend, Fitz John Porter, and William B. Franklin to command the other corps. The JCCW protested, but the president prevailed.

McClellan, feeling more confident, began to move his troops but then briefly altered course. The Confederates suddenly evacuated Manassas and Centreville to form new lines of defense for McClellan's anticipated attack. McClellan decided to occupy these abandoned forts to give his soldiers "some experience on the march." Earlier, Lincoln and the JCCW had urged him to attack the positions, but he had refused. They were too well defended, he said, by large bodies of Rebels who occupied strong fortifications with bristling guns. Congressmen, including many members of the JCCW, went to view these "strongholds" that McClellan had feared. To their surprise, they found evidence that only small forces had occupied them. Further, the fortifications were piles of dirt, and the dreaded guns were logs painted black! McClellan was humiliated. Even his friends began to doubt his abilities and his loyalty. The JCCW demanded his removal. If he had not known about the wooden cannon he was incompetent, they argued; if he had known, he was disloyal.

On March 11, Lincoln relieved McClellan of his position as general in chief but kept him as commander of the Army of the Potomac. All generals of departments were to report to Stanton, who now held the powers previously wielded by McClellan.

In a cabinet meeting, Stanton referred to McClellan as an imbecile, a traitor, and a force for evil. But in a note to McClellan he reassured him not to move until he was "fully ready" and that he had "no firmer friend" than the secretary of war. Such actions by Stanton were devilish hypocrisies, of course, and they were followed by a Stanton-JCCW plot to ensure McClellan's failure in the Peninsula campaign. "McClellan is in danger, not in front but in the rear," presidential secretary John Hay recorded in his diary.

Accordingly, Wade approached Lincoln and complained that McClellan wasn't leaving enough men to defend Washington. The senator advised taking Blenker's division away from McClellan and adding it to the army of Maj. Gen. John C. Frémont, which was guarding the approaches through

The U.S. Capitol, with its unfinished dome, is pictured during the first years of the war. Within its walls, the Republican-controlled Joint Committee on the Conduct of the War plotted to assure the failure of the Peninsula campaign and discredit McClellan.

the Shenandoah Valley. Lincoln, who was determined to provide for the capital's safety, accepted the proposal. McClellan consequently lost ten thousand men for the Peninsula campaign. This was just the first step by Stanton and the JCCW to cripple McClellan's army so badly that he could not succeed. The politicians who called Little Mac a traitor had themselves become traitors.

Before leaving for the Peninsula, McClellan listed the troops he was leaving behind to defend Washington—twenty thousand in the capital and forty-five thousand in the Shenandoah Valley, where the enemy would have to pass.

Maj. Gen. Ethan Allen Hitchcock, a recently appointed consulting military expert in Stanton's office and chairman of the newly established Army Board, reviewed the list and responded to McClellan: "If the force designated is in your judgment sufficient, nothing more would be required." It was a quick and perhaps honest judgment from a general who had recently written in his diary that Stanton came to his office and "shutting the door behind him, stated to me the most astounding facts, all going to show the astonishing incompetency of General McClellan. I cannot recite them; but the Secretary stated fact after fact, and I felt positively sick."

Brig. Gen. James S. Wadsworth, commander of the capital's defenses, was surely aware of McClellan's list and Hitchcock's implied endorsement of it. But he was a Republican politician from New York who despised McClellan. Wadsworth delivered the list and his analysis of it to Stanton. He contended that the assigned troops were "entirely inadequate and unfit" for the city's defense. They could not repel a Rebel attack, he said. "Washington was in danger," and McClellan was at fault.

Hitchcock, who had earlier refused to criticize McClellan's arrangements, chimed in. McClellan, he said, had not followed Lincoln's instructions. The capital was not properly protected.

When this information reached Lincoln and his cabinet, they reportedly were scared "almost out of their senses." With Stanton, Wadsworth, and the JCCW all pleading with Lincoln to order another of McClellan's corps to remain in Washington, he acquiesced. The president authorized Stanton to detain either McDowell's or Sumner's corps, and Stanton chose McDowell's corps of thirty thousand men.

Lincoln had not been informed about the forty-five thousand Union troops in the Shenandoah that the enemy would have to overpower before attacking Washington. This misunderstanding, which Stanton and Wade did nothing to dispel, necessitated a blistering letter from Lincoln to McClellan. He mistakenly accused Little Mac of violating the March 8 presidential order to secure the capital but then urged him to speed up his movements and "strike a blow."

Lincoln and the Radicals had now reassigned forty thousand of McClellan's men, about one-third of his army on the eve of the crucial campaign. With that reduction, the Radicals obviously did not expect

Senator Benjamin Wade of Ohio chaired the Joint Committee on the Conduct of the War. He and other Radical Republicans on the committee gave misleading information to the president that caused him to reassign a third of McClellan's army on the eve of the Peninsula campaign.

McClellan to be able to strike much of a blow on the Peninsula. It was all a devious political plan.

McClellan, without those forty thousand troops, still had a large enough force to accomplish his objectives. He was never outnumbered, although he thought otherwise. He was frequently outsmarted. His basic problem was psychological. Afraid of losing battles and wasting the lives of his men, he constantly pleaded for reinforcements. But with his existing troops he inflicted heavy casualties on the Confederates, lost only one battle in the Seven Days' campaign on the Peninsula, and probably could have marched into Richmond.

What he lacked was not manpower but guts. Even when he won battles—which he often did—he retreated instead of advancing, afraid that to advance was to commit suicide. But when he retreated, he did so with skill. He was never routed. He was a master at maintaining defensive positions but a miser at throwing knockout punches when he had his opponent on the ropes. Perhaps he would have acted differently if he had had those additional forty thousand troops. But he did not have them, and he failed to accomplish his mission.

The Radical Republicans in their secret sessions probably rejoiced and took credit for McClellan's embarrassing "strategic withdrawal" from the gates of Richmond to a base on the James River and eventually his total abandonment of the Peninsula. Playing hardball politics to the hilt, the Radicals even went so far as to downplay McClellan's successes and those of other Democratic generals and to give exaggerated credit for those victories to Republican officers. The Radical Republican press cooperated. Horace Greeley's correspondent for the *New York Tribune*, Samuel Wilkeson, admitted that his policy in his dispatches at the beginning of the Peninsula campaign was to disparage and belittle McClellan, but then what he saw changed his mind, and he issued a story censuring the administration and the Radicals for weakening McClellan's army. Somebody, he said, wanted McClellan to fail. Meanwhile, in Washington, the Radicals spread rumors of McClellan's disloyalty and called him "unfit for his position or worse."

The prosecution of the war was now about politics, and the Democratic press screamed that McClellan was being sabotaged by the Radical Republicans—sabotaged because they did not want a Democratic general to win the war. They wanted a Democratic scapegoat to serve as a warning to other generals who did not think as they did. Navy Secretary Gideon Welles called it a clever scheme to remove McClellan and replace him with a Radical Republican general. Lincoln, the Democrats said, had acted as the tool of Radical plotters, and the Democrats would never trust the president again. *Harper's Weekly* opined, "It is impossible to exaggerate the mischief which has been done by . . . civilian interference with military movements."

The Radicals undoubtedly believed that if McClellan had defeated the Rebels and won the war, three outcomes were likely: slavery would continue with peace on any terms, McClellan would become president, and the Democrats and the South would rule for years to come. They couldn't allow that to happen. Their schemes to undermine McClellan and assure his colossal failure made them dangerous political goats to be feared.

4

THE SEVEN DAYS' BATTLES: JUNE 26–JULY 1, 1862

STONEWALL'S FIVE STRIKEOUTS

MAJ. GEN. GEORGE B. MCCLELLAN's massive Peninsula campaign in the spring and early summer of 1862 could have ended the Civil War. It didn't because of bad decisions, bad intelligence, bad weather, and a new field commander named Robert E. Lee.

Lee could have destroyed McClellan's army and perhaps saved the Confederacy. He didn't because of poor staff work, poor coordination among his top commanders, and most of all, the chronic tardiness of Maj. Gen. Thomas J. "Stonewall" Jackson.

In March 1862 McClellan landed the Army of the Potomac at Fort Monroe on the tip of the Virginia Peninsula—a narrow strip of land between the York and James rivers southeast of Richmond. Moving slowly and cautiously he pushed the Rebels up the Peninsula past the historic areas of Yorktown, Williamsburg, and Jamestown to within six miles of Richmond. When heavy rains stalled his advance, half of his army crossed the Chickahominy River before it became impassable. The split army presented an opportunity Confederate commander Joseph E. Johnston couldn't pass up. He attacked McClellan's weaker right flank on May 31 at a woody, mucky place called Seven Pines (also known as Fair Oaks).

The battle, with forty-two thousand men engaged on each side, was a tactical draw. Both sides suffered heavy losses: six thousand Confederates and about five thousand Federals. McClellan spent the day confined to bed with neuralgia and a recurrent attack of malaria. Johnston, near the front, was carried off the field with a bullet through his shoulder and a shell fragment in his chest.

Near panic, Confederate president Jefferson Davis turned over the army's command to his military adviser, fifty-five-year-old Robert E. Lee. Immediately Lee ordered a retreat into the defenses around Richmond, where he put his men to work at digging trenches and strengthening the fortifications ringing the capital.

The attack at Seven Pines, combined with Allan Pinkerton's erroneous intelligence reports, convinced McClellan that he was heavily outnumbered. Pinkerton, a private detective who had set up the army's secret service, was the general's counterespionage director. McClellan relied upon Pinkerton—a mistake to some degree responsible for McClellan's lackluster performance to come. McClellan sincerely believed he lacked the manpower to take Richmond and called repeatedly for reinforcements. "If anything happens to this army, our cause will be lost," he wrote to his wife. At the time McClellan's troops numbered about one hundred thousand; Lee's about sixty-one thousand.

More than forty thousand men had been withheld from McClellan mostly for political reasons (see chapter 3), but Secretary of War Edwin M. Stanton hypocritically wired McClellan that "my desire [has always been] to aid you with my whole heart, mind, and strength." To placate McClellan, Stanton indicated that he had dispatched Brig. Gen. George A. McCall's division to join the army on the Peninsula.

Lee needed time to plan and to augment his army. And he got it. It rained the first ten days of June, washing out bridges and flooding the bottoms. McClellan's big guns were immobilized, unable to move in the water and mud. "The men are working night and day, up to their waists in water," he informed Washington. Lincoln asked when he was going to attack. "The moment McCall reaches here and the ground will admit the passage of artillery," McClellan responded.

On June 18, with McCall at hand, McClellan wired: "After tomorrow we shall fight the rebel army as soon as Providence will permit." He wrote to his wife: "I will push them in upon Richmond and behind their works. Then I will bring up my heavy guns, shell the city, and carry it by assault."

While McClellan was making promises, Lee was mapping strategy. On June 12 he sent Brig. Gen. James Ewell Brown "Jeb" Stuart with twelve hun-

Union troops relax at Maj. Gen. George B. McClellan's Federal encampment on the Pamunkey River in May 1862.

dred carefully selected cavalrymen on a reconnaissance to find Brig. Gen. Fitz John Porter's Fifth Corps and determine the strength and location of the Union right. Stuart discovered that the Union flank was "in the air" (exposed to attack). He continued his ride on a complete circuit around McClellan's army. His four-day mission covered a hundred miles. He destroyed wagonloads of Union supplies and captured 170 Union soldiers and 260 horses and mules.

Lee couldn't have asked for more. He now knew where to attack and whom he wanted to lead the attack: Stonewall Jackson.

Earlier that spring, when Lee was Davis's military adviser, they had worked out a strategic diversion to keep McClellan from getting sizable reinforcements. Jackson was to take an army of at least seventeen thousand men to the Shenandoah Valley, engage Union forces in battle, and so threaten Lincoln and Stanton that they would divert sixty thousand soldiers from other tasks and disrupt Maj. Gen. Irvin McDowell's plan to link up with McClellan's right wing on the Peninsula. Three times McDowell was ordered to reinforce McClellan, and three times those orders were superceded by orders to stay put because of the threat Jackson posed in the Valley.

And what a threat it was. His brilliantly executed Valley campaign is still studied in military schools. In about fifty days Jackson marched his army four hundred miles and with little rest threw them into battle. His men outmaneuvered three separate Federal armies with a combined strength of thirty-three thousand and won five major battles. In four of them he brought superior numbers to the scene of combat, often shuttling Maj. Gen. Richard S. Ewell's force by railroad to the Valley to strengthen his combat power. Jackson's men gained a sense of pride and began calling themselves "foot cavalry" because they seemed to move as fast on foot as others did on horseback.

Jackson's victories created what historian James M. McPherson called "an aura of invincibility" around him and his foot cavalry. He became larger than life in the eyes of both Northerners and Southerners.

In his reports to Richmond, Jackson always credited God with his victories. Very religious, he sometimes refused to march or fight on the Sabbath. He did not smoke, drink, or play cards. He looked common, wore ragged uniforms, and scorned military display. A harsh disciplinarian, he demanded much from his men. That is, except during the Seven Days' campaign on the Peninsula.

Brig. Gen. Jeb Stuart's four-day reconnaissance around McClellan's army on the Virginia Peninsula enabled Robert E. Lee to know where to launch his attack.

LIBRARY OF CONGRESS

On June 16, Lee sent for Jackson and his foot cavalry. His instructions were:

> The present . . . seems to be favorable for a junction of your army with this. If you agree with me, the sooner you can make arrangements to do so the better. In moving your troops you can let it be understood that it was to pursue the enemy in your front. Dispose those to hold the Valley so as to deceive the enemy, keeping your cavalry well in their front, and at the proper time suddenly descending upon the Pamunkey [River]. . . . I should like to have the advantage of your views and to be able to confer with you. Will meet you at some point on your approach to the Chickahominy [River].

Jackson rested on Sunday, June 22. At midnight he mounted his horse and, accompanied by a single courier, rode rapidly toward Richmond for a conference with Lee. Using a relay of commandeered horses, he reached the city shortly after 1 p.m. He was dusty, stiff, and tired from nearly fourteen hours in the saddle.

At 3 p.m. he met with Lee and the other three division commanders—forty-one-year-old Maj. Gen. James "Old Pete" Longstreet, tall, dogged, and opinionated, with a spotty record in the field; thirty-seven-year-old Maj. Gen. Ambrose Powell Hill, a first-rate combat officer known as "Little Powell" because of his slimness; and forty-one-year-old Maj. Gen. Daniel Harvey Hill, Jackson's brave, sharp-tongued brother-in-law.

Lee, in a manner calm and stately, explained his plan for a bold initiative and then left the room so the generals could discuss it among themselves. Longstreet asked Jackson to set the date, since his troops were the only ones not on the scene. They agreed on Thursday, June 26, at the earliest possible hour. Jackson, after drinking a glass of milk, returned to the saddle and rode all night in a heavy rainstorm—his second consecutive sleepless night—to rejoin the Valley soldiers moving to meet him. But only the van of his army was where it was supposed to be. The main force was about fifteen miles away, marching slowly on muddy roads broken by swollen streams.

Jackson had less than forty-eight hours to bring them together and get them into position. Yet he was in no hurry. He needed sleep. He gave a few orders to his staff and then rode to a nearby plantation, took off his wet uniform, read part of a novel, and went to bed.

Battle of Beaver Dam Creek (June 26, 1862)

Lee had assigned Jackson one major mission. At 3 a.m. on June 26, with Stuart's cavalry screening his movements, Jackson was to swoop down on Fitz John Porter's exposed flank and force him to evacuate his main line. When A. P. Hill heard Jackson's guns, he was to cross the Chickahominy and drive through the Union forces in Mechanicsville. Then Harvey Hill and Longstreet would be able to cross uncontested to the north side of the river. They would form on each side of A. P. Hill, and the united Confederate line of fifty-five thousand men would force Porter's thirty thousand to retreat. The Rebels then would seize McClellan's base at White House Landing. McClellan, cut off from his supplies, would have to come out of his entrenchments and fight the Rebels on their terms and at a place of their choosing.

Lee was taking a big risk. The plan required expert coordination and execution by all his subordinates. About three-fourths of the Rebel forces would move away from McClellan's front and take position on his northern flank. If McClellan discovered the movement and was aggressive and smart, his seventy-five thousand men south of the river could overcome the thirty thousand Confederates on their front and smash through them to Richmond.

Lee knew McClellan was overly cautious and, in all likelihood, would not attack. But if he did, Lee was confident that his thin line of trenches could withstand an assault by superior numbers long enough for Lee to regroup and reposition. He told Davis: "If [they] will hold as long as [they] can at the entrenchments, and then fall back on the detached works around the city, I will be on the enemy's heels before he gets here." Davis approved the plan. The risk was great, Davis knew, but not so great as the possibilities for gain.

Lee's plan, if successful, could crush McClellan's army. Jackson was the key. Timing was critical. Jackson had the farthest distance to cover, and everyone had to wait until he made the first strike. Thus began what is known as the Seven Days' battles.

Jackson was to strike Porter's flank in the early morning. The other three Confederate divisions established their positions under cover of darkness. Lee watched from an observation post on the crest of a low ridge overlooking the river. He could see the Yankee outposts on the opposite bank. They were at ease, lolling around, not doing much of anything. It was time for Jackson

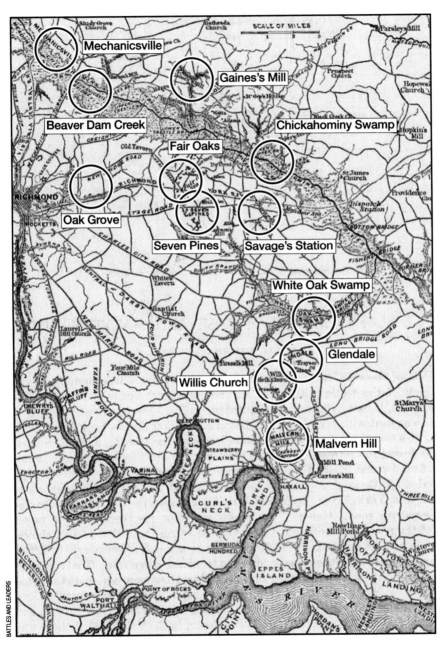

This map shows the region where McClellan's Peninsula campaign bogged down as well as the scenes of the Seven Days' battles that thwarted that campaign. The sites of the major conflicts leading up to the Seven Days' battles and the battles themselves are highlighted with circles.

Stonewall Jackson's brilliantly executed campaign in the Shenandoah
Valley was followed by five *"disastrous and unredeemable"*
failures in the Seven Days' campaign.

VIRGINIA STATE LIBRARY

to attack. But there was no sign of him and
no sound of his guns.

Shortly, Lee received a message that
Jackson's foot cavalry was three hours behind schedule. Jackson blamed it on poor
roads and hostile forces. A. P. Hill sent a message to one of his brigades: "Wait for Jackson's
notification before you move unless I send you
other orders." The hours passed. Another message
came; this one for the commander of Hill's detached brigade: Jackson was
six hours behind schedule. By noon that margin was gone. By 3 p.m. there
still was no Jackson.

Jackson's tardiness remains a mystery, regardless of the conditions he
was encountering. He had always obeyed orders to the letter. He once kept
an entire column of troops waiting in line to march while he stared at his
watch, unwilling to move one second before the time specified. But on this
day he had not moved at all.

More things went wrong. A. P. Hill, usually quick and impulsive, had
been unusually patient, frozen by the battle plan. Wearing his battle shirt—a
red wool deer-hunter's shirt—he decided to fight. Acting on his own at 3 p.m.
he led sixteen thousand men across the river and through Mechanicsville with
only minor skirmishing. In the distance his men saw the Yankees well positioned on the banks of Beaver Dam Creek, six miles from Richmond. The
banks were high, almost perpendicular; the approach was across open fields.

Hill's brigades struck at Porter's right flank and left center but got
nowhere. The Yankees' lead volleys from the steep brushy banks across the
narrow stream forced the Rebels to retreat. One of Harvey Hill's brigades
rushed to their support and was mowed down. Jackson should have been attacking the Union flank during the fighting, but no one knew where he was.

Lee's "grand assault" was a gory disaster witnessed by Jefferson Davis
and a cavalcade of Richmond politicians. Despite equally matched numbers, the Rebels were badly beaten, with 1,350 killed or wounded, compared to 361 for the Yankees. They were beaten primarily because Jackson's

18,500 troops were not there to unhinge the Federal line along the ridge. Jackson's failure caused confusion among the other commanders in carrying out the complex plan. A. P. Hill's forces, with some help from Harvey Hill, had borne the fight by themselves. Even Lee had been of little or no help.

So, where was Jackson? Actually, just a few miles away, but ten hours behind schedule.

On the night before the battle, Jackson halted about seven miles short of where he was supposed to be, then prayed through the night instead of

---

From Hero to Goat Within Weeks

Maj. Gen. John B. Magruder, known as "Prince John" because of his inflated ego, was both a Confederate hero and a goat during the Peninsula and Seven Days' campaigns.

His heroics evolved from his skills as an actor.

In a diversion during the Mexican War, he staged a performance of Shakespeare's *Othello* with himself in the lead role and Ulysses S. Grant as Othello's wife, wearing crinolines and a wig.

During the Peninsula campaign, at Yorktown, Magruder deceived George B. McClellan about the strength of the Rebel forces by marching small numbers of troops past the same position multiple times. He also moved around his artillery frequently and fired when Union troops were sighted. The ruse delayed McClellan's advance for many weeks. Magruder was praised by his then commander, Joseph E. Johnston.

Magruder applied similar antics south of the action at Gaines's Mill. He moved his twenty-two thousand troops from one location to another, along with fake wooden guns, and also ran a railroad back and forth throughout the night. "I am pretty tired," a Confederate corporal wrote home after marching in circles, "to show ourselves to the enemy at as many different points of the line as possible." The charade worked. McClellan held back seventy thousand men from the battle at Gaines's Mill, fearing Magruder's "superior force" would attack him. Unnecessarily unnerved, McClellan withdrew from Gaines's Mill, giving Robert E. Lee the victory.

Magruder's magnificence was short-lived. Possibly because of heavy drinking, he performed poorly in the Seven Days' battles at Savage's Station, Glendale, and Malvern Hill. At Malvern Hill, he became confused and marched three units away from the action. It took James Longstreet three hours to persuade Magruder he was wrong and to reverse the march.

As part of Lee's reorganization of his army after the Seven Days, he ousted Magruder and reassigned him to command the District of Texas, New Mexico, and Arizona.

resting. On this day his foot cavalry took seven hours to march just seven miles. They had to deal with felled trees across roads and burned bridges across creeks, but these obstacles should not have impeded these seasoned warriors. They often fought after marching twenty miles in a day.

Jackson finally arrived at his initial objective, Hundley's Corner, at about 5 p.m. It was nearly three miles from the battle line. Jackson could hear the roar of guns in the distance. But with only three hours of daylight remaining, he encamped for the night without notifying Lee of his arrival. He was exhausted. He had had only a total of ten hours' sleep in the past four nights. His men, too, were worn out from the Valley campaign, body-rattling railroad travel, and marching in oppressive heat and humidity over dusty roads with little water. Still, they had been given an assignment; Jackson had agreed to the date; and they had failed to do their duty because Jackson had failed to prod them. Apathy and lethargy had overpowered his iron discipline.

Battle of Gaines's Mill (June 27, 1862)

The Rebel fiasco gave McClellan two opportunities. He could take the offensive the next day, June 27, and go after the Rebel army and/or the Confederate capital. He wired Stanton: "The firing has nearly ceased. . . . Victory of today complete and against great odds. I almost begin to think we are invincible."

Strategically, however, he acted otherwise, rejecting the advice of subordinates who urged an attack. Instead, McClellan retreated. He ignored his opportunities because he feared he was heavily outnumbered. Devious maneuvers and diversions by Maj. Gens. Benjamin Huger and John B. Magruder helped create that illusion, as did McClellan's knowledge that Jackson was in the area. Jackson's presence and reputation probably intimidated McClellan, along with his belief that Jackson's force was much larger than it actually was.

Proud to be holding his own under such false assumptions, McClellan ordered Fifth Corps commander Fitz John Porter to take an even stronger defensive position than he had on the previous day. Porter chose some high ground behind Boatswain's Swamp, a boggy stream enclosing a horseshoe-shaped position of great natural strength. It was near Gaines's Mill, a brick-and-timber structure along Powhite Creek. McClellan told Porter to hold Gaines's Mill at all costs, then he wired Stanton that his army was "so concentrated that it can take advantage of the first mistake made by the enemy."

Lee planned to pursue McClellan, but he didn't know exactly where he was, and he still hadn't heard from Jackson. In desperation Lee sent a staff officer to find Jackson and tell him to continue his march eastward beyond the Union flank. About 9:30 a.m. Lee's anxiety subsided as he came upon Jackson and A. P. Hill talking in a country churchyard. Hill left, but Lee dismounted to confer with Jackson. Lee expected McClellan to make a stand at Powhite Creek, about a mile ahead, and he instructed Jackson to march to Cold Harbor, three and a half miles to the east. If Lee was correct, Jackson would then be behind the Yankees and able to cut them off or damage their flank as they came past him. Jackson nodded and rode on.

Lee was attempting another complex coordinated attack against the front and rear of Porter's corps. The flawed plan placed too much dependence upon the suddenly undependable and sleepy Jackson.

Jackson's four divisions were to attack the Union right (as he should have done the day before) while Harvey Hill came in on Jackson's flank and hit Porter's rear and cut off his line of retreat to McClellan's base at White House Landing. A. P. Hill was to assault Porter's center, and Longstreet was to

At Gaines's Mill, Confederate brigades unexpectedly encountered three separate lines of Yankee infantry and a hill crowned with guns. The Rebels turned and ran. That evening Lee resorted to a general assault that broke the Union line and forced their retreat.

LESLIE'S

This illustration shows the departure of the Federal flotilla from McClellan's abandoned base on the Pamunkey River to a more secure position on the James River. Accidentally burned was a house that was the home of Martha Custis when she married George Washington.

make a feint against the left. If Porter shifted troops to meet Jackson's threat, Longstreet and all fifty-five thousand Rebels were to advance against Porter's thirty-five thousand Yankees.

Like the day before, A. P. Hill's bloodied division would bear the brunt of the attack. They advanced around 3 p.m. intending to strike Porter's right center. Jackson meanwhile wandered lost in the pine woods.

Four of A. P. Hill's brigades penetrated deep into the open swampy areas, expecting to encounter Porter's exposed and vulnerable right. But Porter's flank wasn't where Lee expected it to be. Instead, Hill's brigades came face to face with a powerful fortress: three separate lines of Yankee infantry, dug one above another in a two-mile convex arc known as Turkey Hill. The height was crowned with guns facing the open field. Along its front was Boatswain's Swamp.

Lee didn't even know this place existed. It wasn't on his maps or Hill's. But Hill's men knew about it now as they were bombarded with rifle and artillery fire. They turned, ran, and stumbled back wild-eyed.

When Longstreet arrived, he recognized the difficulty of attacking over this terrain. He chose to wait until Jackson could attack on Hill's left.

Jackson was less than a mile away. Unfortunately for the Rebels, he was confused, and he and his foot soldiers just stopped, uncertain as to what action to take.

Jabs and counterjabs followed—minor fights with brigades attacking and withdrawing. By 4 p.m. the Yankees appeared to be in control. They had pinned down an entire division. It looked as if the Rebel attack was breaking up. Then, for the first time that day, Lee did something. Still waiting for Jackson, he ordered Longstreet to support A. P. Hill's right. Surprisingly, one of Jackson's division commanders suddenly showed up and on his own initiative supported Hill's left, adding strength to the faltering line.

Jackson finally arrived late in the afternoon but was disoriented following a day of pointless marching and countermarching. He and Lee made contact around 6 p.m. What Lee said to him is unknown, but Jackson's soldiers finally joined the battle line.

At 7 p.m. Lee resorted to a general assault involving fifty thousand troops going forward in concert. They gained ground. They reached the creek. They waded across it. They struggled up the banks, tossing their guns ahead of them.

Lee called upon Brig. Gen. John Bell Hood's Texas brigade to help break the Union line. With one of the most courageous charges of the war, Hood's brigade opened a gap in the center of the line, as did Brig. Gen. George E. Pickett's brigade on its second attempt of the day. The rest of the line collapsed. Lee's victory cost him nine thousand, most of them from A. P. Hill's division.

Fresh Union brigades from across the Chickahominy prevented a rout, and Porter withdrew his men and guns across the river during the night, burning the bridges behind him. He left behind sixty-eight hundred casualties.

McClellan wired Stanton: "I have lost this battle because my force was too small. I am not responsible for this." But he was. During the preceding two days of fighting, McClellan held back seventy thousand men. They were idle, doing nothing.

While the heavier action occurred north of the river, John B. Magruder again tricked McClellan about the size of the Rebel force south of the river. For that reason, McClellan kept those seventy thousand men in reserve in case this "superior" force attacked him. Magruder's force actually consisted of only twenty-two thousand men. To persuade Yankee observers that this force was many times its size, Magruder ordered an infantry unit to march in a wide circle for several hours and for his officers to call out orders to imaginary regiments in the woods. They lit extravagant campfires and made bold reconnaissances.

Union generals took the bait and warned McClellan about a strong Rebel force on their front. The predictable McClellan failed to counterattack, despite having overwhelming numbers. That night McClellan abandoned his base at White House Landing and ordered his entire army to withdraw toward a secure base he planned to erect at Harrison's Landing on the James River. There he would have the Union navy at his rear. His movement was a clear signal he would not try to capture Richmond by a siege and artillery bombardment. His siege guns required rail travel, and there was no railroad from the James.

McClellan's withdrawal is difficult to justify. It continues to puzzle military historians. He had withstood fierce Confederate attacks and was in a strong position. He had deployed only one of his five corps in battle. For whatever reason, Lee had unnerved him.

Even more strange is the telegram he sent to Stanton. It included this statement: "If I save this Army now I tell you plainly that I owe no thanks to you or any other persons in Washington—you have done your best to sacrifice this Army." The military telegraph office omitted this sentence from the copy delivered to Stanton.

While Stanton didn't like McClellan and had withheld thousands of troops he could have had, McClellan's existing force was strong enough to defeat Lee and capture Richmond. The problem was McClellan, not Stanton.

Battle of Savage's Station (June 29, 1862)

While McClellan was acting badly, Lee was roaring like a lion. On June 29, the Confederate commander formulated another complex plan. He intended to intercept and destroy McClellan's army before it reached the James. Lee put nine divisions on the march. They were to converge by six different roads against the retreating Bluecoats. Muddy roads, faulty maps, and, again, Jackson's slowness would frustrate Lee.

The Confederates caught up with elements of McClellan's army at Savage's Station, on the Richmond and York Railroad, just three miles south of the Chickahominy. There the Federals were preparing for the difficult march through and around White Oak Swamp. Two corps with full artillery

BATTLES AND LEADERS

As McClellan's army was retreating toward the James River, Lee caught up with the Federals' rear guard at Savage's Station. Stonewall Jackson's absence and Lee's poor staff work limited the assault to halfhearted stabs that were easily repulsed.

support protected a field hospital and the southward passage of McClellan's wagon train of supplies and wounded.

Lee supposedly ordered Jackson to attack from the north and Magruder from the west. Magruder, realizing he was outnumbered, sent orders down the line for "each commander to attack the enemy in whatever force or works he might be found." He expected Jackson's assistance at any moment.

Yet again Jackson disappointed Lee. He failed to show up at the proper time. Jackson had wasted an entire day resting his men and rebuilding a bridge over the Chickahominy, even though a suitable ford was available nearby. Huger also was late, and Longstreet and A. P. Hill were lost. Lee had ordered Longstreet to take the Darbytown road and cut off the Yankees' retreat to the south. Longstreet couldn't find the road. It took its name from a local farmer who called himself Darby when his actual name and the sign on the road was spelled "Enroughty." Hill, ordered to follow Longstreet, was equally confused and lost precious time. If Lee had given his division commanders local guides, these problems could have been averted.

Magruder opened the battle alone, using less than half his division. No reinforcements were around. His halfhearted stabs at the Union rear were easily repulsed, and he was soundly defeated. Lee sent Magruder a sharply worded note: "I regret that you have made so little progress today in the pursuit of the enemy." Meanwhile, McClellan's army continued its strategic retreat.

Some historians argue that Jackson's absence on the battlefield that day was due more to Lee's poor staff work than to Jackson's lethargy. They believe that Jackson was not aware of an order for him to attack and that Lee did not make any concerted attempt to find Jackson.

Battle of Glendale (June 30, 1862)

By noon on June 30 most of McClellan's army had maneuvered through and around White Oak Swamp Creek, but there was a traffic jam at Glendale that was complicated by the uncoordinated withdrawal. Lee, not one to give up easily, decided to strike at this bottleneck—a rear guard of four Union divisions. He directed seven divisions to converge on them near Frayser's Farm. This plan, too, would be badly executed.

Lee's plan to destroy McClellan's army before it reached the James was thwarted when Jackson's twenty-five thousand men failed to show up at Willis Church (Glendale). Needing to cross White Oak Swamp (pictured), Jackson ignored reports of suitable crossings and napped.

LIBRARY OF CONGRESS

Benjamin Huger, slowed by road obstructions, never reached the battlefield. At the same time, John B. Magruder seemed to be plagued by indecision. Stonewall Jackson, with twenty-five thousand men, again failed to do his part. Approaching White Oak Swamp from the north—an obstacle he had to cross—Jackson attempted to rebuild a bridge over the creek but found this unfeasible when Union artillery and sharpshooters fired on his infantry.

Jackson's brigade commanders found suitable crossings upstream and downstream, and Brig. Gen. Wade Hampton personally reported one of the possibilities to Jackson, who asked if the crossing could be bridged. Hampton replied yes, but only for infantry. Jackson instructed him to build the bridge. A work crew of some fifty soldiers cut down dozens of trees and fashioned a crude footbridge. Hampton galloped back to notify Jackson and found him sitting on a log, motionless. Hampton volunteered to lead the advance over the new bridge. Jackson, however, "sat in silence for some time, then rose and walked off in silence." Hampton, mystified, rode back to his troops.

Jackson sat down under a large oak and slept for an hour. After dark, while eating supper with his staff, he fell asleep again, this time with a biscuit in his mouth. Several minutes later he woke up and stood stiffly. "Now, gentlemen," he announced, "let us at once [go] to bed, and rise with the dawn, and see if tomorrow we cannot do *something*."

Two miles to the south, the divisions of Longstreet and the ever-present A. P. Hill attacked McClellan's flank in the late afternoon. President Davis, Lee, Longstreet, and their staffs observed the action on horseback until they came under heavy artillery fire. The party withdrew with two men wounded and three horses killed.

On the battlefield, Longstreet chose not to strike with a concentrated force. Instead he sent in brigade after brigade, piecemeal. With ferocious assaults, including hand-to-hand combat, they gained some ground and even took a thousand prisoners before being repulsed. Superior Yankee numbers ultimately made the difference. Confederates lost thirty-five hundred killed or wounded, twice as many as the Federals. Jackson's twenty-five thousand men certainly could have changed the outcome, especially if Huger's and Magruder's forces had also shown up.

Twenty-five years later, Longstreet placed the blame on Jackson. "[He] should have done more for me than he did."

Lee wrote in his official report, "Could the other commands have cooperated in the action, the result would have proved most disastrous to the
enemy."

Several days later Jackson wrote to his wife: "During the past week I
have not been well, have suffered fever and debility, but through the blessing of an ever-kind Providence, I am much better today." It was the only
time he ever admitted to a physical weakness.

Two weeks after the battle of Glendale, Jackson walked into a room
where staff officers were discussing the Seven Days' campaign. One of them
wondered why Jackson did not go to the aid of Longstreet and A. P. Hill.
Jackson responded bluntly: "If General Lee had wanted me, he could have
sent for me."

McClellan himself missed the Glendale battle. He sat in the comfort of a
gunboat on the James River and organized his new supply base. Having left
his troops with few orders, they fended for themselves. Perhaps that accounts for their success in thwarting Lee's plans.

Battle of Malvern Hill (July 1, 1862)

On the morning of July 1, Jackson seemed alert and ready for action,
having finally succeeded in crossing White Oak Swamp. He rode up to a
cluster of horsemen in the yard of Willis Methodist Church. Waiting for
him on horseback were Lee, Longstreet, A. P. Hill, Harvey Hill, and Magruder. Lee was irritable. Referring to the enemy as "those people," he
growled: "If those people got away [it's] because I cannot have my orders
carried out!"

Lee was determined to make one more thrust to destroy McClellan's
army. "We must push south," he asserted, sure that his army would find the
Yankees in another defensive position.

About thirty thousand Rebels were to advance in columns of four on a
single, narrow road through thickly wooded country. The countryside was
traversed by a swamp passable at only a few places, and those were difficult
crossings in themselves. Lee decided that the brunt of the attack would fall
upon the commands of Huger, Jackson, and Magruder, since they had not
been in action the day before. Longstreet's and A. P. Hill's divisions would
stay in reserve. Jackson was to lead the march.

Lee was not feeling well and asked Longstreet to ride with him in case it
became necessary for Longstreet to assume overall command.

LESLIE'S

Lee attacked the Federals at Willis Church expecting to use the forces of Jackson, James Longstreet, and A. P. Hill. The Federal line (pictured) repulsed the onslaught. The battle might have turned out differently if Jackson's troops had been engaged.

As Lee predicted, McClellan's army again had taken a strong defensive position. The Federals were staked on Malvern Hill, close to the James River and three miles south of Glendale. The hill, about 150 feet high, was actually a long plateau, three-quarters of a mile across the northern face and a mile and a quarter deep. Flanked by deep ravines, it could only be attacked frontally and uphill across open fields with a gradual ascent of about a half-mile to the crest.

As Jackson's columns came around a curve a quarter of a mile from Malvern Hill, Union shells exploded in front of them. Jackson rapidly deployed the troops, placing part of his force on the left of the Confederate battle line, with the remainder in reserve to go where needed. He was convinced that an assault from his sector was out of the question. Longstreet recommended positioning sixty cannon to achieve a cross fire on the Yankee position. Lee approved the placement.

The Confederate batteries opened fire in piecemeal fashion and were quickly knocked out by counterfire from the Union guns massed almost hub to hub. Jackson tried to place his guns to counteract the Federal artillery and dismounted several times to help roll cannon into place. John G. Gittings, a

LIBRARY OF CONGRESS

Union troops stood their ground against Confederate frontal assaults at Malvern Hill on July 1. The Union victory was so decisive that McClellan's generals believed they could take Richmond the next day. Instead, McClellan fell back to his supply base, thus ending his campaign.

volunteer aide who was steering a line of infantry, noted that Jackson's "face was aflame with passion . . . and his voice rang out sharp and clear."

Jackson encountered Brig. Gen. Chase Whiting casually smoking a cigar. "Move your guns forward!" Jackson ordered.

Whiting hesitated. He said only sixteen of his fifty guns had arrived and shouted at Jackson, "Those gunners won't live in there five minutes."

Jackson demanded, "Obey your orders promptly and willingly."

Whiting snapped, "I have always obeyed my orders promptly, but not willingly under such circumstances!" Reluctantly, he directed his battery commanders to move onto the field.

In a matter of minutes, the gunners and all sixteen pieces were blown asunder. "Great God!" Whiting exclaimed. "Won't some ranking officer come and save us from this fool!"

Lee's battle plan—his worst of the war—called for a major assault to drive the Yankees off the hill. It was to be based on one brigadier's opinion. Lewis A. Armistead's brigade occupied the center of the Confederate line. If, in his opinion, the Federal position had been sufficiently weakened by artillery fire, he was to charge "with a yell," and the other commanders were to "do the same."

Rebel artillery, however, was poorly utilized. The head of Lee's artillery reserve, Brig. Gen. William Nelson Pendleton, did not look for advantageous positions for his guns. He chose to await orders from Lee, but he received no orders. As a result, more than eighteen batteries in the reserve were never used. Pendleton was later accused of making himself inaccessible so that no orders could reach him.

As both sides continued to exchange artillery fire, Jackson and Harvey Hill decided to have a picnic. They sat atop a fence rail and ate biscuits and syrup.

Magruder, meanwhile, had lost three hours in getting to the battlefield. He had taken the wrong road.

By 2:30 p.m. the Yankees dominated the artillery exchange with no evidence of weakening. An officer in the Fifth New Jersey observed that the Southern artillerists "did not even get their guns unlimbered before our guns drove them like a flock of frightened sheep into the woods."

As Lee pondered what to do, he received word that Armistead had charged against the center of the Union line. The men came within 150 yards of the Federals before being driven back.

Around 4 p.m. Magruder's troops finally arrived on the field and, following Lee's original orders, assumed they were supposed to attack—which they did.

Longstreet later said that Lee had determined that no attack would dislodge the Yankees from Malvern Hill. Lee apparently canceled the attack but changed the order late in the afternoon, when he mistakenly assumed that certain Union troop movements indicated a withdrawal. Neither of these orders apparently reached his field commanders. Thus Armistead attacked, and two brigades in Magruder's division followed him. The three brigades—thirty-five hundred men—were swept by infantry and artillery fire. They wavered. Jackson, following Lee's original directive, then ordered Harvey Hill's ten-thousand-man division to join the charge. Unprotected, they too were struck unmercifully by deadly accurate artillery fire.

In a letter home, a North Carolina soldier wrote, "The enemy mowed us down by fifties."

A Massachusetts officer recorded, "We murdered them by the hundreds but they again formed and came up to be slaughtered."

Lee described the scene in gentler terms in his official report:

Orders were issued for a general advance at a given signal, but [obstacles] prevented a proper concert of action among the troops. [Harvey] Hill pressed forward across the open field and engaged the enemy gallantly, breaking and driving back his first line; but a simultaneous advance of the other troops not taking place, he found himself unable to maintain the ground he had gained against the overwhelming numbers and numerous batteries of the enemy. Jackson sent to his support his own division and that part of [Richard S.] Ewell's which was in reserve, but owing to the increasing darkness and intricacy of the forest and swamp they did not arrive in time to render the desired assistance. Hill was therefore compelled to abandon part of the ground he had gained after suffering severe loss and inflicting heavy damage upon the enemy.

On the right the attack was gallantly made by Huger's and Magruder's commands. Two brigades of the former commenced the action; the other two were subsequently sent to the support of Magruder and Hill. Several determined efforts were made to storm the hill. . . . The brigades advanced bravely across the open field, raked by the fire of a hundred cannon and the musketry of large bodies of infantry. Some [brigades] were broken and gave way, others approached close to the guns, driving back the infantry, compelling the advanced batteries to retire to escape capture, and mingling their dead with those of the enemy. For want of concert among the attacking columns their assaults were too weak to break the Federal line, and after struggling gallantly, sustaining and inflicting great loss, they were compelled successively to retire. Night was approaching when the attack began, and it soon became difficult to distinguish friend from foe.

Lee's emphasis on lack of "a proper concert of action among troops" reflected his own failure. Harvey Hill described the battle more succinctly: "It was not war; it was murder. My recollections of Malvern Hill are so unpleasant that I do not like to write about it. Twas a mistake to fight." A mistake indeed. Lee and Jackson had mismanaged the troops at hand. About fifty-six hundred Rebels were killed or wounded. The Yankees lost about three thousand.

That night, Lee asked Magruder, "Why did you attack?" Magruder replied, "In obedience to your orders, twice repeated." Lee did not respond.

That same night Jackson ate a small dinner in the front yard of a nearby farm and then lay down and was quickly asleep. Near 1 a.m. concerned officers rode into the yard. The Confederate lines were in disarray and would be destroyed if McClellan attacked the next day. They squatted around Jackson, waiting for him to wake up. One general finally yelled into his ear. Jackson responded, "Please let me sleep. There will be no enemy there in the morning." Events proved him to be right.

McClellan's protégé Fitz John Porter and others wanted to mount a counterattack the next day and take Richmond, but McClellan said no. Porter executed the withdrawal from Malvern Hill before dawn on July 2 and continued to Harrison's Landing, where McClellan's army was too protected for Lee to assault. As Lee explained to Jefferson Davis, "As far as I can see there is no way to attack him to advantage."

Lee, after seven days of fighting, lost a fourth of his army—twenty thousand Southerners, won only one battle (Gaines's Mill), but knocked the Yankees from the gates of the Confederate capital. He wrote to Jefferson Davis: "Our success has not been as great or as complete as I could have desired. Under ordinary circumstances the Federal Army should have been destroyed."

That army might have been destroyed if Stonewall Jackson had been *the* Stonewall Jackson of Bull Run and the Valley campaign. His failure in the Seven Days' campaign was, in the words of one historian, "complete, disastrous, and unredeemable." He was the Confederate goat of the campaign.

HARPER'S WEEKLY

Northern frustration over McClellan's failure to take Richmond (and thus end the war)—as well as his withdrawal after the Seven Days' battles—found expression in this *Harper's Weekly* cartoon, which depicted Secretary of War Edwin M. Stanton as a goat.

That phenomenon has a separate entry for Jackson in *The Civil War Dictionary*: "Jackson of the Chickahominy was a phrase used to distinguish the brilliant Jackson of the Valley from the ineffective Stonewall Jackson who failed five times during the Seven Days' battle."

Lee was clearly upset with Jackson's performance. But he obviously sensed the greatness in the man. When he reorganized his army into two corps in the aftermath of the Seven Days, he appointed Jackson to command one and Longstreet the other. Jackson would redeem himself in battles to come at Fredericksburg, Second Bull Run, Antietam, and Chancellorsville.

McClellan was the Federal goat. Initially, he had nothing to fear but fear, and that fear consumed him. All he had to do to defeat Lee and take Richmond was to issue a simple order—"Advance!" But he waited too long, and then it was too late. He was beyond redemption.

5

PORTER VERSUS POPE

BY THE SUMMER OF 1862 the Union's politicians and generals were, figuratively speaking, either in bed with each other or in the divorce courts. Radical Republicans ran the Joint Committee on the Conduct of the War. Maj. Gen. George B. McClellan, a Democrat, was failing miserably on the Virginia Peninsula. The JCCW and the Radicals reasoned that if one Democratic general was bad, then all Democratic generals must be bad. These Democrats were conservatives who opposed emancipation, were inclined to make cynical remarks about the government, and believed that radical politics had no place in the conduct of the war. Secretary of War Edwin M. Stanton wanted the wholesale dismissal of such "weak-kneed traitors."

What followed was a reign of terror—a campaign launched by Radical Republicans to destroy the Democratic generals through court-martials, high-profile smear campaigns, War Department dismissals, and congressional denunciation. Their primary target was McClellan, whom some had begun calling King George. With his problems on the Virginia Peninsula, the king was about to lose his crown. In the meantime, the JCCW had been grooming a successor and anointing him with Radical oil. He was Maj. Gen. John Pope, a Republican (of course) fresh from successes on the western front. As commander of the Army of the Mississippi Pope had scored important military victories at New Madrid, Missouri, and Island Number 10, which opened the Mississippi River to Northern commerce almost to Memphis.

On the recommendation of the JCCW, Lincoln summoned Pope to Washington. The general dazzled the right people, from the president to the

Radical politicos. With a commanding figure, piercing eyes, and an air of self-confidence, he proffered advice on military questions, took potshots at McClellan, and boasted he could decimate the Rebels in a single battle.

On June 26, Lincoln created a new army, the Army of Virginia, and placed Pope in command. The JCCW wanted more; the members meant to make Pope commander of the eastern army. To do so, they had to shove McClellan out of the way. With the collapse of McClellan's campaign in July and his army entrenched at Harrison's Landing, the Radicals demanded his removal and "a thorough change in the manner of carrying on the war." Treasury Secretary Salmon P. Chase said that McClellan "has cost us fifty thousand of our best young lives" and was "the cruelest imposition ever forced upon a nation." Stanton was in a like mood. They paraded Pope before the JCCW, and he thrilled them by endorsing Radical war aims and advocating harsh treatment for Rebels.

Stanton, who handled public relations for Pope, wrote a proclamation for him to issue to the Army of Virginia. Its most famous line boasted: "I come to you from the West, where we have always seen the backs of our enemies; from an army whose business it has been to seek the adversary; and to beat him when he was found; whose policy has been attack and not defense. . . . Success and glory are in the advance, disaster and shame lurk in the rear."

While politicians approved of Pope's bravado, such statements made the general instantly unpopular with the soldiers in the ranks. By inference, this pronouncement was a slap in the face to the men who had recently faced Stonewall Jackson in the Shenandoah Valley.

Meanwhile, Lincoln's general in chief Henry W. Halleck went down to McClellan's camp on the James River on July 25 and delivered an ultimatum: either attack Richmond with his army slightly augmented by new troops or withdraw and join Pope. McClellan wasn't about to attack without substantial reinforcements, so on August 3 he was directed to send his troops to Pope. Stanton and Pope had triumphed. Pope, referring to Lee's soldiers, claimed he could now "bag the whole crowd" at one swoop.

Maj. Gen. Fitz John Porter was among McClellan's commanders and officers who went grudgingly. They neither liked nor respected Pope. The thirty-nine-year-old Porter was McClellan's youngest corps commander and a loyal favorite with "Little Mac." Porter's Fifth Corps did the heaviest fighting on the Union side in the Seven Days' battles and suffered the most casualties. He especially distinguished himself at Malvern Hill. A New Englander who had taught artillery and cavalry at West Point, Porter appeared to be a rising star among Federal commanders. But by placing him under Pope, Halleck was clouding his future.

Two weeks earlier, Porter had written to a Washington insider, J. C. G. Kennedy: "I regret to see that Gen. Pope has not improved since his youth and has not written himself down, what the military world has long known, as an ass." Pope, he said, would never reach Richmond except as a prisoner of war. Porter said such views should be heard in Washington, but he warned Kennedy "never to disseminate them as mine." The letter wound up in the hands of Lincoln and Stanton, and Stanton passed it on to Pope!

Multiplying future problems that would endanger his career, Porter regularly sent military and political commentaries to the editor of the Democratic *New York World*. In one he described Pope as a tool of the Radical Republicans dominating the government and as "a vain man (and a foolish one) . . . who was never known to tell the truth when he could gain his object by a falsehood."

Now, Porter had to serve under the man he despised. His Fifth Corps was among the first of McClellan's units to hook up with Pope. It would not be a happy union.

As Fitz John Porter's corps advanced upon Stonewall Jackson, James Longstreet's corps enfiladed Porter's ranks with shot and shell. Three times Porter made vigorous attacks and was repulsed with heavy losses.

LESLIE'S

Porter didn't help his cause by making other derogatory statements about Pope in the telegraphic link to Washington. The link went through Maj. Gen. Ambrose E. Burnside, who held the Federal position on the Rappahannock River. With comments intended only for Burnside, Porter wrote: "It would seem . . . that [the enemy] was wandering around loose, but I expect they know what they are doing, which is more than anyone here or anywhere knows. . . . I wish myself away from it, with all our old Army of the Potomac, and so do our companions." Burnside forwarded the reports to Lincoln and Stanton. Porter's loose tongue, combined with his politics and actions to come, would bring him to trial on the gravest of charges.

* * *

As the threat to Richmond from the east subsided, Lee became concerned that Pope's army might attack Richmond from the north. On July 13 he sent Stonewall Jackson with two divisions north to Gordonsville to be in position to oppose Pope if he decided to move south. Shortly, Lee learned from a deserter that McClellan's army was boarding transports and leaving Harrison's Landing. Lee correctly concluded that McClellan and Pope were joining forces. That could be disastrous for the Confederacy.

Lee's solution was to attack the Army of Virginia before the merger. On August 13 he ordered the remainder of his army to Gordonsville to form with Jackson. Then on August 25 Lee gambled on a clever tactical move. Splitting his army, he sent Jackson with half of it, twenty-four thousand men, on a brilliant maneuver—a long arcing flank march around Pope's right and to his rear. This placed Jackson's force between Pope's army and Washington, cutting Pope's lines of supply and communication.

At the rail junction of Manassas, twenty-five miles west of Washington, Jackson looted and destroyed Pope's undefended supply base, a square mile of warehouses containing supplies of every description, from rations and quartermaster goods to munitions, liquor, and medical supplies.

Jackson then abandoned his exposed position for a hiding place on a wooded ridge a couple of miles west of the old Bull Run battlefield. One soldier later recalled that they were "packed [in there] like herring in a barrel." They lounged about, playing cards and enjoying the supplies they had taken from the warehouses.

Jeb Stuart's cavalry had maintained liaison between Jackson and Lee, so Jackson knew that James Longstreet's advance units would join him on the morning of August 29. Jackson would await Longstreet's arrival and the consolidation of the army under Lee.

Pope by now was aware of Jackson's destruction of the Manassas supply center, but Jackson had seemingly vanished. Pope sent a division to look for him, and it stumbled onto his hiding place on the evening of August 28. In a fierce fight at dusk the outnumbered Yankees inflicted considerable damage before withdrawing. The battle was a stalemate.

Pope was convinced he had trapped Jackson. To concentrate the bulk of his army against him, Pope issued orders for nighttime marches to unite his army. Fitz John Porter and Philip Kearny were ordered to begin their marches at 1 a.m. Because Porter's men had just completed an all-day's march and were exhausted, Porter waited until 3 a.m. to give them more time to rest. This delay was within the normal discretion allowed a corps commander, and nothing was affected by the delay, but Pope would later cite this as one of several charges against Porter.

Kearny, a socially prominent New Yorker who had also been part of McClellan's Peninsula campaign, notified the courier who brought the orders to march to "tell General Pope to go to hell. We won't march before morning." That was not within his normal discretion. Then a conflicting order came from the commander of the Third Corps, Maj. Gen. Irvin McDowell, who instructed Kearny to "hold your position." Disobeying both orders, Kearny fell back and then became lost in the woods all night.

Of these three generals, only Porter would be charged with disobedience. During that fateful day, Porter's friend McClellan was in Washington, resisting Halleck's orders to rush to Pope's aid with another corps from the Army of the Potomac. McClellan told Lincoln he should stay and defend Washington and let Pope "get out of the scrape by himself." He told others he would not send his men to the battlefield because it would be throwing good money after bad. He didn't want to waste men for a failed cause.

Pope was determined to bag Jackson on August 29, before Longstreet reached the field, which Pope incorrectly estimated would happen on August 31. But instead of waiting until his forces were concentrated in front of Jackson, Pope launched a series of attacks with no more than thirty-two thousand men available. He hurled his divisions against Jackson in piecemeal assaults that were poorly coordinated and badly led. The twenty-two thousand Rebels, concealed and sheltered in the trenches of an unfinished railroad track, repulsed each attack, with heavy casualties on both sides.

Pope wanted McDowell and Porter to turn Jackson's right flank while the rest of the army struck his center and his left. But they did not receive their orders until noon, and Pope said nothing about attacking. The orders were to advance and halt, departing from the directive only "if any considerable advantages are to be gained."

McDowell's thirty thousand troops were slow arriving. Only a few of his regiments saw action, and that was in a moonlight skirmish. Porter, on the other hand, chose not to attack, which seemed to be an option available to him.

Pope issued another dispatch to Porter at 4:30 p.m.:

Your line of march brings you in on the army's right flank. I desire you to push forward into action at once on the enemy's flank and, if possible, on his rear, keeping your right in communication with General [John F.] Reynolds. The enemy is massed in the woods in front of us, but can be shelled out as soon as you engage their flank. Keep heavy reserves and use your batteries, keeping well closed to your right all the time. In case you are obliged to fall back, do so to your right . . . so as to keep you in close communication with the right wing.

Both orders to Porter were based on Pope's assumption that the enemy was Jackson, and only Jackson. Porter knew that Pope was wrong and therefore did not attack. Porter had discovered that Longstreet's corps of twenty-five thousand men was squarely across his designated line of advance, outnumbering him nearly three to one. If Porter had attacked with his nine thousand men as Pope ordered, "I suppose we should have cut him to pieces," Lee said after the war.

Pope should have known of Longstreet's presence through effective reconnaissance, but he didn't. Pope wired Halleck:

We fought a terrific battle . . . which lasted with continuous fury from daybreak until dark. . . . Our troops are too much exhausted yet to push matters, but I shall do so in the course of the morning. . . . The enemy is still in our front, but badly used up. . . . [The enemy] stood strictly on the defensive, and every assault was made by ourselves. Our troops behaved splendidly. . . . The news just reaches me from the front that the enemy is retreating toward the mountains. I go forward at once to see.

John Pope had bragged he could "bag the whole crowd" at one swoop. Instead, the crowd (the Army of Northern Virginia) bagged him at Second Bull Run, ruining his career. McClellan's inaction also contributed to Pope's defeat.

As darkness fell, Porter moved to the main line. Before dawn he met with Pope and explained why he hadn't attacked as ordered, warning Pope about Longstreet's corps. Pope, however, refused to believe him. Pope remained convinced that Longstreet was nowhere near the battlefield and would not arrive until the evening of August 30 or 31.

Believing Jackson was retreating toward the mountains, Pope had prepared for a major assault at sunrise, and it would go forward. Porter would be heavily engaged.

Pope had ordered McDowell to lead a two-pronged pursuit, contesting Jackson's presumed retreat from two directions. Porter's corps and two of McDowell's divisions would go one way, and Samuel Heintzelman's corps and McDowell's other divisions would go another. "Press Jackson vigorously during the whole day," Pope urged his commanders. The pursuit began at 2 p.m.

Pope had made several erroneous assumptions. Contrary to the Union commander's thinking, the Rebels were not retreating, and Jackson had moved his troops to another position—in woods at the base of a mountain—to give them some rest. Longstreet remained where he was, apparently still unseen by Pope, but eager for a confrontation—as was Lee.

While Lee was working on a plan to move around Pope's right, Jeb Stuart rushed in to report that the Federals were massing along Jackson's front. Jackson also had observed this activity, but he expected nothing to come of it. He was wrong. Just before 3 p.m. the Federals came charging at Jackson in three separate waves, stronger and more determined than they had been the previous day.

Jackson received urgent requests for reinforcements all along his two-mile front. At several points his men ran out of ammunition and were throwing rocks in a last-ditch effort to hold the line. Others snatched rifle cartridges from the dead and wounded. Lines wavered. Jackson, who had no reserves, appealed to Lee to send help from Longstreet. The Federals continued to fight with redoubled fury, striking Jackson's line again and again, as if taking out their bitter resentment of Pope and McDowell on the Rebels.

Then eighteen guns of Longstreet's artillery reserve fired on the Union troops, striking the closely spaced rows of startled Federals who had been unaware of this danger to their flank. Now, Pope realized that Longstreet was on the scene. Decimated by the artillery fire, the second and third lines of Federals retreated in disorder. Then the first line wavered and gave ground.

With Jackson no longer needing reinforcements, Lee ordered an all-out counterstrike. Longstreet was already in motion, and his twenty-five thousand men bore down on the enemy. That charge started Jackson's men forward. It was the largest simultaneous mass assault of the war. On both sides, the widespread Rebel jaws began to close.

Porter's Fifth Corps was on the Federals' exposed flank. Two New York regiments were on his left as a shield against disaster; they bore the brunt of Longstreet's assault at the hands of John Bell Hood's Texans. One Union regiment of 490 Zouaves suffered 347 casualties, including 124 dead—the largest percentage of men killed in any Federal regiment in any single battle of the war. Altogether, Porter lost 2,100 men, about a quarter of his force.

Pope was surprised and unprepared. His left flank was crushed; his army fell back to Henry Hill, scene of the hardest fighting in the battle of First Manassas thirteen months earlier. Confederate battle flags "danced after the Federals as they ran in full retreat," Hood reported to Lee, calling it "the most beautiful battle scene I have ever beheld." Lee noted gravely: "God forbid I should ever live to see our colors moving in the opposite direction."

That night Pope, no longer boasting, decided to pull back toward Washington. Federal casualties totaled 16,054 from a total force of 65,000. Pope left 2,000 wounded on the field. The Confederates lost 9,197 out of a total of 55,000.

Maj. Gen. Fitz John Porter, McClellan's "pet," became Pope's scapegoat for the defeat at Second Bull Run. Pope and Secretary of War Stanton successfully conspired to have Porter court-martialed as an example for all Union generals who were members of the Democratic Party. It took Porter twenty-three years to clear his name.

To the demoralized rank-and-file Federals, the blame lay with Pope and McDowell. McDowell had been deeply involved in the decision-making behind Pope's failure on the battlefield. He made at least two costly mistakes. McDowell supposedly knew that Longstreet's corps was marching toward the battlefield but was tardy in notifying Pope, and he ordered the removal of a division from the left flank immediately prior to Longstreet's decisive attack. Soldiers accused McDowell of treason and threatened to shoot him. Some said that whenever Confederates saw McDowell's hat they conserved their ammunition because they were convinced that his record of poor command would accomplish more than their fire.

Pope and McDowell, in turn, blamed Porter and McClellan for lack of cooperation and refusal to obey orders. Lincoln agreed with Pope that McClellan's inaction was "unpardonable." The young Napoleon had "wanted Pope to fail," the president told one of his private secretaries. Lincoln and Halleck, however, decided to put McClellan in charge of the Washington defenses and later reunited the two armies under him. The president relieved McDowell of command and transferred Pope to Minnesota. Later, McDowell was exiled to California.

Stanton and the Radicals were in a frenzy over the loss of Pope and the retention of McClellan. Lincoln said he was "greatly distressed" at having to take these actions, but while McClellan had "acted badly . . . he has the Army with him. We must use what tools we have. . . . If he can't fight himself, he excels in making others ready to fight." Lincoln had taken note of the army's reaction when McClellan rode out to greet the dispirited troops returning to Washington. One soldier noted that enlisted men "threw their caps high into the air and danced and frolicked like school boys. . . . The effect of this man's presence was electrical and too wonderful . . . to give a reason for it."

Pope did not go quietly to Minnesota. "The treachery of McClellan and his tools" are responsible, he exclaimed. He put in motion a scheme to have McClellan's pet, Fitz John Porter, court-martialed. Pope blamed his failure to smash Jackson's army on August 29 on Porter's failure to attack Jackson's right flank—a failure Pope insisted was responsible for the Rebel victory at Second Bull Run. Porter, he asserted, was guilty of disobeying an order and misbehavior before the enemy.

Stanton and the Radical Republicans were eager to help Pope. They needed an example for other Democratic generals and a cure for "McClellanism," a disease they defined as bad blood and paralysis infecting much of the officer corps of the Army of the Potomac, a disease making men too cautious, too hesitant, too unwilling to fight, and inclined to overestimate enemy strength. They succeeded, and a general court-martial to try Porter was scheduled to convene in Washington in November.

Historian Stephen W. Sears analyzed the trial in his insightful and thought-provoking book *Controversies and Commanders*. He noted that anyone reading the trial transcript would be surprised if the court found Porter guilty—but it did. The verdict was predictable because the nine generals sitting in judgment were predictable. Stanton had packed the court to guarantee a conviction. The generals were:

1. Maj. Gen. David Hunter, a Republican, an abolitionist, an enemy of McClellan
2. Maj. Gen. Ethan Allen Hitchcock, who had opposed McClellan's Peninsula campaign and admitted to being cowed by Stanton's bullying
3. Brig. Gen. Silas Casey, whom McClellan had demoted for his failures on the Peninsula
4. Brig. Gen. Napoleon Bonaparte Buford, Pope's chief of cavalry whom Treasury Secretary Salmon P. Chase promised a promotion and an army posting for his son if he voted guilty
5. Brig. Gen. Rufus King, who disobeyed orders from McDowell at Second Bull Run and should have been disqualified for this conflict of interest
6. Brig. Gen. James B. Ricketts, a personal enemy of Porter who served under McDowell at Second Bull Run
7. Brig. Gen. James A. Garfield, a future president, who, as a protégé of Secretary Chase, was predisposed to vote guilty
8. Brig. Gen. Benjamin M. Prentiss, a hero at Shiloh and a leader of Missouri's Republican Party, who was a rare independent thinker on the court
9. Brig. Gen. John P. Slough, a hot-tempered politician expelled from the Ohio General Assembly, a brigade commander in the Shenandoah Valley, and recently made a brigadier general of volunteers

Stanton's friend Joseph Holt, judge advocate general of the army, was the chief prosecutor. A simple majority was required for conviction; a two-thirds majority was all that was required for the death penalty.

The Republican and Democratic press acted as if the proceedings were a political contest between McClellan and Pope. Horace Greeley's Washington correspondent wrote that Porter should be shot. The Democrats screamed that Holt and Hunter were denying Porter a fair hearing. They called the trial an underhanded scheme to attack McClellan.

The major charge against Porter was his failure to attack on August 29 after receiving Pope's 4:30 p.m. order to do so.

Pope's nephew, Douglass Pope, testified that he delivered Pope's 4:30 dispatch within half an hour of its writing, which, if true, gave Porter adequate time to launch at attack. But Porter, his staff, and his field commanders all insisted that the message arrived about 6:30, near sunset, and at that time it was too late to mount an attack before dark. Porter said he could prove the time by a message he sent back to McDowell, but he had no copy, and McDowell said he did not remember it. It would turn up fifteen years later in McDowell's papers.

Even if Porter had received the message earlier, he said he could not have attacked at any time that day because his path was blocked by a superior Confederate force. That was true even though Porter couldn't prove it. He had not discovered the enemy's strength, and he had not reported to Pope that day what he had actually encountered. He reported the next morning, but Pope did not believe him.

McDowell was the prosecution's chief witness. More interested in saving his own skin than in seeing justice done, he made several false statements and remembered only what was advantageous to him. He had to look out for himself because he was facing a court of inquiry in the same building about his own military record. If he supported Porter's version of events, he would be admitting his own mistakes. (The court of inquiry cleared McDowell of culpability, possibly as a reward for his testimony against Porter.)

McDowell's testimony was based on the premise that he had trouble "remembering." He could recall hardly anything the defense wanted him to remember. He said events had to be connected to "some important things, such as daylight and darkness" in order for him to remember them.

On all the main points of contention in the Porter case, the defense produced the larger number of witnesses and more authoritative ones than did the prosecution. Pope's own testimony was self-damaging. It became clear that he did not know the positions of his own troops or those of the enemy and that he had issued orders without knowing much about the real situation on the battle lines. For example, he flatly denied Porter's contention that Longstreet was on the battlefield when he issued orders on August 29.

There was nothing, he said, to prevent an attack by Porter's Fifth Corps. He was wrong on both counts.

Ambrose E. Burnside was asked about Porter's anti-Pope comments in the dispatches Burnside had forwarded to Washington. Burnside said he found nothing unusual about them; everybody in the Army of the Potomac had talked that way about Pope. That did not help Porter's cause, but before these judges nothing could have.

Porter was found guilty under two articles of war—failure to obey lawful orders and misbehavior before the enemy. Only Prentiss cast a dissenting vote in the final tally. His vote damaged both his political and military clout.

Porter was the first army general to be convicted by general court-martial since the War of 1812. He was sentenced to be cashiered from the army "and to be forever disqualified from holding any office of trust or profit under the Government of the United States." Lincoln approved the verdict without comment.

"Porter's frame of mind was un-officer-like and dangerous," wrote Capt. Charles Russell Lowell to a friend. "This sort of feeling was growing in the army, and the Government and the Country felt that it must be stopped. Porter was made the example."

For the next twenty-three years Porter tried to clear his record. He continually applied for a rehearing based on evidence newly discovered or not available at the time of the trial. Again politics intervened. He remained committed to the Democratic Party, and as long as the Republicans were in power, he wasn't likely to get anything he wanted. After Ulysses S. Grant became president, he surprisingly did nothing to help Porter even though he earlier had stated that Porter suffered "a very great injustice." Grant's successor, Rutherford B. Hayes, ignored Porter's concerns initially but then took an action of sorts.

In 1878, Hayes appointed a three-man board of army officers to rehear the case. The Schofield Board, named after its senior officer, John M. Schofield, heard 142 witnesses and recreated the Second Battle of Bull Run, supplemented by accurate maps of the field of battle. These maps, testimonies, and official reports of Confederate officers threw new light on the circumstances as they existed in Porter's front on August 29. Longstreet confirmed that his entire command had been there on that day. Other witnesses furnished important facts McDowell could not remember. Douglass Pope recanted his story at the trial that he had delivered Pope's message to Porter shortly after 4:30. He admitted he had gotten lost on the way. The board wrote in its report:

> The fact is that Longstreet, with four divisions of 25,000 men was there on the field before Porter arrived with his two divisions of 9,000 men; that the Confederate general-in-chief was there in person at least two or three hours before the commander of the Army of Virginia himself arrived on the field, and that Porter with his two divisions saved the Army of Virginia that day from the disaster naturally due to the enemy's earlier preparations for battle.
>
> If the 4:30 order had been promptly delivered, a very grave responsibility would have devolved upon General Porter. The order was based upon conditions which were essentially erroneous and upon expectations which could not possibly be realized.
>
> What General Porter actually did do . . . now seems to have been only the simple necessary action which an intelligent soldier had no choice but to take. It is not possible that any court-martial could have condemned such conduct if it had been correctly understood. On the contrary, that conduct

Nine generals were handpicked by Secretary of War Stanton to guarantee the conviction of Fitz John Porter. The trial was an underhanded, political scheme to attack McClellan's supporters.

HARPER'S WEEKLY

was obedient, subordinate, faithful, and judicious. It saved the Union army from disaster on the 29th of August.

Piece by piece the case against Porter fell apart. On every charge, the board agreed with Porter. It criticized him only for his insulting comments about Pope. That, the board said, "cannot be defended." In a personal note to Porter, Schofield wrote, "The cold terms of an official report could but faintly express the feeling which my associates fully shared with me when we fully realized the magnitude of the wrong under which you had so long suffered." The board accordingly recommended to the president that he set aside the findings and sentence of the court-martial and restore Porter to his rank in the service from the date of his dismissal.

When Hayes, a Republican, appointed the Schofield Board, congressional Republicans were outraged. To placate them, he submitted the board's proceedings and conclusions to Congress for action. That year and for the next several years, bills to provide relief for Porter were proposed and defeated. One Republican senator mirrored the feelings of others when he exclaimed, "If we pass the Porter bill the widow of the North will point to the empty chair at the table where the father once sat who was slain in the battle because Fitz John Porter lingered and lagged behind and failed to add strength to the conflict."

James A. Garfield's administration was of no help, but after Garfield's assassination, the new president, Chester A. Arthur, issued a presidential pardon to Porter in 1882. Porter was then able to hold public office. A relief bill also passed both houses of Congress, but in a weird flip-flop, Arthur vetoed it. He had suddenly remembered that he was a Republican.

The Democrats finally came into power in 1884. Two years later, President Grover Cleveland signed an act "for the relief of Fitz John Porter." The House of Representatives had passed it by a vote of 113 to 11, the Senate by 30 to 17.

Porter's twenty-three-year battle was over. He was no longer the scapegoat for the Union's defeat at Second Bull Run.

6

BURNSIDE'S BLOODBATH

YOU'RE FIRED!" PRESIDENT LINCOLN probably wanted to say personally to George B. McClellan, commander of the Army of the Potomac. But he chose a more diplomatic course and sent a War Department emissary to deliver orders for "Little Mac's" removal. McClellan's demotion was due to his failure to pursue and destroy Robert E. Lee's Army of Northern Virginia after the Union's slim victory at Antietam in Maryland on September 17, 1862.

Actually, the battle was a tactical draw, but Lee quietly withdrew his exhausted army across the Potomac on the night of September 18. If McClellan had followed Lincoln's order to get moving and "cross the Potomac and give battle to the enemy," he could have gotten between the Rebels and Richmond and confronted Lee in a fight to the finish. But he didn't. His feeble pursuit took him eight days just to reach and cross the river, a feat Lee accomplished in one night. That was the last straw for Lincoln. He was tired of trying "to bore with an auger too dull to take hold."

On November 7, Lincoln replaced McClellan with Maj. Gen. Ambrose E. Burnside as commander of the Army of the Potomac. Burnside was McClellan's scapegoat for not achieving a decisive victory at Antietam. McClellan accused Burnside of being so slow in following orders that his twelve thousand troops took seven hours to subdue five hundred Georgians at the Rohrbach Bridge on Antietam Creek and then attack Lee's right flank. The delay, according to McClellan, prevented a rout of Lee's army.

Maj. Gen. Ambrose E. Burnside replaced George B. McClellan as commander of the Army of the Potomac on November 7, 1862. The two had once been close friends, but they became distant after McClellan blamed Burnside for the army's failure to win decisively at Antietam.

Burnside could have crossed on shallow fords downstream, but he fixated on the narrow bridge. On the opposite side, five hundred Georgians were dug into a steep embankment facing the bridge. Burnside foolishly ordered his men forward in columns that were easy targets for the Georgia sharpshooters. The first column was cut down before it reached the bridge. But Burnside stuck to his plan and sent more columns forward. They suffered the same results. After two hours of such idiocy, some Union soldiers sought cover behind a low stone wall and fired back at the Rebels. Scores of others then rushed the bridge and made it across. The Georgians retreated.

Getting twelve thousand men over the bridge took time, but Burnside had them reassembled quickly. At 3 p.m. they attacked and within an hour were on the verge of crushing Lee's right flank. Only Lee's foresight and McClellan's lack thereof prevented that from happening.

Early that morning Lee had sent an urgent message to Maj. Gen. A. P. Hill at Harpers Ferry to bring his division to Antietam. Just as Burnside was minutes from victory, Hill's division appeared on Burnside's left flank, where Burnside had positioned a regiment of raw Connecticut troops. Hill struck them with a massive force. The regiment collapsed, as well as Burnside's advance. His men panicked and ran toward the bridge.

It didn't have to happen. McClellan had two corps he never used at Antietam. If he had supported Burnside with a push by the Fifth Corps, the outcome probably would have been different, and McClellan would have had his decisive victory. Burnside, too, was at fault. Had he crossed Antietam Creek earlier than he did, he could have destroyed Lee's right flank before Hill's arrival. These failures made goats out of both McClellan and Burnside. But despite Burnside's mistakes, McClellan still could have ended the war on September 18 by engaging two full corps of fresh, unused troops to smash Lee's battered army either on the battlefield or during

Lee's retreat. To cover his own ineptness, McClellan filed a report severely critical of Burnside.

Once over the bridge, Burnside was courageous and aggressive, as he was in the spring of 1862 when he commanded land and naval forces that had captured Roanoke Island, New Bern, and Beaufort along the North Carolina coast. The success of that complex operation brought him to Lincoln's attention as a soldier of promise.

Lincoln wanted a field commander he could trust and work with. And to avoid morale problems, the president wanted someone who was not hostile to, controlled by, or as slow as McClellan. Another plus for Burnside was his lack of political opinions. Lincoln assumed he would probably escape the wrath of Radical Republicans and the Joint Committee on the Conduct of the War. Among existing corps generals, Burnside seemed the best choice.

Lincoln generally sized up persons accurately, but in this case, he underestimated the extent to which Burnside's flaws could overshadow his strengths and undermine a major military operation.

"Burn," as the general was called, was thirty-eight, six feet tall, and for many years, a close friend of McClellan. He graduated from West Point in

Burnside issues orders to his staff immediately after assuming command of the Army of the Potomac. To others he acknowledged he wasn't "fit for so big a command, but would do his best."

LESLIE'S

1847, eighteenth in a class of thirty-eight. After six years of routine assignments, he left the army to go into business, making breech-loading carbines he had invented. Within four years that venture was bankrupt.

Before this financial crisis, he received his worst personal shock when his fiancée, a lovely Kentucky girl, accompanied him to the altar and responded to the minister's final ceremonial question with an emphatic, "No!"

McClellan, who was chief engineer of the Illinois Central Railroad, pulled some strings to land a job for Burnside there, and before long he was the railroad's treasurer. Then the war broke out. Rising from the ranks of the Rhode Island militia, Burnside organized the First Rhode Island Infantry, commanded a brigade at First Bull Run, and secured the North Carolina coast for the Union.

Burnside was good at following orders, but he was bad at deviating from them when the situation warranted. And although he lacked military imagination and flexibility, he applied these characteristics to his appearance. Heavy dark brown hair covered the lower sides of his nearly bald head and flowed down the sides of his face as bushy, muttonchop whiskers. The whiskers then curved up to cross below his nose, forming an elaborate mustache. This hairstyle, minus a beard, made him famous and was responsible for the coinage of the word *sideburns*, which was an inversion of his name.

Unlike most generals, Burnside was modest, shy, and unsure of his abil-

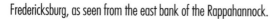

Fredericksburg, as seen from the east bank of the Rappahannock.

ity to lead an army of one hundred thousand men. He twice declined Lincoln's offer before accepting it, and then became nervous and depressed. Many years later, Ulysses S. Grant wrote in his memoirs that Burnside was "an officer who was generally liked and respected. He was not, however, fitted to command an army. . . . No one knew this better than himself."

When a group of generals congratulated Burnside, he responded by telling them he knew he was "not fit for so big a command, but would do his best." A few moments later the generals talked among themselves, and several shook their heads and wondered how they could have confidence in a leader who had no confidence in himself.

Knowing Lincoln wanted offensive action during the autumn months, Burnside fretted, worked long hours, and became physically ill. But he drafted a plan for review by General in Chief Henry W. Halleck, Lincoln's military adviser. Burnside proposed to move the army east from near the Blue Ridge Mountains to Warrenton, then make a diversionary move directly southwest to Culpeper Court House, before heading southeast to Fredericksburg, an important rail crossing and prosperous old colonial town of four thousand residents on the banks of the Rappahannock River.

Historically significant, Fredericksburg had been the home of George Washington's widowed mother, Mary; the place where James Monroe had his law office; and where Robert E. Lee had courted Mary Custis, the great-granddaughter of George Washington's wife, Martha. The town was fifty miles from both Washington and Richmond. If Burnside could cross the river and capture Fredericksburg, his army would be in a good position to advance to the Confederate capital.

"Old Brains" Halleck didn't like the plan and didn't think Lincoln would either. So Halleck went to Burnside's headquarters at Warrenton to talk it out. Burnside stubbornly insisted on going to Fredericksburg, and Halleck reluctantly agreed to forward the plan to Lincoln for a decision.

Lincoln reminded Burnside that taking Richmond would not end the war; his objective should be to engage and defeat Lee. But Lincoln wanted to show support for his new commander, so he agreed to Burnside's plan with one stipulation. Halleck wired Burnside: "The President thinks the plan will succeed if you move rapidly; otherwise not."

Lincoln realized that Burnside's only chance of success was to cross the Rappahannock and be on the way to Richmond before Lee's army could confront him. The Army of Northern Virginia was now split. Stonewall Jackson's corps was in the Shenandoah Valley to protect Virginia's breadbasket, and James Longstreet's corps was east of the Blue Ridge but near primary rail lines. Burnside would have a head start if he didn't dillydally. Burnside understood and believed he could cross the river before Lee could bring up Longstreet to obstruct him and certainly before Jackson could arrive.

The bold plan had the potential of ending the war in a single day. But that required brilliant generalship.

To cross the four-hundred-foot-wide Rappahannock, Burnside told Halleck he needed pontoon bridges—temporary bridges resting on floating pontoons that were lashed together and anchored in the waterway—and so Halleck ordered a large number of them to be transported to Falmouth, on the northeast side of the river from Fredericksburg. Burnside gave Halleck a deadline for delivery, and "Old Brains" assured "Burn" that the pontoon train would be at Falmouth when his army got there.

Meanwhile, Burnside prepared to execute the campaign. To reduce the number of generals reporting to him, he reorganized the Army of the Potomac into three Grand Divisions under unlikely commanders—sixty-five-year-old Maj. Gen. Edwin "Bull" Sumner, a white-haired former cavalryman described by McClellan's military adviser, the Count of Paris, as having "an air of stupidity that perfectly expressed his mental state"; boastful, conniving Maj. Gen. Joseph Hooker, whom Burnside hated; and Maj. Gen. William B. Franklin, who acted bewildered and confused at Antietam and was perceived as slow moving, apathetic, and not eager to fight.

A week after Burnside's appointment, and a day after Lincoln approved his plan, Burnside had Sumner on the move; the rest of the army followed over the next two days. Old Bull, without McClellan to slow him down, marched his veterans to Falmouth in less than three days, arriving on November 17—not bad for a forty-mile march. No Confederates were there, which was good news for Sumner and Burnside, but there were no pontoons there either, and that was bad news.

Sumner, although old and unimaginative, could think clearly. Arriving first, it seemed logical to him to ford the river and take the heights above Fredericksburg before Lee could beat him there. Sumner had ample time to establish a strong, fortified bridgehead. If he had been allowed to do so, the battle of Fredericksburg probably would not have occurred.

Sumner's men discovered that the river was easily fordable upstream. They had observed stray cows crossing without difficulty. So Sumner sent

General in chief Henry W. Halleck did not like Burnside's plan to cross the Rappahannock and capture Fredericksburg. Either through incompetence or malicious intent, Halleck failed to deliver on time the pontoon bridges Burnside needed to cross the river.

word to Burnside that he could wade across and take the town without a fight. Burnside objected and said to stay where he was. With dark storm clouds moving in, Burnside was afraid that Sumner could become isolated on the opposite side before Hooker and Franklin arrived to cross. The pontoons would be there any minute, Burnside said, and the entire army would have plenty of time to cross the river before Lee arrived. Burnside was wrong.

Burnside arrived in Falmouth with the main body of the army on November 19. The army positioned itself on Stafford Heights, from which observers could see the spires of picturesque Fredericksburg. But they couldn't see any pontoons, because there weren't any. If the army had forded the river then, it could have been on the road toward Richmond at least a full day ahead of Longstreet, who didn't arrive in Fredericksburg with half his corps until the afternoon of November 21. That would have forced Lee and Longstreet to rush to battle while Stonewall Jackson was at least a hundred miles away. And that could have been the decisive battle of the Civil War. But Burnside foolishly refused to cross the river without pontoons. He wasn't about to modify his game plan.

Until now, Lee had been outgeneraled by Burnside. But Burnside's failure to exploit his early advantage would prove costly and save Lee's hide.

Where were the pontoons?

Since Halleck was responsible for delivery, he was especially at fault. Whether from malicious intent or lackadaisical bungling, Halleck's requisition for the pontoon-bridging equipment was mailed, not wired, on November 6 to the supplier near Harpers Ferry, and he did not receive the request until November 12, a loss of six critical days. Thirty-six pontoons reached Washington on November 14, and the commander of engineers, Brig. Gen. Daniel Woodbury, wired Burnside that "one train would start on the morning of November 16 or 17" and that another would be ferried down the Potomac to Aquia Landing. The first train, however, did not start

Pontoon supplies were ferried down the Potomac to Aquia Landing and then transported overland to Falmouth, on the northeastern bank of the Rappahannock, across from Fredericksburg. The weeklong delay was devastating for Burnside's plans and gave Lee enough time to collect his army and dig in.

until November 19, a loss of three more days. When rain and mud slowed its progress, it was diverted to the Potomac and floated down the river. Woodbury later testified he was not aware of any urgency. No one had told him when Burnside would be moving toward Fredericksburg.

On November 22, the rains came, the river rose rapidly, and the waterway was no longer fordable. On November 25 the remainder of Longstreet's corps arrived, and he occupied Fredericksburg.

Both armies faced each other across the river, engaging in "watchful waiting." Confederates passed the time by digging in and having snowball fights. Union bands broke the monotony one night playing "Hail Columbia," "The Battle Hymn of the Republic," and of all things, "Dixie," the last prompting cheering and laughter on both sides.

Finally, on November 27 the pontoons and building materials showed up. If they had arrived on November 19 or 20, the army could have crossed the river with little resistance. "But now," Burnside notified Halleck, "the opposite side of the river is occupied by a large Rebel force under General Longstreet, with batteries ready to be placed in position to operate against the working parties building the bridge and the troops in crossing."

Nevertheless, the engineer in charge later testified they could have thrown two bridges across the river on the night of November 27 without interference from the enemy if Burnside had consented. He didn't.

Burnside's message to Halleck included this dismal admission: "I cannot make the promise of probable success with the faith that I did when I supposed that all parts of the plan would be carried out."

Burnside was so mentally paralyzed by having lost the element of surprise he didn't know what to do, even though he had the tactical advantage—110,000 troops compared to about 40,000 with Longstreet. When Jackson's corps reached Falmouth on December 1—having marched 150 miles in twelve days—the Confederate strength grew to more than 75,000.

Burnside had given Lee the gift of time, and the Confederate commander used it wisely to choose the perfect defensive position—four miles of high ground in the steep hills south and west of the town. That gave Longstreet's corps a broad range of fire over a half-mile stretch of open fields the enemy would have to cross. Lee hoped the Yankees would assault this position, but he didn't think they'd be that stupid. He expected them to bypass the town and move farther downriver. To his surprise, they didn't budge.

Lee then strengthened his resistance to their anticipated river crossing so that Jackson's corps would have time to connect with Longstreet and extend the Confederate line another three miles. Jeb Stuart's cavalry brigades were posted on both flanks of the line.

Directly behind the town was Marye's Heights—two hills, one rising steeply from the flat plain. Along their face ran a sunken road fronted by a stone wall. It would become a formidable Confederate position. With the town situated directly between the two armies, Lee advised the local citizens to evacuate, which they did.

Lincoln, growing impatient, wired Burnside on November 25: "If I should be in a boat off Aquia Creek at dark tomorrow evening, could you, without inconvenience, meet me and pass an hour or two with me?"

They conferred twice—at Aquia Creek on November 26 and in Washington on November 27. Little is known about what was said, but it appears that Lincoln advised Burnside to cross the river and attack the enemy *if* Burnside thought he had a fair chance to succeed.

Burnside regarded the attempt as "somewhat risky." Lincoln urged him to use his best judgment.

Burnside planned to cross directly in the enemy front in early December. It would take Lee by surprise, he said. He reasoned that Union artillery positioned on Stafford Heights would prevent Lee from mounting infantry maneuvers to hinder the bridge builders. The Army of the Potomac would run several bridges simultaneously, from the northern and southern edges of town and another a mile beyond.

Burnside issued oral instructions to his commanders on December 10. He told them where to go but not much else. Sumner was directed to take Fredericksburg and strike the Rebels on the heights beyond the town. Franklin was to occupy the plain south of town and then maneuver the Confederate right (Jackson) off their high ground. Hooker's division would be held in reserve and intervene where needed.

Burnside apparently didn't have a well-rounded, detailed plan as to how the attack should be pressed. And his generals apparently didn't pursue the matter by asking relevant questions about their specific responsibilities and options. They did, however, give their opinions. The dominant reaction was, "We don't like it." One brigade commander said, "If you make the attack as contemplated, it will be the greatest slaughter of the war; there isn't infantry enough in our whole army to carry those heights if they are well defended." A member of Sumner's staff added, "The carrying out of your plan will be murder, not warfare." Burnside, while jarred by their reaction, ordered them to follow the plan.

The upstream bridge builders began their work of placing and anchoring pontoons in the wintry predawn darkness and dense fog of Thursday, December 11. Confederate pickets in Fredericksburg heard the noise and alerted William Barksdale's Mississippi brigade. They were positioned in and near buildings throughout the town. As the fog lifted, their musketry rang out, toppling the leading engineers into the water and forcing others to scamper back to the shore. The unarmed pontooneers kept trying to return to their work, but each time they were cut down or driven back.

Union artillery on Stafford Heights retaliated with a two-and-a-half-hour bombardment of nine thousand shells into the town. A correspondent wrote, "The earth shook beneath the terrific explosion of the shells, which went howling over the river, crashing into houses, battering down walls, splintering doors, and ripping up floors." It wrecked and burned houses but had little effect on the sharpshooters, who found cover in cellars and rifle pits. After the shelling, they rose from the rubble and targeted the bridge builders.

In desperation, Union infantrymen volunteered to paddle across the river and dislodge the snipers. They succeeded, established a bridgehead, and engaged them in bitter street fighting that continued through the remaining daylight hours. Meanwhile, more Union infantrymen ran across the completed bridges and drove the riflemen out of town, house by house. But sixteen hundred Southerners had held up Burnside for an entire day.

Franklin's three lower bridges had been completed by 11 a.m. with little opposition. He could have passed a couple of divisions over quickly and swung north to scatter the sharpshooters. But Franklin waited five hours before sending any brigades across. Burnside countermanded this crossing because of the delay in completing the upper bridges, and Franklin's advance elements marched back across the river to their original position.

Burnside's first written battle orders were as imprecise and incomplete as his earlier oral instructions. Franklin, for example, received this order: "After your command has crossed, you will move down the old Richmond road, in the direction of the railroad, being governed by circumstances as to the extent of your movements. An aide will be sent to you during your movements."

Burnside did not state Franklin's objective in clear, unmistakable language. He made no reference to his earlier oral instruction to maneuver Jackson's corps off their high ground. Sumner's and Hooker's written instructions were equally deficient.

Burnside was placing his army close to the Confederates without ordering them to fight and without telling them what to do if the enemy attacked. Franklin, Sumner, and Hooker should have received clearly defined orders that allowed reasonable discretion to them and to their corps commanders. But they didn't.

By nightfall on December 11 Burnside could have moved most of his army across the river. Instead he chose to wait until morning.

Maj. Gen. Edwin "Bull" Sumner and his division arrived first at Fredericksburg, but they were forbidden by Burnside from fording the river. Had Sumner been allowed to cross, the battle of Fredericksburg probably would not have occurred.

As fog shrouded the valley on December 12, the long blue lines of men began crossing the swaying bridges. Union guns on Stafford Heights fired over their heads to keep the Rebels from interfering. By noon, as the fog lifted, Lee could see them clearly. Realizing the battle would be fought the next day, he sent for Jackson's other two divisions.

As the Federals arrived by the thousands in Fredericksburg with nothing in particular to do, they turned into undisciplined mobs. They looted. Breaking into private homes, they slashed paintings; smashed furniture, pianos, and glassware; snatched women's lace-trimmed underwear from bureau drawers; stole clothing, blankets, and family treasures; dumped flour and molasses on rugs; and threw Bibles and other books into the streets. To Southerners, this plundering reinforced their stereotype of the barbaric damn Yankees. The wanton destruction, said the *Richmond Enquirer*, was further proof that the true Yankee was "a compound of cant, cunning, treachery, avarice, cruelty, and cowardice."

Union regiments cross the Rappahannock in boats to drive Confederate sharpshooters out of town so that the pontoon bridges can be completed for use by the main army. Rebel sharpshooters were killing the unarmed engineers working on the bridges.

LIBRARY OF CONGRESS

Lee, now knowing Burnside's intentions, shifted his troops for the battle on Saturday, December 13. His full army would be united and ready to fight.

At sunset on December 12, Sumner and Hooker had 57,000 men facing Longstreet's 41,000 on the heights. Franklin had 51,000 opposing Jackson's 39,000. More than 140 Federal cannon lined Stafford Heights, and another 190 accompanied the attacking columns. It was less than two weeks before Christmas and one day before many of the fun-loving Yankees would be ready for coffins.

On the late afternoon of December 12, Burnside left his headquarters to meet with Franklin and his corps commanders, Maj. Gens. John F. Reynolds and William F. Smith. The three generals submitted what they regarded as their only sensible attack plan—to form two assault columns on either side of the Richmond road and to turn Lee's right flank (commanded by Jackson), no matter what the cost. Burnside gave his tacit approval, and the generals worked most of the night on details for their divisions.

At 7:45 a.m., Franklin, Reynolds, and Smith received written orders from Burnside ignoring their plan and reinstituting his original directives to keep their Grand Division "in position for a rapid movement down the old Richmond road" and "to send out at once *a division* at least" to seize "if possible" Prospect Hill, which was on Jackson's far right.

Sumner was to assign one division to march straight toward Longstreet and take Marye's Heights. Two of Hooker's divisions were to stand by at the bridges Franklin would use to cross the Rappahannock. Then, after occupying Prospect Hill and Marye's Heights, Franklin and Sumner were to place their artillery there and force Lee to abandon his position and retreat to the south.

With eighteen divisions on hand and ready for action, Burnside had decided to use only two. With all that power at his disposal, Burnside would try to win without using it.

Why? Burnside hadn't grasped the complexity of the situation. From his headquarters across the river and far removed from the potential battlefields, he did not seem to know much about the terrain, the obstacles, or the positions of Lee's army. Nor did it seem to occur to him that Lee was likely to concentrate his resources against the limited Union assaults.

It didn't require a military genius to know better than to send a cat to conquer a lion, which is exactly what Burnside ordered by committing a powerful force piecemeal. Further, by using the words, "if possible," he was acknowledging his own uncertainty, and that did little to inspire his troops or to build confidence in his leadership.

But Burnside had spoken, and Franklin, Sumner, and Hooker had their duties to fulfill. To pierce Jackson's line at Prospect Hill, Franklin chose Reynolds's corps. Reynolds, in turn, selected the division commanded by his friend Maj. Gen. George Gordon Meade. Although this division of Pennsylvanians was the smallest in the corps—only forty-five hundred men—it was one of the best in the army.

Meade was ready to advance by 8:30 a.m. under cover of the heavy morning fog. Brig. Gen. John Gibbon's division was assigned to support Meade. All of Franklin's other divisions would stand in readiness. Meade surely assumed they would join the attack and envelop the Rebel position.

Slowed by enemy fire almost at once, Meade's division plodded forward until his men came within six hundred yards of the railroad at the base of the high ground on which Jackson's corps was posted. There they were held up for two hours until Reynolds's artillery silenced the resistance. Resuming the advance, they encountered gunners on Jackson's right. After an artillery slug match, Meade reached the foot of the slope. Gibbon, on the right, ran into point-blank fire at the railroad embankment. He was wounded and brought back on a stretcher. Two of his brigades became confused and retreated.

Meade's Pennsylvanians encountered a wide stretch of wet, spongy ground A. P. Hill had left unmanned, thinking it impenetrable. But Meade's troops slogged through it. After pushing forward, they found a seam in Jackson's line along a wooded ravine, penetrated Hill's defenses, and scattered the startled Rebels while taking several hundred prisoners. This could have been a major breakthrough if supporting troops were thrown in. They weren't.

Burnside had goofed again by his inadequate preparations and poor communications. Franklin, too, was at fault. In spite of Burnside's restrictive directive, Franklin should have seized the moment and rushed forward some of his unemployed divisions to exploit Meade's success. Franklin also had an entire corps of twenty-five thousand men nearby, but for the most part, this corps sat out the battle. With that power and depth properly engaged, the battle of Fredericksburg might well have had a different ending.

In contrast, A. P. Hill wasted no time in sending for help, and Jackson quickly dispatched Brig. Gen. Jubal Early's division and other brigades to plug the gap. They came on the run and counterattacked Meade's troops as they were sweeping northward along the lower ridge. These yelling gray-

HARPER'S WEEKLY

Street fighting cleared Brig. Gen. William Barksdale's Mississippi brigade from Fredericksburg. Then the Federal skirmishers broke into private homes and looted the town.

backs struck Meade's front and both flanks. The attack drove the Pennsylvanians back through the boggy gap and into the open fields. The Rebel pursuers fired viciously at the Federals' rear and flanks.

Meade's troops might have been wiped out if Brig. Gen. David B. Birney's division, idle on the sidelines, had not responded when the Pennsylvanians streamed toward them. The combination of Birney's support and the Rebels' coming into range of the Union artillery halted the counterattack. Birney inflicted more than five hundred casualties. But Meade had suffered a severe mauling, losing more than a third of his men while accomplishing nothing.

Lee watched nervously from his hilltop command post during the breach in the line and sighed with relief when it was repaired. He said to Longstreet, "It is well that war is so terrible—we should grow too fond of it." Longstreet, whom Lee called "my old warrior," was, at age forty-one, fourteen years younger than Lee. But on this day Lee looked young and dapper with a glow of victory on his face.

While Lee was full of zip, Franklin seemed full of fear. After Meade's costly venture, Franklin was not about to deliver another attack. Instead, he formed a tight defensive line and decided his day's work was over. Then a courier delivered an order from Burnside to renew the attack. Franklin replied that "any movement to my front is impossible at present. The truth is, my left is in danger of being turned. What hope is there of getting reinforcements across the river?" That was a bizarre question since Franklin had only employed three of his eight divisions offensively and had not used an entire corps of twenty-five thousand men.

Burnside read the note and exclaimed, "But he must advance!" He dispatched another courier to Franklin with an order to move forward on his entire front—in other words, to make a grand assault. Franklin refused. He repeated that he was in grave danger, and he didn't have time. The sun was setting, he said, and it would soon be dark. He may have felt that any order from Burnside could not be regarded as intelligent.

Franklin was right on one point: he was susceptible to an attack by Jackson. But Franklin certainly had adequate troops to deal with any assault. Jackson was itching to strike the inactive bluecoats. If all those thou-

Pontoon bridges farther down the river were completed with little opposition for use by Maj. Gen. William Buel Franklin's division. After his advance elements crossed, Burnside countermanded the crossing because the upper bridges weren't ready, and Franklin's troops marched back to their original position.

sands of Federals weren't going to approach the ridge, he wanted to go after them. "I want to go forward," he said, "to attack them—drive them into the river." Lee approved it, and Jackson initiated it. But he canceled the attack when he realized that Union artillery fire from Stafford Heights could annihilate his men.

Franklin's troubles paled compared to the bloodletting at the other end of the battlefield. At Marye's Heights, Sumner obeyed Burnside's orders to take a single division and attack Longstreet's position. Longstreet was well prepared. His artillery had wide fields of power. His infantry was protected by the terrain and by a long four-foot-high stone wall in front of a sunken road along the forward slope of the hill. North Carolinians manned this natural trench, standing in two parallel lines along the wall. Both the wall and the sunken road were invisible to the attackers.

One of Longstreet's battalion commanders declared that the fields in front of them were so thoroughly targeted by the artillery on the ridge and the rifles of the infantry at its foot that "not even a chicken could live to cross." His grim prophecy was accurate. If Burnside had conducted a few reconnaissances, he surely would have come to the same conclusion. Any other general would have grasped the efficient killing ground approaching Marye's Heights.

HARPER'S WEEKLY

Maj. Gen. William Buel Franklin is one of the many goats of
Fredericksburg. He failed to reinforce Maj. Gen. George Gordon
Meade after Meade had succeeded in penetrating Stonewall
Jackson's defenses.

Bull Sumner dutifully ordered the Second Corps to advance against this line, en-
trusting the mission to Brig. Gen. William
H. French's division. These bluecoats
marched out of the outskirts of town and
started up the gentle slope toward Marye's
Heights some eight hundred yards distant. About
halfway there they encountered their first obstacle—a
drainage ditch crossable only by bridges—and suffered substantial losses
from Longstreet's artillery. Those who survived the crossing then encountered a barrage of rapid-fire volleys from behind the stone wall.

Still, French's men surged forward as masses fell against the Confederate
sheet of flame. Some got as close as two hundred feet to the wall before being
forced back. While they retreated, French's second brigade advanced past
them and suffered the same fate. Another brigade then tried and also failed,
essentially wiping out French's division. They were replaced by Brig. Gen.
Winfield Scott Hancock's division. By this time four ranks of Georgians and
North Carolinians stood behind the wall, loading and shooting in such a
fashion as to create nonstop, machine-gun-like torture. Thousands of Union
soldiers lay dead or wounded in front of the wall. Even those who were not
shot fell to the ground to avoid being killed. Behind Hancock came Brig.
Gen. Oliver O. Howard's division, and they also were slaughtered.

"We marched up against a shower of shot and shell," said a New Jersey soldier, "and what a horrible sight it was to see men mowed down by
the dozens."

"It can hardly be in human nature for men to show such valor," noted a
newspaper reporter, "or generals to manifest less judgment."

Burnside, who never saw the front himself, ordered Hooker to send two
more divisions against the stone wall. Hooker, who had seen the front,
begged Burnside to withdraw the order because the stone wall could not be
taken. Burnside refused to alter his plan. So two more divisions struck at
Marye's Heights and struck out in the process.

Wave after wave of blue soldiers had fought courageously and hope-lessly, making six successive assaults in division strength—forty thousand men repulsed by six thousand Rebels, with the ghastly carnage before the wall totaling more than sixty-three hundred. Hooker suspended the attack, refusing to sacrifice more men needlessly.

During the bitter-cold night hundreds of uninjured Federals who had hugged the ground in front of the wall hustled back to their lines. Burnside used the darkness to send another division to hide close to the stone wall and make an early morning assault. In a Halloweenish kind of night, they rolled the frozen bodies of the dead in front of them to form human breast-works for protection in the fight to come. Around them they could hear the moaning cries of the wounded on the ice-cold ground. Farther down the line, ragged Confederates replenished their clothing by scavenging coats, uniforms, blankets, and even underwear from the dead.

When the morning fog lifted, the Yankee division found themselves much closer to the wall than they intended to be—less than a hundred yards. Immediately pinned down by Rebel fire, they had to lie there all day in an uncomfortable and hazardous position. "We were unable to eat, drink, or attend to the calls of nature," one officer reported. "Raising a head or arms drew fire instantly. Even stretcher bearers were hit."

Burnside himself actually crossed the river that night to inspect the front. He believed he could break Lee's line by continuing the attacks. He sent out orders to do so. Recrossing at 4 a.m. to his headquarters, he wired Washington: "We hold the first ridge outside the town, and three miles below. We hope to carry the crest tomorrow." Earlier that night Lee wired Richmond that he expected Burnside to renew the battle at daylight.

Burnside rose early Sunday morning and was immediately confronted by Sumner. "General," he said, "I hope you will desist from this attack. I do not know of any general officer who approves of it, and I think it will prove disastrous to the army."

Taken aback, Burnside later wrote, "Advice of that kind from General Sumner, who had always been in favor of an advance whenever it was pos-sible, caused me to hesitate."

When the other Grand Division commanders gave the same advice, Burnside reacted with despair. He spoke wildly about personally leading a desperate all-or-nothing charge against the stone wall. Talked out of it, he retired to his tent. One of Franklin's corps commanders, Maj. Gen. William

F. Smith, followed him and found him pacing back and forth, convulsed in agony, mumbling, "Oh! oh those men! Oh, those men!"

"What men?" Smith asked.

"Those men over there [across the river]. I am thinking of them all the time."

Burnside finally took the advice of his commanders and chose not to fight. After all, they had taken the town of Fredericksburg. That was a victory of sorts, and he was reluctant to give it up. So the army sat there for two days while Burnside stroked his bushy whiskers, perplexed and distraught and pondering what to do next.

Sunday evening Lee conferred with Longstreet, who had known Burnside in the peacetime army. Lee remarked, "General, I am losing faith in your friend, General Burnside."

At sunset "a magnificent aurora borealis made its appearance, tinging the heavens blood red," according to a Richmond newspaper. This natural beauty of the northern lights contrasted starkly with the ghastly ugliness of the unburied Northern dead stripped of their clothing and the haunting cries of the wounded, many of whom froze to death that night.

The next morning Burnside called for a truce so he could collect and bury the dead and care for the wounded. Later that day he realized his situation was hopeless and his only viable choice was to withdraw from Fredericksburg to the north side of the river. Tears streamed down his face when he gave the order. As he rode past his men, an aide called for three cheers for Burnside. No one responded.

His once grand Army of the Potomac, now battered, recrossed the river unmolested during a violent winter storm of wind and rain and took up the bridges behind them. The retreat was conducted so quietly and quickly that the Confederates weren't even aware of it. The storm had covered the noise. Lee, who had anticipated another assault, regretted he had allowed the enemy to escape without punishment. He wrote to his wife, "They suffered heavily, as far as the battle went, but it did not go far enough to satisfy me." He could only claim "having checked the enemy without destroying him, and the vulgar glory of our having killed and wounded several thousand men more than we had lost."

Lee and Jackson rode into Fredericksburg that afternoon and were angered by the rampant vandalism they witnessed. "What can we do?" a staff officer asked.

"Do?" replied Jackson. "Why, shoot them." He later added: "We must do more than defeat their armies. We must destroy them."

Lee's army took up collections to relieve the suffering of the town's civilian population. They raised more than eleven thousand dollars.

The battle statistics were embarrassingly awful and lopsided. With 106,000 Federals opposing 75,000 Confederates, Federal casualties totaled 12,653, most of them in front of the stone wall. Confederate casualty estimates range from 4,600 to nearly 5,400. The battle stands as one of the worst defeats in the history of the U.S. Army.

The slaughter at Fredericksburg moved Lincoln to say, "If there is a worse place than Hell, I am in it." Letters from soldiers revealed a morale crisis: "I am sick and tired of disaster and the fools that bring disaster upon us. . . . My loyalty is growing weak."

The major goats who brought disaster upon the Union were Halleck, Burnside, and Franklin. Burnside's campaign plan probably would have been successful if Halleck had delivered the pontoons on time. By ordering them via mail and by not conveying a sense of urgency to the commander of engineers, Halleck displayed unforgiving incompetence.

Even without pontoons, Burnside squandered other options and other

Defenders behind this stone wall below Marye's Heights mauled attacking Federal regiments.

opportunities available to him. Civil War historian Edward J. Stackpole noted Burnside's failure to "think imaginatively, . . . take calculated risks, and improvise ingeniously." The unexpected triggered Burnside's mental collapse and exposed his deficiencies. He was strangled by stubbornness and instability. Having lost the advantage, he poorly mismanaged the battle and subjected his troops to monstrous slaughter.

Franklin deserves a share of the blame for failing to reinforce Meade after he had penetrated Jackson's defenses. Franklin had enormous resources that lay idle as men in blue perished. Franklin's lack of communication with Burnside during the entire day of the battle was irresponsible. He made no effort to offer suggestions, request instructions, or to have his orders modified. The Joint Committee on the Conduct of the War heaped all blame on his shoulders, partly because of his close ties to McClellan, whom they disliked passionately, but also because they believed Burnside's plan would have succeeded if Franklin had used more troops.

Nevertheless, it was Burnside's battle, and it was his bungling that led to the bloodbath.

On the Southern side, A. P. Hill was a goat for leaving a huge gap in the Rebel line. The breach could have spelled disaster for the Confederates. Jack-

Confederate Gens. Robert E. Lee, George E. Pickett, Stonewall Jackson, and James Longstreet observe the battle of Fredericksburg.

son, who probably knew the gap existed, loudly condemned Hill, adding to the enmity between them and the problems Lee faced within his command.

The winter of 1862–63 was the winter of Northern discontent. Many in the North blamed both Lincoln and Burnside.

Burnside blamed himself and said so in a letter to Halleck. He wrote: "To the brave officers and soldiers who accomplished the feat of . . . recrossing the river in the face of the enemy, I owe everything. For the failure of the attack I am responsible."

Burnside requested a meeting with Lincoln and said he would publish a letter taking all the blame for Fredericksburg. Lincoln was pleased that a general would relieve him of any responsibility for the disaster.

Hooker, Franklin, and other officers not only blamed Burnside but wanted him removed from command. They argued that he was incompetent and dangerous.

On December 30 two brigadier generals—John Newton and John Cochrane—informed Lincoln that Burnside was preparing to cross the Rappahannock again, that the army distrusted his ability, and that his proposed move would result in another disaster.

Shocked by their visit and what they told him, Lincoln wired Burnside: "I have good reason for saying you must not make a general movement of the army without letting me know." Burnside rescinded the orders for his advance and met with Lincoln in Washington on New Year's morning.

Lincoln, without divulging the names of Newton and Cochrane, told Burnside that none of the leading generals had any faith in his proposed move. Lincoln himself expressed misgivings and sent for Halleck and Secretary of War Edwin M. Stanton to join the conference.

While Burnside was still alone with Lincoln, he acknowledged he lacked the confidence of his major officers and therefore should be relieved. He then added a scorcher by stating that Halleck and Stanton also lacked the confidence of the army and the country and ought to be removed. Burnside put that opinion in a letter to Lincoln, but the president refused to formally receive it.

The four-man conference continued for two days but reached no decision. Burnside returned to camp determined to make the crossing but wanted official permission to execute it. He wrote two letters—one to the president offering to resign if he didn't approve it, and one to Halleck requesting general directions. Halleck's evasive response was that he advised a crossing some place at some time, as early as possible, with all or part of the army, if the movement could be made on favorable terms. Lincoln approved Halleck's letter and wrote to Burnside: "Be cautious and do not understand that the government is driving you."

On January 20, 1863, Burnside sent his army upstream toward shallow fords he should have used in November. He planned to cross the Rappahannock and sweep down on Lee's left flank. One problem surfaced—mud, lots of it—from torrential, chilling rains. The whole army bogged down in what was later called the "Mud March." Wagons and artillery pieces could not move on the impassable roads. Snow and freezing rain sapped the men's desire to fight as they settled into makeshift camps. Three days after starting the advance, Burnside called if off.

Back in Washington, Burnside attempted to dismiss Hooker, Newton, and Cochrane from the service and told the publisher of the *New York Times*, Henry J. Raymond, that if Hooker resisted, he would swing him before sundown. Raymond informed Lincoln of Burnside's intentions, and the president said he would stop Burnside from issuing the order.

One of Burnside's aides reminded him that he didn't have the authority to dismiss an officer, that only the president could do that. So on January 24 Burnside presented Lincoln with the dismissal order and his resignation and told him he could accept either one, but that he would not go on as things stood.

Lincoln said he'd discuss the matter with advisers and think about it overnight. He asked Burnside to return the next morning. Lincoln undoubtedly realized that Burnside was destroying the army's morale and creating confusion and chaos among the principal officers.

The two men met just after Lincoln had finished breakfast. The president told Burnside he had decided to relieve him from command and replace him with Hooker. Lincoln, however, asked Burnside not to give up his commission. "General . . . we need you," he said. The president was being overly nice and overly confident in the general's usefulness to the Union.

Burnside would go on to attain military success at Knoxville, Tennessee, but to perform poorly at Spotsylvania and Petersburg in 1864. Better off in politics, he left the army and later became governor of Rhode Island and a U.S. senator.

7

CHANCELLORSVILLE: MAY 1–5, 1863

PORCH POST WOES

NORTHERNERS CALLED MAJ. GEN. Joseph Hooker "Fighting Joe." It was a well-deserved sobriquet for the fightingest general in the army. He had won brevets for gallantry during the Mexican War and had a solid record of successful leadership during the Seven Days' battles and at Second Bull Run and Antietam. In these campaigns he was fearless and quick to adjust to changing situations. He never hesitated to go into battle with his men. They admired him. So did the powerful Joint Committee on the Conduct of the War.

Six feet tall, handsome, and clean shaven, this forty-eight-year-old bachelor was a ladies' man who frequently paid for his pleasure. That perhaps was his major vice, but he had no shortage of troublesome qualities. Stubbornly independent, Hooker was brash, loud, a braggart, and overly critical of superiors. Most of his fellow generals didn't trust him. When he met Lincoln after First Bull Run, he blurted out, "I was at Bull Run . . . and it is no vanity in me to say that I am a damned sight better general than any you had on that field." He mocked George McClellan as an "infant among soldiers." He observed that Ambrose Burnside had a brain the size of a hickory nut. While serving under Burnside, Hooker bad-mouthed him to influential Washingtonians and complained about the army's inefficiency. Hooker also was constantly at loggerheads with Henry W. Halleck, general in chief of the Union armies. Their dislike for each other dated back to their days together in California, when Hooker charged Halleck with "schemes of avarice and plunder" related to land claims.

When Lincoln appointed Hooker commander of the Army of the Potomac in January 1863, he did it without consulting Halleck or Secretary of War Edwin M. Stanton. And Hooker accepted the position only after being assured he could deal directly with the president on substantive matters. Lincoln, fully aware of Hooker's sharp tongue, handed him a letter in which he observed: "There are some things in regard to which I am not quite satisfied with you. . . . You have taken counsel of your ambition and thwarted [Burnside] as much as you could, in which you did a great wrong to the country. [That] will now turn upon you. Neither you nor Napoleon, if he were alive again, could get any good out of an army while such a spirit prevails in it. . . . And now beware of rashness, but with energy and sleepless vigilance go forward and give us victories."

The president directed his new commander to use the entire army to crush Lee. Other generals had attacked piecemeal to no avail. Lincoln also required Hooker to take the offensive as soon as possible, while not leaving Washington unprotected.

Hooker miraculously restored the confidence and morale of the army in just two months. He fed, clothed, and housed them better than did his predecessors. He gave them more furloughs. He created unit badges. He developed an effective intelligence service (a network of riders, scouts, and informants), replaced Burnside's Grand Divisions with a corps structure, and organized the cavalry into a corps of twelve thousand horsemen. By the spring of 1863 his army numbered 134,000 men—the "finest army on the planet," he boasted, adding, "May God have mercy on General Lee, for I will have none."

Lee's Army of Northern Virginia and Hooker's Army of the Potomac were basically in the same positions they held after the devastating December 1862 battle of Fredericksburg—on opposite sides of the Rappahannock River, a major waterway blocking the Federals' advance to Richmond.

For his first great offensive, Hooker planned to finesse the Rebels out of their strong defensive line in Fredericksburg and destroy them. He would advance in three directions. Ten thousand cavalrymen under Brig. Gen. George Stoneman were to raid Lee's rear and shatter his railroads and communications with Richmond. Three corps of forty thousand men, temporarily under Maj. Gen. John Sedgwick's command, were to cross the

Rappahannock below Fredericksburg and make a major demonstration against the town to keep most of Lee's army in its earthworks there. Hooker, meanwhile, would secretly send upstream the bulk of his army—seventy thousand infantry—to cross the Rappahannock and the Rapidan rivers and make a wide sweeping march to get around and behind Lee. Moving through the area known as the Wilderness, they would head for a cross-roads called Chancellorsville, which was ten miles west of Fredericksburg. They would then attack Lee's rear and flank while Sedgwick attacked Lee's front.

Hooker believed these multiple threats would force Lee to abandon his defensive line along the river and retreat or be trapped along its banks. With Lee out in the open and retreating, Hooker confidently boasted that his superior army would annihilate the Army of Northern Virginia and then move on to take Richmond. Hooker's reinvigorated officers were equally enthusiastic. Everyone believed, said one of them, that "Lee is in our power."

Lincoln hoped they were right, but the president was not overconfident. "The hen is the wisest of all the animal creation," he observed, "because she never cackles until *after* the egg is laid."

On April 29 Sedgwick began putting elements of his command over the river below Fredericksburg. Hooker and his three corps forded the Rappahannock and Rapidan upstream and began their wide sweep, taking them

Maj. Gen. Joseph Hooker's main army of seventy thousand infantry made a wide sweep to get around and behind Lee's army while another forty thousand feigned an advance at Fredericksburg to hold Lee there.

LESLIE'S

This sketch by Edwin Forbes depicts the first confrontation at Chancellorsville. Hooker was so stunned by the presence of Confederate forces here that he withdrew from this position.

into the Wilderness—a wet, spongy forest of dense trees and thick brambly underbrush difficult to get through. The area was crossable only on a few turnpikes and roadbeds of wooden planks laid over log rails to avoid the mud. But the Army of the Potomac executed these difficult maneuvers quickly and efficiently.

Lee did not begin to grasp Hooker's real intentions until that night. When cavalry leader Jeb Stuart brought news of Hooker's movement across the Rapidan, Lee realized that the Federals had stolen a march on him and were headed toward Chancellorsville. He saw that he was in serious trouble. His sixty thousand men could be trapped between two forces that outnumbered him more than two to one. He did not know which force would attack first, but he knew that if he maneuvered to face one assault, the other force could consume him from the rear.

Late on the afternoon of April 30, Hooker and his army set up camp around the Chancellor family tavern and home. The crossroads was not a town but a large building in a clearing, with woods and the wilderness around it. The house belonged to a well-known Virginia family, but its only current occupants were several women. An Iowa private recalled: "Upon the upper porch was quite a bevy of ladies in light, dressy, attractive spring costumes. They scolded us audibly and reviled us bitterly. [They] pleaded pitifully to be carried to a place of safety." Hooker and his staff took over the ground floor.

Just two miles from the mansion, the Wilderness opened up near Lee's flank and rear. Maj. Gen. George Gordon Meade's Fifth Corps had reached Chancellorsville earlier that afternoon and was preparing to attack. He spoke enthusiastically to Maj. Gen. Henry W. Slocum, commander of the Twelfth Corps. "This is splendid," said Meade. "We are on Lee's flank, and he does not know it. You take the Plank Road toward Fredericksburg, and I'll take the turnpike, or vice versa as you prefer, and we will get out of this Wilderness." Slocum stunned Meade by delivering orders from Hooker that they halt their advance even though several hours of daylight remained.

Hooker, overly confident, wanted his army to rest. He believed he had surprised Lee and was on the verge of a huge victory. Tomorrow they would advance to the open ground to await Lee and fight the battle. He issued a statement to his army: "Our enemy must either ingloriously fly, or come out from behind his defenses and give us battle on our own ground, where certain destruction awaits him." While Hooker rested, he advised Sedgwick to attack in Fredericksburg "when feasible for success" and to drive Lee back to him.

Brig. Gen. Alfred Pleasanton, commander of the First Division of the Cavalry Corps, later wrote:

> Up to this time General Hooker's strategy had been all that could have been desired. He had outflanked the enemy and had surprised him by the rapidity of his movements. At 2 o'clock on the 30th of April, General Hooker had ninety chances in his favor to ten against him. . . . [He] had it in his power at that time to have crushed Lee's army and [end] the war. The Army of the Potomac never had a better opportunity, for more than half of its work had been done before a blow had been struck, by the brilliancy of its strategy in moving upon Chancellorsville.

By not moving on April 30 and waiting until May 1, Hooker lost the element of surprise and gave Lee time to react. "The golden moment had been lost," Pleasanton said in hindsight. He was right. Lee was no longer surprised. When no strong movement had been made against his lines in Fredericksburg, he concluded that the main threat must be from Hooker's corps at Chancellorsville.

Lee considered two options: retreat to a better defensive position or attack part of Hooker's army. The prudent choice was to retreat. That's what Hooker expected him to do. But Lee was not inclined to do the expected. He saw Hooker's army divided and therefore vulnerable. Lee decided to defend Fredericksburg with a small force and to counterattack the main Union army while it was still in the Wilderness around Chancellorsville.

Leaving feisty Jubal Early with ten thousand infantry to oppose Sedgwick's forty thousand in Fredericksburg, Lee ordered Stonewall Jackson to move westward with the remainder of the Rebel army. They left their camps at daylight on May 1. Their mission was to block Hooker's roads out of the Wilderness and take the battle to him.

Without Early's ten thousand troops, Lee had only fifty thousand effectives to confront Hooker's main army. Lee was without Lt. Gen. James Longstreet's corps and two divisions; they had been dispatched to the Virginia coast to be ready for an anticipated Union attack there.

That same morning, Hooker's army marched eastward from Chancellorsville toward Fredericksburg. Within two miles they were out of the tangled forest and on wide, open ground near a small building called Zoan Church. The Federal commanders liked this area. Here they could form battle lines and not be handicapped by the Wilderness. Here they could wait for Lee's expected retreat and attack him.

In a bizarre coincidence, Jackson's corps marched into the same open ground at the same time; his force accounted for two-thirds of the army Lee had at his command. The two forces collided. The Rebels fired first. A sharp skirmish followed. The Union force, which was greater in numbers and artillery, had the advantage in this open country. And they took it. They advanced. Their frontline commanders sent reports of their progress back to Hooker at the Chancellor house. Then, just as the Federals were about to break through the Rebel position, they received orders from Hooker to retreat to Chancellorsville. The commanders were stunned at first, then furious. "Fighting Joe" Hooker had lost his nerve and, with it, a splendid opportunity to smash the Rebels and perhaps end the war.

The clash with Jackson apparently confused Hooker. It wasn't supposed to happen this way. He believed the bulk of Lee's army was still at Fredericksburg. The Confederates should have been retreating, not attacking. He panicked. Then he changed his entire plan. Instead of attacking, he would wait to be attacked. He called up his reserves, bringing his total at Chancellors-

Hooker had all the advantages but one: intelligence. A fellow officer said of him: "He could play the best game of poker I ever saw until it came to the point where he should go a thousand better, and then he would flunk." He also flunked at Chancellorsville.

ville to about eighty thousand men. He ordered them to dig in. They entrenched their five-mile line from flank to flank along a dirt road in the middle of the forest.

Had Hooker used his cavalry more effectively, he surely would have known that he had twice as many men as Jackson. But lacking that information, he seemed to anticipate a gigantic force striking him at his doorstep. Instead, he had sent nearly all his cavalry on a raid that frightened Richmond officials but otherwise accomplished nothing significant. The horsemen would have been more useful providing reconnaissance in the Wilderness. Hooker's thinking was also swayed in part by exaggerated reports from reconnaissance balloons of large Rebel columns "moving on the road toward Chancellorsville." These reports were magnified by Rebel deserters who provided misinformation of major reinforcements linking up with Lee.

Sedgwick, meanwhile, had not yet launched the demonstration called for at Fredericksburg, even though he had four times as many men as did the Rebels left on Marye's Heights. Sedgwick's inaction was not necessarily his fault; Hooker's instructions had not been precise. Consequently, the day was wasted. It was not until the next afternoon that Hooker issued clear orders for Sedgwick to cross the river and engage the Confederates on the heights.

While Hooker dithered, Lee deliberated over his next move. His engineers advised him that the Union center was too strongly entrenched to be assaulted. Then cavalryman Jeb Stuart rode into camp and exclaimed he had uncovered Hooker's western flank. This right flank—the Eleventh Corps commanded by Maj. Gen. Oliver O. Howard—was "in the air," wide open to attack. The Union flank was exposed, not anchored on any defensible terrain, but situated in a heavily wooded area that Hooker considered impenetrable.

That night Lee and Jackson sat on empty hardtack boxes and conferred by campfire. "How can we get at those people?" Lee asked Jackson, fully aware that they were heavily outnumbered. They studied a map for a suitable route through the scrub oak and thorny undergrowth. They couldn't find one.

"Show me what to do, and we will do it," Jackson said. Lee then drew a line westward from their present site and past the enemy's front and around the enemy position. That would enable Jackson to attack the Union flank head-on and roll it up toward the center. But they still had to find a way through the wilderness without being observed.

At four o'clock in the morning the two generals met again, this time with a cartographer and a local resident. They marked an exact route requiring a march of some twelve miles. It was a track used to haul charcoal for an iron-smelting furnace. Jackson approved the route.

Lee asked, "What do you propose to make this movement with?"

"With my whole corps," Jackson replied, "with Stuart's cavalry covering the march."

This was one of the most daring decisions of military history. The bold plan defied all the rules of warfare. Lee would split his army again. In broad daylight, Jackson would be taking thirty thousand infantry and artillery and marching across the enemy's front. His strung-out column would be vulnerable to attack, and he would be out of contact with the rest of the army for most of the day. Only thirty-two cannon and fifteen thousand men would remain under Lee, not counting Early's ten thousand in Fredericksburg. Hooker's force of ninety thousand might attack at any time.

After weighing the odds, Lee said, "Well, go on."

It was a huge gamble. If Hooker became aware of what was happening, he would surely exploit his six-to-one numerical advantage and launch an all-out attack before the widely divided Confederates could reunite. But Lee assumed correctly that Hooker would remain inactive until he was attacked.

In the other camp, Hooker expected

Robert E. Lee won his greatest victory under seemingly insurmountable odds at Chancellorsville. Gambling on Hooker's inaction, Lee divided and maneuvered his greatly outnumbered forces to give them superiority where he chose to attack.

LIBRARY OF CONGRESS

Lee to attack either the center of his line or his left flank, so he beefed up those sections. After inspecting preparations the next day on his big white high-stepping horse, he was handed reports of Confederate movements to the south, across the front of his defensive lines. His scouts had spotted Jackson's six-mile-long assemblage of infantry, artillery, and supply trains along a stretch of road that disappeared into the woods. Noting on a map that the road veered west beyond the trees, Hooker concluded that Lee was in fact retreating.

The Union army commander sent Maj. Gen. Daniel E. Sickles with two divisions from his Third Corps to investigate the movement as well as a courier to tell Howard "to be vigilant" in protecting his western flank. Hooker advised Howard to advance his pickets for purposes of observation "as far as may be safe to obtain timely information of their approach."

Just after the courier left, Hooker received a dispatch from Howard. He said he had sighted a Rebel column moving westward and that he was "taking measures to resist an attack from the west." Those measures amounted to nothing more than posting two guns and nine hundred men at the far end of his line.

Shortly, Sickles reported he had pierced the tail end of the "retreating" Rebel army and captured men and wagons. But most of the column, he said, had continued westward and was out of reach. Although some of the captives bragged that the Federals would "catch hell before night [after] Jackson gets around on your flank," Hooker remained confident that Lee was in full retreat.

Instead, the bulk of Jackson's corps gathered in formation in the underbrush of the Wilderness. Union scouts observed them and rushed messages to Howard. The thirty-two-year-old former mathematics professor at West Point did nothing to strengthen his right or to verify the reports. He assumed, as did Hooker, that Lee's army was retreating toward Richmond. Any Rebel presence in the underbrush was nothing more than a trick to cover the retreat, Howard opined. He, like Hooker, regarded that briary area as impenetrable and dismissed the reports.

Howard's Eleventh Corps was made up primarily of freethinking, harddrinking German immigrants who had fled religious oppression back home. They resented Howard's tough discipline and religious fervor, especially his attempts to change their worldly ways by preaching to them. Howard's physical appearance didn't set well with them either. He was slightly built with a pale complexion, high shrill voice, and fidgety gestures. His troops didn't like him. Their morale was the lowest of any corps in the army.

Around 5:15 p.m., with only about two hours of daylight left, Jackson launched the attack. His men were to keep moving, keep up the pressure, and roll up the Union flank.

It was the dinner hour for the Eleventh Corps. They had stacked their weapons, set up their tents, and were cooking their meals. Suddenly, scores of deer and rabbits ran toward them out of the underbrush, and the men pointed and cheered, wondering what had scared the animals. They didn't have to wait long to find out. From the Wilderness they heard bugles sounding a charge, followed by the thunderous Rebel yell of thirty thousand men. Before the startled Federals could react, Jackson's troops—in a formation two miles wide—charged out of the "impenetrable" thicket and swooped upon Howard's corps.

"They ran like sheep," wrote Capt. Benjamin Leigh, a member of A. P. Hill's staff, and threw away "their arms, knapsacks and everything of which they could divest themselves."

Howard tried to rally these frantic wild-eyed men. A visitor from Hooker's staff urged him to fire at his own men to stop the rout. Howard refused. "Halt and form!" he shouted, but they ignored him.

"Press them! Press them!" Jackson yelled to keep his men moving and to prevent the enemy from forming. The Rebels pressed and stormed and broke the enemy trench lines as they advanced. A Third Corps mule train joined the charge and stampeded through Union positions.

Hooker, chatting with his staff three miles away, didn't know that his right flank was in turmoil. Then one of his officers routinely looked westward through his field glasses and couldn't believe what he saw. "My God! Here they come!" he exclaimed. "Fighting Joe" in fevered tones promptly called up Sickles's division, which had been left in reserve, and ordered it to stem the rout.

As night set in, both sides found themselves in puzzling situations. Confederates fired upon their own men. A Pennsylvania cavalry rode into the midst of a Rebel brigade and had to cut their way out with sabers and pistols. Sickles's two divisions moved between Confederate and Union lines and were fired upon by Federal artillery before moving back. Jackson's flanks came within Union forces. If he had advanced, he would have been surrounded. Instead, the darkness and Union artillery fire forced him to halt the charge.

Gradually, the Union line was reinforced and strengthened with the arrival of the First and Twelfth Corps and the deployment of numerous guns. The Federals then held the advantage and should have counterattacked. But Hooker, confused by darkness and inept reconnaissance, withdrew to a shorter line.

Hooker chose to stay put but ordered Sedgwick to drive Jubal Early's defenders from Fredericksburg and to attack Lee from the rear. Hooker believed that Sedgwick's twenty-three thousand fresh troops coming in on Lee's rear would be a decisive attack.

While Hooker was entrenching for the night, Jackson, aided by a rising full moon, pondered launching an attack before sunrise. Having completed what he regarded as "the most successful [flank] movement of [his] life," Jackson was buoyed to fulfill two objectives: to prevent Hooker from fording the Rappahannock and to reunite his own army with Lee's so that the combined Rebel force could assault the trapped enemy.

By firelight, Lee and Jackson made one of the most daring strategic decisions of military history.

BATTLES AND LEADERS

Stonewall Jackson's daring march of thirty thousand infantry and artillery across the enemy's front enabled him to rout Oliver O. Howard's Eleventh Corps. It was the most successful flank movement of his life. A few hours later he was mortally wounded. This photograph, the last one taken of him, was made two weeks earlier.

Jackson and his staff rode eastward in search of a route by which his troops could cut off any Federal retreat. Coming within the sound of Federals working on breast-works, Jackson's entourage turned around and was joined by Hill and his staff. As they rode toward their own lines through dense woods dotted with clearings, soldiers from a North Carolina infantry unit apparently mistook them for Union horsemen and opened fire.

Hill and one of Jackson's officers shouted: "Cease firing! You are firing into your own men!"

The Tar Heel commander yelled back: "It's a lie! Pour it into them boys!" And they did. They fired a second volley. Jackson was struck by three bullets; two hit his left arm and one hit the left hand. The Carolinians then stopped firing, supposedly discovering their error. But the gunfire attracted the attention of a Union battery, and canister and shell also fell on Jackson's party. Hill was hit in both legs. Several men were wounded. Fourteen horses were killed.

The survivors somehow managed to carry Jackson and Hill to a nearby aid station. Jackson's medical director, Dr. Hunter McGuire, was there. He took one look at Jackson and decided to prepare him for surgery, during which he amputated Jackson's left arm. Jackson was then moved to Guiney's Station, a supply depot south of Fredericksburg. McGuire notified Lee of Jackson's injuries and the loss of his left arm. Lee said dejectedly, "I have lost my *right* arm."

With Hill incapacitated as well, Lee called on Jeb Stuart to assume command of Jackson's corps. Stuart, who had not been briefed on Jackson's plans, requested advice. Jackson replied through a messenger, "Say to General Stuart he must do what he thinks best." Stuart ordered the corps to halt the attack and wait for daylight.

Lee issued orders for the next day. "Those people must be pressed. . . . [Give them] no time to rally. . . . Dispossess them of Chancellorsville, which will permit the union of [our] army."

Jackson was expected to recover. But he developed pneumonia and died eight days later, May 10, in the presence of his wife and infant daughter. When told he was about to die, the deeply religious general said: "It is all right. . . . It is the Lord's Day; my wish is fulfilled. I have always desired to die on Sunday." Moments before death he said, "Let us cross over the river and rest under the shade of the trees."

Some historians have wondered if the friendly fire was accidental or intentional. Capt. Benjamin Leigh of Hill's staff said at the time that he didn't know if they were shot at "because our troops mistook us for a body of Federal cavalry, *or for some other reason.*" Every time Jackson's party passed through the clearings in the woods, they were briefly in full moonlight. Jackson's attire and silhouette made him instantly recognizable. He wore a distinctive visored cap from the Virginia Military Institute; he rode a small horse; and he leaned forward in the saddle like a jockey. Historian Webb Garrison in *The Unknown Civil War* noted that "men close enough to take aim on Jackson's party should have recognized the general and Little Sorrel [his horse] the instant they were spotted."

When Hill and others screamed out to cease fire, his voice and Virginia accent should have removed any doubt about which side they were on. The second fatal volley then was fired. Only Jackson was hit three times, as if he were singled out.

Hated as much as he was loved by his officers and men, Jackson was a tyrannical commander. He inflicted harsh military discipline. Anyone not doing exactly what he was told to do was accused of mutiny. Troublemakers were shot. He forced his men to cover as much ground on foot as did men on horses, and to do so regardless of the rain, mud, heat, dust, or winter winds. He drove hungry men as hard as those who were well fed. And after marching all day, his men were required to polish their weapons before going to sleep.

They admired Jackson the victor in battle, but at times they despised Jackson the commander. The possibility that he was shot deliberately cannot be ruled out.

* * *

At daybreak on Sunday, May 3, Stuart resumed the attack. He engaged Sickles's Third Corps and Slocum's Twelfth Corps and pressed forward in an attempt to reunite the divided wings of the Confederate army. Sickles's divisions, although fiercely assaulted the previous night by both friend and foe, fought to hold their position on high ground, but Hooker ordered them to withdraw. This created an opening for the two wings of Lee's army to unite. But that would not occur for some time.

Stuart secured the hill abandoned by Sickles, mounted forty guns, and raked the Federals at Chancellorsville with sweeping gunfire. Hooker rushed reinforcements to critical points and rode the lines to motivate his troops. The battle seesawed back and forth, but by 9 a.m. momentum favored the Rebels after Stuart committed his last reserves and drove a wedge into the center of the Union line.

The battle was still winnable for the Union—but not for long. A wooden pillar did them in. Hooker was leaning against it on the porch of his headquarters. From there he had a commanding view of the field. He had just been handed a call for more reinforcements when a cannonball struck the post and split it. In Hooker's words, the strike hurled half of the post "violently against me . . . which struck me . . . from my head to my feet."

Hooker lay unconscious for about forty minutes. When he regained consciousness he tried to mount his horse but collapsed. He was carried to the rear.

Maj. Gen. Abner Doubleday later wrote that Hooker "suffered great pain and was in a comatose condition" for a long time. He added that Hooker's mind "was not clear, and they had to wake him to communicate with him." The general apparently suffered a severe concussion.

Second Corps commander Darius N. Couch, the senior general on the field, was called to the scene, but Hooker was briefly alert when he arrived, and so Couch returned to his post. Hooker collapsed again and was out for about thirty minutes before Couch was sent for again. During the hour that had elapsed since Hooker was struck down, his command was struck mute, unable to respond to calls for reinforcements or to provide instructions. The battle had peaked. The Federals needed but did not get reinforcements. The corps commanders had to fight on the defensive. The Confederates gained control.

Lee's divided wings drew closer together and trapped two Union divisions in a pocket. They overwhelmed one and battered the other. Then ex-

LIBRARY OF CONGRESS

On May 3, these Union guns supported John Sedgwick's assault that carried the stone wall and Marye's Heights behind Fredericksburg.

ploding shells started brush fires that flamed out of control, burning the wounded where they lay. Both armies briefly ceased fighting to rescue hundreds of wounded men threatened by the fires.

By late morning the Federals were rebounding. Meade met with Couch and proposed what might have been a devastating attack on Stuart. Meade's Fifth Corps, in reserve, sat near an exposed Confederate left flank. But Couch told him that Hooker's last order was to leave the field. The news shocked Meade, but he had no choice but to comply. Maj. Gen. John F. Reynolds's First Corps also was available and not used.

Had these two corps been engaged, the Federals could have won; without them, victory was nearly impossible. If Hooker had been his usual self, he perhaps would have used these resources effectively. But his condition made it impossible to respond intelligently. All he could do was turn over partial command to Couch. While Couch wanted to counterattack, Hooker, affected by clouded reasoning, ordered him to pull back, placing their right flank on the Rapidan and their left on the Rappahannock.

Lee, with his army reunited, rode past the burning Chancellor house, cheered by celebrating Rebels. It was his greatest triumph to date, but the job wasn't finished. Lee was about to order an attack on the main Union line when couriers notified him of Union troops to his rear: Sedgwick's Sixth

Corps—the largest corps in Hooker's army. Their presence disrupted Lee's plans for a grand assault and forced him to split his army again. Lee sent Maj. Gen. Lafayette McLaws's division to hold back Sedgwick.

Sedgwick's troops had just done something that Burnside had failed to do at the battle of Fredericksburg in December. In a fierce bayonet charge, they trounced the Rebels at the stone wall below Marye's Heights and then carried the heights itself, defeating Early's ten thousand troops and capturing more than a thousand prisoners.

With Brig. Gen. John Gibbon's division holding the heights, Sedgwick sought to fulfill Hooker's orders to rush to his support. That meant marching about fourteen miles on a road vulnerable to Rebel skirmishers on a ridge parallel to the road. From these heights the soldiers were able to slow Sedgwick's advance by spreading out on the ridge, then ridge hopping, thus appearing to be stronger than they actually were. Sedgwick should have forged ahead, but he was caught up in a bluffing game.

Sedgwick stalled long enough for McLaws's division to arrive and

Jeb Stuart assumed command of Jackson's corps and engaged Daniel E. Sickles's Union corps on the morning of the third day of the battle.

LESLIE'S

thwart his advance. Sedgwick then established defenses and told his troops to bed down. Having moved too slowly, he had placed them in danger. Hooker later accused Sedgwick of procrastinating. That, said Hooker, "gave the enemy time to concentrate and stop him before he had moved over half the distance, and I consequently got no help from him."

Col. Huntington Jackson of Sedgwick's corps offered another perspective. They expected help from Hooker, but never got it. He said it "was understood throughout the corps that as soon as it should become engaged with the enemy Hooker would immediately attack in his front, and prevent any reinforcements from being sent against Sedgwick. All during that Sabbath day and the next the sound of Hooker's guns were eagerly listened for." They never heard them. Jackson said, "The feeling became widely prevalent that the Sixth Corps would be compelled to take care of itself." That became difficult.

Splitting his army again, Lee directed Stuart, who had twenty-five thousand troops, to keep Hooker's seventy-five thousand men nested in their breastworks while Lee personally led the remaining twenty-one thousand Rebels in an assault against Sedgwick's force. The divisions of McLaws, Early, and Maj. Gen. Richard H. Anderson were to attack Sedgwick simultaneously from the south, east, and west and destroy him.

The Confederates attacked at 6 p.m. on May 4. But Lee's plans disintegrated when McLaws lost his way in a maze of thickets and Anderson's men shot at each other in confusion in the Wilderness. Lee ordered another attack that night, but a thick fog prevented it.

Lee resumed his advance in the morning but couldn't find Sedgwick's troops. They had disappeared. Realizing his precarious situation, Sedgwick had withdrawn his entire corps across the river during a thick fog on hurriedly constructed pontoon bridges. Gibbon meanwhile abandoned his possession of Fredericksburg and crossed the river there.

Sedgwick's recrossing was in obedience to an order from Hooker dated May 5 at 1 a.m., and received by Sedgwick at 2 a.m. At 1:20 a.m. Hooker sent another order to Sedgwick countermanding the first order. Sedgwick received it at 3:20 a.m., but by then almost his entire command had withdrawn across the Rappahannock under the earlier order. Hooker had wavered too long before deciding to bring the whole army to Sedgwick's support in an all-or-nothing effort to gain a decisive victory. "My last chance was frustrated," he said later.

Exploding shells in the Wilderness started fires that spread to brush and dry leaves. Fighting ceased so that soldiers on both sides could carry wounded men from the path of the fires. Still, many of the wounded burned to death.

Hooker, still in a delirium much of the time, should have come to Sedgwick's aid during the earlier battle. Hooker and the seventy-five thousand men in his wing did nothing all day long.

That same night, at a council of war, Hooker's corps commanders voted to counterattack. Hooker rejected their vote and decided instead to retreat across the river. Assisted by low visibility from stormy weather, his entire army crossed to safety during the night and early morning of Wednesday, May 6.

Lee, meanwhile, rejoined Stuart's twenty-five thousand men. Together they had planned to attack Hooker on May 6—but he was gone.

It was another astounding victory for Lee and another wasted opportunity for the Army of the Potomac. While accomplishing nothing strategically, Lee lost thirteen thousand men (22 percent of his force) compared to seventeen thousand for the Federals (15 percent). Outnumbered two to one before the battle, Lee traded casualties at too close a rate and at a much higher percentage than did the Federals. He couldn't afford to continue such losses. Nor could he afford the grievous loss of Stonewall Jackson. Still, the battle of Chancellorsville is regarded as Lee's most brilliant victory, with "130,000 magnificent soldiers so cut to pieces by less than sixty thousand half-starved ragamuffins," as Horace Greeley described it. But it fell short of Lee's goal to annihilate the Army of the Potomac.

After Chancellorsville, Abraham Lincoln appeared broken, dispirited, and ghostlike. He clasped his hands behind his back and paced back and forth in his office, exclaiming, "My God! My God! What will the country say! What will the country say!" What it said was reflected in the words of Radical Republican Charles Sumner: "Lost, lost, all is lost!"

For the Union, Hooker was the primary goat. Although mentally disabled at a crucial point in the battle, he was the commander and had to accept ultimate responsibility. He had all the advantages, but he made critical tactical errors and mismanaged his opportunities. Throughout the battle, he failed to ever marshal more than half his power against the enemy. To his credit, he had developed a good plan. To his discredit, he executed it well for only one day. When Lee and Jackson surprised him by fighting instead of retreating, Hooker was caught off-guard. Then after being struck senseless, he botched the entire operation.

Cavalry commander Pleasanton was probably correct when he surmised: "Had the First Corps, which had not been engaged, and the Fifth Corps, still fresh, been thrown into action [on May 3] when Lee's troops were exhausted from the struggle, they would certainly have made Chancellorsville what it should have been—a complete success." But there was no one to order these thirty thousand men into the fight, and another golden opportunity was lost.

Hooker, however, refused to accept the blame for his defeat. Contrary to what others have written, inadequate and spurious evidence does not support their claim that he said, "I lost confidence in Hooker, and that is all there is to it." He never slighted himself, but he was quick and perhaps right to blame others for performing poorly. His goats for the defeat at Chancellorsville were his lieutenants—George Stoneman of the cavalry, Sixth Corps commander John Sedgwick, and Eleventh Corps commander Oliver O. Howard.

Stoneman's raid to wreck Lee's railroad lifeline and cut his communications was a dismal failure. Straying from his mission, he segmented his powerful column into small units incapable of doing major damage. Aside from engaging in a few skirmishes and burning some bridges, canal boats, and tobacco houses, the Union horsemen had negligible results. Yet it was Hooker who chose to send them on a raid when they could have been a major force on the battlefield. Still, Hooker unofficially removed Stoneman from his command and sent him to Washington to seek "medical treatment" for hemorrhoids, an unfortunate ailment for a cavalryman.

Stoneman partially salvaged his reputation in late 1864 by leading successful raids into southwestern Virginia to destroy ironworks and saltworks serving Lee's army. In the 1880s he served a single term as governor of California, after which he became estranged from his wife over her infidelity. Camp Stoneman near San Francisco is named in his honor. From it, hundreds of thousands of soldiers departed to fight in World War II and the Korean War.

Sedgwick, bluffed and outsmarted by a small group of Confederates, should have been able to come to Hooker's assistance before Confederate reinforcements under McLaws made that impossible. But why did Hooker need Sedgwick's twenty-five thousand troops when he had thirty thousand other troops he never used? And why didn't Hooker rush troops to reinforce Sedgwick on May 4, when the Rebels were closing in on him? He had the manpower, but he didn't use it.

Sedgwick, generally regarded as brave, competent, and hard fighting, removed any doubts about his military skills by commanding the Union left wing on the third day at Gettysburg and performing brilliantly in other operations. Tragically for the Union, he was killed by a Rebel sharpshooter at Spotsylvania in 1864.

Howard's negligence led to everlasting humiliation for his Eleventh Corps. After being overrun, the mostly German unit was nicknamed "the flying Dutchmen." Hooker encouraged one of Howard's division commanders,

Maj. Gen. Carl Schurz, to use his influence with Lincoln to oust Howard. Lincoln disagreed. "Give him time, and he will bring things straight," he told critics of the thirty-three-year-old general.

At Gettysburg two months later, Howard still hadn't gotten things straight. His corps lost three thousand men—half of them captured—even though he was aware of the enemy approaching him. Howard later fought at Lookout Mountain and Missionary Ridge and led the Fourth Corps in Maj. Gen. William T. Sherman's Atlanta campaign. Sherman was so impressed with Howard that he made him commander of the Army of the Tennessee. After the war, Howard was superintendent of West Point and then founding president of Howard University, which was named for him. He was a slow bloomer, but he finally fulfilled Lincoln's belief that he would "bring things straight."

After Chancellorsville and Hooker's charges against Howard, Sedgwick, and Stoneman, they turned on Hooker in a classic case of generals fighting among themselves to preserve their reputations. Congressional Democrats clamored for Hooker's removal while the Radical Republicans defended him.

Despite the complaints against Hooker, Lincoln retained him as commander of the Army of the Potomac until other developments surfaced. He said he was not disposed to throw away a gun because it misfired once. Then Hooker clashed with Lincoln over military strategies. Lincoln urged Hooker to hit the Confederates as they drove north for Pennsylvania. Hooker was reluctant, falsely claiming he was outnumbered and unable to fight unless he received large numbers of reinforcements. Hooker also wanted assurance

Goats or scapegoats? For the defeat at Chancellorsville, Hooker blamed his chief lieutenants—the Sixth Corps's John Sedgwick (far left), the Eleventh Corps's Oliver O. Howard (near left), and the cavalry's George Stoneman (right). Stoneman's raid to wreck Lee's lifelines was a dismal failure, but Hooker should never have sent him away from the battlefield. Sedgwick brilliantly carried Marye's Heights but then was prevented from aiding Hooker by a small force that outsmarted him. Of the three, Howard is the major goat. His negligence humiliated his corps.

that Halleck had no power to order his movements. Lincoln refused, saying, "I shall direct him to give our orders, and you to obey them." Hooker then asked permission to abandon the defenses of Harpers Ferry so those troops could join his army. Lincoln and Halleck said no. Hooker apparently was afraid of Lee and looking for an excuse to get rid of his command.

Lincoln had had enough of Joe Hooker. He relieved him on Sunday, June 28, 1863, and replaced him with George Gordon Meade.

For the Confederacy, the goat award for Chancellorsville must go to the North Carolina infantry regiment that wounded Stonewall Jackson. Whether deliberately or unintentionally, they severely damaged the Southern cause by removing Lee's ablest commander and one of the South's greatest heroes. Jackson was irreplaceable.

8

BLAME LEE, NOT STUART

AFTER THREE HOT, SULTRY July days in the small town of Gettysburg, Pennsylvania, the Union army under Maj. Gen. George G. Meade defeated the Confederate army of Gen. Robert E. Lee. The bloody battle helped to turn the tide of the war.

In the aftermath, no one in the South wanted to blame their revered general for the defeat, but the only way to make Lee look better was to denigrate others. A cult developed to do just that. Finding a scapegoat would not only spare Lee but also deflect from the failure of others in command. The scapegoat they named was Maj. Gen. James Ewell Brown "Jeb" Stuart, the flashy thirty-year-old commander of the Confederate cavalry.

Historians today are sharply divided on the extent to which Stuart was at fault. Some say:

- He was on a joyride around the Union army, causing him to be late for the battle of Gettysburg.
- Without Stuart, Lee had no cavalry to do the main army's reconnaissance.
- Stuart disobeyed orders.

All are "patently false" states former Gettysburg park ranger–historian Mark Nesbitt in his book *Saber and Scapegoat,* in which he builds a compelling case supporting his conclusions. Nevertheless, a cadre of Confederate officials and sympathizers have spread these fabrications with such skill that they have been picked up as fact and popularized in Civil War films and videos and even school textbooks.

The charges against Stuart originated with distorted reports written by Lee's military secretary, Col. Charles Marshall. His loyalty to Lee trumped his fairness to Stuart. A comparison of Lee's "orders" with his "reports" supports this contention. Orders govern the actions of subordinates; reports should tell what actually happened but are often biased.

At a social gathering in Baltimore about twenty-five years after the war, Marshall raised eyebrows by commenting that he tried to have Stuart court-martialed. He recommended it in the official Gettysburg report he drafted for Lee. In the plainest language he argued that Stuart deserved to be shot. Marshall then falsely stated that Lee ordered Stuart to move along the Confederate army's flank, and that Stuart disobeyed and chose to ride around the Union army, pursuing glory and fame.

Marshall was taking information out of context. He knew better. Stuart actually pursued the only course his orders allowed.

Maj. Gen. Henry Heth, who more than anyone else was responsible for the battle of Gettysburg—as will be noted later—added more fiction to

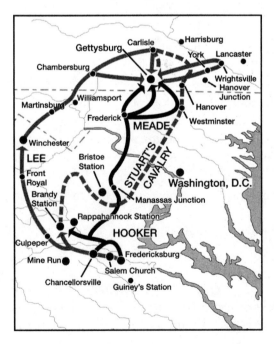

This map shows Jeb Stuart's ride around the Union army as well as the line of march toward Gettysburg for both the Union and Confederate armies. The gray line, through Winchester, was Lee's invasion route into Pennsylvania.

Marshall's reports with an article, "Causes of Lee's Defeat at Gettysburg," published in the *Southern Historical Society Papers* in July 1877. He falsely asserted, "In the opinion of almost all the officers of [Lee's] Army of Northern Virginia, [the reason for defeat] can be expressed in five words—*the absence of our cavalry.*" Col. John S. Mosby, the heroic "Gray Ghost" of the Confederacy, retorted, "I would rather say it [the reason for defeat] was due to the presence of Heth!"

Stuart was a brilliant cavalry commander, "the best cavalryman ever foaled in America," observed Union Maj. Gen. John Sedgwick, and probably the most famous cavalryman of the Civil War. In stature, Stuart was six feet and weighed about 190 pounds. He had light brown hair worn rather long, a full flowing beard, and a ruddy complexion. Flamboyant by nature, Stuart wore a regulation gray uniform profusely decorated with gold braid and topped with a broad-brimmed black felt hat. The hat was pinned up at the side with a star from which drooped a large ostrich feather. He wore a

Jeb Stuart was called "Beauty" by his admirers. The cavalry leader's flamboyant attire included a broad-brimmed black felt hat with a star from which drooped a large ostrich feather. His uniform was decorated with gold braid, a two-inch shield on his left breast, and a chain attached to a small stiletto.

LONDON ILLUSTRATED NEWS

Jeb Stuart has been maligned by writers who claim that his "joyride"
around the Union army made him late for the battle and
responsible for Lee's defeat. Actually, Lee ordered the ride, and
Stuart left substantial cavalry with Lee to meet his needs.

LIBRARY OF CONGRESS

two-inch-wide shield on his left breast. It
held a chain attached to the handle of a
small stiletto, the blade of which passed
through the buttonholes of his coat. A
Union signal officer wrote in his diary: "To
us his self-assumption and bombastic exagger-
ation of dress invited contempt."

Stuart led the cavalry in the Army of Northern
Virginia's battles in the Peninsula campaign and at Second Bull Run, Antietam, Fredericksburg, Chancellorsville, Gettysburg, and the Wilderness. An
innovator of cavalry strategy and tactics, he twice led his command around
Maj. Gen. George B. McClellan's army. At Second Bull Run he lost his famed
plumed hat and cloak to pursuing Federals. In a later Confederate raid, he
overran the headquarters of Union army commander John Pope and captured Pope's full uniform as well as orders that provided Lee with valuable
intelligence. On several occasions Yankee lead bored holes in his clothes.
Luckily he escaped injury when a Yankee minié ball whizzed across the
front of his face, shaving off half his mustache.

Stuart, who was married with children, has been accused of pursuing
the attention of women and currying their favors, but there is no evidence
of impropriety. In a letter to his wife, he wrote, "If you could see the straw-
berries, bouquets, and other nice things the ladies send me you would
think me pretty well off." In another letter he wrote of ladies "begging for
autographs." He asked his wife, "What shall I do?"

A Virginian of high morals, he held deep religious beliefs and disdained
liquor. At West Point, he was called a "Bible class" man. Yet he was a natural
scrapper and often accepted challenges to fight larger students, usually losing but always coming back for more. Classmates said he had a never-give-
up attitude.

Stuart earned the respect of the academy's superintendent, Robert E.
Lee, and became a favorite of the entire Lee family. He was a frequent guest
at the superintendent's home for dinners and seasonal parties. Stuart espe-

cially liked Lee's daughter Mary Custis and admired her "beauty and sprightliness." Their friendship would last for the rest of his life.

Given the high regard that Lee and Stuart held for each other, it is unimaginable that Stuart would have intentionally disobeyed him in the Gettysburg campaign.

* * *

During the last month of 1862 and the first six months of 1863, Lee carried out one of the most brilliant military campaigns in history, smashing huge Union armies at Fredericksburg and Chancellorsville and winning the South's undying love. (See chapters 6 and 7.)

In June, Lee's advance units were moving up the Shenandoah Valley, and his main army east of the mountains was preparing to head toward the Valley and then northward. On June 9, Union cavalry under Maj. Gen. Alfred Pleasonton surprised Jeb Stuart's horsemen at Brandy Station, southwest of Washington in northern Virginia. It became the largest cavalry engagement in American history as twenty-two thousand mounted men clashed for twelve hours along the Rappahannock. The battle was a standoff. The Federals retired without discovering Lee's infantry camped nearby, but they had learned that the Confederates were on the move.

In Washington, Lincoln was distressed. He hadn't heard from Joseph Hooker, commander of the Army of the Potomac, so he telegraphed Hooker, urging him to hit the Rebels at some point on their line of march. He wrote: "If the head of Lee's army is at Martinsburg and the tail of it on the plank road between Fredericksburg and Chancellorsville, the animal must be very slim somewhere. Could you not break him?"

The next day the Confederates captured Winchester and Martinsburg and were approaching the Potomac. If they continued in that direction they would cross through a

Maj. Gen. Henry Heth was, more than anyone else, responsible for the battle of Gettysburg. Ignoring Lee's order not to force a battle on July 1, the impulsive general took his division and a battalion of artillery into the town supposedly to look for shoes. Instead he found Union cavalry waiting for him.

ALL LIBRARY OF CONGRESS

narrow strip of Maryland and then into Pennsylvania. Lee again would be invading the North!

Under great anxiety, Lincoln again wired Hooker, passed the information to him, and added, "I would like to hear from you."

Hooker panicked. He had a superior force but was convinced he didn't. On June 23, he conferred in Washington with Lincoln, Secretary of War Edwin M. Stanton, and General in Chief Henry W. Halleck. They discussed whether or not to hold Harpers Ferry at the northern end of the Shenandoah Valley, on the southern side of the Potomac. Halleck said the position was expendable; Lincoln and Stanton disagreed. Hooker followed instructions and ordered a corps to move toward Harpers Ferry. Then his chief of staff returned to the capital to declare that Hooker would not fight without reinforcements. Lincoln consulted with Halleck and agreed it was unwise to detach any more men from Washington. They feared such a move would endanger the capital.

Hooker asked to be relieved. He said he had been assigned too much to do. He couldn't cover Washington and Harpers Ferry and fight a superior army. Lincoln sensed correctly that Hooker was afraid to fight Lee and wanted out. He complied and relieved the general of his command on June 28. He replaced him with George Gordon Meade, age forty-eight, a general highly respected by the top brass. Stanton noted that Meade was from Pennsylvania, the likely site of the next major battle. Lincoln reportedly said, "And he will fight well on his own dunghill."

Meade's written instructions from Lincoln were to keep in mind that his

Before Stuart began his swing around the Yankees, he assigned three cavalry brigades to ride with Lee's army. These brigades of nearly nine thousand troopers were commanded by brigadiers Beverly H. Robertson (far left), Albert G. Jenkins (near left), and John D. Imboden (right). Robertson was ordered to be readily available to Lee to fulfill his needs. Jenkins led advance units into Pennsylvania. Imboden covered Lee's left flank.

army was the covering force for Washington and Baltimore as well as the striking force against the enemy. Meade said that he would move toward the Susquehanna River and fight the Confederates if they turned east.

* * *

Lee chose to invade Pennsylvania for four reasons: England might recognize the Confederacy if he won a major battle in the North; the campaign would maneuver the Yankees out of Virginia, thereby preventing Federal campaigns there during the summer; a successful strike into the North might prevent reinforcements from reaching Ulysses S. Grant and cause him to loosen his siege of Vicksburg; and Lee could gather supplies for his army from Northern sources, thereby providing relief for Shenandoah Valley farmers who had fed Confederate armies for two years. In the North, Lee would seize food, livestock, clothing, and wagons from civilians and give worthless Confederate scrip in exchange. He also would seize freed blacks and send them south into slavery.

In mid-June, Lee was still in the Shenandoah Valley with the corps of Lt. Gens. A. P. Hill and James Longstreet. The latter was holding the mountain gaps, and Jeb Stuart was guarding the approaches to them east of the Blue Ridge. In that position, Stuart came under Longstreet's orders. The Union army, while Hooker was still in command, was spread out from Leesburg (near Washington) to Thoroughfare Gap in the Blue Ridge.

On June 22, Lee wrote twice to Lt. Gen. Richard S. Ewell, the forty-six-year-old career officer who commanded the vanguard of the Confederate invasion. The first letter directed him to march "toward the Susquehanna" by way of Emmitsburg, Chambersburg, and McConnellsburg. Chambersburg was twenty-seven miles from Gettysburg. "Toward the Susquehanna" was the same direction Meade prepared to move six days later.

The second letter repeated orders Lee gave earlier that day to Stuart. These orders expressed Lee's concern that the Federals would get across the Potomac "before we are aware." He said, "If you find that he is moving northward, and two [of your] brigades can guard the Blue Ridge and take care of your rear, you can move with [your] other three [brigades] into Maryland." Then Stuart was to "take position on General Ewell's right, [be] in communication with him, guard his flank, keep him informed of the enemy's movements, and collect all the supplies you can for the use of the army." Lee believed the Union army was still on the Virginia side of the Potomac; he was essentially ordering Stuart to ride around it to get to Maryland.

Stuart's orders were sent through Longstreet. Thus he seemingly endorsed Lee's orders while emphasizing that Stuart should "take the proposed route in rear of the enemy." Longstreet feared that if Stuart crossed the Potomac at Ewell's rear, the movement would disclose their plans. So he was advising Stuart to ride around the Union army regardless of where it

Invading the North, Lee's Confederate cavalry crossed the Potomac on June 11, 1863, followed by the main army of one hundred thousand men in marches that occupied ten to twelve days.

LESLIE'S

was relative to the river. Since Lee's secretary, Charles Marshall, transcribed Lee's orders, he had no basis for stating years later that Stuart's ride around the Union army violated Lee's orders. Marshall knew better.

Lee issued more orders on June 23. As Stuart passed around the enemy, he was to do all the damage he could and cross the river east of the mountains. Then "after crossing the river, you must move on and feel the right of Ewell's troops, collecting information, provisions, &c. . . . I think the sooner you cross into Maryland, after tomorrow, the better."

That meant Stuart was to cross the Potomac as soon as possible after June 25 and then ride ninety miles to Emmitsburg, Maryland, where he was to meet Ewell. At the earliest, Lee could not have expected to hear from Stuart until June 28 or 29. Stuart was supposed to be out of touch, and Lee understood that. The combined orders were consistent on one point: Stuart must ride around the Union army.

Late that night, during a drenching rainstorm, Stuart received more orders as he slept under a tree at the rear of his headquarters. (When advised to move to shelter by his chief of staff, H. B. McClellan, Stuart replied: "No! My men are exposed to the rain, and I will not fare any better than they.") These new orders informed Stuart that Jubal Early (the advance division of Lee's right wing) would move on York, Pennsylvania, and that Stuart should place his cavalry as speedily as possible with them. This was a change from the earlier order instructing Stuart to place his command with Ewell at Emmitsburg, Maryland. The new order required a longer ride, more time to get to York, and a longer time to be out of touch with Lee.

The letter noted that the roads leading northward were clogged with Confederate troops and artillery, thus Stuart would be delayed if he accompanied them. It would be faster, Lee suggested, for Stuart to pass *around the enemy's rear.* In that case, he should expect to hear from Early after Early's arrival in York, where the army was likely to concentrate. Lee ordered Early to "look out" for Stuart "and endeavor to communicate with him." That made Early at least partially responsible for reconnecting his army with Stuart's cavalry.

McClellan, who delivered Lee's letter to Stuart, later wrote that its "whole tenor gave evidence that the commanding general approved the proposed movement [around the enemy's rear] and thought it might [produce] the best results, while the responsibility of the decision was placed upon General Stuart himself."

Stuart agreed with Lee and chose to swing around the Yankees. To fulfill Lee's need for cavalry close to him, Stuart divided his brigades. Roughly half of his cavalry would ride with the army, and the other half—three brigades— would accompany Stuart on his sweeping ride around the rear and eastern side of the Union army.

So Stuart ordered Brig. Gen. Beverly H. Robertson's three thousand men to follow Lee, keep on his right flank, and be available to Lee to do any task Stuart would have done if he had been there. Stuart gave Robertson explicit written instructions for all conceivable contingencies and urged him to stay in close touch with Longstreet by relays of couriers. Brig. Gen. John D. Imboden's brigade of two thousand was to cover Lee's left flank. And Brig. Gen. Albert G. Jenkins thirty-eight hundred troopers were to lead Ewell's advance into Pennsylvania.

Close to nine thousand troopers would be within a day or two's ride of Lee. He had ample cavalry support. They were under Lee's and Longstreet's direct command, not under Stuart's. Again Marshall had lied when he said that Lee had no cavalry to do the main army's reconnaissance. Lee had plenty, and Gettysburg scholar Edwin Coddington believes he misused them. "For all the use he made of them," Coddington wrote in *The Gettysburg Campaign*, "they might as well not have been around."

Lee, for example, kept Robertson's cavalry in the mountain gaps in Virginia for five days and did not order them to join him in Pennsylvania until June 29. Instead of keeping two brigades behind in Virginia, he should have had at least some cavalry accompany his infantry in his right and rear. That's what Stuart ordered them to do, but that's not how Lee used them.

After the war Longstreet wrote to Stuart's chief of staff: "Your paper . . . shows Gen. Lee's authority for the movement of his cavalry, and that those movements were well

John Buford's two cavalry brigades were the first Federals in Gettysburg when Henry Heth's Rebel division and artillery approached the town on July 1. Buford held off the enemy force, which was twice the size of his, for two hours and was about to give way when John Reynolds's First Corps arrived and engaged the Rebels.

conducted, rapidly, and vigorously executed, that Stuart left more cavalry with us than we actually used—a fact not known to me heretofore—and that therefore it was peculiarly unjust, not to say cruel, in all who have assailed Stuart, as the cause of the failure of the Campaign."

Jeb Stuart, following Lee's instructions to do all the damage he could while riding around the Union army, cut the Baltimore and Ohio Railroad supply line; disrupted communications and other supplies in the rear of the Union army; immobilized two Yankee brigades, artillery, and cavalry in Lee's rear at Carlisle, Pennsylvania; and rattled the gates of Washington and Baltimore. Near Rockville, Maryland, Stuart captured an eight-mile-long wagon train loaded with oats, corn, hams, bacon, and whiskey. During the swing, he also took four hundred prisoners and fought several skirmishes.

Unexpected skirmishes near Fairfax Court House in Virginia on June 27 and at Westminster, Maryland, on June 29 delayed Stuart's advance by a day and a half. Both encounters were fierce. The Eleventh New York Cavalry at Fairfax Court House, though outnumbered ten to one, fought until every man was "ridden down, shot down, or cut down," wrote an observer. None escaped. The First Delaware Cavalry at Westminster displayed "an almost suicidal bravery" before backing off, an eyewitness wrote.

At Hanover, Pennsylvania, Stuart was nearly captured. When he jumped his mare over a hedge and into a large field of high timothy, he found himself within a few feet of some thirty Yankees. They ordered him to halt. Ignoring the order, he turned his horse and leaped over a fifteen-foot-wide ditch and escaped.

If Marshall regarded these dangerous action-packed successes as "Stuart's joyride" seeking fame and glory, he was wrong. Stuart was fulfilling his mission.

Unfortunately, many historians have ignored Lee's actual orders to Stuart and focused instead on Marshall's reports, which

John F. Reynolds was considered by many to be the army's best general and was himself a candidate to replace Hooker as commander of the Army of the Potomac. A native of Pennsylvania, he brought his corps to Gettysburg but was killed by a bullet in his forehead shortly after he conferred with Buford.

Lee apparently never read in detail, even though they bore his signature. Lee hated paperwork. Writers, by using Marshall's words as Lee's, have distorted history. Marshall was protecting Lee from blame while unjustly transferring blame to Stuart.

Lee meanwhile received information from a spy hired by Longstreet that five Union corps were north of the Potomac. They were following Lee. That's exactly what Lee wanted—to lure them out of Virginia. And contrary to later reports attempting to blame Stuart for not keeping Lee informed, Lee was very much aware of what was happening around him. He knew that Stuart was incommunicado and in great danger and that other cavalry officers were supposed to be keeping him informed. Couriers from Stuart's cavalry brigades assigned to Lee brought him information almost daily.

As late as July 1, Lee was seemingly unconcerned about the need for cavalry closer to him. He wrote to Imboden, whose cavalry brigade had been assigned by Stuart to cover Lee's left flank, telling him not to rush and to take the necessary time to organize and refresh his troops for a day or two.

Lee, with Meade on his tail, decided to reunite his scattered corps near Gettysburg. Meade, who was receiving accurate intelligence of Lee's movements, assumed the Confederates were preparing to attack the Army of the Potomac. Meade hoped to determine the battlefield and secure the most favorable positions. He preferred a line along Pipe Creek in northern Maryland because of its excellent defensive terrain, but first he wanted to strike elements of Lee's army before they were reunited. So he issued orders for his army to move toward Gettysburg. By dawn on July 1, both armies were heading for the same crossroads town. Gettysburg was a prosperous community served by a dozen roads that converged from all directions.

Two brigades of Union cavalry commanded by Brig. Gen. John Buford arrived at Gettysburg on June 30. Buford immediately noted the strategic value of this crossroads village flanked by defensible ridges and hills. Seminary Ridge, west of the town, ran north and south for more than two miles. It was named for the Lutheran seminary at its crest. Cemetery Ridge paralleled it, commencing below the town. On its northern end was Cemetery Hill. At its southern end, two miles distant, was a rocky, wooded eminence known as Little Round Top. Below it was Big Round Top. The ridges overlooked a rolling valley of peach orchards, wheat fields, and hay meadows.

Buford posted his brigades on high ground northwest of Gettysburg. He expected the Confederates to approach from this direction and prepared

If the South needed someone other than Lee to blame for their defeat at Gettysburg, Lt. Gen. Richard S. Ewell would have been a more logical choice than Jeb Stuart. Ewell's failure to attack the Federal forces gathering on Cemetery Ridge enabled them to reinforce and hold a strong position. On the next day Ewell ignored Lee's order to make a demonstration against Cemetery Hill and, instead, sent his whole corps in a general attack that was ill managed, uncoordinated, and doomed to failure.

to receive them. He also sent word to Maj. Gen. John F. Reynolds to move quickly to join him. Reynolds commanded the infantry corps closest to the village.

While Buford was getting organized in Gettysburg, Stuart and his cavalry rode into Dover, Pennsylvania, twenty-four miles to the east. They were about six miles from York, where they were supposed to link up with Early's infantry. Stuart, to his surprise, learned that Early had passed through Dover, headed for York, but then backtracked and moved west toward Gettysburg. Obviously Lee's plans had changed, so Stuart sent a courier to contact Early.

On the evening of July 1, Stuart approached Carlisle, twenty-five miles north of Gettysburg in search of food for his men, many of whom were too exhausted to continue after seven days in the saddle. The wagon train Stuart had captured was available, but he wanted to conserve it for the rest of the army. In the meantime he awaited word from Early.

Near Gettysburg on the previous night, June 30, Confederate Maj. Gen. Henry Heth supposedly asked his superior, A. P. Hill, if he objected to his going into Gettysburg to look for shoes for his footsore troops. Heth later said Hill replied, "None in the world"—four words responsible for the terrible ordeal to follow. Yet both Heth and Hill knew that a Confederate vanguard had scoured the area for shoes five days earlier. And not a word about shoes appeared in Hill's official report.

On July 1, at 5 a.m., Heth took his entire division and a battalion of artillery toward Gettysburg. No one has adequately explained why Heth would take such a large force if his only purpose was to find shoes. Both Hill and Heth had received orders from Lee not to force a battle on July 1; the Confederate army was too scattered for a general engagement.

Heth disobeyed Lee's order. By doing so he set in motion a chain of events that started the battle of Gettysburg. Heth's previous claim to fame was commanding a numerically superior force that was soundly defeated in a battle in western Virginia. He also would later blame Stuart for Lee's defeat at Gettysburg.

When Heth's division came marching out of the west, Buford's cavalry was ready for them. The Union horsemen fought dismounted, from behind fences and trees, and held off a force twice their number for two hours. By late morning Buford's tired troopers were beginning to give way when the lead division of Reynolds's First Corps arrived and brought the Rebel assault to a standstill. Reynolds, while leading his troops into place, was killed by a bullet to his forehead. This was one of the most crucial Union casualties at Gettysburg; Reynolds was considered by many to be the army's best general.

More Union columns arrived on either side of the Round Tops. Cemetery Ridge immediately in front of them was theirs for the taking.

Heth soon found himself outnumbered and sent for reinforcements. Every Confederate division in the area converged upon Gettysburg. Lt. Gen. Richard S. Ewell's Second Corps came up fast from the Susquehanna and was met by the Union's Eleventh Corps commanded by Maj. Gen. Oliver O. Howard. By early afternoon some twenty-four thousand Confederates confronted nineteen thousand Federals along a three-mile arc west and north of Gettysburg. Lee, who arrived late in the afternoon, envisioned another Confederate victory and authorized Hill and Ewell to send in everything they had.

Howard's right flank collapsed, and his Eleventh Corps retreated in a disorganized dash. Whooping Rebels drove them helter-skelter through the streets of the town and up Cemetery Hill. Union artillery and a reserve brigade Howard had posted there stopped the onslaught.

With the rest of the Federal army hurrying toward Gettysburg, Lee knew he had to drive the Yankees off Cemetery Hill before reinforcements made it impregnable. He gave Ewell discretionary orders to attack "if practicable." Ewell chose not to do it. He didn't want to risk a hastily organized assault. Stonewall Jackson, had he been alive, wouldn't have hesitated.

As night approached, the Union army strengthened its position on this high ground through the leadership of Maj. Gen. Winfield Scott Hancock, a cool, composed corps commander known as "Hancock the Superb." He set up a desperate line of defenses on the northern, eastern, and western slopes. From the west face the line extended two miles south to Cemetery

Ridge. When Meade arrived later that night, he and his generals felt they were in good shape. Meade decided to stay and fight here rather than fall back to Pipeline Creek.

If Ewell had attacked and succeeded as Lee envisioned, the Rebels would have gained the higher position, and that could have altered the outcome at Gettysburg. If the South wanted someone other than Lee to blame for the forthcoming defeat, Ewell was a better candidate than Stuart. Ewell had a chance to make a difference, but he refused to gamble. Stuart that afternoon still didn't know what was going on.

The earliest documented verbal comment about Stuart's whereabouts came from Lee himself around 10 a.m. that day. At Cashtown, five miles from Gettysburg, Lee said: "I cannot think of what has become of Stuart; I ought to have heard from him long before now. He may have met with disaster, but I hope not. In the absence of reports from him, I am in ignorance as to what we have in front of us here."

His last sentence, if quoted correctly, was not entirely true. Stuart's orders were not to connect with Lee and the main body but to connect with Early. Lee had been receiving scouting reports from other cavalry commanders.

Shortly after noon on July 1 Lee was informed of Stuart's location. He immediately sent a dispatch to him. When Stuart received it after dusk, he directed several brigades to proceed at once to Gettysburg. Then he began the all-night ride. Stuart's ordnance officer, John Cooke, accompanied him. He called the ride "the most severe I ever experienced" and later wrote:

> General Stuart and his staff . . . passed over mile and mile asleep in the saddle. At dawn, the General dismounted in a clump of trees and said, "I am going to sleep two hours," and wrapping himself in his cape simply leaned against a tree and was immediately asleep. Everybody imitated him, and I was awakened by the voice of one of the couriers, who informed me that "the General was gone." Such was the fact—Stuart had risen punctually at the end of two hours, stretched himself, mounted, and ridden on *solus*, a wandering Major-General in the heart of Pennsylvania!

On the night of July 1, Lee and Longstreet argued over their plan of action. Longstreet had studied the Union defenses and concluded that an attack could not succeed. He wanted to swing around the Union position and

Lt. Gen. James Longstreet was an easy target for Southerners looking for goats for their loss at Gettysburg. The only non-Virginian holding high command in Lee's Army of Northern Virginia, Longstreet was accused of insubordination and slowness in executing Lee's orders.

take a stand between Meade's army and Washington. This would force Meade to attack the Army of Northern Virginia in *its* preferred position.

"No," said Lee, determined to attack head-long. "If the enemy is there tomorrow, we must attack him."

"If he is there," replied Longstreet, "it will be because he is anxious that we should attack him—a good reason, in my judgment, for not doing so."

Longstreet, the only non-Virginian to hold high command in the Army of Northern Virginia, would suffer numerous barbs from Virginians for years after the war. They accused him of insubordination and of slowness in executing Lee's orders. They were looking for another goat—anyone other than Lee.

By the morning of July 2, sixty-five thousand Confederates faced eighty-five thousand Yankees. All was quiet as battle plans were readied. A detachment of 250 cavalrymen from Brig. Gen. Wade Hampton's brigade arrived before dawn. It reported to Lee and was assigned to Longstreet. Lee and Longstreet thus had adequate cavalry for any scouting necessary to determine where the Union army was forming. But they were not used for that purpose. Instead they were told to guard the roads in Longstreet's rear, watch his flank, and "do whatever came to hand." Lee apparently had all the information he needed.

Stuart and Lee finally made contact that afternoon. There are no documented records of their immediate exchange. Accounts from Stuart's family indicate that Lee greeted Stuart by saying, "Well, General Stuart, you are here at last." While this greeting can be interpreted in various ways, it likely reflects Lee's affection for Stuart and his relief that Stuart was safe.

Some writers have stated that Lee wanted Stuart near him once the fighting started. But Lee's actions do not support that claim. Instead of assigning Stuart a role with the main army, he assigned him to the flanks. He was to guard the Confederate left from the Union cavalry and to map the terrain.

Lee certainly was concerned about his cavalry, but his concerns were probably over the cavalry with Imboden, Robertson, and Jenkins. On July 1 they were not with Lee; they had become separated when a division of Ewell's corps entered a road blocking Longstreet's line of march. Their absence hampered Lee's movements. Longstreet later wrote that "so vexed was [Lee] at the halt of the Imboden cavalry at Hancock, in the opening of the campaign, that he was losing sight of Pickett's brigades as a known quantity for battle." Imboden, who did not arrive at Gettysburg until noon on July 3, probably would have gotten there faster if he had not taken time to destroy railroad bridges and parts of the Chesapeake and Ohio Canal.

After Stuart's cavalry was in position, pickets from Hampton's brigade reported a large Union force headed toward the Hunterstown crossroads four miles from Gettysburg, probably to descend upon the rear and left flank of the main Confederate army. Stuart ordered Hampton to check the enemy's movements.

After passing through Hunterstown without incident, Hampton's rear guard was attacked and forced back by Michigan cavalry regiments. They were led by twenty-three-year-old Brig. Gen. George A. Custer. He was a tall, lithe trooper with long, curly yellow hair and an elaborate velvet-trimmed uniform with scarlet cravat. One observer said that Custer looked like "a circus rider gone mad."

Four companies from the main Confederate column then charged into the Yankees and began to drive them back with the help of dismounted Rebel skirmishers along the road. Custer was nearly killed. His horse went down, and he was trapped beneath the dead animal as a Confederate rode toward him. Only one Yankee trooper was near Custer. He shot the Confederate and hoisted Custer upon his own horse.

The battle continued at dusk and into the night. Around 11 p.m. Custer changed positions to bolster the Union left flank. The fighting on July 2 is covered in chapter 9. That action started in the late afternoon when Longstreet launched his attack on Meade's left and Little Round Top. Union Maj. Gen. Daniel E. Sickles created major problems for Meade when he disobeyed orders and advanced his Third Corps a half mile from the main Union line. About half of his corps was wounded or killed. Rebels then moved on Little Round Top, where spirited and creative resistance held it for the Union.

As night fell on July 2, Lee and Meade prepared their armies for a major battle the next day. Meade followed the advice of his generals: stand our ground, stay on the defensive, give Lee no more than another day to strike, and then either take the offensive or move away from Gettysburg. Meade strengthened his center, where he expected to be attacked since Lee had failed in attempts to turn his right and left flanks. He was correct. Lee was convinced that an all-out attack on the Union center would work. One more push, he said, and "those people" will break.

Longstreet commented that "Lee's blood was up," and when his blood was up there was no stopping him. Even though Lee was weakened by a bout with diarrhea, he believed he and his men were invincible. He had come north in quest of a decisive victory, and he was determined not to leave without it. His army had pummeled one Union general after another. Lee expected them to do it again on July 3.

Lee's judgment was not at its best.

Scapegoating Longstreet to Sanctify Lee

After Robert E. Lee's death in 1870, former Confederate Gen. Jubal Early led a movement to blame James Longstreet for the defeat at Gettysburg and even for the Confederacy's defeat. Determined to make Lee the holiest of Southern icons, Early and other never-say-die adherents of the Lost Cause looked for scapegoats to remove any blemishes that tarnished Lee's luster. While some went after Jeb Stuart and Richard S. Ewell, Early and his small band of followers targeted Longstreet through their writings and speeches. They noted that Longstreet had opposed Lee's invasion of Pennsylvania and had tried to persuade Lee not to order Pickett's Charge at Gettysburg. Longstreet, of course, was right, but he had questioned Lee, and when Southerners learned that, they didn't like it.

Early, it should be noted, was relieved of his command in the Confederate army in March 1865 in response to mounting public pressure against him. "Old Jube" had been soundly whipped by Philip H. Sheridan at Winchester, Fisher's Hill, and Cedar Creek and routed by George A. Custer at Waynesboro.

Longstreet, on the other hand, was Lee's most reliable commander during the Seven Days' battles and was instrumental in achieving Confederate victories at Second Manassas and Chickamauga. But Early and his supporters kept such heroics in the background.

Longstreet was worried. His men would have to march nearly three-fourths of a mile, in clear view across broad fields, then up the slopes of Cemetery Ridge against a barrage of Yankee guns. He objected and argued strenuously against it. He urged Lee to maneuver around Meade's left. Lee refused. He was adamant. His order was to take three divisions and drive them like a wedge into the Union center. "They're there, and we're going to strike."

The other part of Lee's plan called for Stuart to protect the rear of the Confederate left flank and to distract Meade by fighting his way northward and into the rear of the Union lines. Then, if the grand assault succeeded, Stuart could surprise the retreating troops and assure a complete victory. Some historians have stated that Stuart's mission was to attack the Union rear at the same time Longstreet launched Pickett's Charge. But no one knew exactly when that would occur, and there was no feasible way to signal Stuart.

Longstreet combined Maj. Gen. George E. Pickett's division with the divisions of Brig. Gen. J. Johnston Pettigrew and Maj. Gen. Isaac R. Trimble—a

After the war, Longstreet handed Early more ammunition to use against him by committing three unforgivable sins in the eyes of Southerners. He became a staunch Republican; he campaigned for Ulysses S. Grant in the presidential election of 1868 (for which Longstreet was rewarded with federal patronage jobs); and he wrote a memoir in 1896 criticizing not only Lee but also another Southern hero, Thomas J. "Stonewall" Jackson. These "dastardly deeds" erased Longstreet's noble service during the war and transformed him into one of the South's most hated men.

Thus, because of Early's efforts and Longstreet's support and service to the federal government after the war, no statue or monument exists in the South to honor the man dubbed by Lee as his "Old Warhorse," with one exception—Longstreet's name is on a highway overpass in the state of Georgia.

Only after media mogul Ted Turner turned Michael Shaara's novel *The Killer Angels* into a movie did Longstreet's reputation rise from Early's scrap heap to its proper place in history. In the movie, Longstreet was portrayed as the voice of reason at Gettysburg—a voice ignored by Lee, to his regret. Inspired by the film, a private group raised funds and commissioned a statue of Longstreet. Today, that statue guards a picnic area at Gettysburg. It is one of only two statues in the park honoring Confederate generals.

The other is of Robert E. Lee.

total of 12,500 men. Lee told Longstreet that Pickett's fresh division should lead the assault. The combined force was to advance after the Confederates fired a horrific two-hour barrage from 159 cannon along Seminary Ridge. It began at 1:07 p.m. The cannon were supposed to soften up the Union defenses at the point of attack. Despite the barrage, the Confederates overshot the Union infantry lying behind stone walls and breastworks. Men farther back were hit. As Meade was having lunch, an orderly serving him was struck by a shell that tore him in half.

The Union artillery fired back for a while and then fell silent to conserve ammunition and to lure the Rebels into the open field. Confederate commanders assumed they had silenced the Yankee batteries. The thirty-eight-year-old Pickett had never before led a division into battle. He was eager to win everlasting glory. Around 3 p.m. he asked Longstreet if his men should go forward. Longstreet, knowing that it was a desperate endeavor, was unable to bring himself to speak the order. With tears streaming down his face, he just sat there on his horse and nodded his head. Then Pickett gave the order: "Up men, and to your posts. Don't forget that you are from old Virginia."

With parade-ground precision, 12,500 men moved out. It was a mile-wide, eye-catching panorama. They were silent as they marched at a brisk pace across the open fields. They were forbidden to fire or give the Rebel Yell until they were close to the enemy. It was the greatest infantry assault of the war. The Yankees saw an ocean of armed men sweeping toward them. "Don't fire too fast," they were told. "Let them come up close before you fire and then aim slow."

As the first Rebels came into range, the Yankees began intense shelling and ferocious volleys of small-arms fire from all sides. The Union artillery on Little Round Top and Cemetery Ridge opened fire. Eleven cannon and seventeen hundred muskets went off at once. Single bursting shells destroyed ten men at a time. Entire regiments disappeared. Shells exploded in clusters of Confederates, sending heads, arms, and legs flying into the air. Still the Rebels pushed on.

Portions of two Confederate brigades penetrated the Federal line after rushing up the rocky slope and over a stone wall and dirt mounds. Among them was Brig. Gen. Lewis A. Armistead, who held his sword high over his head and called for his men to follow him. About 150 got over the wall. All were killed or captured. Armistead was mortally wounded as he placed his hand on a Yankee cannon. On the spot he fell is a monument marking what is called "the high water mark" of the Confederacy.

The Yankees held their ground, and the Rebels under heavy fire ran back to Seminary Ridge. Of the 12,500 who made the charge, only about 5,000 returned. As the survivors staggered back, they encountered Lee and Longstreet working to form a defensive line. They expected Meade to counterattack.

"All this has been my fault," Lee told the men with tears in his eyes. "It is all my fault. It is I who have lost this fight, and you must help me out of it the best way you can. All good men must rally." Fortunately for Lee, Meade did not attack. One reason he later gave was his concern about Stuart's presence somewhere in his rear.

At midday Stuart had ridden eastward as he tried to carry out his orders to place his troopers at the enemy's rear. In that position he would either attack or harass the expected Union retreat. Riding with him were the brigades of Cols. John R. Chambliss and Milton J. Ferguson. The brigades

Pickett's Charge against Union forces on Cemetery Ridge was the greatest infantry assault of the Civil War and Lee's worst mistake. Nearly half of the attacking force was killed, wounded, or taken prisoner. "All this has been my fault," Lee told his men with tears in his eyes.

of Brig. Gens. Wade Hampton and Gen. Fitzhugh Lee followed at a short distance behind. Altogether, there were just over six thousand sabers.

Around 2:30 Stuart was about three miles east of Gettysburg, near the Federals' right rear. Stuart saw horsemen in the distance and decided to intercept them and eliminate any blockage to the enemy's rear. He quickly developed a plan. He posted Chambliss behind a screen of woods and used Ferguson's men as bait, dismounting and placing them around a large barn. With the Federals focused on Ferguson's men, Chambliss would attack, followed by Hampton and Fitz Lee, who were to remain under cover until signaled. It was a good plan, but it didn't evolve as expected.

The approaching Federal cavalry was much stronger numerically than Stuart assumed. There were three brigades—five thousand strong—and they were armed with repeating carbines.

The bait—Ferguson's men—had not taken adequate ammunition (only ten rounds each), and they exhausted this quickly. To prevent their capture, Stuart had to send in Chambliss prematurely.

Hampton and Fitz Lee, who were supposed to be out of sight, disclosed their presence while too far away to achieve surprise. The Federals withdrew from the fighting around the barn and formed ranks not only to receive the charge but also to move out to meet it.

The Union brigades consisted of two from Brig. Gen. David Gregg's division and one from Brig. Gen. H. Judson Kilpatrick's, which was made up of four Michigan regiments. These latter regiments were commanded by Custer, the brash but colorful last man of the West Point Class of June 1861.

"Come on, you Wolverines!" Custer shouted and charged, his yellow ringlets streaming in the wind. A Federal observer described the scene: "As the two columns approached each other, the pace of each increased, when suddenly a crash, like the falling of timber, betokened the crisis. So sudden and violent was the collision that many of the horses were turned end over end and crushed

LIBRARY OF CONGRESS

Maj. Gen. George E. Pickett never forgave Lee for ordering the grand assault on July 3. Years later Pickett said, "That old man had my division slaughtered."

their riders beneath them. The clashing of sabers, the firing of pistols, the demands of surrender and cries of the combatants filled the air."

The head-on collision and saber-to-saber conflict brought both gray and blue columns to a standstill, with both sides losing about 250 men. Stuart recognized the futility of the fighting and withdrew his troopers to the ridge from which they had charged. The Federals let them go. Stuart then backtracked six hours and went into bivouac.

Both cavalries declared success. Gregg reported: "Defeated at every point, the enemy withdrew." Stuart overstated the results, reporting that "the enemy's masses vanished before them like grain before the scythe." He said he withdrew only when he was "good and ready."

Stuart, however, had failed to accomplish his mission of reaching the enemy's rear. But as things turned out, even if he had done so, he wouldn't have had anything to do there. Lee's grand plan had been thwarted.

Both armies were exhausted. On July 4 they collected their wounded and began burying their dead. Many different estimates exist on the number of casualties. The Union reported 3,155 killed, 14,529 wounded, 5,365 missing—a total of 23,049 casualties, more than one-fourth of Meade's army of 88,289. Confederate estimates amounted to 28,063 killed, wounded, or missing, more than a third of Lee's army of 75,000. About 7,000 Rebel wounded were left behind to be cared for by Union surgeons and volunteer nurses.

It was the first open-field defeat for the Army of Northern Virginia, and it was Lee's last venture into the North and his last offensive operation of the war.

Pickett never forgave Lee for the futile charge that bears his name. Years later he said of Lee, "That old man had my division slaughtered."

Longstreet later wrote: "My heart was heavy. I could see the desperate and hopeless nature of the charge and the hopeless slaughter it would cause. . . . That day at Gettysburg was one of the saddest of my life."

Lee passed the buck only once. Speaking to Imboden, he said that if Pickett's division "had been supported as they were to have been—but, for some reason not yet fully explained to me—were not—we would have held the position, and the day would have been ours." This was a misstatement on his part. Lee himself had refused to allow A. P. Hill to throw his corps into the assault.

Clearly, Lee was to blame, not Jeb Stuart and not James Longstreet. Lee certainly knew that frontal assaults were usually doomed; the weaponry available to well-placed defenders would mow down the attackers. But Lee was desperate. He gambled and lost.

After the war, Lee told Wade Hampton, "General Stuart was my ideal of a soldier. . . . He was always ready for any work, and always reliable." *Always reliable.* Lee would not have said that if he believed that Stuart was primarily or partially responsible for the defeat at Gettysburg. Lee knew he wasn't.

Lee was responsible. He admitted it and went so far as to submit his resignation to Jefferson Davis. Davis wisely rejected it.

Lee, as great a general as he was in other battles at other places, was not invincible. He was human. At Gettysburg, hampered in part by physical ailments—diarrhea, rheumatism, and chest pains—he made mistakes.

He was wrong to order Pickett's Charge.

He was wrong when he failed to effectively use the cavalry (minus Stuart) that accompanied him to Pennsylvania.

He was wrong in not using Stuart more strategically on July 2 and 3.

And he must assume major responsibility for disorganized and poorly coordinated troop movements. Lee had given vague and discretionary orders, often verbal, leading up to the battle and even during the three days of fighting. This system had worked well for him in the past, especially when he had Stonewall Jackson to rely upon, but it failed him at Gettysburg, with Jackson having died seven weeks earlier.

Southerners were wrong in their unwillingness to attribute any blame to Lee while making Stuart the principal scapegoat for their loss at Gettysburg. The real problem at Gettysburg—the goat—was Robert E. Lee. It was his worst-fought battle.

9

GETTYSBURG—DAY 2: JULY 2, 1863

VERBAL SHOOT-OUT

O N THE SECOND DAY of the three-day battle at Gettysburg, Union commander George Gordon Meade issued an order to Daniel E. Sickles, a
politician turned general. Put simply, Sickles was to place his Third Corps of
more than eleven thousand men in a position to lengthen the Union line
south along Cemetery Ridge to Little Round Top and to occupy that hill if
practicable. That order, Sickles's response to it, and the result have triggered
arguments among historians, generals, and politicians from 1863 to the
present day. Sickles's actions were either a stupendous blunder or a sound
maneuver, depending upon one's viewpoint.

Little Round Top was strategically significant. If the Rebels controlled
it, their artillery could fire down on the entire Yankee line as far north as
Cemetery Hill. That advantage would almost guarantee them victory at
Gettysburg.

Brig. Gen. John Geary's Union division had been separated from the
Twelfth Corps at the north end to lengthen the southern end and defend Little
Round Top. Now, with Sickles's corps approaching the field, Meade ordered
Geary to move his division back to its corps at the opposite end of the line;
Sickles's corps would replace Geary's division. Geary waited for some time to
be relieved by Sickles, but the notorious New York politician never came.
Growing impatient, Geary sent a staff officer to find Sickles and explain to him
the importance of the position and the need for him to relieve Geary as soon

as possible. The staff officer found Sickles and requested that someone from Sickle's staff inspect the ground so that Sickles could immediately deploy his troops. Sickles responded that he would attend to it in due time. But hours passed, and no officer or troops came. Geary, his patience exhausted, followed orders and withdrew his division to rejoin the Twelfth Corps.

Around noon Sickles appeared at Meade's headquarters and said that he didn't know where to take his corps. This infuriated Meade. Sickles had been issued instructions three times, the last by one of Meade's staff shortly after Geary's messenger had seen him. Meade again explained where Sickles was supposed to be—specifically: "Your right is to be on Hancock's left (thereby lengthening the Union line), and your left is to be on Round Top." Meade pointed out the hill to him. Sickles understood and left.

Sickles found the position, studied it briefly, and decided he didn't like it. It was on low and marshy ground. Gazing uphill, he observed a broad knoll more than a half mile due west. Its crest was about twelve feet higher than the ground where he stood. But by advancing to it, he thought he could prevent the Confederates from taking it.

The position on the knoll was precarious at best, potentially devastating at worst. Its only cover was the foliage of a peach orchard. Rebel artillery from either side could easily bludgeon everything on that bald hump. Furthermore, Sickles would be on a salient, separated from the rest of the army.

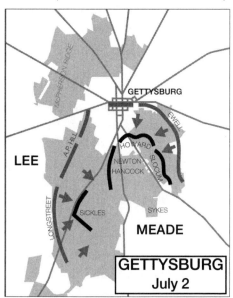

If he moved to that location, he would create a huge gap in the main Union line—a weak point that would be vulnerable to attack—an attack that could quash the Union army.

Shortly before 3 p.m. on what had been a relatively peaceful day for the center of the Union line, Sickles decided on his own to move forward and occupy the knoll. He was aggressive by nature but short on common sense. Other Union troops relaxing on the northern half of Cemetery Ridge were surprised

Maj. Gen. Daniel E. Sickles, commander of the Third Corps of the Army of the Potomac, was the Union goat at Gettysburg. His colossal blunder on the second day of the battle came perilously close to disaster for the Union army. An astute politician, he claimed he was actually a hero of the battle and that Meade was the goat.

to hear drums off to their left. They saw Sickles's eleven thousand men advancing in military precision across the open field in formal battle order with flags aflutter and bugles blowing.

Brig. Gen. John Gibbon, commander of the Second Corps, observed the scene and wondered if he had missed an order for his corps to advance. Maj. Gen. Winfield Scott Hancock, on his horse alongside Gibbon, said, "No. . . . Wait a moment and you'll see them tumbling back." Another officer noted that Sickles's Third Corps "stuck out like a sore thumb" and moaned that it was an outright invitation to disaster.

Sickles's new position was similar to that of a V. Its apex was in the Peach Orchard, and its left was anchored in a maze of boulders known as Devil's Den. These terms would soon be eternally etched in military history.

Robert E. Lee wanted his army to take and hold the Round Tops at the southern end of the Union line. Several hours earlier, at 11 a.m., he ordered James Longstreet to position his troops to assault the Federal left flank— the flank Sickles was supposed to occupy at the southern end of Cemetery Ridge. Lee expected Meade to pull troops from his right flank to reinforce the left, and if that occurred, Richard S. Ewell had orders to attack the Union right. Under this scenario, Lee believed both Union flanks would crumble, and Meade would be defeated. Longstreet was agonizingly slow in assembling his six brigades for the attack. He finally launched the attack at 4 p.m. with fifteen thousand yelling Rebels. In their path now was Sickles's isolated smaller corps, which had just advanced to the knoll near the Peach Orchard.

What followed over the next few hours was some of the war's bloodiest fighting in the Peach Orchard, in a wheat field east of the orchard, and at Devil's Den. "It was a perfect hell on earth never to be equaled [or] surpassed," wrote Pvt. Robert H. Carter of the Twenty-second Massachusetts. The battle wrecked Sickles's corps, which suffered more than forty-two hundred casualties—nearly half of its troops. Hancock's prediction had come true as Sickles's survivors came "tumbling back" from the salient.

A fresh Federal division led by Brig. Gen. John C. Caldwell was rushed into the fight. It, too, suffered mightily, losing three of its four brigade commanders. In disorganized fighting, regiment fought regiment, driving each other back and forth across the hotly contested ground.

While Sickles was riding his line, a cannonball struck his right leg just above the knee and left the limb hanging in shreds. He fell hard to the ground but saved his own life by ordering a tourniquet made from a saddle strap. As men lifted him onto a stretcher, he heard a rumor he was dead. He quelled it by asking a stretcher-bearer to light a cigar for him. With the stogie clinched between his teeth, he puffed it repeatedly to prove to his men that he was alive.

Meanwhile, Meade's chief engineer, Brig. Gen. Gouverneur K. Warren, spotted a crisis in the making. Sickles's advance had left both Round Tops unprotected at the south end of Cemetery Ridge. Warren surmised at once that Little Round Top was the key to the entire Federal line. But there were no Union combat troops there!

Confederate Col. William C. Oates also saw that Little Round Top was undefended. From that position he knew he could blow apart the Union army. His Alabama brigade moved unopposed down and around the Union left and raced up the slopes to secure the hill.

Acting quickly, Warren persuaded Maj. Gen. George Sykes, commander of the Fifth Corps, to rush a brigade to the crest. The 140th New York, which had just arrived on the field after a long march, made it to the crest of Little Round Top just in time to meet the charging Rebels. Warren continued to search for regiments to dispatch to the scene. After a furious fight from behind boulders and fallen trees, the force he cobbled together eventually repulsed the Rebels.

At the far left of the New York brigade was Col. Joshua L. Chamberlain's Twentieth Maine, consisting of 360 men. Chamberlain was a modern languages professor on leave from Bowdoin College. Taking cover behind boulders, his men prepared to hold their position against a force at least ten times their number. "They were pouring a terrible fire upon us," a Union soldier later wrote. "The air was alive with lead." Five times the Rebels drove Chamberlain's men back, and five times the Twentieth Maine fought their way forward again. Within an hour and a half, a third of Chamberlain's men fell.

Hearing gunfire from the rear of Little Round Top, Chamberlain assumed the hill was being surrounded. His ammunition was nearly gone. He had to advance or retreat. Resorting to an unusual tactic, he ordered his men to fix bayonets. Then while the right of his line held straight, he had his left lurch down the hillside, all the while wheeling to the right "like a great gate upon a post," as one soldier later recalled.

The Alabamians were startled, shocked, not sure what to do. The front ranks dropped their weapons and surrendered. Others behind them turned and ran. Then from the left came another horrifying surprise to the Rebels. The Twentieth's Company B, which Chamberlain thought had been killed or captured, rose and fired from behind a stone wall. Bullets from different directions struck the Rebels. They ran for their lives. Little Round Top was secure.

A mile to the north, another Alabama brigade threatened the center of the Cemetery Ridge line. The gap created by Sickles's unauthorized advance

Sickles, a lifelong womanizer, neglected his wife, who then had numerous liaisons with Philip Barton Key, son of the author of the national anthem. Sickles, then a congressman, retaliated by confronting and shooting Key three times. The final, fatal shot was fired as Key lay on the ground, begging for mercy. At his trial, Sickles pleaded temporary insanity and was acquitted.

Teresa Bagioli married Sickles in 1852, when she was fifteen. Years earlier Sickles had seduced her mother and blackmailed her father. In 1859, after killing Teresa's lover, Sickles publicly forgave her and agreed to stay married to her. He, of course, continued to have affairs with other women.

HARPER'S MAGAZINE

to the Peach Orchard was about to be punctured. Only 262 men from one regiment—the First Minnesota—were on hand to face the oncoming brigade. They charged the 1,600 Alabamians and held them back until reinforcements arrived. Hancock plugged the gap, ending the Confederate attack along the southern half of the battlefield. These close calls reflected the horrendous problems resulting from Sickles's unauthorized forward move.

The fighting finally ended on July 2 after the Federals repulsed an attack by Ewell's corps on the Union's right flank. Ewell, who had a prosthetic right leg, added some humor to an otherwise humorless day after being hit in the leg. He never flinched. "It don't hurt a bit to be shot in a wooden leg," he sang out.

Except for the loss of Sickles's indefensible salient, the Union line was secure. Each side had about nine thousand casualties. All the Confederates had to show for this carnage was the area once held by Sickles—the Peach Orchard and Devil's Den. "We haven't been as successful as we wished," Longstreet told an inquirer.

Sickles's disobedience, however, could easily have been disastrous for the Union. What saved the day was the initiative and coolness of Union officers from Meade down (except for Sickles) and the uncoordinated and disjointed assaults led by Confederate commanders.

Yet Sickles was not about to accept any blame for disobeying Meade's order, advancing his corps, and jeopardizing the Union army. For the rest of his life he resorted to ruthless tactics to smear Meade and portray himself as the hero of Gettysburg. With considerable success, Sickles made Meade look weak and indecisive. The victory at Gettysburg, Sickles argued, was not due to Meade's generalship but in spite of it. These distortions and others reflected Sickles's despicable character and career.

Sickles was a product of Tammany Hall, the graft-ridden Democratic machine that controlled New York politics. In 1857, he was elected to the U.S. House of Representatives. Five years earlier, thirty-three-year-old Dan Sickles married the stunning fifteen-year-old Teresa Bagioli—after getting her pregnant. Years earlier, Sickles had seduced Teresa's mother and black-mailed her father, a wealthy, well-known singing teacher. Teresa, polished and sophisticated for her age, spoke five languages. Sickles, the son of a New York patent lawyer, was a corporate attorney with good looks, a dash-ing manner, and persuasive skills.

Committed to marriage but not to monogamy, Sickles was a lifelong womanizer. In 1853 he accepted a governmental assignment to London, left his pregnant wife at home, and took with him Fanny White, his favorite New York prostitute and madame. He presented White to Queen Victoria using as her alias the surname of a political opponent. Sickles returned to America in 1855, became a member of the New York state senate, and was censured by the state assembly for escorting Fanny into its chambers.

Sickles's neglect of his young wife, as well as her knowledge of his dal-liances, led her to fall into the arms of widower Philip Barton Key, the U.S. attorney for the District of Columbia and the son of Francis Scott Key, au-thor of "The Star-Spangled Banner." They had numerous liaisons, first at the Sickles's mansion and later at a nearby home he rented for the purpose of their get-togethers. In 1859, then Congressman Sickles learned through a poison pen letter of his wife's torrid affair. By the double standard of the era, it was all right for him to have affairs, but horribly scandalous for her to en-gage in such deceit.

Around 2 p.m. on February 27, 1859, Sickles peered from a window of his home on Lafayette Square, near the White House, and saw Teresa's lover signaling her with a white handkerchief. Enraged, Sickles grabbed two der-ringers and a revolver, ran out of the house, and shot Key three times. He deliberately fired the fatal shot as Key lay bleeding on the ground and beg-ging for his life. Among the dozen witnesses to the murder was a presi-dential page, who immediately informed President James Buchanan. The president, who was on a first-name basis with Sickles, dispatched the page on an extended trip abroad. One of the most scandalous trials of the cen-tury followed.

Sickles's legal team was headed by Edwin M. Stanton, who later became Lincoln's secretary of war. Stanton put forward a temporary insanity plea, the first time such a defense was used in the United States. It worked. Sickles was acquitted of murder, and cheers reverberated throughout the crowded courtroom.

Sickles subsequently stunned Washington society by publicly forgiving his unfaithful spouse and agreeing to stay married to her. "I shall strive to prove to all that an erring wife and mother may be forgiven and redeemed," he said.

At the outbreak of the Civil War in 1861, Sickles's desire to repair his public image, combined with his patriotic fervor, motivated him to raise and organize four regiments for Federal service. As thanks for his efforts he was commissioned a brigadier general. In Washington, his mesmerizing demeanor appealed to Mary Lincoln, and she invited him to her salons and séances.

Sickles's war service began in Joseph Hooker's division during the Peninsula campaign. Soon, Hooker and Sickles were fast friends. In February 1863, shortly after Lincoln installed Hooker as head of the Army of the Potomac, Hooker passed over more deserving officers and made Sickles commander of the Third Corps. Hooker, like Sickles, was a notorious ladies' man. His army headquarters was said to resemble a rowdy bar and bordello. Sickles's own headquarters was considered to be even worse. Four months later Lincoln replaced Hooker with Meade, but Sickles retained his position.

After being hit in the leg by a cannonball at Gettysburg, Sickles was carried off the field. His leg was amputated that afternoon by a battlefield surgeon. On Sickles's insistence, he was transported back to Washington. He reached the capital on July 4. Although in severe pain, he eagerly provided his version of the great Union victory. It was the beginning of his campaign to smear Meade and to ensure that his version of what had happened on July 2 would prevail. He took full advantage of his severed leg to enhance his reputation as a war hero. And true to his character, he donated the leg to an army medical museum and courted women by escorting them there to see it.

Meade's official report to General in Chief Henry W. Halleck, Lincoln's military adviser, gently reprimanded Sickles for his disobedience. He noted that Sickles had "not fully apprehended" his instructions and had advanced his corps three-quarters of a mile in front of Hancock's left and one-quarter of a mile in front of the base of Little Round Top. Halleck's version of the report had a sharper edge on it. He wrote: "General Sickles, misinterpreting his orders, instead of placing the Third Corps on the prolongation of the

On Day 2 of the battle of Gettysburg, Sickles was ordered to place his corps of eleven thousand men so as to extend the Union line to Little Round Top, the summit of which is shown here. Instead, Sickles advanced to an isolated position that became "a perfect hell on earth never to be surpassed."

Second, had moved it nearly three-quarters of a mile in advance—an error which nearly proved fatal in the battle."

Sickles bristled. He had his version of events, and he told it to congressmen, the press, and the president. He argued that his movement away from Cemetery Ridge was correct because it disrupted the Confederate attack, redirected its thrust, and effectively shielded their real objective, Cemetery Hill.

Sickles became a darling of the Congressional Joint Committee on the Conduct of the War—a committee dominated by Radical Republicans and controlled by Sen. Benjamin F. Wade (Ohio) and Sen. Zachariah Chandler (Michigan). Wade, Chandler, and their Radical associates were uncompromising abolitionists who made political war on anyone who wasn't.

In late February 1864, the JCCW, urged on by Sickles, initiated an investigation of Meade's generalship of the Army of the Potomac. Their secret agenda was to gather sufficient evidence to make Meade the goat of Gettysburg, encourage Lincoln to remove him from command, and replace him with his predecessor, Joe Hooker. Hooker shared the JCCW's political views, and in their eyes, he was the better choice for army command.

The first officer to testify was, not coincidentally, Sickles, Hooker's close friend. Talking at length about the second day of fighting at Gettysburg,

Sickles falsely asserted that Meade didn't issue him any orders, even when Sickles asked for them. He said he dropped by Meade's headquarters that morning and "was satisfied from the information which I received" that Meade intended to retreat. This was untrue, but it was what the committee wanted to hear. Sickles claimed that the line he occupied was not taken through "misinterpretation" of orders. "I took it on my own responsibility."

Knowing the JCCW's interest in restoring Hooker to command of the Army of the Potomac, Sickles talked about the "near-disastrous" implications of removing Hooker three days before the battle of Gettysburg. He said the rank and file had "entire confidence" in Hooker.

The next witness, Maj. Gen. Abner Doubleday, also was an opponent of Meade, probably because Meade had removed him as commander of the First Corps. Wade asked Doubleday to explain why he had been relieved. He responded: "General Meade is in the habit of [placing] his personal friends in power. There has always been a great deal of favoritism in the Army of the Potomac. No man who is an antislavery man or an anti-McClellan man can expect decent treatment in that army as presently constituted."

This is the view of Devil's Den, where Sickles's left flank was anchored in a maze of boulders. At Devil's Den and in the nearby Peach Orchard and Wheat Field, Sickles had more than forty-two hundred casualties—nearly half of his corps.

The third witness, Brig. Gen. Albion P. Howe, was a former division commander in the Sixth Corps. He attributed the victory at Gettysburg to the Union's strategic position. Meade, he said, did little to win the battle. "There was no great generalship displayed; there was no maneuvering, no combination," Howe asserted.

Wade and Chandler had heard what they wanted to hear. They met with Lincoln and Stanton, called Meade incompetent, demanded his removal from command, and recommended that Hooker replace him. That didn't happen, and Secretary of War Edwin Stanton assured Meade it would not happen.

The forty-eight-year-old Meade probably didn't care whether or not he was removed. He had no desire for the high command thrust upon him three days before the battle, and he had no interest in partisan politics. He was candid, reliable, and capable. To him, duty came first.

Meade became a soldier by chance. He was born in Spain, where his father served as a U.S. naval agent. Much of his boyhood was spent in near poverty in Philadelphia. He preferred a career in law but couldn't afford it. A free education was available at West Point, and he was accepted after his second application.

Once he had his commission, he joined an artillery regiment and served for a year in Florida, where he was sick with fever much of the time. He tried civil engineering for six years, found it more difficult than he expected, and returned to the army because he knew of no better way to support his family. He saw action in the Mexican War, held various engineering posts during the 1850s, and at the outbreak of the Civil War accepted a brigadier's commission. While commanding a brigade of Pennsylvania infantry, he was shot in the hip at Glendale during McClellan's Peninsula campaign. He recovered sufficiently to command a division at Antietam and Fredericksburg and to lead the Fifth Corps at Chancellorsville. But the wound troubled him for the remainder of his life.

On June 28, 1863—three days before the battle of Gettysburg—a messenger from Lincoln informed him he had been chosen to replace Hooker as commander of the Army of the Potomac. At Gettysburg he deserved praise for demonstrating great tactical skill in troop placement and the use of reserves to bolster threatened places in his line. Fighting primarily on the defensive, he gave the Army of the Potomac its first undeniable large-scale victory. It was the largest battle ever fought on the continent and one of the most impressive victories ever scored. Meade deserved the credit for the victory, but Sickles was determined to claim it for himself.

Meade was hot tempered, and his subordinates were often targets of his temper. That may have accounted for the willingness of some of them to testify against him before the JCCW. He was like a firecracker, noted one of his staff officers, always going bang at someone near him. Meade described himself as "an old snapping turtle." His unchanging expression reminded one observer of someone with a toothache biting into a hard apple.

Meade probably looked and felt that way when he arrived in Washington on March 4, 1864, and learned of "certain grave charges" made against him by Sickles, Doubleday, and Howe. But when he appeared before the JCCW, only Wade was there, and he informed Meade there were no charges against him. The committee, Wade said, was simply gathering information about the battle to include in their history of the war. Wade, of course, was being devious.

Meade's testimony recounted Sickles's corps being in the wrong position far in advance of Cemetery Ridge. Meade said that he had issued orders to Sickles three times to form on Hancock's left to prolong the line south to Little Round Top and to occupy Little Round Top if practicable. Instructions were first given early on July 2. Later that morning, Meade sent an officer to find out if Sickles was in position. The officer reported that there was no one there. Meade then sent the officer back to find Sickles and give him the same instructions previously issued. A little later, Sickles appeared at Meade's headquarters and received these orders from Meade himself.

Meade expressed no desire to penalize or censure Sickles in any way. "I am of the opinion that General Sickles did what he thought was for the best," he said, "but I differed from him in judgment. And I maintain that subsequent events proved that my judgment was correct, and his judgment was wrong."

While Meade was struggling with Sickles's nastiness and the unfriendly committee, Lincoln appointed Ulysses S. Grant as commander in chief of all Union armies. Grant could have based his operations in Washington, but he detested its political atmosphere. The only viable option was to set up his headquarters in the field with the Army of the Potomac. Meade would continue as commander of that army, but Grant would direct its strategies.

Returning to Washington to dine with Lincoln and Grant, Meade asked the JCCW for another opportunity to provide additional evidence. He appeared on March 11 and distributed copies of his orders of June 30 and July 1. These orders proved that Meade had no intention of withdrawing the army once contact was made with the enemy. Sickles's assertion that Meade planned to retreat on the morning of July 2 would appear "almost incomprehensible," Meade said, when compared to the exertions made on the night of July 1 to concentrate his army at Gettysburg. Meade also testified that his corps commanders had met with him on the evening of July 2 and agreed with his strategy to remain on the field and await further attacks by the enemy before assuming the offensive.

Interestingly, the next day the *New York Herald* published an article on the battle of Gettysburg that highlighted Sickles's heroism. The author, identified only as "Historicus," claimed to be an eyewitness who wanted to "vindicate history" and do justice "to the survivors." The article praised Sickles for significant successes on both July 1 and 2. It said that on the first day Sickles's corps arrived on the field at an opportune time. The article implied that the corps's presence brought an end to the fighting. In fact, the corps reached the battlefield long after the fighting was over.

The writer repeated Sickles's version of July 2 as he had told it to the committee: he had no orders on placement, and Meade was planning to

This 1900 painting by H. A. Ogden shows Lt. Gen. James Longstreet on July 2 giving orders to his staff to relay to troops in the distance. Little Round Top is in the background.

LIBRARY OF CONGRESS

Maj. Gen. Gouverneur K. Warren, Meade's chief engineer, quickly recognized that Sickles's movement had left both Round Tops unprotected and that Little Round Top was the key to the entire Federal line. He persuaded the commander of the Fifth Corps to rush troops to the crest.

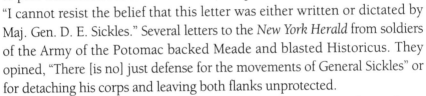

retreat. The writer added more imaginary zingers. Sickles, Historicus implied, had saved Little Round Top. He allegedly was the first to act on his own when Confederate columns were spotted moving toward the hill.

Meade wasn't about to allow such nonsense to pass unnoticed. He wrote to the War Department: "I cannot resist the belief that this letter was either written or dictated by Maj. Gen. D. E. Sickles." Several letters to the *New York Herald* from soldiers of the Army of the Potomac backed Meade and blasted Historicus. They opined, "There [is no] just defense for the movements of General Sickles" or for detaching his corps and leaving both flanks unprotected.

The outcry in defense of Meade provoked Historicus to resurface with another article slandering Meade. He stated that information presented to the JCCW was "known to be so ruinous to the Commander of the Army of the Potomac that it will be a singular indifference to public opinion on the part of the government if he is allowed to remain longer in that important post."

Sickles, the well-connected Tammany Hall politician, had more tricks up his sleeve. He advised Chandler, his closest supporter on the JCCW, to call upon Maj. Gen. Daniel Butterfield to testify. Butterfield served both Meade and Hooker as chief of staff. Butterfield was an ally and shared many character traits with Sickles and Hooker. He also participated in their sexual escapades at army headquarters.

Displaying loyalty to Hooker and disloyalty to Meade, Butterfield described Meade as "dazed and confused" when named commander of the Army of the Potomac. More likely, it was Butterfield who was dazed while under the influence of too much liquor. Meade, said Butterfield, embraced Hooker's campaign plans with only minor changes. Therefore, according to Butterfield, Gettysburg was really Hooker's victory, not Meade's, even though no one anticipated a battle there.

Butterfield, of course, concurred with Sickles's allegation that on July 2

Meade was preparing to withdraw: "General Meade directed me to prepare an order to withdraw the army from that position." But, he said, after the battle began in front of the Third Corps, the impending retreat was not discussed further. He acknowledged that the order may have been for emergency use only, but he believed the fighting on the afternoon of July 2 prevented withdrawal.

Meade returned to the JCCW to contend that Butterfield "misapprehended" their discussion. Yes, said Meade, he had directed Butterfield to study the roads in all directions and to draw up eventuality plans. But no, it was not his intent to retreat. Otherwise, why would he have ordered Maj. Gen. Henry W. Slocum, commander of the Twelfth Corps, to examine the area in his front for a possible attack?

At 9:30 a.m. on July 2 Meade had asked Slocum to report from Culp's Hill on "the practicality of attacking the enemy in that quarter." When Slocum replied an hour later that the terrain on the right, though excellent for defense, was not favorable for attack, Meade abandoned the notion of taking the offense and embraced the benefit of implementing a strong defense.

Meade concluded that Butterfield's "excess of zeal and desire to do more than he was called upon to do" may have prompted him to compile a retreat order. But, said Meade, "I did not sanction it, and I was not aware of it."

Brig. Gen. John Gibbon, commander of the Second Corps, noted that Butterfield asked him to read the draft of an order he had just prepared. When he started to read it and realized it pertained to a withdrawal, he knew that was not Meade's intent. Gibbon said he responded with, "Great God! General Meade does NOT intend to leave this position!" Gibbon said Butterfield admitted that it was prepared so that a plan was in place if a withdrawal became necessary.

Meade's adjutant general, Seth Williams, also said it was a contingency plan that was never distributed. All of Meade's actions, he said, led to the "irresistible conclusion" that Meade intended to stay and fight.

Generals Warren, Hancock, and Sedgwick and artillery chief Henry Hunt all testified that they were not aware of any order to retreat. And all of these generals were aware of the order to Sickles to extend the Union line south to Little Round Top. Even the chief of staff for the commander of the Second Division of Sickles's corps later wrote that it was "common knowledge before noon" on July 2 at division headquarters that Meade had ordered Sickles "to continue Hancock's left and cover Round Top."

Despite all of this testimony disputing Sickles and corroborating Meade's testimony, the JCCW's report at war's end was unfavorable to Meade. Biased, as might be expected, the report insinuated that Sickles's forward movement prevented a disastrous flanking attack by the enemy. The report also criticized Meade for "wasted opportunities" to attack Lee after Pickett's failed charge.

The Meade-Sickles debate raged on for many years after the war as Sickles and his supporters continued their efforts to distort history and sanctify Sickles's actions. In 1869, John Watts DePeyster published an article praising Sickles's "intelligence, experience, and consequent cool judgment" by advancing his troops and forcing Longstreet into a frontal assault rather than flanking the Army of the Potomac. Also that year, Col. William W. Grout spoke at the Reunion Society of Vermont Officers and stated that Meade was upset with Sickles because his advance "precipitated the [battle] and prevented the possible retreat of [Meade's] army to Pipe Creek."

The editor of the *Burlington (VT) Free Press*, Col. George G. Benedict, listened to the speech and became so outraged by Grout's unjustified claims that he published several editorials supporting Meade. In response, Meade wrote a lengthy personal letter to Benedict, asking him to not disseminate it.

For the next thirteen years, the issue was relatively quiet while Sickles was occupied with postwar endeavors. His career struck its first postwar bump in 1867 when President Andrew Johnson removed him from command of the Carolinas' military district, where Sickles's job was to enforce Reconstruction. He was fired for "overzealousness." As minister to Spain from 1869 to 1873, he wielded considerable influence in the Spanish court and had a well-publicized liaison with the deposed queen of Spain, Isabella. Later, as chairman of the New York State Monuments Commission, he was forced to resign amid rumors of embezzlement. However, while in that position, he did much to bring about the National Battlefield Park at Gettysburg, a site he visited often during his life.

Meade, meanwhile, died in 1872 from complications of the hip wound he received a decade earlier. He was fifty-seven.

Sickles returned to the speakers' platform in 1886. Spinning his Gettysburg distortions, he addressed the Third Army Corps Union in Boston on April 8. Championing his Third Corps advance far in front of the Union line, he declared it was the best way to defend Little Round Top. He announced: "I simply advanced out on to the battlefield and seized Longstreet

Little Round Top would have been carried by the Rebels if the 140th New York hadn't arrived just in time to repulse them and if Col. Joshua Lawrence Chamberlain's heavily outnumbered 20th Maine hadn't used imaginative tactics on the extreme left to turn them back. Both of these close calls resulted from Sickles's disobedience of Meade's orders.

by the throat and held him there." He neglected to say that he had disobeyed orders regarding his position and that he lost nearly half of his corps and came perilously close to causing the Union army to be defeated.

Sickles also spoke at Gettysburg on July 2, 1886. There he said the Rebel attack would have been a complete surprise to Meade had it not been for Sickles's vigilance in discovering Southern preparations to flank the Union army out of its strong position. He said that by moving his corps to the higher ground, he was responsible for Longstreet's frontal assault. And that assault, Sickles surmised, prevented the flank move and gave Meade time to bring up reinforcements to occupy Little Round Top. This was hindsight on Sickles's part. No large units were in his front until just before 3 p.m., when a Confederate division emerged from the woods to discover Sickles's men already in position there.

One of Meade's aides, Col. James C. Biddle, responded to Sickles's two speeches with an article in the *Philadelphia Weekly Press*. His main point was: "The real and serious accusation is against General Sickles . . . to the effect

Maj. Gen. George Gordon Meade led the Army of the Potomac to its first undeniable large-scale victory in the largest battle ever fought on the continent. His dour demeanor reminded one observer of someone with a toothache biting into a hard apple.

that on July 2, 1863, he, through igno-rance, or from a worse motive, disobeyed the orders of General Meade, his com-mander, and by that disobedience imperiled the safety of the army, which was saved from serious disaster by the energy of General Meade in sending and bringing reinforcements from other portions of the line."

Former Confederate Maj. Gen. Lafayette McLaws couldn't resist writing his own response and striking at political generals always seeking fame. He argued that if Sickles had followed orders and taken the position Meade as-signed to him, Little Round Top would have been made unconquerable, and the Confederate attack that almost seized the hill probably would have been canceled, avoiding countless casualties on both sides. He said that Sickles's move almost led to disaster on the Union left. "It would, therefore, appear that the arrangements of the troops made by General Meade, which contemplated the occupation of Round Top, were the best possible to meet all emergencies."

The third response to Sickles's Gettysburg speech came from the news-paper editor to whom Meade had confided back in 1869. George Benedict was so irate over Sickles's exhortations that he felt compelled to publish Meade's private letter to him. Meade wrote that he had hoped to avoid any controversy with Sickles and Butterfield "though both [have sought] to dis-tort history for their purposes." Meade said that the so-called retreat plan was formulated to prevent the terrible possibility of Lee's getting between the Army of the Potomac and Washington. Then Meade revealed a new piece of information he received after the war from Geary. Before moving his division to Culp's Hill, Geary was ordered to await relief by Sickles's corps. When that relief was not forthcoming, one of Geary's staff officers ex-plained to Sickles where his corps should be. That was when Sickles prom-ised to move "in due time." Instead, in due time, he rode to Meade's headquarters and asked where he was supposed to be! This information established conclusively that Sickles was repeatedly given the same order and that he deliberately disobeyed it.

Sickles's response to Meade's letter appeared in the *New York Times* on August 14. Sticking to his old arguments, Sickles claimed to quote from Meade's official report to disprove some of Meade's statements. These so-called quotes, however, did not exist. Sickles made them up.

Second Corps commander Gibbon rebuked Sickles in the June 1891 *North American Review*. After explaining the nature of military orders, Gibbon declared that Sickles's corps was "in a position to which it was not ordered by General Meade." He elaborated: "In cases of this kind there is and can be but one rule in armies. If a soldier is ordered to go to a certain point on a field of battle, he goes there if he can. If he does not get orders to go there, he does not go, with the one single exception that overwhelming necessity requires him to make the move, when he is so situated that he cannot solicit or receive the orders of his commanding officer."

Sickles's distorted version of July 2 was frequently repeated as fact by historians throughout the twentieth century. Finally, in 2003, Richard A. Sauers destroyed many commonly accepted myths by examining the evidence in detail in his book *Gettysburg: The Meade-Sickles Controversy*, a rich resource for much of the material in this chapter on the postwar controversy. Sauers, a military historian who began his research with no preconceptions, concluded that Sickles spun a contrived tale. He disobeyed an order, he completely ignored Little Round Top, and by moving forward, he jeopardized the entire Federal line. Sickles, Sauers said, successfully deflected attention from his own shortcomings by unfairly attacking his superior. Sickles's dirty politics damaged Meade's reputation and created a false picture of what happened at Gettysburg.

As for Sickles's charge that Meade was weak and indecisive, Brig. Gen. Henry J. Hunt, Meade's chief of artillery, wrote to Brig.

Maj. Gen. Daniel Butterfield was chief of staff to both Joseph Hooker and George Meade. An ally and carbon-copy of Sickles and Hooker, he participated in their sexual escapades at army headquarters. On Capitol Hill, he testified against Meade and supported Sickles's false assertions.

Gen. Alexander S. Webb, who commanded a brigade in the Second Corps: "[Meade was] right in making his battle a purely defensive one; right, therefore, in taking the line he did; [and] right in not attempting a counterattack at any stage of the battle. . . . Rarely has more skill, vigor, or wisdom been shown under such circumstances as he was placed in."

After the battle, diarist George Templeton Strong rejoiced that "the charm of Robert Lee's invincibility is broken. The Army of the Potomac has at last found a general that can handle it, and has stood nobly up to its terrible work in spite of its long disheartening list of hard-fought failures. . . . Government is strengthened fourfold at home and abroad."

Meade deserves the credit and praise for the victory at Gettysburg. He had fought for the nation's life and not only saved it but won a tremendous victory that energized the North. The victory was his to claim. After untangling fact from fiction, it is clear that Sickles was the goat in blue that day. He deserves the blame for imperiling the Union line and almost causing a spectacular disaster.

10

SHOO, SHOO, GENERAL LEE

NEWS OF THE UNION victory at Gettysburg electrified the North. "I never saw such excitement in Washington," wrote one journalist. It was the most celebrated Fourth of July in the nation's history. President Abraham Lincoln jubilantly issued a press release announcing the "great success" at Gettysburg and urging "that on this day, He whose will, not ours, should ever be done, be everywhere remembered and reverenced with profoundest gratitude."

Back in Gettysburg, late in the day on July 3, generals on both sides debated what to do after Pickett's Charge turned into Pickett's Rout. Gen. Robert E. Lee frantically regrouped his troops into a defensive position on Seminary Ridge. His biggest concern following his gravest mistake was: can we hold this line if they attack?

Union cavalry commander Alfred Pleasonton advised George Gordon Meade to attack: "I will give you half an hour to show yourself a great general. . . . Order the army to advance, while I take the cavalry and get in Lee's rear, and we will finish the campaign in a week." But Meade would have no part of it. "How do you know Lee will not attack me again?" he asked. "We have done well enough." Pleasonton, eager to do more, continued to argue for an attack. If we nail them down, he said, they will be obliged to surrender. Meade ignored his plea but invited the cavalryman to ride with him to Little Round Top.

The troops cheered as Meade approached them, and Pleasonton inter-
preted that to mean "they expected the advance." Maj. Gen. Winfield Scott
Hancock, wounded in the battle, made a similar appeal. From his stretcher
he dictated a message to Meade, urging him to hurl the Fifth and Sixth
Corps at Seminary Ridge without delay. Maj. Gen. John Sedgwick's Sixth
Corps, the largest in the army, had been engaged minimally and would be a
logical choice. "The enemy will [then] be destroyed," Hancock predicted.
Meade's only response was to express regrets Hancock had been wounded.

Meade later wrote that he did not want to follow Lee's bad example "in
ruining himself [by] attacking a strong position." The attackers at Gettysburg had been decimated. He didn't want to suffer the same fate.

Henry J. Hunt, the artillery chief whose guns had stopped Pickett's
Charge, agreed with Meade: "To change from the defensive to the offensive
after an engagement at a single point . . . on the assumption that Lee had
made no provisions against a reverse, would have been rash in the extreme." Gouverneur Warren, Meade's chief engineer, also concurred: "[We
felt] we had saved the country for the time and that we had done enough;
that we might jeopardize all that we had done by trying to do too much."

Meade's army had already paid a high price for its success, and he was
reluctant to risk another encounter with the old gray fox for whom he had
considerable respect. Meade's casualty lists included a staggering loss of
men of rank: his most aggressive corps commanders—John Reynolds
(killed), Hancock and Daniel E. Sickles (wounded)—as well as sixteen
brigade and division commanders and three hundred field and company
grade officers. Four of the seven corps had been shot almost to pieces. One-
fourth of the Federal army had been killed or captured and another one-
eighth was unaccounted for.

Meade's judgment was that his army could not at this time launch a
major assault. Thus he did not advance swiftly and, after a council of war
with his senior generals, postponed an attack. The corps leaders voted to
hold their present ground until it was certain that Lee was retreating. Meade
assented.

Lee, no less battered than Meade, still had twenty-nine brigades in fairly
good condition, but eight were shattered in Pickett's desperate charge. All of
his cavalry were with him now. "We'll fight them, sir, till hell freezes over,"
said one Rebel, "and then, sir, we will fight them on the ice." But Lee had
lost seventeen of his fifty-two generals, eighteen colonels, and more than a

third of his army, probably about twenty-eight thousand men. Further, he was low on food and had only enough ammunition for one more day of heavy action. His only choice was to retreat.

By candlelight in his tent, Lee pored over maps and chose his routes. Despite his exhaustion, he personally visited each commander and issued detailed written instructions. They would hold their ground the next day, July 4, thus giving their wounded a head start, and then they would march out under cover of darkness. "We must return to Virginia," he told Brig. Gen. John D. Imboden, a Virginia-born lawyer and cavalry leader who helped to cover the retreat.

On the morning of July 4, all was quiet as the Confederates built and maintained a continuous line of defense along Seminary Ridge. "Will the Yankees attack?" they kept asking each other. They didn't. About 1 p.m.

As part of the Confederate withdrawal from Gettysburg, Brig. Gen. John Imboden's cavalry escorted Lee's seventeen-mile-long wagon train of supplies and wounded men over rough and rocky roads to Williamsport, Maryland, where they planned to cross the Potomac into Virginia.

BATTLES AND LEADERS

clouds rolled in and heavy rain streamed down from the darkened sky. The storm cleansed the grass of blood and spared the soldiers from further slaughter.

Lincoln reasoned correctly that Lee had been badly beaten. But the president wanted more—complete and total victory by pursuing Lee and forcing his surrender. Lincoln's jubilation faded when a copy of Meade's congratulatory message to his troops came across the wire. Meade had told his troops "our task is not yet accomplished." He said he looked to the army "for greater efforts to drive from *our* soil every vestige of the presence of the invader." Lincoln's hands dropped to his knees, and in an anguished tone he said: "Drive the invader from our soil! My God! Is that all?. . . . The whole country is our soil!" Dispatches from generals operating with Meade convinced Lincoln that their purpose was to get the enemy across the river without risking a battle, while Lincoln's objective was to prevent the enemy's crossing and to destroy him.

Three days later, Lincoln learned that Maj. Gen. Ulysses S. Grant had taken Vicksburg and that the Mississippi River, from Cairo to New Orleans, was once more in Union hands. The war could end that very month, Lincoln opined, if Meade caught up with the Rebels before they crossed the Potomac, fought just one more battle, and annihilated Lee's army.

On Sunday, July 5, Meade determined that Lee had withdrawn from Gettysburg. But he did not know if Lee was retreating or maneuvering for an attack. The Union commander regarded Lee as cocky, cagey, and wily. Perhaps Lee still had some trick up his sleeve. This thought was reinforced by a wounded officer's report that he overheard Rebels planning to feign retreat and then ambush the Yankees coming after them. Meade had learned to beware of Lee when he seemed most vulnerable. Further, Meade did not want to digress from his orders to "maneuver and fight in such a manner as to cover the capital and Baltimore." So rather than chase Lee, Meade chose to march south, forty miles into Maryland, toward Frederick—a route avoiding the Appalachian passes well-defended by the Rebels—and then to move northwest and hopefully encounter Lee before he crossed the Potomac. This movement would ensure that the Federals stayed between Lee and the capital. He also ordered cavalry under John Buford and H. Judson Kilpatrick to harass Lee's retreat.

Meanwhile the Confederate withdrawal was well underway. Imboden's cavalry was escorting a seventeen-mile-long wagon train of supplies and wounded men. They were traveling west on slow-going mud roads toward Chambersburg and then turning south to Hagerstown for a Potomac crossing near Williamsport, Maryland, a total distance of about forty miles. The infantry took a shorter southwesterly route via Fairfield to the same destination. Units of Jeb Stuart's cavalry guarded both flanks and secured the mountain passes.

Altogether, Lee had about fifty thousand effectives, and he assumed correctly that Meade was being heavily reinforced from nearby Northern states. In a matter of days, Lee expected Meade to have an army twice the size of his own.

By July 6, the wagons had made good headway and advanced to Williamsport. It had not been a pleasant trip for the wounded on board. Imboden later wrote they had not eaten for thirty-six hours, and "their torn and bloody clothing, matted and hardened, was rasping the tender, inflamed, and still oozing wounds. Very few of the wagons had even a layer of straw in them, and all were without springs. . . . From nearly every wagon . . . came such cries and shrieks as these: 'Oh, God! Why can't I die?' 'My God, will no one have mercy and kill me?'"

Unable to cross the Potomac because of high water from recent rains, the wagons parked at the foot of a hill. Imboden had to protect the wagons for more than a week until the Potomac receded enough to be passable. In normal times, a person could wade across the stream at this point.

At Hagerstown, about seven miles north of Williamsport, Stuart's cavalry drove back Union horsemen with a saber charge as they prepared to attack Confederate infantry. Then as Buford's division came to within a half mile of the Confederate wagons, Imboden's artillery repulsed them. As Buford reorganized for another attack, the Rebels counterattacked and Buford retreated. Stuart's and Imboden's cavalry successes on July 6 were significant. Lee had invaded the North primarily to gather supplies. If he had lost the wagons, his campaign would have been a total failure.

By July 7 the main Union army was approaching Frederick, Maryland. Meade refreshed himself with a hot bath in a hotel and put on fresh clothes for the first time in ten days. He wrote to his wife: "From the time I took command till today, I . . . have not had a regular night's rest, and many nights not a wink of sleep, and for several days did not even wash my face and hands, no regular food, and all the time in a state of mental anxiety. Indeed, I think I have lived as much [the past few days] as in the last thirty years."

BATTLES AND LEADERS

Waiting for the Potomac to become fordable, Lee parked his several thousand wagons and ambulances in this bottomland between the Chesapeake and Ohio Canal and the river at Williamsport, Maryland.

Meanwhile, General in Chief Henry W. Halleck and Meade exchanged pointed messages:

Halleck to Meade: "You have given the enemy a stunning blow at Gettysburg. Follow it up, and give him another before he can reach the Potomac. . . . There is strong evidence that he is short of artillery ammunition, and if vigorously pressed he must suffer."

Meade to Halleck, from Frederick: "My army is assembling slowly. The rains of yesterday and last night have made all roads but pikes almost impassable. Artillery and wagons are stalled; it will take time to collect them together. A large portion of the men are barefooted. . . . I expect to find the enemy in a strong position, well covered with artillery, and I do not desire to imitate his example at Gettysburg and assault a position where the chances were so greatly against success. I wish in advance to moderate the expectations of those who, in ignorance of the difficulties to be encountered, may expect too much. All that I can do under the circumstances I pledge this army to do."

Halleck to Meade (one hour later): "There is reliable information that the enemy is crossing at Williamsport. The opportunity to attack his divided forces should not be lost. The President is . . . anxious that your army should move against him by forced marches."

Meade to Halleck: "My army is and has been making forced marches, short of rations and barefooted. . . . I repeat that I will use my utmost efforts to push forward this army."

Halleck to Meade: "Do not understand me as expressing any dissatisfaction. On the contrary, your army has done most nobly. I only wish to give you opinions formed from information received here. . . . If Lee's army is so divided by the river the importance of attacking the part on this side is incalculable. Such an opportunity may never occur again. . . . You will have forces sufficient to render your victory certain. My only fear now is that the enemy may escape."

The rains stopped on July 8, and Meade was getting reinforcements. His ranks numbered eighty-five thousand, with at least ten thousand more coming.

Meade to Halleck: "This army is moving in three columns, the right column having in it three corps. . . . I think the decisive battle of the war will be fought in a few days. In view of the momentous consequences, I desire to adopt such measures as to my judgment will tend to ensure success, even though they may be deemed tardy."

Halleck to Meade: "Do not be influenced by any dispatch from here against your own judgment. Regard them as suggestions only. Our information is not always correct."

Halleck to Meade: "[More troops are on the way.] I think it will be best for you to postpone a general battle till you can concentrate all your forces and get up your reserves and reinforcements. . . . Beware of partial combats. Bring up and hurl upon the enemy all your forces, good and bad."

This last dispatch from Halleck to Meade would have troubled Lincoln had he seen it. Halleck thought Meade wise to follow Lee cautiously. Lincoln didn't. He wanted Meade to move quickly and attack the Confederates before they crossed the Potomac.

Meade followed Halleck's orders.

By July 8, Lee's main army had arrived at Williamsport. Having no place to go, with the enemy at his front and the rising river at his back, Lee dug in behind formidable fortifications. His engineers laid out defensive positions that extended three miles in each direction from the town. James Longstreet's corps held the left flank from a position on high ground; A. P. Hill's corps held the center; and Richard S. Ewell's corps, the right. Stuart's massed cavalry reinforced the flanks and patrolled the front. Lee, concerned for the wounded, collected all ferryboats in the region and used them to transport the injured to the opposite bank in Virginia.

On July 9, much-needed ammunition arrived from Winchester, Virginia, and was transported to Lee by the ferries. But there was no food or forage in the shipment. Lee's men were now on half rations; his horses on grass and standing grain.

On July 10, Stuart repulsed a Federal advance in seven-hour fighting.

Lee wired Jefferson Davis: "With the blessing of heaven, I trust that the courage and fortitude of the army will be found sufficient to relieve us from the embarrassment caused by the unlooked-for natural difficulties of our situation." From scouts, Lee learned that Federals were on the march from Frederick.

On Sunday, July 12, Lee sent a message to Stuart: "Keep your eye over the field, use your good judgment, and give assistance where necessary."

That afternoon selected divisions from Meade's Second, Fifth, and Sixth Corps were ready for probing action against a Rebel-held wheat field. A Pennsylvania chaplain, seeing the preparations, protested to Meade: "As God's agent and disciple I solemnly protest. I will show you that the Almighty will not permit you to desecrate this sacred day. . . . Look at the heavens; see the threatening storm approaching!"

The storm came in quickly with loud thunder and dramatic lightning. Meade canceled the attack. To Halleck, Meade wrote: "It is my intention to attack them tomorrow unless something intervenes to prevent it."

Something did intervene that night. Meade called a council of war to discuss what he should do. Five of Meade's seven corps commanders said

they weren't ready to fight. They wanted more information on Lee's position. Surely, Meade knew that he ought to attack, yet he and his subordinates seemed overly concerned about being defeated. Meade reported to
Halleck, "I shall continue these reconnaissances with the expectation of
finding some weak point upon which, if I succeed, I shall hazard an attack."

While he was searching, the river subsided. In the meantime, Halleck
responded, "You are strong enough to attack and defeat the enemy. . . . Act
upon your own judgment and make your generals execute your orders. Call
no councils of war. It is proverbial that councils of war never fight. . . . Do
not let the enemy escape."

Lincoln, waiting nervously at the War Department for dispatches from
Meade, predicted, "They will be ready to fight a magnificent battle when
there is no enemy to fight."

On July 13, as Meade planned to begin reconnaissances the following
morning, Lee prepared to cross the Potomac. His engineers had created a
bridge of improvised pontoons by tearing down abandoned houses for their
timbers, which were then linked and floored. At 4:15 p.m., Lee gave Stuart
his orders: "I know it to be a difficult as well as delicate operation to cover
this army and then withdraw your command with safety, but I rely upon
your good judgment, energy, and boldness to accomplish it, and trust that
you may be as successful as you have been on former occasions."

Stuart was. His cavalrymen manned the trenches and parapets as the
wagons and foot soldiers crossed the river. Depending on the threat, Stuart's
troopers could mount their horses and move swiftly to whatever position
was advisable. By midnight the entire army had crossed.

Meade erred in following the advice of his generals when he should
have been leading them. He demonstrated a severe lack of aggressiveness.
When he finally did go forward on the morning of July 14, he couldn't find
Lee's Army of Northern Virginia. They were gone. Across the river. A river
that once again was rising. To Halleck, he reported, "Your instructions as to
further movements, in case the enemy are entirely across the river, are desired."

Never was Lincoln so disappointed and so furious. "If I had gone up
there, I could have whipped them myself," he exclaimed. "Our army held
the war in the hollow of their hand and they would not close it," he fumed.

Walking across the White House lawn with Gideon Welles, secretary of
the navy, Lincoln seemed both sad and angry. He had expected and dreaded

this awful news. "There is bad faith somewhere . . . What does it mean, Mr. Welles? Great God! What does it mean?"

Later, still festering, Lincoln asserted, "Meade and his army had expended their skill and toil and blood up to the ripe harvest, and then allowed it to go to waste." Rhetorically he asked, "Don't they realize that their primary purpose is to destroy enemy armies?" To Lincoln that was a basic military principle, and he couldn't understand why his generals failed to grasp it.

Halleck wired Meade that Lee's escape without another battle had "created great dissatisfaction in the mind of the President" and that only Meade's energetic pursuit of Lee would remove from the president's mind the impression that the pursuit so far had not been active enough. Meade, taking this message as a censure, responded: "Having performed my duty conscientiously and to the best of my ability, the censure of the President conveyed in your dispatch . . . is, in my judgment, so undeserved that I feel compelled most respectfully to ask to be immediately relieved from the command of the army."

Halleck replied that his telegram "was not intended as a censure, but as a stimulus to an active pursuit" and that it was not sufficient cause for Meade to apply for relief. Meade withdrew his resignation.

The president immediately drafted a long letter to Meade, expressing gratitude for his "magnificent success" at Gettysburg and regret that anything he had said had pained the general. But, wrote Lincoln, "I do not believe you appreciate the magnitude of the misfortune involved in Lee's escape. He was within your easy grasp, and to have closed upon him would, in connection with our other late successes, have ended the war. As it is, the war will be prolonged indefinitely. . . . Your golden opportunity is gone, and I am distressed immeasurably because of it." Lincoln did not sign or send the letter, but he retained it among his records.

The president eventually calmed down and spoke of Meade "as a brave and skillful officer, and a true man" who was responsible for repelling the Confederate invasion. He realized that perhaps he was expecting too much of this general who had been in command only three days prior to the battle and had lost some his ablest subordinates.

Historians have argued over whether or not an attack on the strong Confederate position would have succeeded. Meade, after examining the abandoned earthworks, concluded that his forces would have been re-

Union cavalrymen march Confederate prisoners of war to Frederick, Maryland. The building in the upper right was probably used as a Union hospital. Supply wagons and ambulance trains are parked in front of it.

pulsed. Certainly, an attack would have had heavy casualties. But all attacks carry risk. Success is rarely guaranteed. The potential value of this one was well worth the risk. Generals such as Ulysses S. Grant and William T. Sherman would not have hesitated to take that risk. The opportunity to end the war was too great to pass up.

In retrospect, Lee's getaway without a showdown from Meade was unforgivable. Both generals had exhausted armies, but Lee kept his moving until he reached the Potomac. He then put his troops to work building fortifications while waiting for the river to recede. Meade moved sluggishly but still had time to launch a major attack. He lacked courage and determination. With nearly 106,000 men, many of them fresh reinforcements, he was afraid of Lee's 59,000, none of whom were fresh and all of whom were near starvation.

For Meade it was "good enough" to prevent Lee from destroying the Army of the Potomac and to force him out of Pennsylvania. For Lee, considering the circumstances and the trap he was in, it was certainly good enough to escape to Virginia. His army had survived despite the loss of seventeen generals, nine dead and eight wounded.

Meade, the victor at Gettysburg, was the goat at Williamsport. As Lincoln wrote in his unsent letter, Meade had "stood and let the flood run down, bridges be built, and the enemy move away at his leisure without attacking him."

During discussions with Meade weeks later in Washington, Lincoln displayed his grim humor by asking Meade: "Do you know, general, what your attitude towards Lee for a week after the battle reminded me of?"

"No, Mr. President, what is it?" replied Meade.

"I'll be hanged if I could think of anything else," said Lincoln, "than an old woman trying to shoo her geese across a creek."

Meade, by Lincoln's directive, would not seek a decisive battle in Virginia in the summer of 1863. Lincoln told Halleck that if Meade with a far superior force could not smash the enemy in the North, he certain could not attack successfully in the South. Lincoln had lost confidence in Meade's ability to be aggressive anywhere.

To ease his mind, Lincoln composed a doggerel, "Gen. Lee's Invasion of the North":

> In eighteen sixty three, with pomp,
>   and mighty swell,
> Me and Jeff's Confederacy, went
>   forth to sack Phil-del,
> The Yankees they got after us, and
>   give us particular hell,
> And we skedaddled back again,
>   and didn't sack Phil-del.

11

THE CRATER: JULY 30, 1864

"CLAPTRAP AND NONSENSE"?

T HE UNION'S NEW GENERAL in chief, Ulysses S. Grant, engaged Robert E. Lee in a bloody campaign in northern Virginia during the spring and summer of 1864. Grant, who was trying to get between Lee and Richmond, was relentless despite severe losses. At the battle of the Wilderness, for example, he lost seventeen thousand to Lee's eleven thousand. And at Spotsylvania, eleven thousand fell compared to four thousand Southern casualties.

The two armies, seldom out of sight of each other, maintained a constant rhythm of marching and fighting during four weeks in May. This relentless, ceaseless warfare forced Lee to fall back step by step to a dusty crossroads known as Cold Harbor, about six miles northeast of the Confederate capital. Both armies were exhausted and haggard.

After indecisive skirmishes on June 1 and 2, Grant launched a massive assault at 4:30 a.m. on June 3. A major breakthrough could have ended the war.

Grant assumed that Lee's army was worn out and would be whipped. He was mistaken. Impatient and overconfident, he failed to do any reconnaissance or special preparation for the attack. Some of Grant's troops, however, were so lacking in confidence that they pinned slips of paper with their names and addresses on their uniforms so their bodies could be identified after the fighting. Fifty thousand Federals (out of 117,000 available for duty) moved against an army of 30,000 (out of 60,000 available).

Rebel artillery saw the Yankees coming and fired everything they had at them. Then, during a hellish ten minutes of butchery, Rebel infantry entrenched in well-protected zigzag fieldworks shot at them from three directions simultaneously. The battle lasted about an hour; it was actually over in about thirty minutes. More than 7,000 Federals fell. Confederate losses were under 1,500. Lee had stopped Grant cold.

Grant admitted defeat and called off further attacks. That night he said, "I regret this assault more than any I have ever ordered." It represented incredibly poor generalship on the part of the seasoned warrior. Moreover, the disaster destroyed morale among his battle-weary troops. "The men feel . . . a great horror and dread of attacking earthworks again," said one officer. Reflecting on what the army had been through in the past four weeks, Capt. Oliver Wendell Holmes Jr. wrote: "Many a man had gone crazy . . . from the terrible pressure on mind and body."

After several days of both armies staying in position, Grant made up for his ineptness at Cold Harbor by conceiving one of the most daring and skillfully executed movements of the war—a movement that completely fooled Lee. During the evening of Sunday, June 12, Grant quietly and cautiously pulled out his army from Cold Harbor. With one corps left behind to cover the movement of the rest of the army, more than one hundred thousand troops marched east and south of Lee and crossed over the James River headed for Petersburg. Situated twenty-three miles south of Richmond, the city was the hub of five major railroads that linked the Confederate capital with many Southern cities. Grant believed that if he could take this back door to Richmond, Lee would have to abandon his capital and reestablish another supply line.

Lee was deceived and unaware of the magnitude or destination of Grant's move. The Confederate commander sent most of his troops to the outskirts of Richmond, expecting an attack in that area. Thus, when the first Federals approached Petersburg on June 15—sixteen thousand troops under Maj. Gen. William F. "Baldy" Smith—only three thousand Rebels under Gen. P. G. T. Beauregard were there to protect the city.

Grant ordered Smith to attack quickly. Three thousand Rebels, he reasoned, couldn't stop sixteen thousand Federals. So Smith attacked. But poor maps, confused orders, delays, and missed opportunities by commanders combined with a courageous Confederate defense saved Petersburg. Smith bungled the attack so badly that he was relieved of field

Here at Cold Harbor, Virginia, Gen. Ulysses S. Grant made his worst mistake and suffered the worst defeat of his career. His ill-conceived assault cost him seven thousand casualties, compared to Lee's fifteen hundred. Grant recovered to conceive a daring movement that fooled Lee.

command. With the arrival of more Federal troops, Grant ordered assaults on June 16 and 17, but they also failed.

Lee finally realized that the bulk of the Army of the Potomac actually was south of the James near Petersburg. He ordered two corps to the city.

Grant, by this time, decided he couldn't take Petersburg by assault. He began a siege.

Immediately under Grant at Petersburg were Maj. Gen. George Gordon Meade (the victor at Gettysburg), who commanded the Army of the Potomac, and Maj. Gen. Ambrose E. Burnside (the goat of Fredericksburg), the army's former commander who now led the Ninth Corps. Part of the Union line held by Burnside's corps lay within 150 yards of a four-gun Confederate redoubt known as Elliott's Salient, because Brig. Gen. Stephen Elliott's South Carolinians were entrenched there.

Early in July, at Grant's request, Meade asked Burnside if he thought it was feasible to attack the Rebels in his front. Burnside said yes but advised waiting until he completed the construction of a mine. The innovative Burnside explained that instead of going through or around Lee, he had in progress a project to go under the Confederate entrenchments. This idea startled Meade, who discussed it with Grant.

Burnside noted that if Grant insisted on an immediate offensive, its best chance of success was from Burnside's position. He then qualified his statement, adding, "if it is left to me to say when and how the two other corps shall come in to my support."

Meade took offense at the remark and shot back that he, not Burnside, was in charge of the Army of the Potomac, and he would make such decisions. Burnside apologized, and Meade promised to promote "harmony and

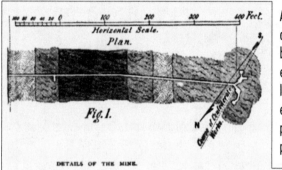

A coal miner proposed tunneling under a Rebel stronghold at Petersburg and blowing it up. His commander, a civil engineer, drew up these plans for the longest military tunnel ever to be excavated. Meade's engineers said the project was impossible. They refused to provide supplies or other assistance.

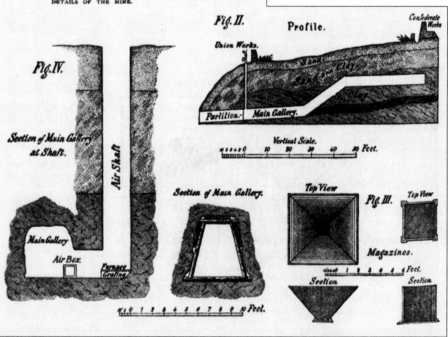

good feeling" among the corps commanders and himself. It was a promise unlikely to be kept by the irascible Meade, known throughout the army for his unruly temper and frequent quarrels with senior subordinates. Neither Grant nor Meade expressed enthusiasm for the mine concept, but they allowed it to proceed.

The mine was the brainchild of a coal miner in the Forty-eighth Pennsylvania, a regiment made up primarily of volunteers from the anthracite fields of Schuylkill County. Seeing the Rebel stronghold about 150 yards from his trenches, he exclaimed, "We could blow that damned fort out of existence if we could run a mine shaft under it."

His commander, Col. Henry Pleasants, overheard him. Pleasants was a civil engineer with some expertise in railroad tunneling. He drew up a sketch and showed it to his division chief, Brig. Gen. Robert B. Potter, who passed it along to Burnside. The corps commander told Pleasants to start digging. Some four hundred men worked in around-the-clock shifts to move dirt and rock at the rate of forty to fifty feet a day.

Pleasants said the work could have been done in half the time if they had been given the proper tools, yet Meade refused to provide them. Since Meade had not officially approved the project, his staff would not cooperate with tools and supplies, and Meade did not encourage them to do so.

Meade's chief engineer, Maj. James C. Duane, frankly commented that the project was absurd, and his engineers regarded it as "claptrap and nonsense." Such a long mine couldn't be dug, he said, because there was no way to ventilate it or prevent the walls from collapsing. Duane, in fact, had written a manual for military engineers. It listed forty basic tools miners needed, but he wouldn't provide any of them or any other material to Pleasants. The Pennsylvania miners were left to their own devices.

Pleasants, with the help of regimental blacksmiths, contrived his own picks. He made barrows out of hardtack boxes. He confiscated a lumber mill in unoccupied territory to cut timbers and planks to shore up the gallery walls and roof. And he borrowed a surveyor's instrument—a theodolite—from a civilian when Meade's engineers couldn't spare one of theirs. Pleasants needed it to be sure that the mine didn't overshoot the fort. To draw an accurate reading, he crawled out on the picket line—a risky act with enemy sharpshooters less than fifty paces away.

Meade's staff wouldn't even provide wheels for the barrows, so the men had to carry the dirt and debris out of the tunnel—eighteen thousand cubic

feet of it! Of course, as the tunnel grew longer, they had to haul the stuff farther—a cumbersome, backbreaking chore.

When Pleasants ordered six tons of explosives, Meade sent four. And
when the regimental commander requisitioned a thousand yards of safety
fuse, he received common blasting fuse that had been cut into short
lengths. Pleasants had to splice it every few feet. The fuse lines were readily
available from the manufacturer, but again, Meade and his staff were
uncooperative.

Meade, an engineer himself, regarded Pleasants as a crackpot and told
Burnside so. But Meade was wrong. Pleasants knew exactly what he was
doing, and he did it superbly.

When the miners finished, they had a shaft 511 feet long—the longest
military tunnel ever excavated. The tunnel was twenty feet below the surface, five feet high, four feet wide at the bottom, and two feet wide at the
top. At its end they dug left and right lateral galleries, each about forty feet
long, creating four powder chambers in each wing directly under the enemy
fort and its flanking trenches.

The hard work done, Pleasants distributed 320 kegs of black powder
among eight connecting magazines and sandbagged them to direct the explosion upward. By the evening of July 28 everything was ready for
detonation.

Meade and Grant, surprised by Pleasants's success, authorized Burnside
to explode the mine and attack with his corps through the resultant gap.
Burnside was ecstatic. He saw this as an opportunity to redeem his failure at
Fredericksburg. He could capture Petersburg and win the war.

Burnside's battle plan after the explosion called for Brig. Gen. Edward
Ferrero's division of African American troops to lead the attack through the
gap into the Confederate line. After penetrating the ruins of the Rebel defenses, they were to spread out, left and right, and sweep the adjoining lines
of any resistance. Three other divisions then would come up, move unopposed onto the high ground behind the blasted entrenchments, and proceed to take Petersburg.

Ferrero, a Spanish immigrant and former New York dancing instructor,
had fought under Burnside in North Carolina and had joined Grant's army
at Vicksburg and Knoxville. His division was the largest and freshest of the
four, with nine fully officered regiments. The other three divisions, all
white, had been in the trenches and under fire for thirty-six days, averaging

thirty casualties a day. Burnside feared they would advance only when they felt it was safe and then they'd stop and dig in.

Although the African American division had never attacked a fortification, Burnside was confident they were the least likely to waver among the four divisions. He and Ferrero had two weeks to prepare them. As fairly new recruits, they had to learn complicated footwork, such as mastering a right or left wheel in double column. They did, and they also completed other training on schedule. They knew what to do, when to do it, and how to do it. They were eager "to show the white troops what the colored division could do," said one of their officers.

Burnside met with his division commanders on Friday afternoon, July 29, to give them final instructions for the assault scheduled before dawn the following morning. He was unusually enthusiastic. In the meantime, Grant and Meade had finally recognized the opportunities and ordered two other corps to stand by to assist in exploiting the breakthrough. Further, they assigned 144 field pieces, mortars, and siege guns to support the assault. And Grant sent Maj. Gen. Winfield Scott Hancock's corps and two of Maj. Gen. Philip H. Sheridan's divisions to create a diversion on the north side of the James to pull several of Lee's divisions away from the immediate area.

As Burnside was concluding his battle conference, a courier dashed in with an order from Meade, approved by Grant. It was explicit: don't use Ferrero's black troops to spearhead the assault. Instead, Meade directed him to choose one of the white divisions. Meade lacked confidence in his African American soldiers. The task of charging entrenchments, he believed, required combat-hardened troops. Grant later added another reason to justify this last-minute decision: "If we put the colored troops in front and [the attack] should prove a failure, it would then be said, and very properly, that we were shoving those people ahead to get killed because we did not care anything about them."

Brig. Gen. Edward Ferrero's division of African American troops was to lead the attack after the explosion. Well trained and ready, they were canceled at the last minute by Generals Grant and Meade, who lacked confidence in them. Instead of being first, the African American division would be the last of four divisions in the assault.

Brig. Gen. James H. Ledlie, the army's most incompetent divisional
commander, was chosen by lot to lead the assault. As soon as his
division advanced, Ledlie abandoned them and rushed to the
rear to hide and get drunk.

In a double whammy that nearly paralyzed Burnside, Grant and Meade also
voided Burnside's plan to clear the Confederate trenches. They directed the attack to
focus on the crest of a hill—known as Cemetery Hill—less than a mile behind the Confederate line. At that time, nothing stood between
the hill and Petersburg.

With the assault scheduled in less than twelve hours, Burnside was so
shaken that he lost control over the operation. Ferrero's African American
division was well prepared and ready; there was little time to prepare any of
the three other divisions for the lead role. Burnside no doubt wondered
why Meade and Grant had waited until the last minute to meddle in his
plans; they knew it would be difficult for him to adjust his assault orders on
such short notice.

Flabbergasted, Burnside told his division commanders to draw straws
to determine who would replace Ferrero's division at the lead. It was a bad
decision. The draw went to Brig. Gen. James H. Ledlie, a man regarded as
the army's most incompetent divisional commander. In fact, the Senate held
up Ledlie's confirmation as a brigadier until he pulled a few political strings.
Surely Burnside knew this, but he gave no indication of it.

Burnside told Ledlie his mission was to occupy Cemetery Hill as quickly
as possible, before the Rebels could regroup. The divisions of Brig. Gens.
Robert B. Potter and Orlando Willcox were to follow him, and Ferrero was to
bring up the rear. That was the extent of Burnside's instructions. Ledlie, Potter, Willcox, and Ferrero could use their discretion in accomplishing the objective. Shortly before 3 a.m. on July 30 the four divisions were all in place,
with other corps standing by. About fifteen thousand troops were ready for
the assault.

At 3:15 a.m. Pleasants entered the tunnel and lit the ninety-eight-foot
fuse. He expected the blast to occur at about 3:30. It didn't. He waited until
4 a.m. Still nothing happened. Two men bravely went into the tunnel to

find the problem: a burned out fuse at one of the splices. They fixed it, relit it, and ran for the entrance. They had just reached the tunnel opening when the eight-thousand-pound charge erupted at 4:44 a.m.

A Union officer described the scene: "A slight tremor of the earth for a second, then the rocking as of an earthquake, and, with a tremendous blast . . . a vast column of earth and smoke shoots upward to a great height, its dark sides flashing out sparks of fire, hangs poised for a moment in midair, and then, hurtling down with a roaring sound, showers of stones, broken timbers and Blackened human limbs."

Immediately the Federal guns—110 cannon and 54 mortars—boomed with a deafening sound along a two-mile line. Confederate troops on both sides of the crater fled in terror. Ledlie's vanguard momentarily panicked and moved backward, rather than forward, until the officers calmed the men's fears and started them onward. As soon as they were in motion, Ledlie abandoned them. He ran to a shelter behind the lines where he opened a bottle of rum and began to drink; he never rejoined his troops. Meanwhile, the advancing Federals had only the vaguest notion of what was expected of them.

Ledlie's troops encountered one problem immediately: Burnside had failed to order the division commanders to clear their defensive obstructions in front of their earthworks. As a result, Ledlie's command couldn't advance on a broad front. They had to break formation and go through a quickly improvised ten-foot passage into no-man's-land.

All they had to do to take Cemetery Hill was to keep moving. The bulk of Lee's army remained north of the James. Only a small force of Rebel infantry lay to the right and left of the crater. But after sprinting a hundred yards, the Federals stopped and gawked in awe and shock at the edge of a twelve-foot wall of dirt—their attention riveted on what had once been the Confederate fort. In its place now was a gigantic crater—170 feet long, 60 feet wide, and 30 feet deep. At its base were 278 dead, wounded, dazed, and mangled Confederates. The detonation had buried an entire Rebel regiment and an artillery battery.

So awestruck were Ledlie's soldiers that they were frozen in place at the sight of the strange spectacle. Instead of advancing around the crater to roll up the broken Rebel flanks, some of them entered the crater to extract partially buried Rebels. Then, when a small group of defenders opened fire, more of Ledlie's shell-shocked men darted into the crater for shelter. Most of them stayed there and settled in on the far side. One soldier later observed,

"The bottom and sides . . . were covered with a loose sand, furnishing scarcely a foothold, and for this reason, as well as that of the narrowness of the place, it was with great difficulty that the troops could pass through it."

Confusion reigned. Unit commanders who had entered the crater along with their men now issued conflicting instructions. No one urged the men forward, but a few advanced on their own initiative. A regiment of engineers began digging a covered way back to their own lines.

Meanwhile, part of Burnside's second division under Brig. Gen. Simon Griffin passed through the dense dust and smoke with some confusion before coming up against an expanse of Rebel trenches. They drove the Rebels back and advanced three hundred yards into the Confederate line. This gave Ledlie's men the opportunity to push for the crest of Cemetery Hill. Instead, they climbed into the works Griffin had just taken and refused to go farther.

Ledlie apparently never told his brigade commanders what they were supposed to do. His commanders later said that they heard nothing from him about moving beyond the captured works. Ledlie probably was at least partially drunk when he received his instructions and fully drunk once the battle began.

Burnside notified division commanders Potter and Willcox to move regardless of what Ledlie's men did. They went forward briefly in an effort to sweep the trenches of Rebels, but they were forced back by concentrated volleys and converging fire on the ground between the crater and the Union trenches. Some of them also sought shelter in the crater. Shortly, several thousand Federals were crammed into the steep-walled hole in the ground. Heavy fire kept them there and blocked any further Union advance. Willcox's division was stalled in the trenches to the left of the depression; Potter's was caught up on the right.

A dispatch to Burnside about the refusal of Ledlie's men to advance inadvertently ended up in Meade's hands. He urged Burnside to send in all of his corps as well as Maj. Gen. Edward O. C. Ord's Eighteenth Corps.

Burnside said he would push forward his corps as soon as possible. Ord couldn't move, however, because of heavy foot traffic in and near the covered passway. It was blocked by Col. Zenas Bliss's brigade of Potter's division, by casualties coming back, and by the massed troops inside the crater. Bliss's failure to be with his brigade probably accounted for its poor placement. In other words, the situation degenerated into a disorganized mess.

Next, Meade inquired if Maj. Gen. Gouverneur K. Warren's Fifth Corps

The explosion created a hole 170 feet long, 60 feet wide, and 30 feet deep. Casualties included an entire Rebel regiment and an artillery brigade. This photograph was taken a few weeks after the fighting.

should go in. Burnside said they should form in readiness. Burnside and Warren met at the front, and Warren suggested that his corps proceed on the left. Since Burnside felt he didn't have the authority to tell another corps what to do—a fact Meade had emphasized earlier—Burnside sent an inquiry to Meade, who responded that someone should move quickly—Warren had been ready to move for three hours. Meade also demanded to know what had prevented Warren's advance. He wrote: "I wish to know the truth and desire an immediate response." Burnside replied that Meade's remark was unofficerlike and ungentlemanly and implied that he was hiding the truth. Meade then asked for a copy of Burnside's dispatch as evidence for official charges against him.

While this was transpiring behind the Union lines, Confederate Gen. P. G. T. Beauregard rushed up reinforcements and artillery and formed in a low-lying area behind the crater. Also, most of the bolted Rebels returned to their posts in the flanks of the excavation.

About 7:30 a.m. Burnside's fourth wave—Ferrero's African Americans—charged into the fray, but their progress was slowed by a steady flow of retreating comrades. Complicating matters further, Ferrero was not with his troops. After ordering the charge, he left his men and joined Ledlie in a bombproof shelter a quarter mile away. Most of Ferrero's men swung around the crater in the manner they had rehearsed and drove toward the high ground, joined by some of Brig. Gen. John Turner's division from the Tenth Corps.

With these black and white troops poised to assault the Confederates, Gen. Simon Griffin chose to attempt another assault on Cemetery Hill. As they pushed their way through the swirl of smoke, this Federal force was met head-on by a brigade of Virginians under Maj. Gen. William Mahone. Enraged by the sight of black soldiers in uniform, the Virginians lost all respect for the rules of warfare. When a colonel saw black soldiers advancing over the bodies of dead Southerners, he rallied his regiment in a vicious charge amplified by the Rebel Yell. They drove the blue line into a large trench, fired pointblank volleys into the ditch, and then pounced on the Yankees with their bayonets.

The stunned freedmen who survived the onslaught "broke up in disorder and fell back to the crater," a witness reported. Rebels bayoneted several who tried to surrender. Others were beaten up. The African American division lost a third of its men—1,327 out of just under 4,000.

Ewell's Fiery Blunder

On April 2, 1865, Richmond fell. But not before the Confederates destroyed their own capital city.

Lt. Gen. Richard S. Ewell was responsible. He ordered his troops to burn tobacco warehouses—an act more harmful to Southerners than Federals. The flames quickly got out of control and spread to adjacent houses and shops and the city's business district.

Meanwhile, the troops torched and bombed their warships in the James River. Then the army's arsenal exploded. Shells soared high into the air like fireworks. They fell ablaze, starting more fires.

As a Confederate brigade crossed Mayo's Bridge, Gen. Martin W. Gary shouted, "All over, good-bye; blow her to hell." Soldiers ignited tar-filled barrels under bridges, and fires from two railroad bridges burned into the night. Altogether the fires set by Confederate troops destroyed some eight hundred buildings.

Ewell later denied that his troops started the fires, but the evidence that they did is substantial.

Burnside called for help and asked for the Fifth Corps to be sent in immediately. But Grant and Meade regarded the battle as already lost. Grant himself had witnessed Ferrero's men repulsed. He directed Meade to cancel further attacks and to order Burnside to withdraw his corps to its old line. Meade rode to Burnside's headquarters and told him: "The entire opportunity has been lost. There is now no chance of success. These troops must be immediately withdrawn. It is slaughter to leave them there."

Burnside, believing that support for his troops could have countered the Rebel resistance, flew into a rage over the order to withdraw. He maintained the assault would succeed if supported by Warren and Ord. Meade asked Ord for his opinion, and he agreed with Meade.

Grant and Meade returned to their headquarters as Ord and Burnside wrangled over the lost opportunity. Burnside was angry with Ord for disagreeing with him in front of Meade and for not springing his corps into action. Ord replied with an equal show of temper that he could not move his men—that he was "held by the throat." Actually, only a single small regiment stood in the way of an assault on Burnside's right.

Within the crater itself the troops had turned into a mob. In that hot and dusty hellhole more than ten thousand men were crowded hip to hip. They could do almost nothing to defend themselves. Having earlier consumed all the water in their canteens, they suffered greatly from the heat. Some became delirious.

Burnside's withdrawal order reached brigade commanders at about 12:30 p.m. But they saw no way to orderly withdraw the uncontrollable throng. They pleaded for covering fire on their flanks to help them make a mass exit, but all corps commanders except Burnside had been ordered to stand down. And since Burnside had committed his entire corps, all he could offer was artillery support.

The Confederates attempted a second advance on the crater, but Burnside's field guns and a few hundred riflemen stopped them. Then, at 1 p.m., Mahone and Maj. Gen. Bushrod Johnson decided to launch simultaneous attacks on the crater. First, they brought up mortars and fired into the depression. A battery commander recalled, "We could hear them cry out when the shells would fall among them, and repeatedly they would dash out and beg to surrender." Those who survived were covered with the blood and fragments of other men.

The senior officers in the cauldron, convinced they wouldn't have any covering fire for a withdrawal, encouraged everyone to get out the best way they could and make a run for safety. As the trapped Federals prepared to bolt for their lines, Mahone and Johnson made a double assault. They swept into the Yankees in and around the crater, firing volleys and charging with flashing bayonets.

The bottom of the crater piled up with Union corpses. One officer recalled, "Whites and Blacks were squeezed so tightly together that there was hardly standing room. Even many of those killed were held in a standing position until jostled to the ground." The few who emerged from the crater scrambled back to Union lines; hundreds were taken prisoners.

During this struggle, Meade issued several inquiries about the situation at the crater. Burnside, upset with Meade for calling off all support, threw his dispatches to the ground. Only one result was possible, Burnside asserted, and Meade surely knew what that was. He gave Meade the gruesome details the next day. Union losses were estimated at 5,300. The Confederates reported losses of 1,032.

Grant summarized the battle as "the saddest affair I have witnessed in this war. Such opportunity for carrying fortifications I have never seen and do not expect again to have."

Heads had to roll. Grant sent Burnside home on leave. "He will never return whilst I am here," Meade asserted angrily. Burnside's military career was over. Ledlie took a leave of absence and was told to await further orders; they never came. Strangely, Ferrero not only retained his command but also was promoted to major general for "meritorious service."

Meade created a court of inquiry to investigate the disaster. He also brought charges against Burnside for insubordination, stemming from his "ungentlemanly" dispatch and his blowup at Meade's headquarters.

The four members of the court were all friends of Meade. The outcome was predictable. Burnside, they agreed, was primarily responsible. The court cited three failures on his part: not leveling the parapets in his front so that a broad column of assault could sweep across the crater, not pushing Ledlie's division beyond the crater, and not withdrawing Ledlie's division in favor of another when it would not advance (despite the extremely narrow front at the crater, which precluded the withdrawal of individual divisions without pandemonium). Ledlie, Ferrero, and Bliss were censured for remaining behind while their troops attacked.

The court found no fault with Meade but suggested that some officer near the battlefield should have had authority over all the attacking forces. That implied that either Meade should have been at the front to react to new developments or Burnside should have been able to call up Warren's and Ord's forces as needed.

Later the Joint Committee on the Conduct of the War conducted its own investigation. They concluded that the crater debacle was due to Meade's interference with Burnside's plan. Had he left Ferrero's division to lead the attack, with detachments sweeping up the enemy lines to quell the flank threat, the plan ought to have worked. Both Grant and Warren had told them as much.

Grant testified, "General Burnside wanted to put his colored division in front, and if he had done so, I believe it would have been a success." Why, then, did Grant approve Meade's order to replace them? Grant also testified that he knew Ledlie would lead the charge. Yet he did nothing about it even

African American soldiers advance toward and beyond the crater without their commander, Edward Ferrero, who abandoned them and joined Ledlie in the rear. The surging troops were met head-on by a brigade of Virginians who lost all respect for the rules of warfare when they saw African American soldiers in Federal uniforms.

though he thought Ledlie the worst general Burnside had, and he said as much to the committee.

The committee's only criticism of Burnside was choosing the lead division by lot.

Meade and the court of inquiry blamed Burnside. Burnside and the JCCW blamed Meade.

The battle of the Crater had many goats and scapegoats. The goats were:

1. Grant, for allowing Ledlie to lead the assault when he knew he was incompetent and for not requiring Meade to meet personally with Burnside to discuss the change in plans and the choice of the white division to replace the African Americans.
2. Meade, for meddling with Burnside's plan (and doing so just hours before the assault), which resulted in supplanting a division likely to win the day with one whose commander was almost certain to lose regardless of what troops were at hand; for not supporting Burnside adequately; for not being at the front to react expeditiously; and for misjudging Pleasants and not supporting him in the construction of the mine.
3. Burnside, for the failures cited by the court of inquiry, for his means of choosing the replacement of Ferrero's division, and for his loose hand with his division commanders.
4. Ledlie, for abandoning his troops, providing no leadership, and failing to brief his men on what was expected of them.
5. Ferrero and Bliss, for abandoning their troops.

On the Southern side, Mahone deserves credit for the victory. It earned him a well-deserved reputation as one of the best young generals of Lee's army in the last year of the war.

Grant attempted no further major assaults at Petersburg. He settled in for a long siege. It ended with Lee's evacuation of Petersburg and the fall of Richmond.

THE WESTERN THEATER

12

FORT DONELSON: FEBRUARY 13–16, 1862

"GATEWAY TO A GLORY ROAD"

HE TWIN TENNESSEE FORTS of Henry and Donelson commanded bends in rivers and protected Confederate troop positions in western Kentucky and Tennessee. Otherwise they bore little resemblance to each other. Henry, guarding the Tennessee River, was so poorly designed that any rise in the river would flood it. Donelson, just twelve miles away on a high bluff, defended the Cumberland River.

At Donelson, two heavy guns were emplaced on the crown of a hundred-foot bluff, and a battery of twelve guns was dug into the bluff's northern face. Landward, deep gullies and three miles of semicircular trenches provided protection. The fort itself was a rustic stockade enclosing fifteen acres of log huts.

The forts were about eleven miles south of the Kentucky line and seventy-five miles northwest of Nashville, the state capital. The rivers paralleled each other through Kentucky and past the forts and then flowed southward into the Confederate heartland. They were logical avenues for the Yankees to push the Confederates out of middle and western Tennessee and to open a gateway to the Deep South. The forts controlled access to these avenues.

Fort Donelson was within a mile of the sleepy village of Dover, a layover for riverboat traffic. Nearby were major iron-producing areas of the Confederacy. The Clarksville Iron Works, twenty miles east of Dover, produced

Ulysses S. Grant may not have looked like a general, but he quickly
emerged from obscurity to become the Union's best. At Fort
Donelson, he captured an entire army of thirteen thousand
men. It was the largest capture ever made on the continent.

small arms. A foundry turned out cannon-
balls and shells. When the battle came, it
would be one of the most decisive engagements of the war.

Commanding Rebel forces in the western theater was Gen. Albert Sidney Johnston, a
debonair, six-foot Texan with a flared mustache
and deep-set eyes. His seventy thousand troops
manned the line of defense in Kentucky and northern Tennessee. This line
stretched three hundred miles from the Cumberland Gap on the Virginia
border to the Mississippi River in the west. Johnston's base was at Bowling
Green, Kentucky, about eighty miles from Fort Donelson and fifty-five miles
north of Nashville.

Federal forces in the region included an army being put together by
Brig. Gen. Ulysses S. Grant at Cairo, Illinois (where the Ohio flows into the
Mississippi) and the Western Flotilla—a fleet of gunboats at Cairo under
Flag Officer Andrew H. Foote. He was an old-line sailor and religious fa-
natic from Connecticut. Pro-temperance, he cleared his ships of demon
rum and earned a reputation for brimstone sermons and devout prayer.

Ninety miles north of Johnston's Confederate headquarters was the
seventy-five-thousand-man Army of the Ohio at Louisville under Maj. Gen.
Don Carlos Buell. He was a cold, firm disciplinarian. Like George B.
McClellan, he knew how to turn raw recruits into soldiers but was then
slow to use them in battle. Buell could have crushed Johnston's twenty-two
thousand troops at Bowling Green whenever he wished, but neither he nor
his counterpart who headed the Missouri Department, Maj. Gen. Henry W.
Halleck, showed any sensitivity to political urgency or to cooperating with
each other. President Lincoln's frustration in dealing with them was reflected in a note he scribbled on a letter: "As everywhere else, nothing can
be done."

Grant, an aggressive fighter, reported to Halleck, who didn't want to
commit large forces anywhere. Overly cautious, Halleck was once described

as "a large emptiness surrounded by an education." Called "Old Brains" (but not to his face), Halleck had written a book on military strategy and translated similar works. Balding and paunchy at age forty-seven, Halleck was a good administrator and theorist, but not a fighting soldier.

Grant's résumé was the weakest among these officers. It mirrored a "face in the crowd." At five foot eight inches and 135 pounds, with no concern for military "spit and polish," he didn't look like or talk like a general. He didn't curse. His strongest expletives were "doggone it" and "by lightning." He "habitually wore an expression," said one soldier, "as if he had determined to drive his head through a brick wall and was about to do it." His worst habit was smoking. He preferred a long-stemmed meerschaum pipe but later chose cigars and became a chain smoker.

At the age of seventeen, Grant entered West Point after securing a nomination through his congressman. About the only nice thing that could be said of Grant's years at the academy was that he was a good horseman. His major accomplishment was setting a high-jump record on a horse no other cadet could ride.

In 1843 Grant received his commission as a second lieutenant and served in Missouri and Louisiana and earned citations for bravery in the Mexican War. After marrying Julia Dent in 1848, he was assigned to Pacific Coast garrisons where she could not follow, and he was lonely and miserable. When he was reprimanded for heavy drinking, he resigned from the service, allegedly to avoid being dismissed. A failure at almost everything he attempted to do in civilian life, he sold firewood and clerked in his brothers' dry goods store in Galena, Illinois.

Only the desperation of the Illinois governor for experienced officers to train volunteer regiments brought about Grant's return to uniform in 1861. With the aid of his father's political influence, he obtained a commission as colonel. He organized and whipped into shape the Twenty-first Illinois, a group of farm boys accustomed to chasing girls and raiding barnyards for chickens.

Very soon Washington created four new brigadier generals of Illinois volunteers, and to Grant's surprise, one of the stars appeared on his shoulder boards. He was appointed to head the Division of Southern Illinois and Southeastern Missouri. Headquartered at Cairo, Grant constructed a fort on the opposite Kentucky shore and patched together a force of two thousand river men and their boats. On September 6, 1861, he sent them upriver to seize Paducah, Kentucky, under Grant's former West Point instructor, Brig. Gen. Charles F. Smith.

With the Tennessee and Cumberland rivers emptying into the Ohio near Paducah, Grant sought to capitalize on their strategic value. On these waterways he could strike Forts Henry and Donelson and challenge Johnston's defensive line.

Lincoln and others believed that the weakest spot in the line was where the two rivers cut into Tennessee, just above the forts. The location was only about fifty miles south of Paducah.

Grant, eager to put a plan into action, pressed for permission to attack Fort Henry. Foote enthusiastically supported him, but their boss, Halleck, objected. But when Halleck's rival, Buell, allowed Brig. Gen. George H. Thomas to attack the Confederates at Mill Springs, Kentucky, on January 19, 1862—an attack that led to a Union victory—Buell had a "leg up" over Halleck. Determined to prove that his department also could win battles,

Halleck reversed his earlier decision and authorized Grant and Foote to make "a limited expedition" against Fort Henry.

On February 3, 1862, troop transports began moving from Cairo to Paducah, and Foote's flotilla headed toward the fort. Two days later the transports landed Grant's fifteen thousand troops several miles below Fort Henry. They planned to attack it from the rear while gunboats shelled it from the front.

The navy arrived first. Foote's flotilla literally floated into Fort Henry on February 6. Heavy rains had flooded the fort's lower level, leaving only nine guns to fire on the Federals. The boats could fire twice as many. The fort's commander, Brig. Gen. Lloyd Tilghman, recognized the hopeless situation

Flag Officer Andrew H. Foote's seven ironclads and wooden gunboats captured Fort Henry on February 6, 1862, after killing or wounding half of the Confederate defenders. Grant's army, delayed by mud and heavy rain, missed the battle.

HARPER'S WEEKLY

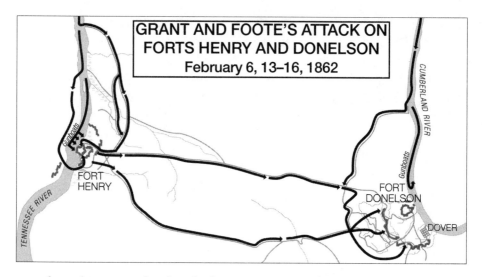

GRANT AND FOOTE'S ATTACK ON FORTS HENRY AND DONELSON
February 6, 13–16, 1862

and sent his twenty-five-hundred-man garrison twelve miles across country to the stronger Fort Donelson on the Cumberland. Tilghman remained behind with one artillery company to fight a delaying action against the four ironclads and three wooden gunboats.

The defenders struck the flotilla with fifty-nine shots. Most were harmless. Shells from the gunboats did far more damage, killing or wounding half of the defenders and disabling nearly all of their guns. At 2 p.m. Tilghman surrendered his small remaining force of twelve officers and sixty-six men. Grant's army missed the battle. They were mired down by mud and heavy rain.

The fall of Fort Henry opened the Tennessee River for Federal advancement southward. But nearby Fort Donelson on the Cumberland still had to be taken. Grant, on his own initiative, decided to remove the obstacle. He penned a short, brusque note to Halleck: "Fort Henry is ours. I shall take and destroy Fort Donelson on the 8th and return to Fort Henry." Halleck moaned to a friend, "It is the crisis of the war in the West!" On the other hand, he rationalized that if Grant lost, it would be Grant's defeat; if Grant succeeded, it would be Halleck's victory. He forwarded reinforcements to Grant.

High waters delayed Grant's advance. With Foote having taken his ironclads back to Cairo for repairs, Grant's land force was in a precarious position. Huddled in crowded camps with their back against swift flood waters, they could have been decimated by a Rebel counteroffensive. But Johnston didn't make the attempt.

With clearing skies and springlike weather on February 11, Grant's army began the march on Fort Donelson without knowing anything about the enemy's strength. Brig. Gen. John A. McClernand led the advance, followed by Charles F. Smith's division. Thinking winter was over, the troops lightened their load by discarding their overcoats and blankets. They'd regret it later.

By evening on February 12, they had formed a semicircle upon hills near Fort Donelson and the nearby town of Dover. At the top of the semicircle was the Cumberland River. When the gunboats arrived, the encirclement would be complete.

The Confederate high command squabbled over strategy. Johnston knew little about Donelson, never having seen it, and relied upon his subordinates for advice. He decided that the fort should be defended, but he personally wouldn't do it. He evacuated his exposed position at Bowling Green and withdrew toward Nashville. He was, in effect, splitting his army, sending about twelve thousand men to reinforce Donelson and the remainder to the Tennessee capital. It was perhaps the greatest blunder of his military career. He defied military logic, which called for either evacuating Donelson or concentrating all available forces against Grant's army.

The reinforcements streamed into Donelson along with four brigadier generals—Gideon Pillow, John B. Floyd, Simon Bolivar Buckner, and Bushrod Johnson. Floyd and Pillow were flamboyant lawyers and politicians who lacked military competency. Floyd had been transferred to Kentucky after losing in West Virginia. Hated in the North for stockpiling Southern

Dover, Tennessee, which was adjacent to Fort Donelson, was a quiet layover for riverboat traffic on the Cumberland before February 13, 1862.

LESLIE'S

arsenals while he was President James Buchanan's secretary of war, Floyd made Donelson an even more tempting target for Grant and the Yankees.

Johnston's choice of Floyd and Pillow to play critical roles at Donelson remains a mystery. It was another major blunder on his part. Grant knew both men and later said about them: "I had known General Pillow in Mexico and judged that with any force, no matter how small, I could march up to within gunshot of any entrenchments he was given to hold. . . . I knew that Floyd was in command, but he was no soldier, and I judged that he would yield to Pillow's pretensions." Pillow, whom Grant called "conceited," was best known for loud, coarse arguments with his commander in the Mexican War.

Prior to Floyd's arrival at Donelson on February 13 to assume command, Pillow had been in charge for four days. During that time he had told his troops, "I will never surrender!" He directed them to "drive back the ruthless invader from our soil." His battle cry was "liberty or death!"

Buckner regarded Pillow as a fool and resented being subordinate to him. He and Bushrod Johnson commanded the two Confederate divisions. They were West Pointers and professional soldiers. At the least, the quartet of generals needed to hold the fort until Johnston arrived in Nashville with the other half of his army.

Grant, meanwhile, assumed from poor scouting reports that he was facing twenty-five thousand enemy troops. Actually, the number was closer to thirteen thousand. With fifteen thousand men in his force, but believing he needed more, Grant sent messages to Brig. Gen. Lew Wallace at Fort Henry to bring over his rear echelon and to Cmdr. Henry Walke to advance his lone gunboat at 10 a.m. as a diversion. Grant wondered why Foote and the main flotilla hadn't arrived. He didn't know they had been struggling against heavy flood currents on the Cumberland and were still several miles from Dover.

Grant's final directive to all subordinates on the morning of February 13 was to avoid battle. He wanted the flotilla in place first. His order was not obeyed; three bloody battles evolved that day.

Conducting what he intended as a simple reconnaissance on the Federal left, Smith employed 10-pounder artillery weapons to goad the Rebels into disclosing their battery positions. He then directed two of his brigades to advance simultaneously to the crest of the ridge facing Buckner's lines. With their visibility hampered by thick timber, they could not gauge the

HARPER'S WEEKLY

The Union's Western Flotilla bogged down in the mud at Fort Donelson. Flag Officer Andrew H. Foote brought his ironclads too close to the shore, causing him to overshoot the shore batteries while making his gunboats easy targets for the Rebels' shorter-range guns. The roar of the land and naval battle was heard thirty-five miles away.

range or extent of the Rebel force. Descending the slope for a better view, they unknowingly came within the enemy's cannon range. An all-out battle ensued. The raw recruits on both sides were taken off-guard by the first rounds and were startled to see wounded and dying men for the first time. Nearly a hundred Federals were killed in the morning action. Repulsed, Smith's brigades withdrew back to the ridge.

On the river, Walke's gunboat opened a long-range fire against the Confederate batteries. That led to a two-hour duel and cat-and-mouse shelling. Two Rebels were killed and five wounded. One of their 32-pounders was shattered. A 128-pound Confederate projectile cut through a bulwark on the gunboat and wounded seamen and burst a steam heater. Another projectile damaged the front traverse wheels.

On the Federal right, McClernand ordered three brigades to merge with Illinois cavalry and push northward toward Fort Donelson. Stymied by hot fire from Confederate artillerists and a six-gun Kentucky battery, McClernand snapped. A scheming Illinois politician who wanted Grant's job, he was overzealous and quick to snatch any opportunity for glory. Thus he deliberately defied Grant's orders and decided to storm the battery and silence it. The Seventeenth, Forty-eighth, and Forty-ninth Illinois charged to within fifty yards of the battery before a murderous crossfire of artillery and

musketry shattered the assault. Some 147 Federals fell. In a dramatic moment, dry leaves caught fire in a no-man's-land where scores of Yankees lay
wounded. Rebels rushed to their aid and rescued the very enemy they had
shot down moments before.

In these three battles of February 13, McClernand, Walke, and Smith accomplished nothing except to build Rebel confidence. Grant was not
pleased. He now knew he confronted a brave and spirited enemy. He needed
Foote's flotilla to equalize the fight and win a quick decision, but he was unsure of its whereabouts. The Rebels, meanwhile, chose not to counterattack
and break the siege. That was a critical mistake in light of the absent flotilla
and the damage to the one gunboat on their front.

The fair and mild weather suddenly changed in the afternoon to cold
rain and sleet and that night to bitter north winds, three inches of snow, and
a temperature of ten above zero. The Confederates shivered in their rifle
pits, and the Yankees huddled around campfires, regretting their discarded
blankets and overcoats. The night was one of terrible discomfort and suffering. Some of the wounded between the lines froze to death.

The USS *St. Louis* was an impenetrable ironclad when engaged in battle at proper distances. Because it
maneuvered too close to Fort Donelson's shore batteries, it was badly damaged. The deck and armor
plating were battered and crushed, a gunpost disabled, and a pilot killed.

On the morning of February 14, Capt. Reuben Ross, who commanded the fort's water batteries, saw smokestacks just around the river bend. He correctly assumed they were transports disembarking Federal reinforcements—ten thousand to be exact. Ross requested permission to fire upon the boats. His request reached Floyd and Pillow as they prepared for a war council, and they forgot about it. Instead, they decided to break free from Grant's encirclement and march southeastward to Charlotte and then to Nashville to join Johnston.

Pillow would lead the assault, with Buckner serving as a rear guard. As might be expected from Pillow's poor leadership record, the Rebels moved out to attack but then returned to their camps. Reportedly, a stray sharpshooter's bullet nearly struck Pillow, and he exclaimed, "Our movement is discovered. It will not do to move out of our trenches under the circumstances." He sent a staff captain to tell Floyd to defer the attack until morning.

According to Maj. Peter Otey of Floyd's staff, Floyd informed Pillow that he had "lost the opportunity not by being discovered, but by the delay in sending the message and the consequent delay in getting a message back to him at this late hour." Floyd, furious with Pillow, asserted that it was now too late to commence an attack, so Pillow should indeed return the troops to the trenches. Otey later wrote, "Here was in my humble opinion the fatal mistake at Fort Donelson."

While the Federal transports unloaded reinforcements, Foote's flotilla of four ironclads and two wooden gunboats moored four miles below the fort. Grant and his staff rode to the landing to meet with Foote aboard his flagship.

Grant left the meeting confident of an easy victory. He issued orders for the gunboats to shell the fort and his land forces to tighten the encirclement to prevent the garrison's escape. He intended to capture every man in the fort.

The flotilla, resembling squat, black bug-shaped vessels, rounded the bend in full view of the fort at about 2:30 p.m. The gunboats mounted fifty-seven heavy cannon against twelve Confederate guns. Observing the obvious, Confederate cavalry commander Nathan Bedford Forrest turned to one of his staff, a former preacher. "Parson," said Forrest, "for God's sake pray! Nothing but God Almighty can save the fort!" Floyd agreed.

The opening shots occurred within minutes. The Federals held the advantage, but they wasted it. Foote brought his ironclads too close to the shore. As a result, they overshot their targets while becoming easy targets for the enemy's shorter-range guns. Each of the gunboats took forty or more hits.

Two were sunk. The others drifted out of the fight. Fifty-four Federal sailors were killed or wounded. Foote himself was struck by shell fragments from a 32-pounder that hit the pilothouse of his flagship, passed through an inch and a half of iron plate, and ricocheted, killing one pilot and injuring others.

The Rebels had won this Valentine's Day river battle. They cheered and celebrated into the night. And rightfully so. They lost no guns and only a few men while performing heroically. For example, when one of their cannoneers dropped his rammer over the parapet during the loading process, he coolly mounted the earthwork and retrieved it, even though a shot from the Federals could have killed him.

The Federal debacle was Foote's fault. He had miscalculated. Had he remained farther out, his ironclads could not have been reached by enemy gunfire, and his longer-ranged ordnance would have pounded the water batteries. But he never admitted his error. Instead, he tried to make Grant the scapegoat by arguing that the flotilla was unprepared for combat, that he had told Grant as much, but that Grant had ordered him to suppress the water batteries, and he had no choice but to obey.

Grant had watched the naval fiasco and was jolted by it. He now had doubts about victory. He wrote to his wife, Julia, that the taking of the fort would "be a long job." He did not know when he might return. He settled in for a siege.

He would have been more cheerful had he known that Floyd and Pillow were equally despondent. They were surrounded on three sides by Union soldiers and on the fourth by the flotilla that, though damaged, still controlled the river.

When Floyd and Pillow first learned of the flotilla's arrival, they expected to be defeated. Floyd telegraphed Johnston, "The fort cannot hold out twenty minutes!" Johnston had wired back, "If you lose the fort, bring your troops to Nashville if possible."

At a meeting that night, Floyd said he had "no doubt whatever" that the whole Yankee force on the Western waters "could and would be concentrated here if it was deemed necessary to reduce out position." He proposed reinstituting their previous plan to dislodge Grant's forces "on our left, and thus to pass our people into the open country lying southward towards Nashville." Their only other choices were to surrender or to stay put and be starved into submission unless saved by a miracle. They decided to try to break out.

Throughout the night they shifted troops to their left to attack and pierce McClernand's force. Pillow was to roll up the flank closer to the river, and Bushrod Johnson's division was to force McClernand's men to flee toward the Union center. Buckner was to clean out Federal artillery positions and attack from the Confederate right, striking the enemy in the flank and rear. Col. Adolphus Heiman's Tenth Tennessee would maintain its position at the Confederate center and serve as a hinge from which the attacks would pivot.

Pillow expected these actions to pin Grant against the river at his downstream landings and provide a large gap in the Union line. The gap would enable Confederate forces to escape from Donelson. He briefed his brigade commanders but left unclear several important details. Were the men to carry rations, blankets, and knapsacks? What was the marching order for the actual escape after the battle? How and when would the retreat commence? Every commander had a different understanding as to what to do after the attack. Pillow, for example, expected his troops to return to their starting points and retrieve equipment and rations before commencing the retreat. Buckner, however, believed the retreat would commence immediately after the assault, with nobody returning to the trenches.

Floyd fully comprehended Johnston's order to save the army. As the senior commander, he was responsible for assuring that clear battle plans were conveyed. He didn't.

In the predawn hours of February 15, Bushrod Johnson's division braved mud, snow, and a biting wind as they took their positions and prepared to mount the attack. With Forrest's cavalry in the lead, some ten thousand Rebels started off at 6 a.m. They marched toward McClernand's right flank—his weakest point. McClernand had planned to strengthen it that day, but Grant had assured him the Rebels would not attack. Grant was wrong.

Brig. Gen. John A. McClernand's Union division suffered the brunt of the Rebel breakout attempt on the morning of February 15. The division was cut to pieces and ceased to exist as a fighting force. Grant was absent from his post for six critical hours that day while conferring with Flag Officer Andrew Foote.

LIBRARY OF CONGRESS

Grant ordered a counterattack to retake the lost position on the Federal right. In this painting by French artist Paul Philippoteaux, Grant watches the action.

Around 7 a.m. the Rebels advanced onto McClernand's position in the woods. After hard fighting for two hours, five Union brigades were driven back nearly a mile. Out of ammunition, McClernand requested reinforcements from Grant and Lew Wallace, commander of the center division.

The couriers reached Grant's headquarters around 8:30 a.m. But Grant wasn't there. During the night, Foote had summoned him for a consultation aboard the flagship. Convinced that the Rebels wouldn't attack in the interim, Grant left orders with his division commanders not to bring on an engagement and to hold their positions until further notice. These orders prevented Charles F. Smith (on the left) and Lew Wallace (in the center) from supporting McClernand's division on the right, which was bearing the full weight of the Rebel assault.

Grant always seemed more interested in what he planned to do to the enemy than what the enemy might do to him, and this style of leadership jeopardized his army more than once. Having not foreseen what the Rebels might do on February 15, he had been absent from his post more than six critical hours while one of his divisions was being mauled and the other two were prohibited by his orders from lending support. Grant's lack of foresight placed his army at great risk. Two couriers galloped for the steamboat landing to find Grant.

Wallace, meanwhile, trumped obedience with common sense, and on his own initiative, he sent reinforcements to McClernand. Strangely, McClernand placed them on reserve. Wallace was baffled and miffed.

Given the situation, it was not difficult for the Southern infantrymen to overpower the Union resistance. Forrest's cavalry, a Tennessee brigade, and a Kentucky regiment moved across a two-hundred-yard open space and smashed into one of McClernand's brigades with brutal fire. The dead "lay as thick as men generally lie in a tent," a Confederate captain discovered later. The Federals left cannon, prisoners, and ambulances in the hands of the Rebels. By 1 p.m. McClernand's division ceased to exist as a fighting force.

Wallace himself saw retreating Federals while chatting with Grant's adjutant astride their horses. A bareheaded officer dashed by shouting, "We're cut to pieces!" Soon an orderly reported roads jammed with wagons and troops. "On the plains we would call it a stampede," he proclaimed.

The Confederate battle line now stretched for a mile, opposed only by small clusters of discouraged Federals trying to survive. The Rebels had achieved their major goal. They not only had a way out of the Fort Donelson trap, but they also had a golden opportunity to destroy Grant's army. Pillow wired Johnston, "On the honor of a soldier, the day is ours!"

Wallace made an inspired effort to stop the advancing Confederates in his sector. He assembled a six-gun battery and infantry units from Illinois, Nebraska, and Ohio on a ridge. They poured a hail of grape and canister into the Rebel brigade coming up the road. The deadly fire forced the Confederates to withdraw. Forrest had a horse shot out from under him and ran away on foot. A Rebel soldier from the Eighteenth Tennessee later wrote, "I can but shudder at the awful condition we were placed in at that time."

Nevertheless, the Confederates had created a large gap through which they could escape. And Buckner was holding Wynn's Ferry Road, the chosen escape route. He expected the garrison to move through the gap immediately and escape toward Nashville. To his surprise and shock, he received a message from Pillow to return to the trenches. Pillow notified Bushrod Johnson to do the same.

Pillow's directive violated Buckner's order from Floyd to hold Wynn's Ferry Road. Irate, Buckner confronted Floyd, who was equally surprised. Floyd then encountered Pillow and demanded: "In the name of God, General

Pillow, what have we been fighting all day for? Certainly not to show our powers, but solely to secure the Wynn's Ferry Road, and now after securing it, you order it to be given up."

Pillow replied that nobody had set a specific time for evacuation. He said they could regroup and move out later. He added that the troops needed rest, the wounded needed treatment, and food and ammunition needed replenishment. Besides, there were reports of twenty thousand fresh Union troops pouring into the battle area, and now was not the time for the combat-fatigued Confederates to be subjected to a fight. Pillow was persuasive, and Floyd agreed that the whole army, including Buckner, should return to the trenches.

Pillow's order and Floyd's acquiescence are puzzling. Perhaps Pillow chose to ignore Johnston's orders and defend his beloved Tennessee to his last breath. Or maybe the tactical success of the morning motivated him to continue fighting until he defeated Grant or received reinforcements. A Kentucky lieutenant said, "Pillow's head was turned with the victory just gained, and he was too shortsighted to see that it was entirely thrown away unless we used it to escape." By withdrawing his troops, Pillow enabled Grant to regroup and take the initiative.

Grant reached his headquarters at 1 p.m. Not surprisingly he found his officers confused and uncertain about what to do, since he had told them to avoid confrontation and had left no one in charge. Grant met with McClernand and Wallace and told them, "Gentlemen, the position on the right must be retaken. Do it." McClernand's command was too dispersed to do much, but Wallace responded, "It is getting late, and what is to be done must be done before night."

He rode among his own division and other units he pulled together. "Are you ready to fight?" he yelled. "We're ready, let 'er rip," they answered, adding, "Forward. Forward." Wallace, a young Hoosier lawyer, courageously led the attack.

Grant then rode to Charles F. Smith's command and found Smith sitting under a tree, waiting for orders. Smith's troops were mulling around, demoralized by McClernand's failure on the right. Grant's appearance and take-charge attitude seemed to electrify them. He issued orders to fill their cartridge boxes, get in line, and prevent the Rebels from escaping. Grant believed that Confederate soldiers were equally disgruntled and that Smith could successfully storm the earthworks on his front. The army that attacks

Brig. Gen. Lew Wallace, a young Hoosier lawyer and future author, led the successful counterattack on February 15 to recover lost ground and drive the Rebels back to their trench line. The way of escape was closed once more.

first will be victorious, Grant declared, "and the enemy will have to be in a hurry if he gets ahead of me."

While he chewed on a cigar, Grant turned to the fifty-three-year-old Smith and asserted, "All has failed on our right; you must take Fort Donelson."

Smith replied, "I will do it." He rode over to the Second Iowa on top of the ridge and shouted: "You must take the fort! Take the caps off your guns! Fix bayonets! I will lead you!"

Marching down the ridge and up the opposite slope, the white-haired general with the oversized snowy mustache led them with his sword aloft and his hat on the tip of his sword. "Come on, you volunteers, come on," he yelled.

"I was nearly scared to death," a Union soldier recalled, "but I saw the old man's white mustache and went on."

The three Tennessee battalions holding the works couldn't believe what they were seeing—surging Yankees with bayonets pointed at them. The Rebels, armed only with double-barrel shotguns, held their fire. Then, when the Federals were only twenty yards away, the Tennesseans turned and ran to a ridge in the rear.

Smith had secured the outer defense line of Fort Donelson without firing a shot. He prepared for the next assault but was held in check by Buckner's division along the second ridge. Both sides fired repeatedly and rapidly at each other until nightfall silenced the action. Smith lost 357 men killed or wounded but was more determined than ever. "We'll take the fort tomorrow," he said.

Meanwhile, Wallace was leading his men in an assault to retake the road and the ground lost earlier that day on the right. Nearly two thousand men squirmed or dashed up a steep frosted slope toward the road. They crept along the ground when under heavy fire and rushed forward when it slackened. They loaded their rifles by rolling over on their backs, then rolled back and fired.

The Rebels taunted them: "Hey there, you damned Yankees. Why don't you come up? What are you waiting for?"

The Yankees weren't waiting for anything. They came up, and the momentum of their drive broke the Confederate line. Forrest's cavalry rushed to the position to conduct a fighting withdrawal to protective trenches. That checked Wallace's drive, but he had recovered the lost ground and driven all the way to the Confederate trench line.

At nightfall both sides were back where they had been that morning. Nearly a thousand Yankees and Rebels had been killed and three thousand wounded. On the frozen ground were dead men, dead horses, and frozen pools of blood. The night was cold and snowy; Grant returned to the comforts of the farmhouse serving as his headquarters.

Throughout the early hours of night the Confederates gathered their dead and wounded and placed them on steamboats with Union prisoners. Near midnight, Floyd ordered the boats to steam upriver

LIBRARY OF CONGRESS

Brig. Gen. John B. Floyd commanded the Rebel forces at Fort Donelson under orders from Gen. Albert Sidney Johnston. Confusion and disagreement among Floyd and Brig. Gens. Gideon Pillow and Simon Buckner led to disaster, however.

for Clarksville and Nashville. By doing so he removed a means of escape for part of his army.

Floyd, Pillow, and Buckner soon gathered at army headquarters. At 1 a.m. Floyd summoned all regimental, brigade, and division commanders to a council of war. With scouting reports of major reinforcements for Grant, the meeting's only agenda item was to finalize plans to escape and save the army. They decided to collect all the commands at 4 a.m. and to cut their way out if necessary. Then disturbing reports arrived that the Federals had reoccupied their previous positions, that Union regiments camped near the only practicable road, that other roads out of town were under water, that frostbite and pneumonia would claim most of the army if it tried to ford icy creeks, and that the chances of escape were "decidedly unfavorable."

Pillow wanted to fight and break through the siege. Buckner, who examined the odds on any gamble, projected a mood of hopelessness. "I cannot hold my position half an hour after an attack," he said. He only had four thousand men. He emphasized that an attempt to cut their way out would cost them three-quarters of the command. "No general has the right to make such a sacrifice of human life," he exclaimed. He proposed surrendering.

Tempers flared. Buckner refused to support any suggestion from Pillow. Floyd swung one way and then another before concurring with Buckner. It was too late to attempt an escape, he said. Pillow reluctantly agreed that they had "only one alternative—capitulation." But he refused to be a part of it. He was afraid of what the Federals might do to him. Floyd also worried about being tried and hanged for his assistance to the South while in Buchanan's prewar cabinet. Buckner declared he would stay with his men and accept his fate, whatever it was. The fate of fifteen thousand Confederates also hung in the balance.

Floyd said to Buckner, " If I place you in command, will you allow me to get out as much of my brigade as I can?"

Buckner replied, "Yes, provided that you left before the enemy received my surrender proposal."

"I turn the command over sir [to you]," Floyd announced to Pillow.

"I pass it," Pillow answered.

"I assume it," Buckner said.

"What should I do?" Forrest asked as he rose in wrath. "I did not come here for the purpose of surrendering my command."

"Cut your way out," Pillow advised.

Forrest, a large, powerful, and fearless man, vowed to escape and to save all that he could.

White flags placed in the trenches before daybreak surprised and infuriated the troops. Some men wept. Officers from the First Mississippi broke their swords and threw them away. One Mississippian wrote in his journal, "So after four days of hard fighting without rest & exposure to severe weather, having defeated the enemy in [nearly] every engagement . . . with no hope of relief, exhausted . . . we yielded to fate and were Prisoners of War."

Forrest gathered his command and offered to lead anyone out of the siege. At 4 a.m. five hundred troopers and two hundred foot soldiers followed him. Using scouts and flankers, Forrest snaked around the Union positions, passed through the snowy woods, crossed an icy, shoulder-deep backwater of the Cumberland, and by 10 a.m. on February 18 had traveled seventy-five miles and reached Nashville. "Not a gun was fired at us," he reported. "Not an enemy was seen or heard."

Back at Donelson, before dawn, Pillow escaped by crossing the Cumberland on a small flatboat. His battle cry had been "liberty or death." He chose liberty. His staff soon joined him, crossing on a steamboat that had just arrived.

Floyd commandeered two steamboats docked nearby. Ironically, one of them carried four hundred Mississippi recruits. The men were put ashore to be surrendered to the Yankees. Floyd and fifteen hundred of his Virginia troops boarded the steamboats and escaped upriver. The boats were only half full. As they were being boarded, Buckner sent word that they must leave at once because the surrender was about to occur. Troops on the bank howled ruefully.

Buckner's formal surrender note proposed "the appointment of commissioners to agree upon terms of capitulation of the forces and post under my command." The surrender party, headed by Maj. Nathaniel Cheairs, was taken before Charles F. Smith. He curtly announced, "I'll make no terms with Rebels with arms in their hands—my terms are unconditional and immediate surrender."

Smith escorted the major to Grant's headquarters and consulted with Grant while Cheairs waited. Grant endorsed Smith's declaration—"no terms to the damned Rebels"—and so indicated in a message back to Buckner. Northern newspapers praised "Unconditional Surrender" Grant, but it was Smith who deserved the credit for proposing it.

Cheairs later wrote that it was "the most disgraceful, unnecessary and uncalled-for surrender during the four years of War."

Surrender details were discussed at breakfast at the Dover Hotel, which had been Buckner's headquarters. Wallace, on his own initiative, broke protocol and rode to the hotel before Grant and without authorization. Grant arrived an hour and a half later and found the two generals enjoying cornbread and coffee. Wallace's breach of military etiquette annoyed Grant and created a permanent rift between them.

Before commencing the formal surrender discussions, Grant and Buckner reminisced about their days together at West Point and in Mexico. Grant then asked why Pillow didn't stay to surrender his command.

Buckner replied, "He thought you were too anxious to capture him personally."

Grant smiled, "Why, if I had captured him, I would have turned him loose. I would rather have him in command of you fellows than as a prisoner."

Buckner had feared that he and others might be treated as traitors rather than as prisoners of war, but Grant assured him that the latter would apply. Prewar friends, Buckner had loaned Grant money in 1854 to help him get home after his resignation from the army. He expected some consideration in return and was pleased to know he wouldn't be hanged. He resented, however, the "ungenerous and unchivalrous" surrender terms. Grant softened Buckner's distress by offering him money out of his own pocket.

"Buckner," he said, "you may be going among strangers, and I hope you will allow me to share my purse with you." Buckner appreciated the offer but said he would not need financial assistance.

In the mass confusion of how to process nearly thirteen thousand prisoners, some Confederates walked unchallenged through the lines and escaped. Among them was Brig. Gen. Bushrod Johnson. He later declared, 'I have not learned that a single one who attempted to escape met with any obstacle."

In addition to capturing an entire army,

The surrender of Fort Donelson was dumped on Brig. Gen. Simon Bolivar Buckner. In a comedic exchange, Floyd and Pillow passed command of the fort to Buckner and then escaped.

When Brig. Gen. Gideon Pillow didn't show up for surrender talks, Grant asked why he wasn't present. After being told he had escaped, Grant jokingly replied: "If I had captured him, I would have turned him loose. I would rather have him in command of you fellows than as a prisoner."

Grant had taken 20,000 arms, 48 artillery pieces, 17 heavy guns, 3,000 horses, 400,000 rations of rice, 300,000 rations of beef, and 400 barrels of molasses. It was the largest capture ever made on the continent.

In Richmond, Jefferson Davis moaned that "events have cast on our arms and hopes the gloomiest of shadows."

In the North, Grant's victory made sensational headlines. "Light Is Breaking, God Speed the Right," declared an Illinois newspaper. Lincoln promoted Grant to major general. In the West, Grant became second in command only to Halleck, who tried to take credit for Grant's victory. In just eleven months, Grant had gone from store clerk to Union hero. His success, however, was due more to Confederate mistakes than to any strategy on his part. At Donelson, he had been a military goat three times: when he assured McClernand it wasn't necessary to strengthen his position because the Rebels wouldn't attack, when he was absent from his post six hours while McClernand's division was being decimated, and when he left orders not to fight while he was absent—the last order contributing to the demise of McClernand's division.

Finally arriving on the scene, Grant did act quickly. He rallied his commanders and troops. He ordered Wallace to retake the position on the right, and Smith to take the fort. They were the real heroes. Smith's courageous assault more than made up for his faulty judgment on February 13 when he disobeyed Grant's order to avoid battle that day. Smith was a goat then, but a hero two days later. Walke and McClernand, who also had disobeyed Grant, remained goats. Further, it was Smith, not Grant, who first proposed unconditional surrender.

Foote became a goat at Donelson for foolishly placing his gunboats too close to the shore. With his shells arcing harmlessly over the fort, the flotilla was useless. Grant had no choice but to call off the assault by water and resort to a siege. Foote's careless mistake contrasted with his notable success at Fort Henry where he, not Grant, was responsible for the Union victory.

On the Southern side, Albert Sidney Johnston deserves the goat label for deciding to defend Donelson with an insufficient force and for placing incompetent commanders in charge of that force. Those commanders—Floyd and Pillow—were incomprehensible goats. Jefferson Davis properly stripped them of their commands. Southerners never forgave Floyd and Pillow for what Capt. John H. Guy of a Virginia artillery unit called "their dastardly conduct and . . . the disgrace of the Surrender."

Pillow was reprimanded for "grave errors of judgment." His worst mistakes were canceling an attack on February 14 prior to Grant's being reinforced, issuing a poorly timed order for retreat at the moment of victory on February 15, and turning over command to a subordinate on February 16 rather than fighting to the finish or surrendering the command himself. Cheairs noted he had heard that Pillow "wished himself dead, and if wishing would do any good, he could have any amount of help."

Pillow's suspension from duty extended until August 22. He was allowed to lead a brigade at the battle of Stones River, but his persistent bickering with his division commander cost him that duty. Then given a small cavalry command in northern Alabama, he marched two thousand men forty-five miles to attack a Federal garrison of only four hundred men, but he failed to capture them. It was his last command.

Floyd, whose fuzzy battle plans hampered the Rebels on February 15, contended that he "suffered the greatest injustice." While "[uttering] no complaint," he blamed Johnston for sending vague and indecisive directives and for ignoring his warnings that the fort was not defensible. Floyd attributed his inability to break the encirclement to reluctant commanders who were paralyzed by fear of heavy enemy reinforcements. He said he chose to evacuate himself and his veteran Virginians because they were more useful to the Confederacy than the untrained officers and regiments from the West.

In 1862, sheet music lyrics appeared about "Floyd's Retreat from Fort Donelson." The closing line was, "He who fights and runs away, May live to run another day." Floyd never returned to duty and didn't live long enough to "run another day." Broken in spirit, health, and reputation, he died on August 26, 1863, at age fifty-seven.

Buckner spent six months as a prisoner of war at Fort Warren, Massachusetts, before being exchanged on August 27. Promoted to major general, he held various commands during the remainder of the war and became known as "Simon the Poet" for his penchant for writing poetry. He was a pallbearer at Grant's funeral in 1885. He later served as governor of Kentucky and ran as the vice presidential candidate on John M. Palmer's Gold Democrats ticket in 1896. At the time of his death in 1914 he was the only surviving Confederate officer over the rank of brigadier general.

At Fort Donelson the Confederacy lost not only an army and tons of military supplies but also the iron and timber resources of its "Great Western Iron Belt." With the Union still pouting over its rout at Manassas in July 1861, these victories in the West demonstrated that the South was not invincible. The Federals—thanks especially to Grant, Wallace, Smith, and their courageous troops—had seized the moment and beaten the proud manifestations of Southern manhood. The triumph at Donelson opened what park historian Benjamin Franklin Cooling called the "gateway to a 'glory road' for the North."

13

SHILOH: APRIL 6–7, 1862

"LICK 'EM TOMORROW"

I HAVE NO DOUBT that nothing will occur today," Brig. Gen. William T. Sherman declared on the morning of April 5, 1862. That's what he assured his thirty-nine-year-old commander, Maj. Gen. Ulysses S. Grant, adding, "I do not apprehend anything like an attack on our position." Sherman's assertion was one of the worst judgments by any general in the war. At that moment he was the goat of goats.

Grant's Army of the Tennessee was positioned along the Tennessee River at Pittsburg Landing in the Volunteer State's bucolic backwoods. This remote location was a few miles north of the Mississippi border and about a hundred miles east of Memphis. The Federals had been here since early March, after Grant's tremendous victories at Fort Henry on the Tennessee River and Fort Donelson on the Cumberland. The latter was the most significant Union achievement of the war to date. These triumphs gave Federal armies access to both waterways and to the rear of the Rebel line.

The Confederates, in danger of being surrounded, moved southward, abandoning all of Kentucky and most of western and middle Tennessee, including Nashville, a major railroad supply center—and the first Confederate state capital to be surrendered. For the North, these events created a broad passageway to the upper Mississippi River and a potential route to the Deep South.

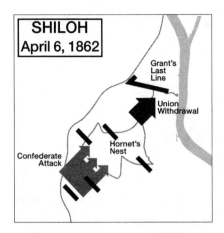
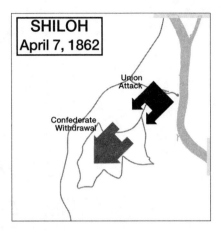

The battle of Shiloh developed into a series of frontal attacks with the left of the Confederate army moving faster than the right. By the end of the first day the Federals had been pushed back to their supply base at Pittsburg Landing, where they were strongly protected by gunboats and heavy artillery. On the second day, Federal reinforcements turned the tide of battle and swept the Confederates from the field.

The commander of the Confederacy's Western Department, Gen. Albert Sidney Johnston, was in hot water, politically and militarily. The Southern press called for his resignation. A year earlier Jefferson Davis labeled him "the greatest soldier . . . then living." He believed that to his dying day. This perception grew from their time together as cadets at West Point when Johnston, two years ahead of Davis, befriended him and Davis responded by idolizing his comrade. Johnston had proved his worth as a Union officer in the Mexican War in the late 1840s and as leader of a major army expedition to California in the 1850s. But when the Civil War broke out, Johnston disappointed Federal officials by joining the Confederate cause. Davis made him the senior field general in the entire Confederate army.

As the winter of 1861/62 morphed into spring, Johnston's Union counterpart in the western theater, Maj. Gen. Henry W. Halleck, ordered Grant and Maj. Gen. Don Carlos Buell to concentrate their forces near Savannah, Tennessee, and the Mississippi state line. Their first goal was to cut a crucial railroad line just south of the state line at Corinth. The line carried Confederate troops and supplies between Memphis and Chattanooga. From the latter city, the railroad connected major regions of the South, branching through Atlanta to Charleston, South Carolina, and Savannah, Georgia, and north through Knoxville, Tennessee, to Richmond, Virginia. A Confederate official called the railroad "the vertebrae of the Confederacy." If this only east-west supply line were cut, the Upper South would be divided and as vulnerable as a person with a broken backbone. Once the railroad was disrupted, the combined armies of Grant and Buell—seventy-seven thousand men strong—would seek to smash Johnston's outnumbered forces.

Grant's army of forty-two thousand arrived first at Pittsburg Landing, adjacent to Savannah. Following Halleck's orders to "strike no blow until we are strong enough to admit no doubt of the result," his troops remained inactive, except for drills and training exercises while waiting for Buell's Army of the Ohio. Buell left Nashville with thirty-five thousand troops, but being no fan of either Halleck or Lincoln, Buell took his time making the 135-mile march.

Halleck, meanwhile, had created other personnel problems. Jealous of Grant's popularity and fame after the capture of Fort Donelson, Halleck had removed him from command on false charges of "neglect and inefficiency" just three weeks after the victory. That didn't set well in the White House. The adjutant general demanded specifics on Halleck's vague charges, but Halleck had only rumors on which to base the allegations. Lincoln intervened, and Halleck dropped the charges. Grant was reinstated and returned to command his army on March 17.

Sherman had had his own problems with Halleck. Earlier, "Old Brains" decided Sherman was crazy and removed him from command of the Department of the Cumberland. Newspapers sensationalized the "crazy Sherman," and the damage to his reputation lingered for years. Actually, Sherman suffered only from mental exhaustion. After much-needed rest at home and pressure from Washington he also was restored to command. Sherman's brother, an influential senator, probably helped his cause. For whatever reason, Halleck concluded that Sherman really wasn't crazy, just high strung and talkative. Plus he noted that the red-haired general had some strange physical quirks: his shoulders twitched, his hands were in constant motion, and his eyes conveyed a wild expression.

Regardless, Grant liked Sherman and admired his courage and brilliance. The two men would develop one of the most successful commander-subordinate relationships in military history.

Grant had allowed Sherman to select the meeting place for the two armies. Thus he chose a site triangular in shape, with the east side bounded by the Tennessee River, the apex by Snake Creek, and the west side by Owl Creek. These waterways provided excellent protection for the army's flanks.

Sherman pitched his headquarters tent alongside a small Methodist log church near the six-mile-wide base of the triangle. The church was named Shiloh, a Hebrew word meaning "place of peace." Sherman's division encamped along the ridges on both sides of the church. From this location they could quickly move south toward the Corinth rail depot as soon as Buell's army arrived.

Sherman and Grant assumed that the Rebels would concentrate at Corinth, dig in, and wait to be attacked. But the Union generals expended no effort to use cavalry to verify their assumptions or determine the size of the Rebel force.

Indeed, Johnston's 44,000 Confederates had gathered at Corinth to protect the railroad. Culled from Confederate commands across the Western Department, they were reorganized into the Army of the Mississippi. They included 9,400 troops under Maj. Gen. Leonidas Polk; 16,300 under Maj. Gen. Braxton Bragg; 6,800 under Maj. Gen. William J. Hardee; 7,200 under Brig. Gen. John C. Breckinridge; and 4,300 cavalry under Col. Nathan Bedford Forrest. This last force, Forrest's horsemen, had skillfully located Grant's army and determined that Buell had not yet reinforced him.

If the Confederates could strike before Buell arrived, they would have a slight numerical advantage and a chance to drive the Yankees out of Tennessee. Johnston, however, vacillated, his spirit broken by past failures, his self-confidence apparently shattered. Had it not been for his second in command, Gen. P. G. T. Beauregard, the battle of April 6–7 probably would not have occurred. Beauregard, a Louisiana Creole with a courtly manner, had earned fame at Fort Sumter and Manassas. Determined to seize the moment, he declared to Johnston: "We must do something or die in the attempt, otherwise all will be shortly lost. . . . . What the people want now is a victory, and we must be determined to give it to them." Persuaded, Johnston gave Beauregard the go-ahead to draw up battle plans to march north to Pittsburg Landing and surprise Grant's army. If successful, they'd finish the job and take out Buell.

The attack was scheduled for April 4. Four corps were to make the one-day march of twenty-three miles on converging roads—a difficult task for green troops led by inexperienced officers, an impossible task when compounded by a torrential storm, shin-deep mud, and confusion over contradictory and ill-conceived orders. The march bogged down, taking two days instead of one.

Bragg, a strict disciplinarian with chronic stomach trouble, lost his temper and probably the contents of his stomach when one of his divisions became sidetracked. Johnston asked him where it was, and Bragg replied it was "somewhere back there." He went to look for it and found it wedged behind troops led by Polk, another of Davis's West Point chums, who had foregone his military commission in favor of an ecclesiastical calling as an Episcopal priest. Polk's troops had refused to yield the right of way, causing Bragg's division to be "lost." With such poor organization, Johnston's troops were not in position until the night of April 5.

Tormented by the delays, Beauregard was ready to call off the attack. He was afraid the army had forfeited any chance for surprise—and surprise was essential for success. Further upsetting him, several men tested their rifles by firing them, creating a racket surely within earshot of Federal outposts. The men, worried about the dampness of the powder in their rifles, should have reloaded instead, but these were green troops, untested in combat.

When Beauregard heard a drum rolling, he sent a messenger to silence

The small Methodist church near Pittsburg Landing was called Shiloh, meaning "place of peace." On April 6–7, 1862, the countryside was anything but that as more than one hundred thousand soldiers clashed here.

it. The soldier returned and reported he couldn't quiet the drummer; the drum was in the Union camp.

With these concerns weighing on him, Beauregard made a last-minute plea to abandon the attack. Johnston, reinvigorated, overruled him. At this point, Johnston didn't care about surprise and curtly announced: "I would fight them if they were a million. . . . Gentlemen, we shall attack at daylight tomorrow." He issued a motivational statement to each regiment. It said in part:

> I have put you in motion to offer battle to the invaders of your country. With resolution and disciplined valor . . . you can but march to a decisive victory over the agrarian mercenaries sent to subjugate and despoil you of your liberties, property, and honor. Remember the precious stake involved; remember the dependence of your mothers, your wives, your sisters, and your children on the result; remember the fair, broad, abounding land, the happy homes and the ties that would be desolated by your defeat. The eyes and hopes of eight millions of people rest upon you. You are expected to show yourselves worthy of your race and lineage; worthy of the women of the South, whose noble devotion in this war has never been exceeded in any time. With such incentives to brave deeds, and with the trust that God is with us, your generals will lead you confidently to the combat, assured of success.

Battle veterans told the green recruits it was time to "meet the elephant"—their expression for going into battle.

* * *

At Pittsburg Landing immediate combat was not anticipated. Grant and Sherman were overly complacent and unprepared for an

LIBRARY OF CONGRESS

Brig. Gen. William T. Sherman assured Grant that the Confederates would not attack Shiloh. Neither he nor Grant fortified their positions or dispatched cavalry to collect information. Compounding the early Confederate success, Sherman was slow to react to news of fighting, but when he became convinced he was under attack, he performed superbly as a defensive leader.

attack. They believed the Rebels were too demoralized to constitute any danger. Thus the Federals did not fortify their position. They did not construct any defensive works—no trenches, no breastworks, nothing to provide cover in case of attack. Nor did they use cavalry to screen and collect information. Yet they were in a highly vulnerable position. If surprised and trapped on the bank of Owl Creek, they could suffer a devastating defeat.

Of the five generals commanding Grant's divisions at Shiloh, only Sherman had either West Point credentials or practical command experience. Three were political brigadiers—Stephen A. Hurlbut, Benjamin M. Prentiss, and William H. L. Wallace. The other, Maj. Gen. John McClernand, was a ruthless wire puller and egotist, intensely disliked by both Grant and Sherman. Interestingly, Hurlbut and Prentiss were Southerners who had moved to Illinois and stood by the Union. They would prove their Union loyalty in a courageous stand later in the day—a stand that saved Grant's army from destruction.

Grant had one other division. It guarded the army's supply depot five miles north at Crump's Landing on the Tennessee. Commanding it was another inexperienced general, Lew Wallace. At age thirty-five, this Indiana lawyer was the youngest major general in the army. He would later write the bestseller *Ben Hur.*

Since Sherman was the only one of the six Union division commanders with a regular army background, Grant left most tactical arrangements to him, while he commuted daily by steamboat from his headquarters in a mansion overlooking a bend in the river at Savannah. The mansion was nine miles from the army at Pittsburg Landing.

During the first few days of April, Grant received reports of enemy activity on a road to the south, but only enemy outposts were spotted. Lew Wallace apparently received a report that Johnston's whole army was on the move. If he informed Grant about it, Grant didn't believe it.

On Friday, April 4, one of Sherman's brigade commanders, Col. Ralph Buckland, took two companies of infantry to scout an area a few miles inland from the landing and was confronted by Alabama cavalry and artillery. Buckland withdrew and reported the incident to Sherman, who angrily rebuked him for overreacting to a minor Rebel reconnaissance force.

On Saturday, April 5, Col. Jesse Appler of the Fifty-third Ohio excitedly told Sherman of hordes of Rebels in the brush. Sherman glared at him and bristled. "Take your damned regiment back to Ohio," he barked. "Beauregard is not such a fool as to leave his base of operations and attack us in ours. There is no enemy nearer than Corinth."

So later that morning Sherman assured Grant that no danger existed, even though Hardee's Confederate corps was now within two miles of Pittsburg Landing. The Rebels were forming in four parallel lines—one for each corps—with a front of three miles and a depth of more than a mile. Hardee was in front, followed by Bragg, Polk, and Breckinridge. As planned by Beauregard, if one line faltered, the next would advance and add its mass to the attack. He intended to drive the enemy by sheer weight of numbers. The critical objective was to turn the enemy's left flank and cut off his line of retreat to Pittsburg Landing, where he could be resupplied and reinforced. By forcing him away from the Tennessee River and toward Owl Creek, they could trap him in vast stretches of swamp and undergrowth and force him to surrender.

* * *

Grant did not visit the camps on April 5. He had sprained his ankle the night before when his horse slipped and fell on his leg during a thunderstorm. As a result, he was in pain and limping on crutches. Anticipating no problems at the camps, he wrote to Halleck that he had "scarcely the faintest idea of an attack being made upon us, but will be prepared should such a thing take place." He wasn't.

Buell, on whom Grant had been waiting, arrived with one division on the night of April 5 and slept on the outskirts of Savannah. His other divisions were scattered on roads within twenty miles. Buell intended to meet with Grant the next morning, Sunday, April 6.

One of Prentiss's brigade commanders, Col. Everett Peabody, couldn't sleep during the night of April 5–6. Feeling uneasy about Rebel sightings, he dispatched a patrol of four hundred Missourians under Maj. James E. Powell to explore a small wagon trail to his front. Around 5 a.m. they entered a clearing about a mile and a half from their camp and encountered a portion of Hardee's skirmish line—elements of the Third Mississippi—and the Rebels opened fire. For the next hour they exchanged blows, each side holding its ground. Powell retreated when he saw what appeared to be Rebel cavalry on his flank. It was actually an escort company searching for a route to bring up artillery.

Powell rushed a messenger to Peabody. Tell him, said Powell, that the enemy was moving in strength and driving him back. Peabody, however, did nothing. He assumed Powell was engaged in just a skirmish.

After Brig. Gen. Benjamin Prentiss's division fell back to their camp shortly after daylight on Sunday, reinforced Confederates advanced furiously upon the camp. The division retreated, scattered and broken.

Prentiss heard the din of battle while eating breakfast. He finished and then rode leisurely to Peabody's headquarters to inquire about the firing. Peabody told him he had sent out a reconnaissance and that they had run into some resistance. Prentiss accused him of precipitating an attack but then ordered companies of the Twenty-first Missouri under Col. David Moore to support Powell's patrol. Moore's column encountered Powell's retreating men, and Moore accused them of being cowards. He demanded that they turn around and join his column, which they did. Moore relieved Powell of command and sent a messenger back to camp to bring up the rest of the regiment. When they arrived, Moore had sixteen companies, enough he said to lick the enemy, and they proceeded four abreast.

By 7 a.m., Moore's companies had marched only a few hundred yards to the edge of a cotton field when heavy fire erupted from the opposite side. Moore was hit in the right leg, shattering the bone. Powell then took back command. Surprisingly, the firing ceased, and the Federals withdrew.

The first major Rebel assault—under Hardee—was scheduled for sunrise at six o'clock, but communication problems and useless skirmishing had delayed it until 7:30. The attack wouldn't be the complete surprise for which

LIBRARY OF CONGRESS

From this sunken road and "hornet's nest," Federal units made an heroic six-hour stand that saved the Union army. They gave Grant much-needed time to post the remainder of his army under cover of siege guns at Pittsburg Landing.

they had hoped. Johnston, however, was confident. At his headquarters he finished a cup of coffee and swung onto his horse. He turned and spoke to his staff, "Tonight we will water our horses in the Tennessee River."

As Peabody's brigade stood at rest in its camp, the men "were soon dumfounded by seeing an enormous force of Confederate troops marching directly toward us," reported Pvt. Charles Morton of the Twenty-fifth Missouri. They advanced slowly, steadily, and silently until they were within about 125 yards. The Federals fired the first volley, blasting a Mississippi and a Tennessee battalion of unseasoned Southern boys. The survivors, "meeting the elephant" for the first time, ran in confusion to the rear, shouting "Retreat! Retreat!"

With some difficulty Johnston and Hardee rallied the command. They moved forward and opened fire. Peabody held his position for a while as both sides inflicted heavy casualties. Then Peabody's flanks were attacked, and he slowly retreated. The Rebels followed and mounted a vicious assault.

Peabody, who had left the camp briefly to look for Prentiss, returned to find his brigade near collapse. While trying to rally his men, he was shot and killed. Then Powell was killed. Prentiss, now on the scene, ordered his troops to fall back and fire from behind trees and bales of hay. Many of them lost their nerve and made a mad dash toward the safety of the river. Those who remained crumbled into isolated pockets before collapsing entirely.

One soldier running to the rear called out to others, "Give them hell, boys. I gave them hell as long as I could."

One who heard him later said, "Whether he had really given them any, I cannot say, but assuredly he gave them everything else he possessed, including his gun, cartridge box, coat, and hat."

By 9 a.m. Peabody's brigade was rolled up, and the Rebels seized his camps. Prentiss escaped the carnage and rode to the camp of his second brigade, commanded by Col. Madison Miller, to warn him of the attack. "Get out your brigade!" he yelled. "They are fighting on the right." Within minutes they were drawn up in line of battle, just barely avoiding a surprise attack. The Rebels struck at 8 a.m. As they advanced toward the Federals up a gentle slope, Miller unleashed a horrific infantry and artillery fire, and the enemy recoiled along its line. Its commander was struck by a cannon projectile and killed. Four more Rebel brigades charged up the hill and "after engaging [the Yankees] for about 20 minutes [we] drove them from their position," said Taylor Beatty of the First Louisiana Regulars. The Rebels had routed Prentiss's entire division.

* * *

The Fifty-third Ohio was in another area of the Federal encampment, on the edge of an old cornfield. It was one of Sherman's regiments. Even though they had heard the sound of guns in the distance, they remained around their breakfast campfires. Its elderly commander, Col. Jesse Appler, had received a report around dawn from a detachment south of the camp. They had sighted an enemy scouting patrol and had heard heavy firing to the left, where Powell was then engaged. They believed that a large enemy force was in their front.

Shortly, a soldier of the Twenty-fifth Missouri ran into the camp bleeding from a wound. He shouted. "Get into line! The Rebels are coming!"

Appler ordered the drummer to summon the men into ranks. While they were assembling, he fired off a message to Sherman. Unaware of any massive attack, Sherman replied sarcastically, "You must be badly scared over there." The Northern press would later publish these words, and some journalists scolded Sherman for making fun of Appler's warning—the second one in as many days.

Appler's Fifty-third Ohio came into line in the old cornfield, joined by other brigades alerted by the colonel. Soon the Rebels were seen crossing the field, and an excited captain reported, "The Rebels are out there thicker than fleas on a dog's back." Appler ordered the line to shift to face them. Then a lieutenant pointed to the right, where he could see bayonets glistening in the morning light. "This is no place for us," exclaimed Appler, as he ordered the regiment to swing back through its camp and form in the woods, lying down in the brush.

At 7 a.m. as the noise of battle grew louder, Sherman and his staff mounted their horses and ventured out to see what was happening. Halting several hundred yards in front of the Fifty-third Ohio, he looked through his binoculars and concluded that a sharp skirmish was underway. To his right, enemy skirmishers suddenly emerged from a creek and fired shots. "My God!" yelled Sherman, "we're being attacked!" He raised his arm as if to ward off a blow and was struck in the hand. Another bullet struck his orderly in the head and killed him. "Hold your ground," Sherman shouted to Appler as he wheeled his horse and galloped back to bring up reinforcements.

By 7:30 a.m. the Rebels and the Fifty-third Ohio were engaged in a fierce clash of rifle fire. Brig. Gen. Patrick R. Cleburne, who commanded Hardee's Second Brigade, led a thousand men toward the Ohioans. But as they charged through the vacated tents, their lines broke, and Appler's troops struck them with a hail of bullets and artillery fire. The Rebels wavered and fell back down the ravine. Cleburne attempted three more assaults, all futile and suicidal. The Sixth Mississippi made the last two charges and lost 70 percent of its men.

With Appler's troops clearly winning the encounter, Appler suddenly went berserk. "Retreat," he yelled to his men. "Save yourselves!" The startled regiment fell back but then rallied and moved up a hill near Sherman's headquarters. Appler, looking dazed, issued senseless orders. The regimental adjutant not only refused to carry them out but also cursed Appler for making them. Appler responded by running away.

Cleburne meanwhile waited impatiently for the second Confederate wave, Bragg's corps, to add its weight to the assault. His corps had become separated from Hardee's by at least a mile during the march. When Bragg's units finally reached the battle line and joined Hardee's men in attacking Sherman's forces, the Federals were in serious trouble. For a few minutes one of Bragg's units had a clear path to get around Sherman's right and into the Yankee rear. Only its sluggish advance prevented it from doing so.

Sherman threw more units into the fight. But the well-placed Rebel infantry and the sight of such a large force caused them to retreat in confusion. The Fifty-third Ohio was among the regiments that streamed to the rear as the Rebels "poured in on [them] like blackbirds into a cornfield," one Ohioan later recalled.

Sherman, remaining cool in the heat of battle, chewed on a cigar as he moved among his troops and encouraged them to stand fast. During the intense fighting—with staggering losses on both sides—his shoulder was grazed by a bullet and three horses were shot from under him. Leaning against a tree, he told an aide: "Tell Grant if he has any men to spare I can use them. If not, I will do the best I can. We are holding them pretty well just now. Pretty well; but it's hot as hell."

The Union division fighting at the Peach Orchard repulsed seven Confederate assaults before being pushed back. The fighting was so intense, men fell in droves.

LESLIE'S

* * *

Grant learned of the action around 7:15 a.m. from a messenger who arrived while he was having breakfast at the mansion. The general stepped outside and heard the sound of distant artillery. He sent notes to Buell canceling their meeting and to one of Buell's commanders, Brig. Gen. William Nelson, whose division had just arrived. He ordered Nelson to move his command to the river opposite Pittsburg Landing. Then with a crutch supporting him, Grant boarded his headquarters boat and headed for the landing. On the way, he stopped at Crump's Landing and ordered Lew Wallace to have his troops ready "at a moment's notice."

When he arrived at the landing at 9 a.m., Grant cringed at the terrible state of affairs. Thousands of frightened raw troops had fled to the rear and cowered below the sheltering bluff along the river. At the front, conditions were even worse. Prentiss's division, attacked on both its front and flank, had dissolved in fragments. That made Sherman's left terribly vulnerable, and Grant double-timed reinforcements to him and other hard-pressed divisions. Grant summoned Lew Wallace, Buell, and Nelson to come as fast as possible. Wallace's orders, however, were unsigned, nonspecific, and slow to reach him. He understood only that he was to come to Shiloh with his division.

Confederate Gen. Albert Sidney Johnston (right) was mortally wounded during the eighth charge at the Peach Orchard. He was succeeded by Gen. P. G. T. Beauregard (left), who had drawn up the ill-conceived battle plan and executed it poorly.

His troops were on the march shortly before noon. But it was not until 2 p.m. that he was told of Grant's perilous situation. Then, with deliberate speed and guidance from his cavalry, he shifted his fifty-eight hundred men and his line of march to join the right of Grant's army as it then rested. With rough terrain in their path, they didn't reach Grant until sunset.

By 10 a.m. Sherman realized his entire division was in jeopardy. With his own camps in danger of being overrun, he withdrew from the area around Shiloh church. Within an hour the whole Union line disintegrated. The Confederates pressed on like "maddened demons," said one Federal soldier, driving the Union right and left back two miles from their starting point.

"We are sweeping the field," Johnston told Beauregard, "and I think we shall press them to the creek."

Grant undoubtedly feared that possibility. He sent repeated appeals to Buell to come quickly.

The Rebels were indeed sweeping the field, actually rolling over anything that got in their way. Many of the Federals found a brief refuge in a shallow pool of water in their path. They crawled into it to quench their thirst and bathe their wounds. So many bled in and around the pond that the water was tinged red by the blood and dubbed the "Bloody Pond."

As each line of Rebels fed its men piecemeal into the line ahead, brigades and regiments became so intermingled that unit commanders lost touch with their own men. This complicated orders and created confusion within the ranks. Probably hundreds or even thousands of Rebels became separated from their units and from the army, thus weakening the Confederate juggernaut. Many of these stragglers wandered in search of food. In the vacated camps they found Sunday breakfasts spread out on tables or still cooking over campfires. So they sat down and ate. Then they foraged through the soldiers' belongings. They seemed especially interested in letters from wives and sweethearts, perhaps curious to find out what Northern girls were like.

With no sign of Buell, the Federal cause seemed hopeless. Johnston anticipated a decisive victory. He might have achieved it had there not been stiff Federal resistance clustered near a sunken road and a peach orchard in full bloom. These men were all that stood between the Confederates and Pittsburg Landing. If they fell, the Rebels could drive the Yankees to Owl Creek, where they would be helpless.

Col. David Stuart's command from Sherman's division had come up earlier near the Peach Orchard to strengthen the defensive position. Its presence startled an advancing Rebel unit, which halted, expecting to be attacked. When Johnston learned of the delay, he reacted quickly. His plan to crush the Union left and drive the Yankees away from Pittsburg Landing had gone awry. The Peach Orchard defenders were stalling the Rebel advance and enabling Grant's army to retreat toward the landing.

To prevent that from happening, Johnston needed to bring more pressure on the Yankees in the Peach Orchard. His only available force was the reserve corps under Breckinridge. He ordered it to dislodge Stuart and all other resistance in or near the orchard. Breckinridge, last in the line of march and far in the rear, would need time to get into position.

Meanwhile, a Rebel brigade routed Stuart but couldn't press forward, because it ran out of ammunition. Three brigades from Hurlbut's and W. H. L. Wallace's commands soon filled the hole in the Union line. Positioned in the orchard, with the cover of trees and some fences, they could only be attacked over open ground.

To Hurlbut's right—at the center of the Union line—Prentiss had come upon an eroded wagon trail—a sunken road—in a patch of dense thickets and tall oaks following the crest of a low hill. The depressed roadway served as a trench, and Prentiss and the remaining fragments of his division scrambled into it to make a stand. The position was a natural bastion, providing cover for the defenders, while the approach was across open fields. Grant noted its importance and told Prentiss to "maintain that position at all hazards." Prentiss understood the deadly seriousness of Grant's order and said he'd do the best he could. His Illinois and Iowa farm boys would make him proud.

Fighting here began about 10 a.m. and lasted without relief until around 4 p.m. In those six hours the fate of the Union army hung in the balance. During the ferocious combat, eighteen thousand Rebels launched eleven massive assaults—all frustrated by Prentiss's forty-five hundred valiant warriors in the sunken road. The constant buzz of rifle and artillery fire sounded like thousands of angry hornets, and one Rebel cried out, "It's a hornet's nest in there!" as his brigade recoiled from one of the assaults. Bragg directed the attacks—all straight-ahead bayonet charges. Brigade after brigade struggled forward across the open field, each being hit by the deadly crossfire. Confederates dropped like leaves in a windstorm, leaving a thickening carpet of dead and wounded.

The same tactics, with the same results, were applied at the Peach Orchard on the Union left, where Breckinridge's advance elements had finally

BOTH: LIBRARY OF CONGRESS

Among the Union heroes at Shiloh were division commanders Brig. Gens. Benjamin Prentiss (left) and Stephen Hurlbut (right). Prentiss's forty-five hundred men in the sunken road held back eighteen thousand Rebels until blasted by sixty-two cannon at point-blank range. Hurlbut's brigades filled a critical hole in the Peach Orchard and later defended Grant's line near Pittsburg Landing. Both men were Southerners by birth.

arrived. Johnston, determined to rally his men and move his line forward, joined Breckinridge at the orchard, which was in full bloom, and launched seven unsuccessful assaults. Bullets were cutting the spring blossoms from the trees so quickly that the cascading peach petals looked like falling snow. Johnston led the eighth charge himself, complete with the Rebel Yell and flags waving. This time they pushed back Hurlbut's left, but only after men fell in droves and the splintered peach trees dropped their remaining blossoms on the dead and wounded.

With the Union left rolled back like a swinging door, the ground was open from the Peach Orchard to Pittsburg Landing, but Prentiss's fierce blows from the Hornet's Nest distracted Breckinridge, and he missed the opportunity. Johnston came out of the orchard with clothes tattered and with a boot sole nearly ripped in half. He remained on the scene for nearly an hour before suddenly turning pale.

When he reeled in the saddle, an aide asked, "General—are you hurt?"

"Yes, and I fear seriously," replied Johnston.

His right boot was full of blood. He had been struck behind the knee by a stray bullet, which severed the femoral artery. A tourniquet would have stopped the bleeding, but the aide didn't know about that, and Johnston

Union wounded and stragglers retreat to the landing passing ammunition wagons going to the front.

had sent his personal physician to attend to a group of wounded Federal prisoners. Sometime around 2:45 p.m., Johnston bled to death. He was the first army commander in American history to die in combat. Although the news was kept secret to avoid upsetting the troops, his death caused a lull in the battle on this flank for about an hour. The command passed to Beauregard, who had been exercising it all day.

The Rebels still couldn't knock out the stubborn Hornet's Nest. Its center, bent back on itself, had not broken. For more than six hours, these determined Midwesterners delayed Beauregard's advance. If they wanted blood, Beauregard would give it to them in the most devastating way he could think of: he'd blast them out. He trained sixty-two cannon on the sunken road at pointblank range and opened fire. The Hornet's Nest exploded in a hail of shattered men. Rebel infantry surrounded the sunken road, and at 5:30 p.m. Prentiss and twenty-two hundred survivors of his division surrendered.

Hurlbut escaped to Pittsburg Landing. But W. H. L. Wallace was mortally wounded while leading a breakout to the landing through a ravine. When the Rebels saw them, they lined the sides and fired indiscriminately. Hundreds perished in the ravine, later known as "Hell's Hollow."

Nevertheless, the incredible stand gave Grant much-needed time to post the remainder of his army under cover of a battery of fifty powerful siege guns massed along the ridge at the landing. And just in time too.

While the Confederates were regrouping, two of their brigades pressed up to Grant's line near the landing. Hurlbut's division, now defending this line, hurled back several assaults with the help of the siege guns and the big guns of the Union gunboats. Finally, the vanguard of Brig. Gen. William Nelson's division from Buell's army arrived and was ferried across the river. They drove the Rebels back.

Bragg, Breckinridge, and Polk—with no word from Beauregard—met and agreed to press forward with a massive assault. By 6 p.m. they were within sight of Grant's batteries and the river. Victory seemed to be in their grasp. They moved slowly before being pinned down by heavy fire from the batteries. Then they heard from Beauregard, who was far in the rear and weakened by a bronchial infection and fever. Break off and withdraw, he ordered. He had concluded that the army was too disorganized and too tired to continue. And with only an hour remaining before sunset, he wanted more time to prepare.

"This is a mistake," Breckinridge told his staff. Bragg was furious too.

Disregarding them, Beauregard wired Jefferson Davis. The Creole boasted that he had won a complete victory. He had Grant where he wanted him, he said, and he'd finish him off the next morning.

Grant spent the night under an oak tree, wrapped in a poncho. Sherman found him there and remarked, "Well, General, we've had the devil's own day, haven't we?"

"Yes," replied Grant. "Lick 'em tomorrow though."

Another officer had recommended retreat before morning. Grant crowed, "Retreat? No, I propose to attack at daylight and whip them."

He had good reasons to be optimistic. That Sunday night, Buell's advance column deployed on the bluffs at Pittsburg Landing. And Lew Wallace's division finally showed up. On Monday, Grant would have twenty-eight thousand fresh troops available to support his battered survivors. Beauregard's effectives had been reduced to about twenty-five thousand.

While Beauregard slept in Sherman's captured tent near Shiloh church, cavalry leader Nathan Bedford Forrest tried to find him and alert him to what his scouts had seen—boats ferrying Buell's brigades across the river throughout the night. Unable to locate Beauregard, Forrest warned the other generals. They ignored him. Forrest predicted, "If the enemy comes on us in the morning, we'll be whipped like Hell."

That night a hard rain commenced—cold, hard rain in torrents—falling on ten thousand wounded, two thousand dead, and eighty-five thousand able-bodied but tired men, including Grant, who continued to huddle beneath a tree. "It seemed like the Lord was running it in," one Yankee noted. Their misery was compounded by lightning, thunder, and the explosion of shells fired every fifteen minutes at the Rebel camps by the Federal gunboats.

On Monday morning Beauregard had a startling awakening from a different kind of thunder—the crack and boom of field artillery and the clatter of musketry, all from a mile-wide line advancing under Buell, who apparently launched the attack on his own initiative, without consulting Grant. Quarrelsome, belligerent, and arrogant, Buell resented being outranked by the coarse general from Illinois.

General Van Dorn a Goat Three Times

Gen. Earl Van Dorn, commander of the Confederate Department of the Trans-Mississippi, became a goat three times before he found his niche.

First, he was ordered to bring his command from Arkansas to Corinth, Mississippi, to participate in the battle of Shiloh. His troops arrived too late.

Second, he chose to attack Union forces at Baton Rouge. He was repulsed, and in the process, he lost the only Confederate ironclad on the Mississippi River.

Third, he attempted a frontal assault at the battle of Corinth in October 1862. It ended in disaster.

Reassigned to command cavalry forces at Vicksburg, he cut Grant's supply lines at Holly Springs, Mississippi, and frustrated Grant's several attempts to capture the city, forcing him to resort to a siege.

Privately, as a ladies' man, Van Dorn had numerous conquests. One was a twenty-five-year-old married woman, Jessie Peters, whose husband, a physician, had been away from home for nearly a year, serving in the state legislature. When the doctor returned, friends told him what had been going on. Peters rode to Van Dorn's headquarters and shot him in the back. The general died four hours later.

Buell's attack took the Rebels by surprise. Breckinridge and Hardee tried to stop him with a charge, but Buell counterattacked so fiercely that he sent the Rebels reeling. Throughout the morning there were more charges and answering charges, but the fresh, well-supplied Federals had the upper hand.

Grant's divisions joined the fight on the right, with orders to "advance and recapture our original camps." They gained ground rapidly before being halted by artillery fire. Soon Buell's men came up with what Sherman called "the severest musketry fire I ever heard," and they resumed the march. By noon, Buell's troops had taken back the Peach Orchard, and Grant's men were approaching Shiloh chapel.

Some Rebel units were so spread out they could assemble only a fraction of the previous day's strength. Beauregard twice seized the colors of wavering regiments and led brigades in desperate assaults, but they were beaten back. Bragg attempted an attack from the Confederate center, but it also failed.

Throughout the day, masses of fresh Yankee troops kept coming into the fight to renew the Federal advances, forcing the Rebels back in disarray. Finally, Beauregard gave the order to withdraw, and his tired, demoralized army retreated in orderly fashion back to Corinth, with their wounded piled into wagons like bags of grain.

With Buell's and Lew Wallace's men on the field, nearly 105,000 men participated in the fighting. Total casualties were around 23,000, making Shiloh the bloodiest battle fought in America up to that time.

Shiloh, the "place of peace," had become Armageddon. One out of every four who had gone into battle had been killed, wounded, or captured. Grant's losses exceeded 13,000; the Confederates', at least 10,000. More than 3,000 lost their lives.

Grant commented that "the ground [by the Hornet's Nest] was so covered with dead soldiers that it [was] possible to walk across the clearing in any direction . . . without a foot touching the ground." Sherman described "piles of dead soldiers' mangled bodies . . . without heads and legs . . . The scenes on this field would have cured anybody of war."

Union soldiers returned to their camps and found them ransacked and in shambles. "I lost my shirts, blankets, letters from home, my testament (mother's gift) and a picture of the girl I left behind," wrote an Illinois private. "I was more indignant over the loss of my girl's picture than I was over the other articles," he added.

Adding to the misery were the groans of the dying and wounded. They were so loud, noted another Illinois soldier, that "sleep was almost impossible."

"No soldier who took part ever spoiled for a fight again," recalled one Union veteran. "We wanted a square, standup fight [and] got all we wanted of it."

With all the carnage, neither side gained an inch of ground. While both sides claimed they had won, Grant held the field and scored a tactical victory of great importance. He had turned back the Confederacy's monumental effort to regain the initiative in the Mississippi Valley.

Before Shiloh, Grant had said, "I consider this war practically over; they're ready to give up." The day after Shiloh he said, "I gave up all idea of saving the Union except by complete conquest."

Both Northerners and Southerners now realized that the nation had a very bloody war on its hands. Both governments needed to reassess what they were going to do. Total war lay ahead.

At Shiloh, who were the goats and the scapegoats? It's difficult to make a distinction between the two categories because of the strange and complex personalities involved and the change of fortunes from the first day to the second. Without question, Grant and Sherman were completely and shamefully surprised, though their armies were not, thanks to the alertness of men like Everett Peabody and Jesse Appler. Nearly every colonel took his men forward and chose a position to meet the enemy. But for much too long Grant and Sherman simply couldn't and wouldn't believe they were under attack. Their firm belief that they would not be attacked reflected their ignorance of the enemy's determination to fight and to do so fiercely and effectively. They were guilty of faulty thinking—expecting the enemy to do what they wanted, that is, to wait for the Federals to attack. It was a familiar military sin, and they paid dearly for it. That makes them the worst kind of goats.

The combination of being surprised and unprepared and suffering heavy losses prompted angry denunciations of Grant in the press and in the halls of Congress. Critics called him incompetent and wondered if he were drunk. Many demanded his ouster.

Grant could easily have made Sherman the goat. Sherman had been more at fault for the surprise than any other officer. Instead, both men denied any wrongdoing. And both supported each other. Such loyalty cemented their mutual respect and loyalty.

Grant praised Sherman's well-deserved defensive leadership on the first day of fighting. That day was the turning point in Sherman's life. He made mistakes, he learned from them, and then he excelled. His magnificence on the battlefield at Shiloh and strong praise from both Grant and Halleck led to his promotion to major general. He went on to become one of the North's best generals.

Lincoln, meanwhile, instructed Secretary of War Edwin M. Stanton to ask Halleck if there was any evidence of misconduct that contributed to the number of casualties at Shiloh. Halleck officially refused to blame Grant, stating somewhat facetiously that the casualties were due to the Confederates. Privately, Halleck said he had never seen a general more deficient in organizational skills. In a letter to Maj. Gen. Ethan Allen Hitchcock, chairman of Stanton's advisory board, he wrote: "Brave & able on the field, [Grant] has no idea of how to regulate & organize his forces before a battle or how to conduct the operations of a campaign."

Halleck's criticism of Grant to a general advising Stanton may have been a backdoor attempt to oust Grant by trying to persuade Hitchcock to convince

These transports brought Maj. Gen. Don Carlos Buell's army to Shiloh. The fresh troops were instrumental in forcing the Rebels back in disarray.

Stanton to apply pressure on Lincoln. Halleck detested Stanton, who in private had berated Halleck as "the greatest scoundrel and the most barefaced villain in America . . . [a person] totally destitute of principle." Both men were intense schemers.

To Grant's credit, he also learned from his mistakes—an unusual plus for Civil War commanders. He implemented precautions previously lacking—trenches, breastworks, and cavalry scouts, among them.

Regardless, immediately after the battle Halleck rushed to Shiloh from St. Louis to take command of the army before, he feared, Grant destroyed it entirely. He replaced Grant with Brig. Gen. George H. Thomas, a former instructor of cavalry and artillery at West Point. Halleck perhaps privately rejoiced over Grant's blunders, resentful as he was of Grant's earlier popularity. Halleck's choice of Thomas was another slap in Grant's face. Grant held a poor opinion of Thomas and suspected him of harboring Southern sympathies. Grant was wrong, however. Thomas's future battlefield successes would prove his loyalty and his valor.

Grant owed much to two other Southerners in his army—Stephen Hurlbut of South Carolina and Benjamin Prentiss of Virginia. Without their heroic stands at the Peach Orchard and the Hornet's Nest, there probably would not have been a second day of battle at Shiloh.

After Halleck took command of Grant's army, he relegated Grant to the meaningless position of second in command and attempted to shame him out of the service. To Grant, his new role was comparable to being under arrest. He didn't like it, but he chose to wait it out.

Halleck sought glory for himself. But he moved so cautiously against the Confederate stronghold at Corinth that by the time he got there, the outnumbered Confederates had escaped without serious harm. It was Halleck's first and last field command.

In July 1862, Halleck was appointed to be Lincoln's military adviser, with the title of general in chief. Lincoln could have chosen more wisely. Halleck would do more harm than good, hampering and harassing his field commanders. Grant, meanwhile, was given independent command of the enlarged District of West Tennessee. It included everything between the Mississippi and Tennessee Rivers, bounded to the north at Cairo, Illinois. Grant was answerable only to Washington.

Lincoln's decision to retain and reward Grant was a gamble since there was little evidence to suggest potential greatness. But Grant, after all, had won a major strategic victory at Shiloh. Pressured by a friend to remove Grant because of poor planning and heavy losses, Lincoln listened to his concerns and then sat quietly for a few minutes before replying, "I can't spare this man; he fights."

When the verbal static over Shiloh died down, the magnitude of the Northern victory became apparent, and both Grant and Sherman emerged as heroes, each staunchly supported by Lincoln. For Grant, it was the beginning of a remarkable ride leading to Appomattox Court House and the White House.

There were other Union goats. Because Jesse Appler ran while winning, his career was finished. Various regimental and company officers faced court-martial and dismissal for displaying cowardice. Grant and other Union officers accused Lew Wallace of dereliction of duty for his tardiness while the Army of the Tennessee was fighting for its life. But Grant later admitted he had never seen the written orders issued to Wallace and therefore was "not competent to say just what order the general actually received." Wallace's alleged slowness made him a scapegoat—a label undeserved.

For the South, the major goats of Shiloh were Johnston and Beauregard. What began as a seemingly lost cause for the Federals turned out to be a lost opportunity for the Confederates. One of Beauregard's major blunders, which Johnston should have corrected, was his battle plan that evenly distributed the troops along the front. This caused confusion when the lines intermingled. To turn the Yankee left, Johnston and Beauregard should have placed more strength on the Confederate right.

Still, they came ever so close to routing Grant's army and probably would have if Beauregard had not called off a final assault in the twilight of April 6. Historians have argued about his decision—one side maintaining he snatched defeat from the jaws of victory, the other contending that fire from the gunboats and siege guns would have slaughtered the Rebels. But in retrospect, a final assault was the only chance Johnston and Beauregard had. On the following day, heavily outnumbered, they had no chance.

Determined to maintain his reputation as the most popular Southern military hero up to that time, Beauregard never admitted defeat. "Untoward events," he said, had saved the Yankees from annihilation. He said his withdrawal was part of a broader strategic plan. But he couldn't fool the people of the South. They gradually turned against him.

Johnston, for reasons known only to him, ignored his responsibility as army commander and gave Beauregard entirely too much authority. Beauregard then squandered it with an ill-conceived battle plan and an incompetently executed strategy. Years later, Jefferson Davis emphasized this in a speech at a ceremony unveiling a statue of Johnston in New Orleans. He said bitterly, "The mistake [Johnston] made was in allowing somebody else [Beauregard] to direct the order of march." Johnston had twelve days to develop his own plan, but he didn't do it. He acquiesced to Beauregard and then rubber-stamped his recommendations.

Finally, Johnston replaced his own command duties with the more limited role of a brigadier and led a charge into a fierce fight at the Peach Orchard. It was perhaps his finest hour as a gallant combat leader, but that wasn't his role. And in doing so, he made it the final hour of his life. That cost the Confederacy a leader whom Davis regarded as the "pillar" among all his generals. While Davis's opinion is debatable, speculation about what might have been if Johnston had lived continues to this day.

Beauregard, to boost his declining ego and image, later claimed credit for many of Johnston's achievements. That antagonized Davis, who was Johnston's biggest cheerleader. From then on, Davis and Beauregard were at either other's throats. Beauregard contributed to his own demise when, after Shiloh, he took a leave of absence without giving notice or asking permission. Davis relieved him of command and replaced him with Bragg.

After Shiloh, it was mostly downhill for the South on the western front. Here, Rebel goats would outnumber Yankee goats, and the Northern soldiers would disprove the widely preached axiom that "a Southern soldier is worth ten Yankees."

14

"A DAMNED SCOUNDREL"

WHOEVER CONTROLS CHATTANOOGA WILL win the war," Lincoln said. The thriving transportation hub just north of the Georgia line was the gateway through the Appalachians to the South's industrial complexes in central Georgia and Alabama. It not only was the South's most important east-west rail connection but also a significant river port. The Tennessee River flowed along the edge of the city before curving to the southwest into Alabama and forming part of that state's border with Mississippi.

Lincoln made Chattanooga a major military objective and chose Maj. Gen. William S. Rosecrans to accomplish it. "Old Rosy," as he was called because of his name and his large red nose, had much to be proud of. As one of George B. McClellan's principal subordinates in the western Virginia campaign, he did more than "Little Mac" to take the area from the Rebels in 1861, sever it from Virginia, and turn it into the state of West Virginia. As commander of the Army of the Mississippi he had defeated Confederate armies at Iuka in September 1862 and at Corinth a month later. Then, when the Army of the Ohio under Maj. Gen. Don Carlos Buell failed to aggressively pursue retreating Confederates in Kentucky in the fall of 1862, Lincoln removed Buell and named Rosecrans to command the renamed Army of the Cumberland.

Lincoln and General in Chief Henry W. Halleck immediately pressured Rosecrans to go after Braxton Bragg's Army of Tennessee. "The government demands action," wrote Halleck, aware of Rosecrans's strange persona—a courageous man who was reluctant to fight.

"Old Rosy" really wasn't old. He was forty-four. He was a brilliant strategist and an incessant worker with boundless nervous energy. He often pushed his staff to work through the night. Always concerned for the welfare of his troops, he earned their respect, and they loved him like a father.

He earned high academic honors at West Point and served eleven years in the old army before poor health forced him to resign his commission in 1853. He thrived financially in the coal industry before returning to the army at the outbreak of the Civil War.

The forty-six-year-old Bragg was a Louisiana sugar planter trained at West Point, where he was graduated fifth in a class of fifty. In the Mexican War he was cited for bravery and distinguished conduct in spite of a temperament that alienated fellow officers. Hard to get along with, he was intolerant of subordinates who didn't promptly obey his orders.

Bragg's unapproachable personality isolated him. As a general, his officers regarded him as an underhanded tyrant who quibbled over trifles. His soldiers resented his iron discipline, but he turned them into some of the South's best-disciplined troops. Allegedly, he once had a soldier shot for killing a chicken. Bragg planned well but often lost his nerve during battles. Some said he was mentally ill.

In late August 1862 Bragg had invaded Kentucky with the political aim of securing enough support from Kentuckians to draw the state into the Confederacy. When that didn't happen, Bragg retreated to middle Tennessee and blamed subordinates for his failure. That started a grudge match within his own high command that never abated. Bragg concentrated the forty thousand men of his Army of Tennessee in and around Murfreesboro, east of the Stones River and about thirty miles southeast of Nashville.

Lincoln wanted Rosecrans to drive Bragg out of middle Tennessee and then secure east Tennessee and its principal cities—Chattanooga and Knoxville—an area having a large population of Union sympathizers. Quick movement was essential to Lincoln's broader strategy of keeping pressure on all Confederate armies so they couldn't reinforce each other. When Rosecrans was slow to get started, Halleck wired him in early December 1862, "If you remain one more week in Nashville, I cannot prevent your removal."

Leaving one division to guard the Tennessee capital, Rosecrans led forty-two thousand troops out of the city on December 26 for the showdown with Bragg. On the cold night before the fighting started, only a few yards separated the opposing armies. Huddled around campfires, the armies sang together "Home Sweet Home." It was the last tune thousands of them would ever sing.

At Stones River the two armies collided and fought savagely in sleet and freezing rain for three days, from December 31 to January 2. Both armies were poorly managed and severely mauled. On the morning of New Year's Eve, for example, thirteen thousand screaming Rebels "swooped down on Yankees [at breakfast] like a whirl-a-gust of woodpeckers in a hail storm," as a Tennessee private recalled. The Union flank retreated three miles before Old Rosy could rush in reinforcements. While he rode along the line rallying his troops, a staff officer beside him was beheaded by a cannonball, and his blood spattered the commander's uniform. Maj. Gen. Philip H. Sheridan's division saved the Union army from destruction, stalling the Rebel attack at a heavy cost to both armies.

Maj. Gen. William S. Rosecrans (on horse at left), a gifted strategist, rallies his troops against a Rebel assault on December 31 at Stones River. His leadership there earned him the "Thanks of Congress." Nine months later at Chickamauga, an error in one of his orders to the front cost him the victory and his command.

In an about-face on January 2, Bragg ordered Maj. Gen. John C. Breckinridge's entire division to attack Rosecrans's left wing, which was commanded by Maj. Gen. Thomas L. Crittenden, who happened to have been a childhood friend of Breckinridge's. Breckinridge argued vehemently against the assault, believing Crittenden's guns on high ground would enfilade his line. But Bragg was adamant. So Breckinridge attacked, and the Federals' massed artillery shattered his division. He lost fifteen hundred men in an hour. Breckinridge never forgave Bragg for ordering this suicidal assault.

Neither side could claim a decisive victory at Stones River. It was a bruising tactical draw and the war's most deadly battle in terms of percentages of casualties. Rosecrans lost thirteen thousand; Bragg, ten thousand. Bragg left the battlefield first and withdrew his army to Tullahoma, Tennessee, a small rail junction thirty miles closer to Chattanooga.

Lincoln, looking for a victory of sorts anywhere, gave Rosecrans his heartfelt thanks for the Union's one bright spot in its winter of gloom following the failure at Fredericksburg a few weeks earlier. He wired Rosecrans, "I

Lt. Gen. James Longstreet's troops arrived at Ringgold, Georgia, on September 18, 1863. On the rails for nine days, they rode in and on top of boxcars. Two days later they routed the Union army at Chickamauga.

can never forget . . . [that] you gave us a hard earned victory which, had there been a defeat instead, the nation could hardly have lived over."

The Confederate commanders spent the winter licking their wounds and blaming Bragg for his poor generalship. They argued that the ground on which he chose to fight offered few advantages to them and far more to the Federals and that he also erred in weakening his forces by spreading them out. Division commander Benjamin F. Cheatham vowed he'd never serve under Bragg again. Breckinridge considered challenging Bragg to a duel.

But Bragg's subordinates were as much or more at fault as he was. Bragg especially blamed his two senior commanders, Lt. Gen. William J. Hardee of Georgia, author of an infantry manual used by both North and South, and Lt. Gen. Leonidas Polk of North Carolina, an Episcopal bishop whose only qualification for command was his close friendship with Jefferson Davis. Their uncoordinated attacks resulted in mass confusion that proved costly to the Confederates. Bragg also condemned Cheatham's drunkenness during the battle; some alleged that Cheatham was so drunk he fell off his horse while leading his men forward. Another general, John P. McCown, was court-martialed for disobeying Bragg's orders, which if carried out should have resulted in a Confederate victory.

Polk and Hardee led a revolt—a near mutiny—against Bragg, complaining to Jefferson Davis and persuading other officers to join them. Davis investigated, found the army's morale high, and retained Bragg. Nevertheless, the animosities reverberated in the Southern press and in the halls of Richmond.

Bragg seemed content to remain inactive at Tullahoma all spring and into the summer. Rosecrans also was sluggish while rebuilding his crippled army. His lethargy enabled Bragg to send reinforcements to Vicksburg, which Grant held under siege. That exasperated Lincoln, along with Old Rosy's delays, and Lincoln let it be known that Rosecrans's job was again in jeopardy. When those rumors reached Rosecrans's camp, he sprang into action. At the end of June he put his army on the march.

During fourteen days of summer rainstorms, Rosecrans conducted a brilliant campaign of clever feints and deceptions. Dividing his army into several strong columns, he threatened Bragg on both of his flanks. Bragg, uncertain where the major assault might occur, chose not to risk another costly fight. He withdrew to Chattanooga where he felt safe in the mountainous terrain.

Rosecrans had successfully driven the Rebels from middle Tennessee, no minor accomplishment. Expecting but not receiving praise from Washington, he was annoyed by a message from Secretary of War Edwin M. Stanton on July 7: "Lee's army overthrown (Gettysburg); Grant victorious (Vicksburg). You and your noble army now have the chance to give the finishing blow to the Rebellion. Will you neglect the chance?"

Rosecrans fired back: "You do not appear to observe the fact that this noble army has driven the Rebels from middle Tennessee. . . . I beg in behalf of this army that the War Department may not overlook so great an event because it is not written in letters of blood."

On August 16, with more nudging from Washington, Rosecrans resumed his marching and maneuvering to gain control of east Tennessee and the rich prizes of Chattanooga and Knoxville. Rosecrans's feints persuaded Bragg that the Federals would cross the Tennessee River north of Chattanooga. Instead Rosecrans marched through mountain gaps and crossed far below the town at four undefended points. He planned to place his army behind Bragg's and force it to react. When Bragg learned he had been duped, that his supply line was in peril, and that Federal forces were crossing Lookout Mountain in his direction, he chose his only viable alternative. He vamoosed, leaving Chattanooga and taking his army to LaFayette, Georgia, twenty-five miles to the south.

Meanwhile, 113 miles north of Chattanooga, Maj. Gen. Ambrose E. Burnside's small Army of the Ohio had come through Cumberland Gap and captured Knoxville. The outnumbered defenders abandoned the city without firing a shot. They retreated south to join Bragg as he was leaving Chattanooga. The many Knoxville citizens loyal to the Union cheered Burnside's arrival.

The two major cities of east Tennessee had been taken with almost no loss of blood. But Rosecrans's rise as a hero was about to be followed by his ghastly descent into the role of a goat. Rosecrans didn't know where Bragg was. But his own intuition and fragmentary intelligence reports convinced him that the Rebels were in a panic-stricken retreat toward Atlanta. Maj. Gen. George H. Thomas, the able commander of Rosecrans's Fourteenth Corps, urged Rosecrans to consolidate their three widely dispersed corps before pursuing Bragg. No, said Rosecrans. Convinced that the Rebels were in full retreat, Rosecrans stubbornly believed he could destroy them with a quick and vigorous pursuit. All elements of Rosecrans's Army of the Cum-

NATIONAL ARCHIVES

Rugged Midwesterners, such as these men, made up the Army of the Cumberland. Despite their determination in the field, their leaders failed them at Chickamauga.

berland would advance from their present positions, wherever they were, looking for Bragg, wherever he was.

Rosecrans's first directive on the morning of September 9 went to Maj. Gen. Thomas L. Crittenden, commander of the Twenty-first Corps. He was to leave a single brigade in Chattanooga and take the rest of his corps in the direction of Ringgold and Dalton, Georgia. Maj. Gen. Alexander McCook, then in Valley Head, Alabama, was to lead his Twentieth Corps toward Summerville, Georgia. And Thomas's corps, positioned north of McCook, was to drive toward LaFayette, Georgia. Surely, Rosecrans assumed, this wide net of infantry would find and strike Bragg's flanks and destroy his army.

These corps would be separated by the equivalent of eighty miles, considering the tangle of ridges and primitive roads. They would be too far apart to assist each other if Bragg's concentrated army were to attack one of the corps. But Rosecrans had not considered that possibility—a possibility that not only put each of his unsupported corps at great risk but also endangered his entire army.

That possibility was about to become a reality. The Rebels were not retreating. Concentrated at LaFayette, they were almost directly in Thomas's path. The two forces were separated only by a gap in Missionary Ridge, a valley (McLemore's Cove), and Chickamauga Creek, named for an Indian word meaning "river of death." The name was prophetic for both armies.

Confederate Gen. Braxton Bragg won the battle of Chickamauga but was severely criticized by his own generals for failing to capitalize on their victory and destroy the Army of the Cumberland.

Jefferson Davis had instructed Bragg to follow a strategy that had worked for Lee—attack the attackers and throw their momentum off balance. To strengthen Bragg, Davis sent him two divisions from Gen. Joseph E. Johnston's idle army in Mississippi and, against Lee's wishes, ordered Lt. Gen. James Longstreet to leave the Army of Northern Virginia temporarily and take two of his divisions—twelve thousand battle veterans—by train to Georgia. The first group left on September 9. The only route available to them was a nine-hundred-mile excursion through both Carolinas and Georgia over at least eight different rail lines. Longstreet would soon be battling Rosecrans, his former West Point roommate.

Earlier, Davis had sent to Bragg a general that Lee and others in Virginia didn't like—the irascible Daniel Harvey Hill. He had replaced Hardee as a senior commander, thereby supplanting one thorn in Bragg's side with an even uglier one.

Breckinridge, who had been in west Tennessee in a failed attempt to save Vicksburg, was called back to Bragg's army for assignment to Hill. Maj. Gen. Patrick R. Cleburne, the impressive Irishman later to be known as the "Stonewall Jackson of the West," also was put under Hill. Polk retained command of his corps.

Two cavalry divisions were placed under one of the great cavalry raiders of the Civil War, Brig. Gen. Nathan Bedford Forrest. Another cavalry division came under the erratic Maj. Gen. Joseph Wheeler, a favorite of Bragg whose abilities were overstated.

When all of these units came together, Bragg had an army of sixty-six thousand, about ten thousand more than Rosecrans. Timing and strategy became critical.

Bragg's plan was to lure Rosecrans's separated columns through the mountains and into McLemore's Cove, a valley south of Chattanooga formed by Lookout Mountain and a spur named Pigeon Mountain. Then his concentrated army could trap and defeat them individually. To bait Rosecrans, Bragg sent "deserters" into Union lines to spread rumors that his army was demoralized and retreating. Bragg's plan should have worked except for one problem. His commanders failed him on September 10 and 13.

On September 10, George Thomas's lead element, Maj. Gen. James Negley's division, did exactly what Bragg wanted him to do. He marched his forty-six hundred troops down Lookout Mountain and into McLemore's Cove—the perfect place to be trapped. Bragg ordered Harvey Hill to attack them from Pigeon Mountain and Maj. Gen. Thomas Hindman from Polk's corps to drive into the cove from the north.

Negley's division should have been annihilated. It wasn't. Hill refused to participate, claiming falsely that the distance was too great and that his best division commander, Patrick R. Cleburne, was ill. Hindman, unaware of Hill's decision, spent the day waiting for him. When Bragg received Hill's message, he promptly sent in Maj. Gen. Simon Buckner's two-division corps. But even then Hindman failed to attack. This was out of character for the usually bold warrior and former U.S. congressman. Instead Hindman called a council of war. Although outnumbering the Federals three to one, both Hindman and Buckner feared they might become trapped. They wanted more information before attacking.

Adding more absurdity to the comedy (or tragedy) of errors, Bragg sent explicit orders to Hindman to attack at dawn on September 11, but the courier gave confusing, garbled instructions. Bragg, Hill, Hindman, and Buckner all became goats. While this was going on, Federal reinforcements arrived, but sensing the hopelessness of their situation, they and Negley's men pulled out of the cove.

Bragg, of course, was enraged by the fiasco. The Confederates had lost an opportunity to destroy two Federal divisions and to cripple Rosecrans's largest corps. Bragg's army wasted another opportunity on Sunday, September 13. On that day Bragg ordered Polk to attack Brig. Gen. Thomas J. Wood's isolated division at Lee and Gordon's Mill, a landmark along Chickamauga Creek. Although Polk had a much larger force, he ignored the orders and demanded reinforcements, insisting he needed them because he was about to be attacked.

Wood's division was part of Crittenden's corps. Had Polk attacked and succeeded, Crittenden's corps probably would have turned southward toward McLemore's Cove. And that movement could have led to the routing of a large portion of the Army of the Cumberland. Bragg's reaction to Polk's inaction was beyond description.

Rosecrans now realized the horrid circumstances he had created for his divided army. With great urgency he ordered his scattered forces to unite. They were spread out along fifty miles of Georgia's backwoods.

The armies of North and South both raced northward along the banks of West Chickamauga Creek. Bragg's objective was to get between the Army of the Cumberland and Chattanooga. Rosecrans was equally determined to prevent that from happening. By September 17, the three Federal corps were finally within supporting distance of each other, with orders to protect their lines of retreat to Chattanooga. Bragg could no longer destroy the Federal army piecemeal. He blamed his officers; they blamed him.

By the morning of September 19, both armies faced each other in a five-mile line paralleling the creek. Early that morning, on the far Union left, George H. Thomas sent two brigades to take out what he thought was a single Rebel brigade isolated on the west side of the Chickamauga. Instead he encountered an entire division supported by Forrest's cavalry. Thomas summoned reinforcements, and divisions of both armies rushed to the scene. In the heavily wooded terrain, more units joined the ferocious but disorganized action. Thick woods limited visibility to about 150 feet, less than the range of a rifle. Cannon were useless. Battle lines did not exist. Often the fighting was hand to hand. Thousands fell on both sides.

Throughout the day Bragg's divisions struck savage blows primarily against Thomas's corps in the thick woods and underbrush on the Union left. The Rebels broke through at several points, but because of Bragg's poor coordination, they became isolated due to lack of support. The breakthroughs collapsed, and the Rebels were pushed back or swallowed up by Union reinforcements.

Bragg was so determined to turn the Union left and get between Rosecrans and Chattanooga that he ignored or overlooked information about a wide gap in the center of Rosecrans's line. Had he attacked with one or two divisions, he could have split Rosecrans's army and put them to rout. But he didn't. Rosecrans filled the gap as the fight continued.

Around 3 p.m. men of Longstreet's corps under Maj. Gen. John Bell Hood joined the melee after marching fifteen miles from the railroad depot at Ringgold, Georgia. In a vicious attack against Rosecrans's right, whole regiments disappeared. But the Federals held the line.

Cleburne arrived with his division around 4:30 p.m. after a daylong march from the south. Bragg, still trying to turn Rosecrans's left, ordered Cleburne to report to Polk on the army's right wing. About 5:30 Cleburne charged out of the thickets in a bloodcurdling assault with rapid-fire weapons. He slammed into Thomas, who slammed right back. An Indiana captain later wrote that the Rebels were "loading and firing in a manner that I believe was never surpassed on any battlefield during the Rebellion." After thirty minutes of hellish fighting, full darkness ended what another Hoosier called "a display of fireworks that one does not like to see more than once in a lifetime."

As day one of the battle of Chickamauga drew to a close, neither side had achieved anything. In "Reminiscences" by Confederate Brig. Gen. John B. Gordon, he wrote:

> To the two armies, whose blood was still flowing long after the sun went down on the 19th, neither of them victorious, but each so near the other as to hear the groans of the wounded and dying in the opposing ranks, the scene was indescribably oppressive. Cleburne's Confederates had waded the

When the two armies fought to a bruising tactical draw at Stones River, dissension mounted in the Confederate hierarchy. Bragg blamed his two senior commanders—William J. Hardee (left) and Leonidas Polk (right)—and they blamed him. Hardee was one of the South's most skilled officers. Polk, a former Episcopal bishop, had no qualifications except his friendship with Jefferson Davis. After Chickamauga, twelve of Bragg's generals signed a petition to Davis urging him to remove Bragg from command.

river with the water to their armpits. Their clothing was drenched and their bodies shivering in the chill north wind. In every direction were dimly burning tapers, carried by nurses and relief corps searching for the wounded. All over the field lay the unburied dead, their pale faces ghastlier by streaks of blood and clotted hair, and black stains of powder left upon their lips when they tore off with their teeth the ends of deadly cartridges. Such was the night . . . of the 19th.

Longstreet himself arrived at the battlefield near midnight. No guides had been sent to the train depot to meet him at 2 p.m. For nine hours he had wandered about, trying to find Bragg's headquarters. He was nearly captured.

Bragg immediately assigned Longstreet to command his left wing. As part of Bragg's surprise reorganization, Hill was demoted and placed under Polk, who—despite his incompetence at Lee and Gordon's Mill—would command the right wing. Bragg blamed Hill more than anyone else for the failure at McLemore's Cove and didn't want to deal directly with him again.

Changes in command were unusual during a major battle. But Bragg had had it with commanders who disobeyed his orders or failed to cooperate and coordinate their actions. Bragg obviously did not consider the possibility that he was part of the problem.

On the Union side that night, Rosecrans feared a catastrophe if he continued the fight with his battered army. But Assistant Secretary of War Charles Dana had come down from Washington as an observer and was present at a meeting of Rosecrans and his senior commanders. No one was about to suggest a full retreat in Dana's presence, so orders were issued to prepare for another fight.

Rosecrans and Thomas expected Bragg to repeat his efforts to cut off their supply and escape route by getting between the army and Chattanooga. They believed that Bragg would again attack Thomas's flank at the north end of the line. Rosecrans reinforced this position, and Thomas ordered his men to cut and pile logs to create a strong defensive barrier.

At dawn on the morning of September 20, Rosecrans's chief of staff, Brig. Gen. James A. Garfield, pointed to the sun and noted its dark red color. "It is ominous," he told Rosecrans. "It will indeed be a day of blood."

Bragg intended to do just what Rosecrans expected—attack the north end of the Federal line. But again his orders were screwed up through con-

BOTH: LIBRARY OF CONGRESS

Rosecrans searched for scapegoats after his defeat at Chickamauga and attempted to pin his failure on corps commanders Alexander McCook (left) and Thomas L. Crittenden (right). Both generals had joined the fleeing horde of Yankees after the Union battle line was pierced. McCook's corps was wiped off the field without resisting. A court of inquiry acquitted them of all charges, but McCook's poor showing virtually ended his military career.

fusion and incompetence. First, Bragg neglected to notify Hill that he was now under Polk. Second, Polk failed to communicate with Hill and other division commanders, including Breckinridge and Cleburne. Breckinridge was supposed to launch the attack at sunrise, but no one had told him in advance. He didn't receive his orders until the time had passed when the attack should already have begun. Consequently, the assault was delayed more than four hours, from 5 a.m. to 9:30 a.m.

Polk later said that Hill wasn't ready because he couldn't be found the night before and wasn't informed about the assault until after sunrise. Hill then complained that he had to do several things before his corps could attack. He had to adjust his line, he said, and let his troops finish their breakfast.

Around 9 a.m. Bragg sent an aide to find Polk. The aide, Bragg said, found him three miles behind the front line, reading a newspaper in a rocking chair and waiting for his breakfast. When Bragg rode to Polk's headquarters to rebuke him, Polk was just then leaving for battle. "My heart is overflowing with anxiety for the attack," he told Bragg with excitement in his voice.

Once the attack was finally underway, Breckinridge delivered mightily. The Kentuckian's three brigades pounded away at Thomas's left flank. Two of them made it around the end of his line before being hurled back by Union fire. It came from behind the breastworks of logs and debris the Federals had worked all night to build.

In a ferocious attack that has become legendary, Breckinridge never let up. The pressure intensified as Cleburne's division lengthened the line of attack on Breckinridge's left, followed by Cheatham's division on Cleburne's left. Through fallen treetops and tangled brush and burning shells, the whole Confederate right, brigade after brigade, furiously assailed the Union breastworks in successive and repeated charges, only to recoil, broken and decimated. Breckinridge needed help, but Polk was under heavy fire at the center of Thomas's well-defended position, and Bragg had placed the Confederate reserves too far south to be helpful.

Four times during these charges the usually cool Thomas called on Rosecrans for reinforcements. And he got them. Old Rosy responded by shifting units from his center—a quiet part of the line—to his hard-pressed left, but he did so without carefully considering the impact on the rest of the line.

In the confusion of battle, a staff officer didn't see a Federal division concealed in the woods on the right and reported a quarter-mile gap there. To fill this imagined hole, Rosecrans ordered Brig. Gen. Thomas J. Wood to shift his division of five thousand men to the left "as fast as possible." McCook, to whom Wood reported, was present when the order was delivered. Wood realized that if he moved "as fast as possible," he would leave a gap nearly half a mile wide in the Federal line—a gap the Confederates could easily exploit. McCook told him he had to obey the order, arguing that Rosecrans's view of the situation must be superior to theirs. McCook said he'd fill the gap with units from his corps, but time would run out before he could act. Rosecrans had made a devastating mistake.

Even before Wood's movement, the weakened Federal center gave Bragg an opportunity that generals dream of. But he

Maj. Gen. George H. Thomas (a Virginian by birth) saved the retreating Union army from annihilation by putting up one of the war's most heroic stands against enormous odds. As a result, he won enduring fame as the "Rock of Chickamauga."

did nothing. He had, however, given his line commanders authority to strike when warranted. Lee's old warhorse Longstreet saw an opportunity, and he took it. With twenty thousand troops at his disposal, he attacked the center of the Federal line.

By a remarkable coincidence and amazing luck—both in timing and in placement—Longstreet's lead division, commanded by Brig. Gen. Bushrod Johnson, unwittingly moved forward exactly at the point Wood's division had left just ten minutes earlier. Johnson overpowered tough resistance on his right front and then found his division in the clear, with no opposition in front of him, just open country. His men surged through, and more butternut soldiers followed with the piercing Rebel Yell. They rolled up Rosecrans's right and drove nearly a mile into the Union rear.

"The scene was unspeakably grand," Johnson wrote in his official report. He described "the rush of our heavy columns sweeping out from the shadow and gloom of the forest into the open fields flooded with sunlight, the glitter of arms, the retreat of the foe, the shouts of our army, the smoke, and the noise of whistling balls and grapeshot and of bursting shell."

By noon, Rosecrans's Army of the Cumberland was split in two and in turmoil. Then when the Confederates on Bragg's left pressed forward, other Union divisions panicked as the enemy approached them from two sides and threatened to cut off their line of retreat. The whole Union right disintegrated. One-third of the blue army broke and streamed northward toward Chattanooga.

Rosecrans saw no hope. The spunk he'd been running on quickly fizzled, and he developed a sudden urge to make himself scarce. He turned to his staff and exclaimed, "If you care to live any longer, get away from here." And that's what he and they did. They left the battlefield and headed toward Chattanooga with the fleeing horde. Corps commanders Thomas L. Crittenden and Alexander McCook joined them.

"McCook's corps was wiped off the field without any attempt at real resistance," an Illinois colonel later testified. The colonel said he saw artillerists cut the traces and abandon their guns in order to make a faster getaway, while others on foot were swept along by the mob, "like flecks of foam upon a river."

Only Thomas and his left half of the Army of the Cumberland held out. Having survived everything Breckinridge could throw at him, he wasn't about to run. He did what he could to cover the retreat of his comrades while being hammered again and again by Breckinridge, Cleburne, and other elements of Longstreet's command.

Concentrating his forces on Snodgrass Hill and Horseshoe Ridge, Thomas put up one of the most heroic stands of the war and won enduring fame as the "Rock of Chickamauga." Cool and determined, he stood his ground against enormous odds and saved the rest of the army that was on the run. But his situation was ominous.

Then another remarkable coincidence developed—this one to Thomas's advantage. A reserve corps under Maj. Gen. Gordon Granger had heard the sounds of battle from their position many miles north. Assuming correctly that the Army of the Cumberland was in trouble, Granger on his own initiative rushed to the sound of guns. His arrival bolstered Thomas and enabled him to hold out until nightfall. Then the fighting ended, and Thomas slipped away toward Chattanooga. His forces joined those who had fled, and they began the defense of what was to become a besieged city.

Thomas was especially hated throughout the South, not just because of his heroics at Chickamauga, but because he was a Virginian—a rare Virginian who, unlike Lee, remained loyal to the Union. By doing so, he was disowned by his fellow Virginians and even by his own family. His sisters turned his portrait to the wall at the family homestead.

The casualties of the battle of Chickamauga were staggering—approximately nineteen thousand for the Confederates (including ten generals) and more than sixteen thousand for the Federals. Each side lost nearly 30 percent of its forces. It was the second-bloodiest battle of the Civil War and the last major Confederate victory. Among the Confederate dead was Brig. Gen. Benjamin Hardin Helm, who had married Mary Lincoln's half sister. Maj. Gen. John Bell Hood lost his right leg. At least half of Bragg's artillery horses were killed.

While the Confederates suffered the most casualties—the result of their ferocious attacks and Thomas's courageous stand—Bragg had inflicted one of the most complete defeats ever suffered by a Union army. Still, Bragg had before him the opportunity to destroy the Army of the Cumberland. Longstreet and cavalry leader Nathan Bedford Forrest urged him to push forward the next morning and confront Rosecrans before he could reorganize and develop defensive fortifications. "Every hour was worth a thousand men," Forrest exclaimed. But that wasn't Bragg's plan. Probably because of the horrifying spectacle of his dead and wounded, he chose to lay siege to Chattanooga and cut off the Federal supply line from Bridgeport, Alabama—a wagon road over the Cumberlands. That, he believed, would force Rosecrans to starve or surrender. (See chapter 15.)

Bragg would fight his own generals rather than Rosecrans. During the week that followed, dissension, bitterness, and recriminations plagued the Confederate hierarchy. Bragg's lieutenants blamed him for failing to follow up to capitalize on their victory, and he accused them of willful ineptitude. They complained individually and collectively to Jefferson Davis and his secretary of war, James Seddon. Leonidas Polk, the bishop-general, wrote of Bragg's "palpable weakness and mismanagement," and James Longstreet stated in a letter to Seddon that "nothing but the hand of God can save us or help us as long as we have our present commander."

A petition signed by twelve generals, including Harvey Hill and Simon Buckner, followed the letters to Seddon. The petitioners claimed:

> Two weeks ago this army, elated by a great victory which promised to be the most fruitful of the war, was in readiness to pursue the defeated enemy. That

From behind a breastwork of logs and knapsacks, George H. Thomas's corps repulsed numerous assaults from elements of Longstreet's command. Thomas's stand enabled the Union army to escape to Chattanooga.

enemy, driven in confusion from the field, was fleeing in disorder and panic-stricken. . . . Today . . . the beaten army, recovering behind its formidable works from the effects of his defeat, is understood to be already receiving rein-forcements, while heavy additions to his strength are rapidly approaching him. Whatever may have been accomplished heretofore, it is certain that the fruits of the victory . . . have now escaped our grasp. The Army of Tennessee, stricken with a complete paralysis, will in a few days' time be thrown strictly on the defensive, and may deem itself fortunate if it escapes from its present position without disaster. . . .

In addition to reinforcements your petitioners would deem it a dereliction of the sacred duty they owe to the country if they did not further ask that Your Excellence assign to the command of this army an officer who will in-spire the army and the country with undivided confidence. Without entering into a criticism of the merits of our present commander, your petitioners re-gard it as a sufficient reason, without assigning others, to urge his being re-lieved, because, in their opinion, the condition of his health totally unfits him for the command of an army in the field.

The next day—October 6—Davis left for Bragg's headquarters, hoping "to be serviceable in harmonizing some of the difficulties existing there." He arrived on October 9.

In Bragg's presence, all four corps commanders told Davis that Bragg must go. Davis, however, kept Bragg and denounced the other generals, calling their complaints "shafts of malice." Polk was suspended for slow-ness and refusal to obey orders. Hill, an ally of Polk and constant critic of Bragg, was relieved and sent to a minor command in North Carolina. Breckinridge replaced him. Davis brought back Hardee from Alabama to replace Polk. Buckner's corps command was abolished, and he was de-moted to leading a division.

Bragg also had a score to settle with the hot-blooded cavalry leader Nathan Bedford Forrest, who was still bitter about Bragg's refusal to follow up the victory. Bragg sent him to head off a supposed Union advance from Knoxville. The threat didn't exist. When Forrest realized that and was on his way back on September 28, he received a dispatch signed by one of Bragg's staff members: "The general commanding desires that you will without delay turn over the troops of your command . . . to Major General Wheeler."

Without reference to the raid Wheeler was about to make on the Federal supply line, the message implied to Forrest that he was about to be relieved of command. Forrest obeyed the order and then dictated and sent through channels a fiery protest. He told the staffer who took it down, "Bragg never got such a letter from a brigadier."

At a meeting with Forrest two days later, Bragg assured him that no affront was intended. He said he'd get his men back as soon as they returned from their mission with Wheeler. Until then Forrest could take a ten-day leave and visit his wife in LaGrange, Georgia, sixty miles southeast of Atlanta. He hadn't seen her for a year and a half.

While at LaGrange, Forrest received an order dated just after his meeting with Bragg. It assigned Wheeler "to the command of all the cavalry in the Army of Tennessee." For Forrest, this was the last straw. He despised Wheeler and nearly fought a duel with him seven months earlier. At the time, Forrest swore he would never again serve under him. Bragg knew this. And he undoubtedly knew that his order would permanently separate Forrest from the troopers he had raised and developed on his own. Forrest, with good reason, was angry. He interrupted his leave and went back to confront Bragg. His staff surgeon accompanied him as a witness.

Bragg offered his hand as Forrest entered his tent on Missionary Ridge, but Forrest declined it. "I am not here to pass civilities or compliments with you, but on other business," Forrest said coldly. Jabbing his rigid index finger in Bragg's direction, he spoke heatedly: "I have stood your meanness as long as I intend to. You have played the part of a damned scoundrel, and are a coward, and if you were any part of a man I would slap your jaws and force you to resent it. You may as well not issue any more orders to me, for I will not obey them. . . . And I say to you that if you ever again try to interfere with me or cross my path it will be at the peril of your life."

Forrest then abruptly left. His doctor companion told him, "You are in for it now."

"No," replied Forrest, "he'll never say a word about it. . . . He'll take no action. . . . I will ask to be relieved and transferred to a different field, and he will not oppose it."

Forrest was right. Bragg probably overlooked Forrest's insubordination for the good of the common cause—to save Forrest's services for the Confederacy. On October 29, Davis approved Forrest's request to be detached from service with Bragg's army and to be transferred to an independent command in Mississippi. But the loss of Forrest heightened the acrimony within Bragg's

Confederate cavalry leader Nathan Bedford Forrest called Bragg a coward and "a damned scoundrel" and warned Bragg not to interfere with him again. Forrest's request to be detached from service with Bragg's army was granted by Jefferson Davis.

command and further weakened Bragg's ability to take on the besieged Union army in Chattanooga.

* * *

Either side could have won the battle of Chicka-mauga. Both armies had too many generals who became goats, and in the end the biggest goat was the Federal commander, William S. Rosecrans. He started the campaign brilliantly with clever feints and maneuvers that confused Bragg and forced him east to Chattanooga and then to Chickamauga. But Rosecrans went awry by scattering his forces and assuming Bragg was in full retreat to Atlanta. Rosecrans's troop deployments and his poor leadership and blunders exposed his army to potential disaster. His flame finally flickered out after his critical error of moving Wood's position to fill a gap that never existed. Then, as Longstreet stormed through the newly created gap and split the Union army, Rosecrans ran from the battlefield while the left half of his army was still fighting. Lincoln aptly described Rosecrans as "confused and stunned like a duck hit on the head."

The Army of the Cumberland was saved only by Thomas's heroic stand and Bragg's overcautiousness and failure to pursue the retreating Federals. But to Rosecrans's credit, he had successfully captured Chattanooga, and that was his original mission.

Rosecrans searched for scapegoats immediately after Chickamauga and attempted to pin the defeat on McCook and Crittenden, the weak commanders of the thirty-four thousand men of the Twentieth and Twenty-first Corps that fled from the battlefield. While their actions were contemptible, they would not have occurred had Rosecrans not created a gap in his line. Rosecrans removed both men from command.

McCook, just thirty-two years old, was a member of the famous "Fighting McCooks" of Ohio—seven brothers and seven cousins who fought for the Union. His forces also had been crushed at Stones River, a factor Rosecrans could not overlook. With two strikes against McCook, Rosecrans was not about to give him a third opportunity, even though he and his men had performed bravely at Shiloh in 1862.

Crittenden's removal aroused anger in his native Kentucky, and the state legislature wrote to Lincoln, demanding a reexamination of the firing of this favorite son. Kentucky, a neutral state at the beginning of the war, declared itself for the Union in September 1861, much to Lincoln's pleasure. Bordering the Ohio River, the Bluegrass State was strategically important. Thus, the legislature appealed to Lincoln, knowing he would not ignore their request. Crittenden was a much better officer than McCook, and he also had fought well at Shiloh. Part of a family with split allegiances, he was the son of a U.S. congressman who remained loyal to the Union. A brother coveted the South and became a Confederate general.

A court of inquiry reviewed the case against McCook and Crittenden and acquitted them of all charges. Their reputations, however, would be eclipsed by the disaster at Chickamauga and the charges against them. Stanton and the War Department refused to return either of them to a battlefield command.

The Confederates, while victors in battle, were stunned by a line of goats, especially Braxton Bragg, Leonidas Polk, D. Harvey Hill, Thomas Hindman, and Simon Buckner. Bragg had the Federals on the ropes several times but failed to deliver the knockout punch. Too often he relied on frontal assaults and other unimaginative tactics, and after having won the battle, he lacked an effective strategy for followup. A competent general with loyal subordinates could have destroyed the Army of the Cumberland. True, Bragg scored a major tactical victory and inflicted one of the worst defeats on a Union army in the war, but he failed to gain any strategic objectives. Further, when a general can literally wipe out an entire army and fails to do so, he has wasted a splendid opportunity. The South needed more from Bragg, and Bragg needed more from his subordinates. But more was not forthcoming.

Hindman and Buckner were goats at McLemore's Cove. Their poor communications, bad judgment, and excessive caution prevented a rout that could have been disastrous to the Union army. Buckner perhaps attempted to mask his failures there by leading the post-Chickamauga anti-Bragg movement.

Hill, a chronic no-show at the cove and for the attack on September 20, received his just reward by being booted to a minor command.

Polk, an ecclesiastic with limited military experience and questionable mental sharpness, had no business commanding half an army. Although at times brave, he had been a liability to a succession of commanders, and he maintained that record under Bragg. Polk and Jefferson Davis had been friends at West Point, but Polk resigned from the army after graduation, never serving in the military. When the war started, Davis offered his old friend a general's commission, and Polk accepted it, believing the South was fighting for a holy cause. At Chickamauga, Polk's failure to obey Bragg's order to attack Crittenden on September 13 and to coordinate the Rebel offensive of September 20 with Hill and Breckinridge prompted Bragg to remove him from command and recommend his court-martial. Davis interceded on Polk's behalf and reinstated him. Friendship apparently meant more to Davis than military experience, intelligence, competence—and results.

15

CHATTANOOGA: NOVEMBER 23–27, 1863

HOOKER ON TRACK, BRAGG DERAILED

XCEPT FOR THE RADICAL Republicans, no one seemed to like "Fighting Joe" Hooker after his humiliating defeat at Chancellorsville. Lincoln, however, was not ready to throw him away. He believed he could be repaired militarily and put to good use. But where and when?

Lincoln suggested giving him a corps command in the army he previously commanded. Maj. Gen. George Gordon Meade, Hooker's replacement, didn't want him. "It would be difficult for Hooker to be quiet under me or anyone else," Meade wrote in a private letter. He regarded Hooker as dangerous, ruthless, and overly ambitious. Besides, Hooker wouldn't be happy being a subordinate to someone who had been a subordinate to him.

The solution, however, wasn't all that complicated. Get him away from the Army of the Potomac and send him to the western theater. The opportunity came when Maj. Gen. William S. Rosecrans needed reinforcements at Chattanooga, Tennessee, for his besieged Army of the Cumberland. Hooker got the nod, along with the Eleventh and Twelfth Corps, which were pulled from the Army of the Potomac. These corps were equally unwanted in the eastern theater after their poor performances at Chancellorsville and Gettysburg.

The entire force—twenty thousand men, artillery, horses, and equipment—traveled twelve hundred miles via dozens of railroad trains and reached the railhead at Bridgeport, Alabama, near Chattanooga during the first week of October 1863. Such a large body of troops had never before been relocated this fast—roughly eleven days—over such a great distance.

A month earlier, Rosecrans's Army of the Cumberland had been badly beaten at Chickamauga in northern Georgia by Braxton Bragg's Army of Tennessee. The shattered Union forces retreated to Chattanooga, on the south bank of the Tennessee River near the Georgia state line. A sharp U-shape bend in the river, combined with mountains on three sides, enabled Bragg's seventy thousand veterans to place Chattanooga under siege. Rather than attack, Bragg chose to starve the thirty-five thousand Federals and force them to surrender.

Lincoln wired Rosecrans: "Be of good cheer. We have unabated confidence in you and your soldiers and officers. We shall do our utmost to assist you." Rosecrans's reply expressed doubt that he could remain in Chattanooga: "Our loss is heavy and our troops worn down. . . . We have no certainty of holding our position here." His negativism disturbed Lincoln. From the president's perspective, the important thing was not that Rosecrans had

Confederates attack a wagon train carrying supplies to Chattanooga. Frequent raids along this slow, treacherous mountain route kept Union soldiers trapped in the town and on a near-starvation diet. When Grant arrived on the scene, his first challenge was to develop a new supply line.

LESLIE'S

been whipped at Chickamauga but that he still held Chattanooga. The city was critical to the Union's war strategy to keep the Confederates out of Tennessee and prevent them from using their most important railroads.

"If we can only maintain this position without [doing anything] more," the president told General in Chief Henry W. Halleck, "the Rebellion can only eke out a short and feeble existence, as an animal sometimes may with a thorn in its vitals."

The Federal position was seriously threatened by Rebel artillery on the mountain heights that controlled access to Chattanooga. Bragg's army occupied the six-mile crest of Missionary Ridge east of the city. Rebel guns on the summit of Lookout Mountain commanded a field of fire on the south and west. Bragg also placed units north of the city and held the west bank of the river at Brown's Ferry, the only access to the city from the west. These positions cut off all avenues of retreat or supply.

In Washington, Lincoln fretted as time passed and the Army of the Cumberland fasted on quarter-rations. A Union officer remembered that "guards stood at the troughs of artillery horses to keep the soldiers from taking the scant supply of corn." He observed that "men followed the wagons, picking up the grains of corn and bits of crackers that fell to the ground."

Faced with a pending disaster, the president consolidated the western armies into the Division of the Mississippi and placed Maj. Gen. Ulysses S. Grant in charge with instructions to deal with the situation in Chattanooga. With the reorganization, Maj. Gen. William T. Sherman would take over Grant's Army of the Tennessee (not to be confused with Bragg's Army of Tennessee), and Maj. Gen. Ambrose E. Burnside would continue his leadership of the Army of the Ohio. In one of his first acts as commander of the Division of the Mississippi, Grant relieved Rosecrans of command. His generalship at Chickamauga was unacceptable, as was his inclination to retreat from Chattanooga. Grant replaced Rosecrans with the "Rock of Chickamauga," Maj. Gen. George H. Thomas. Thomas was directed to hold Chattanooga "at all hazards" against the Confederate siege. "We will hold the town till we starve," Thomas replied.

Sherman, who was in Vicksburg, was summoned to bring seventeen thousand troops to support Grant. And the War Department dispatched Hooker and twenty thousand men from Alabama to protect the Union railroad leading to Chattanooga.

Grant himself arrived in Chattanooga on Friday, October 23. He was not a happy warrior when he discovered that Hooker had been thrust upon him by Lincoln and Stanton. Grant didn't want Hooker around. He wired Stanton that Hooker's "presence here is replete with trouble and danger." Hooker himself later told Radical leader Zachariah Chandler that Grant hated him and that Grant's friends were trying to engineer him out of the army. Nevertheless, Hooker was there, and Grant had to live with it.

Grant's first challenge was to develop a supply line to feed the hungry Federals in the besieged city. Thomas's chief engineer, Maj. Gen. William F. "Baldy" Smith conceived a well-thought-out plan that Grant adopted quickly. Smith led a two-pronged approach overland and down the river, using forces under Hooker and Thomas. Operating under cover of darkness, they headed from different directions toward Brown's Ferry. It was close to the city but beyond the reach of all but the longest-range guns on Lookout Mountain. One of Thomas's columns captured the ferry's Rebel outpost while another column floated downriver in pontoon boats to the ferry. Once there, they anchored them, and an engineering detachment floored them, creating a bridge for the Union troops to cross over.

Then Hooker's and Thomas's forces merged for cleanup operations. They dislodged enemy artillery on Raccoon Mountain and cleared the road of Rebels all the way west to Kelly's Ferry, where the river had curved back to parallel the crossing at Brown's Ferry. This done, the new supply route from Bridgeport to Chattanooga was securely in Federal hands. They called it the "Cracker Line."

On October 30 a small steamboat Baldy Smith put together completed a thirty-mile run from the Union supply post at Bridgeport with a cargo of forty thousand rations. The besieged troops cheered: "The Cracker Line's open. Full rations, boys! Three cheers for the Cracker Line!"

Grant could now go on the offensive, but he didn't want to move until Sherman's seventeen thousand troops arrived from Vicksburg. Bragg, meanwhile, boldly or stupidly sent away nearly one-fourth of his army—Longstreet's fifteen thousand infantry—on a mission to "destroy or capture" Burnside's army in east Tennessee, about a hundred miles northeast. Longstreet protested, concerned that his departure would leave the main body dangerously exposed—a force strung out along six miles around two sides of Chattanooga.

Grant saw that too and hoped to strike and defeat Bragg before Longstreet could attack Burnside and return. In the meantime, Burnside would have to go it alone while being under instructions to keep Longstreet from returning to Chattanooga as long as possible. Burnside did this by skirmishing and falling back, avoiding a major confrontation.

Jefferson Davis, keenly aware of the situation, advised Bragg: "[Don't] allow [Grant] to get up all his reinforcements before striking him." But Bragg did not attack.

On November 15, four of Sherman's five divisions reached Bridgeport, and Sherman rode by way of the Cracker Line to confer with Grant and inspect the area.

On November 16, Burnside continued to avoid a major battle with Longstreet by withdrawing his twenty thousand troops into Knoxville. When Longstreet reached the outskirts of the city the next day, he found the bluecoats skillfully deployed and well dug in. He began a siege of the city.

Back in Chattanooga, Grant prepared for action while the unsuspecting Bragg reduced his force again. This time Bragg shifted eleven thousand men to reinforce Longstreet at Knoxville.

On November 23, troops from Thomas's Army of the Cumberland easily captured Orchard Knob, a hill to the west of Missionary Ridge in Chattanooga, and Grant quickly moved his headquarters there.

Bragg's remaining Confederates controlled Missionary Ridge and Lookout Mountain. Grant's strategy was to place the demoralized Army of the Cumberland at the base of the ridge as a front-line barrier while other Union forces did the real fighting on the flanks. Sherman's Army of the Tennessee was to attack the right flank; Fighting Joe Hooker, the left. Hooker's mission was to carry Lookout Mountain, clear the Confederates out of the valley between Lookout Mountain and Missionary Ridge, and then threaten Bragg's army from the rear (the south end of the ridge).

Three Confederate brigades, occupying the northern slope, held Lookout Mountain. Bragg made no attempt to strengthen these forces. He believed the mountain was impregnable. He was sure that if the Federals tried to attack it, they'd "break their heads" against its rocks. Hooker was hardheaded enough to prove him wrong.

The west side of the mountain confronting Hooker's command was indeed rugged—an obstacle course of boulders, chasms, and timber. Even if there had been no opposing force, troops would have struggled to advance over such terrain. Farther up the mountain, a plateau accommodated a farmhouse. Beyond it was another steep climb. On the east side of the mountain, the slope was more gradual. A good wagon road zigzagged up it, connecting the town with the summit.

Hooker led ten thousand men forward around 8 a.m. on November 24 after a cold, drizzling rain left thick clouds of mist on the mountain. His troops came directly against Maj. Gen. Carter L. Stevenson's division, which was posted on the forward slopes and summit. The Federals outnumbered the defenders six to one, but the Rebels had the high ground—an advantage neutralized by the rugged terrain, which limited their placement of artillery.

"The sound of [Hooker's] artillery and musketry was heard incessantly," Grant noted from his command post. But he couldn't see the action because of the heavy mist that gave the battle its name—the "Battle Above the Clouds."

Joseph S. Fullerton, chief of staff for the Fourth Corps, described the action after Hooker's divisions united in the enemy's field:

> [Hooker's] line, hanging at the base of the palisades like a great pendulum, reached down the side of the mountain to the valley. . . . As it swung forward in its upward movement, the artillery of the Army of the Cumberland, on Moccasin Point, opened fire, throwing a stream of shot and shell into the enemy's rifle-pits at the foot of the mountain, and into the works thickly planted on the plateau. At the same time the guns planted by Hooker on the west side of Lookout Creek opened up on the works which covered the enemy's right. Then followed a gallant assault.

In the daylong skirmish in the fog and mist, Hooker's troops scrambled up the steep mountainside. They advanced over and through deep gullies and ravines and over giant rocks and fallen trees as Rebel gun crews fired with precision into their ranks. But as the Federals drew closer, the Rebels couldn't lower their guns sufficiently to avoid overshooting.

Stevenson reinforced the summit with two brigades, and Maj. Gen. John C. Breckinridge rode over to personally direct the defense. But all the former U.S. vice president could do was hold out until nightfall. After a brief hard fight on the plateau midway up the north face of the mountain, the Rebels fell back, and Hooker called a halt to secure his gains. Daylight had turned into dusk, and Hooker chose to rest his weary men for the next day's fight.

Fullerton observed: "As the sun went down the clouds rolled away, and the night came on clear and cool. A grand sight was old Lookout that night.

LESLIE'S

"Fighting Joe" Hooker redeemed his reputation—tarnished by his earlier defeat at Chancellorsville—by seizing in spectacular fashion the seemingly impregnable Confederate position on Lookout Mountain.

Not two miles apart were the parallel campfires of the two armies, extending from the summit of the mountain to its base, looking like streams of burning lava, while, in between, the flashes from the skirmishers' muskets glowed like giant fireflies."

During the night the Confederate campfires died out, and the Rebels abandoned the mountain. They withdrew eastward from Lookout to join the main Rebel line in the defense of Missionary Ridge.

Hooker had seized the seemingly impregnable Lookout Mountain in spectacular fashion. To celebrate their victory, eight adventurous volunteers from Hooker's Eighth Kentucky Infantry scaled the cliffs before daylight and planted a huge American flag at the mountain's highest point. The morning was cloudless, and the men from the Army of the Cumberland, positioned below on the plain, broke into cheers at the sight of the fluttering flag.

With fewer than five hundred casualties, Hooker had carried the entire mountain, a remarkable feat. His success cleared the way for the primary effort against Missionary Ridge, where the Rebels were strongly dug in. The ridge was all that remained of Bragg's line around Chattanooga.

On November 25, Hooker's troops descended the eastern slope of Lookout Mountain and proceeded southeast across the valley. After a delay of four hours at Chattanooga Creek, where the retreating Rebels had burned the bridge, they continued to Rossville Gap at the south end of Bragg's entrenchment on Missionary Ridge. There, they captured supplies and drove the Rebels from the gap. Late in the afternoon they ascended the southern end of the ridge. Finding the Rebels spread out in pockets, Hooker attacked fiercely. After a few hours of fighting, the Rebels retreated. Many of them surrendered.

While Hooker was succeeding beyond expectations, Maj. Gen. Patrick R. Cleburne had stopped Grant's star general, Sherman, cold at Tunnel Hill at the north end of the ridge. One of the stubbornest fighters in the Confederacy, Cleburne refused to yield an inch of ground to Sherman's twenty-five thousand Federals. Grant expected Hooker to be inept, but not Sherman. Sherman threw in five divisions but could not move over or around the one gray division in his path. After eight hours of fighting and fifteen hundred casualties, he had accomplished nothing.

Grant's grand plan was teetering toward failure. To try to recover, in midafternoon he ordered Thomas to launch a limited assault against the front line of Confederate trenches and rifle pits at the base of Missionary Ridge. Grant hoped this action would prevent Bragg from reinforcing Cleburne. If Thomas succeeded, he was to stay in the trenches and wait for further orders.

Thomas sent twenty-three thousand men in a two-mile front straight at the Rebel line. As they rushed forward with bayonets glistening, the sight was too much for the Rebels in the pits and breastworks. They broke and ran pell-mell up the slopes, disrupting the other lines higher up and at the crest.

Although Thomas's divisions carried the trenches, this placed them in an untenable position. They were now easy targets

Maj. Gen. Patrick Cleburne, the "Stonewall Jackson of the West," stopped Sherman's advance at the north end of Missionary Ridge. Sherman's five divisions of twenty-five thousand Federals could not get around Cleburne's one division.

from above, and Rebel artillery and rifles opened up on them. Col. Frederick Knefler of the Seventy-ninth Indiana recalled: "Nothing could live in or about the captured line of field works. A few minutes of such terrific, telling fire would quickly convert the rifle pits into hideous slaughter pens. There was no time or opportunity for consultation or deliberation. Something drastic must be done—and it must be done very quickly." It was a critical moment in the battle.

Regardless of Grant's orders to stay put, the Cumberlanders weren't about to become sitting ducks. Common sense told them they couldn't stay where they were. They either had to retreat or go forward up the heights. They chose the latter—disproving Grant's expressed concern that they were so demoralized by the battle of Chickamauga that "they could not be got out of their trenches to assume the offensive." On their own initiative—with no orders from Grant or Thomas or anyone else—they spontaneously charged up the four-hundred-foot rocky ridge.

As soon as Grant saw their movement from his command post, he turned quickly to Thomas, who stood by his side, and asked angrily, "Who ordered those men up the ridge?"

Thomas replied in his usual slow, quiet manner: "I don't know; I did not."

Then Grant addressed Maj. Gen. Gordon Granger, commander of the Fourth Corps of the Army of the Cumberland: "Did you order them up, Granger?"

"No," said Granger, "they started up without orders. When those fellows get started, all hell can't stop them."

Grant said somebody would catch hell if this movement turned out badly. Stoically, he turned and watched the ridge as he clamped his teeth on a cigar. He gave no further orders.

On the ridge, the Rebel infantry couldn't use their full fire power out of fear of hitting their own retreating men. And the Rebel artillery was too poorly positioned among the rocks to be effective against the charge. Desperately, the Rebels hurled rocks and lit fuses of shells and rolled them down the slopes. But the Cumberlanders kept coming, with sixty regimental flags flying. "This was their fight," recalled Col. Benjamin Scribner. "Their officers had nothing to do with the advance."

As the Federals reached the summit, they quickly flung themselves up and into the Confederate breastworks before the Rebels realized their presence. As more Federals stampeded the Rebel lines, Bragg's army panicked, broke, and ran. The Cumberlanders, reinvigorated and excited, yelled at their backs, "Chickamauga! Chickamauga!"

Bragg and Breckinridge barely escaped. Bragg, who rode into the melee to try to rally his fleeing men, later wrote: "A panic which I had never before witnessed seemed to have seized upon officers and men, and each seemed to be struggling for his personal safety, regardless of his duty or his character. . . . No satisfactory excuse can possibly be given for the shameful conduct of our troops."

Cleburne had to abandon his position against Sherman to cover the retreat, as Bragg rescued most of his army and fled southward. They didn't stop until they had retreated thirty miles toward Atlanta. That night, in the flickering fire of a Confederate camp, one soldier described Bragg as "scared . . . whipped, and mortified." He was on the verge of annihilation. But Grant did not push his men to pursue the Rebels until the next day, when he ordered Thomas and Hooker to go after them.

Hooker caught up with Cleburne's rear guard at a narrow mountain pass at Ringgold, Georgia, but couldn't push through. With his supplies running out, Hooker called off the pursuit.

Soundly whipped, Bragg telegraphed Jefferson Davis: "I deem it due to the cause and to myself to ask for relief from command and investigation into the causes of the defeat." Davis concurred and replaced him temporarily with Lt. Gen. William J. Hardee and permanently with Gen. Joseph E. Johnston.

Grant wrote in his *Personal Memoirs* that the battle "was won against great odds . . . [and] under the most trying circumstances presented during the war . . . considering the advantage the enemy had of position."

When an observer later told Grant that Southern generals regarded their position as impregnable, Grant replied with a grin: "Well, it *was* impregnable."

Grant's 56,000 Federals captured more than 6,100 prisoners as well as forty pieces of artillery and seven thousand small arms. Confederates reported 361 killed and 2,160 wounded. Union losses were 752 killed, 4,713 wounded, and 350 captured or missing.

The victory didn't happen the way Grant intended, but it succeeded thanks primarily to Hooker, Baldy Smith, and the Army of the Cumberland. Together, they enabled Grant to break the monthlong siege, gain control of the strategic rail center at Chattanooga, and open the gateway to Atlanta. One Southerner observed that the defeat was "the death knell of the Confederacy."

Grant meanwhile ordered some of Sherman's divisions to rush to Knoxville to help Burnside. Longstreet, trying desperately to break Burnside's defensive lines before reinforcements arrived, struck at Fort Sanders and Fort Loudon near Knoxville on November 29. Unsuccessful, and being threatened from the rear by Sherman, he gave up the siege and retreated north to Greeneville, near the Virginia border. From there he could move east or west as the situation warranted.

Having won a double victory at Chattanooga and Knoxville, Grant went on to secure all of Tennessee for the Union. "It would have been a victory to have got the army away from Chattanooga safely," Grant wrote in his *Personal Memoirs*. "It was manifold greater to defeat, and nearly destroy, the besieging army."

Grant withheld praise of Hooker for his strong showing in taking Lookout Mountain, contemptuously writing after the war: "The Battle of Lookout Mountain is one of the romances of the war. There was no such battle

When troops from the Army of the Cumberland spontaneously charged up the slopes of Missionary Ridge, Bragg's army panicked and ran.

In this painting by Thure de Thulstrup, a Swedish-born American artist, Grant (in the upper left) watches the Union advance up Missionary Ridge. Maj. Gen. George H. Thomas is to the right of Grant.

and no action even worthy to be called a battle. . . . It is all poetry." But it wasn't poetry to the men who bled and died on both sides.

Hooker boldly stated at Chattanooga: "I find I am regarded with a great deal of jealousy by those filling high place here." He hoped that his general-ship would carry him through. "I have never yet seen the time that there was no place for a man willing to fight," he said.

More jealousy lay ahead. The following spring Hooker participated in Sherman's Atlanta campaign with his Eleventh and Twelfth Corps consoli-dated into the new Twentieth Corps. Sherman, like Grant, disdained Hooker. Yet Hooker and his corps did most of the fighting on the advance to Atlanta's outskirts. They performed superbly, while suffering the most casualties— more than five thousand. For whatever reason, success seemed to sour Sher-man's attitude toward Hooker. Sherman was determined to get rid of him one way or another.

When Brig. Gen. James B. McPherson, commander of the Union's Army of the Tennessee, was killed in the battle for Atlanta, Sherman bypassed the senior officer on the field, Maj. Gen. John A. Logan, and replaced McPherson with Hooker's nemesis, Maj. Gen. Oliver O. Howard. He was among those Hooker blamed for his defeat at Chancellorsville. If Sherman didn't want Logan because he wasn't a West Pointer, his logical choice was Hooker. He had seniority and the most experience. But as historian Stephen W. Sears pointed out in his book *Controversies and Commanders*, to choose Hooker's former subordinate was a "carefully calculated insult" designed to provoke Hooker's resignation. And that's exactly what happened.

"Justice and self-respect alike require my removal from an army in which rank and service are ignored," Hooker stated in his request to be relieved of duty in July 1864.

The Radical Republicans in Congress accused the Grant "gang" of trying to drive Hooker out of the army. They also charged that Henry W. Halleck had engineered a conspiracy to remove him.

Hooker gave up his command and never returned to the field, but he remained in the service until the end of the war. He retired from the army in 1868 after suffering a paralytic stroke at age fifty-four. Except for his poor performance at Chancellorsville and in the weeks immediately following, Fighting Joe had a brilliant combat record. He not only redeemed himself at Chattanooga and in the Atlanta campaign, but also became a national hero in the process. Hooker did not deserve the catty disrespect shown him by Grant and Sherman. Though they were great battlefield generals—the best in the Union army—they were blatantly wrong in their treatment of Joe Hooker. They seemed to fear him or his mouth more than the enemy. They wanted him to remain a military goat.

The real goat at Chattanooga was Braxton Bragg. Grant noted in his memoirs that victory was accomplished more easily than expected because Bragg made "several grave mistakes: first in sending away his ablest corps commander, with over [fifteen thousand] troops; second, in sending away a division of troops on the eve of battle; third, in placing so much of a force on the plain in front of his impregnable position." Grant also criticized Bragg's "harsh treatment" of his soldiers and his problems in working with subordinates. That, said Grant, led to their "great dissatisfaction" with him "and a disposition to get away if they could."

Among the generals who did get away before the battle of Chattanooga was the great cavalryman Nathan Bedford Forrest. He was promoted to major general and given an independent command by Jefferson Davis. If

Bragg had been able to get along with Forrest, and if he had been active at Chattanooga, the battle might have ended differently.

Bragg's poor leadership may have been due, in part, to his poor health. He suffered from migraine headaches, poor digestion, and rheumatism. While these problems may have contributed to his irascible temper and dour disposition, he probably would have been obstinate, haughty, and erratic even in the best of health.

As the fifth-highest-ranking officer in the Confederacy, much was expected of Bragg. Two months earlier he had inflicted one of the most complete defeats ever suffered by a Union army. Then, at Chattanooga, he bore one of the Confederacy's most humiliating defeats. If he had the right stuff at Chickamauga, he lost it at Chattanooga, a city third in importance only to Richmond and Atlanta.

The loss of this major rail center was devastating to the South and added nothing but misery to the Southerners' observance of the Christmas season. Diarist Mary Boykin Chesnut found "gloom and unspoken despondency hang[ing] like a pall everywhere."

Davis, who apparently never lost his respect for Bragg, made him one of his advisers through 1864. Bragg returned to the field near the end of the war to fight a losing battle against Sherman's forces in North Carolina in March 1865. Often called Davis's pet, Bragg accompanied him in his attempt to escape Union forces after the fall of Richmond. Bragg was taken prisoner on May 9 and paroled shortly thereafter. After the war he worked as a civil engineer in Alabama and Texas and served a four-year term as Alabama's commissioner of public works.

16

SPRING HILL, FRANKLIN, NASHVILLE: NOVEMBER–DECEMBER 1864

HOOD'S "IRRETRIEVABLE DISASTER"

IN THE FALL AND winter of 1864 the Confederates' last hope for success in the western theater depended upon the Army of Tennessee and its battered young leader, thirty-three-year-old John Bell "Sam" Hood. This great army of the West had fought bravely while suffering defeats under a succession of military goats—Albert Sidney Johnston, killed at Shiloh before he could prove himself; P. G. T. Beauregard, who abandoned his command; the irritable Braxton Bragg, who spent too much time fighting his own generals; and Joseph E. Johnston, relieved by Jefferson Davis for not bringing William T. Sherman to battle in the Atlanta campaign.

On July 17, 1864, Davis turned to Hood—the South's newest full general. Stonewall Jackson had called Hood a man to be reckoned with—at least on the battlefield. Known as a hell-for-leather fighter, Hood led the elite Texas Brigade at Gaines's Mill, Second Manassas, and Antietam. At Gettysburg, he led the assault on Little Round Top and lost the use of his left arm. At Chickamauga, he commanded Longstreet's corps and lost his right leg. Now he rode strapped to his horse. While courageous and brilliant as a brigade and division commander, he would be no match for tacticians like Sherman or Grant as head of an army.

After assuming command of the Army of Tennessee, Hood took a thumping in every battle he fought. He wasted his men in fruitless attacks in the defense of Atlanta and then came perilously close to losing his army during a siege.

When he evacuated Atlanta and moved his forty thousand men northward, Sherman countered by sending Maj. Gen. George H. Thomas and a division to Nashville to protect the Tennessee capital and its supply warehouses.

Hood developed a bold, grandiose plan that was also a grand gamble. He would invade middle Tennessee, take Nashville, and continue through Kentucky to the Ohio River. Then he would move eastward to join forces with Robert E. Lee and defeat Grant and Sherman. All was possible—if Hood moved quickly. He didn't because he failed to arrange in advance for supplies. This poor planning delayed him twenty days in Alabama. Heavy rains lashing the countryside also made him immobile. Moving infantry along muddy, rutted roads was impractical. Then came snow, freezing temperatures, and icy winds.

Under these latter conditions, Hood's army left its camp near Florence, Alabama, on November 21 and crossed into Tennessee. With the Confederacy unable to provide new shoes, a fourth of Hood's men wore footwear so rotten that they would soon be marching barefooted.

During this time, Thomas pulled forces into Nashville from garrisons throughout the state. Needing time to consolidate and organize, he detached the two corps of Maj. Gens. John M. Schofield and David Sloane Stanley to Pulaski, Tennessee, eighty miles south of Nashville.

Schofield, who was in command, was expected to scout Hood's movements and delay any advance he might make toward Nashville. If necessary or expedient, Schofield would return to Nashville to bolster Thomas's army.

Schofield was no stranger to Hood. The two had been roommates at West Point, where Schofield excelled and Hood goofed off, graduating forty-fourth in his class of fifty-two. Wild and indifferent to social customs, Hood accumulated 196 demerits in his senior year, just four short of expulsion. But now, as a military hero, the muscular six-foot-two general was praised by Robert E. Lee and adored by young women, many of whom found him captivating.

On the way to Nashville, two rivers were major obstacles for both armies—the Duck at Columbia and the Harpeth at Franklin. If Hood reached Columbia before Schofield and secured the Duck crossings, he would be between Schofield and Thomas and in a position to knock out one and then the other. If he succeeded, he would control Nashville and its supplies. He could then drive to the Ohio, perhaps divert Sherman from his march to the sea, and cross the mountains and support Lee.

The stakes were high. It was potentially a life-or-death situation for the Union. Schofield had to get to Columbia first and across the Duck River to avoid being cut off from Nashville.

Unknown to Schofield until the night of November 21, Hood's army was rushing north and approaching Lawrenceburg, twenty miles due west of Pulaski. Both towns were about the same distance to Columbia and the Duck River. The reports of Hood's location jarred both Thomas and Schofield. They could not imagine an army moving so quickly under such horrible weather conditions.

Now the galloping Sam Hood had the initiative with his fast start against his former West Point instructor, known as "Slow Trot" Thomas. To compensate, Thomas ordered Schofield to act on the defensive and slow down the Rebel army. "We will have to move accordingly without much delay," Schofield wrote that night. At sunrise the next morning, two Federal divisions began their march toward Columbia with artillery and eight hundred wagons. The remaining two divisions, under Stanley, would follow before the next morning. The race was on.

Fortunately for the Federals, Schofield had the most direct route. His lead divisions made it to Columbia on November 24, just ahead of Rebel troopers, and repulsed their attempts to seize the bridges. By the time Hood's main force arrived on November 26, Schofield's army was dug in on the outskirts of town with guns emplaced and breastworks anchored left and right on the river. Hood positioned his army facing the breastworks.

Schofield then outwitted his opponent by crossing the Duck to the north bank during the night of November 27–28 and destroying the two bridges behind him. Shortly afterward, Maj. Gen. James H. Wilson joined Schofield

The Confederate's John Bell Hood could have written a book on how to wreck an army, top to bottom, after his disastrous battles at Spring Hill, Franklin, and Nashville. His mismanagement also cost him the opportunity to destroy a Federal army. He was unparalleled as a successful brigade and division commander, but he was a goat as commander of an army.

Maj. Gen. John M. Schofield, a physicist and Baptist clergyman's son, commanded two corps assigned to scout Hood's movements and delay his advance toward Nashville.

with four thousand horsemen he had organized and trained. The twenty-seven-year-old Wilson, an Illinois-born West Pointer, was one of the Union's most distinguished "boy generals." Thomas had sent him to Schofield to protect the vital railroads and support his army.

Hood, not to be outdone, crossed the Duck three miles above Columbia the following morning and left two divisions to demonstrate in Schofield's front and prevent his rapid withdrawal. Hood would try a flanking movement to get around Schofield, beat him to Spring Hill—about twelve miles north of the Duck—and advance to Franklin and get control of the next obstacle—the Harpeth River. Per this scenario, Hood could either force Schofield to fight from a disadvantage or rush to Nashville and attack Thomas. It was a good plan—on paper.

As Hood moved northward three miles east of the turnpike and parallel to it, Confederate cavalry under Nathan Bedford Forrest made a wide turning movement to keep the Federal cavalry away from the Rebel infantry. Forrest then left one brigade to keep pressure on Wilson while he took forty-five hundred horsemen with him toward Spring Hill to seize it in advance of Hood's infantry. It was another good plan—on paper.

Hood, riding with Maj. Gen. Patrick R. Cleburne's advance column, noticed that his map differed significantly from their route. They were on a crooked backwoods road. Hood summoned a local guide who explained that his map was out of date, that he had missed the direct route, and that the abandoned road they were on was five miles longer than the main road. An aerial view would have shown the absurdity of forty thousand men marching in a zigzag pattern when a good straight road was nearby. Traveling this worst road in the area, the men became "weary and worn out." Hood would be way off schedule.

Meanwhile, Wilson had sent a warning to Schofield about the Confederate movement across the Duck, and Schofield had wired Thomas. "Withdraw to Franklin" was the response. So Schofield directed Stanley, commander of the Fourth Corps, to leave at daybreak with two divisions, the wagon train, and most of the guns. He was to leave one division at Rutherford Creek to guard against an enemy sweep along the creek and to provide cover for the rest of the army, which would soon follow.

The lead elements of the Union wagon train rolled into Spring Hill midmorning on November 29, preceded by four companies of the 73rd Illinois Infantry and 240 men of the 103rd Ohio Infantry. Also in Spring Hill was a new, untried regiment commanded by Lt. Col. Charles C. Hoefling, recently dispatched there from Nashville.

Suddenly, scouts reported swarms of Confederate cavalry approaching, causing grave concern about the threat to the vulnerable supply wagons. Hoefling frantically wired Schofield, who was still at Columbia, that he desperately needed help to defend the village.

Luck intervened. At this crucial time, the Third Illinois Cavalry and three companies of the Eleventh Indiana Cavalry were en route to Spring Hill after guarding the Duck River crossings west of Columbia. Arriving at 11 a.m. and sensing the danger, they rode eastward nearly two miles from town, created a barricade of rails and logs, and deployed in a battle line.

Soon they were joined by a company of the Second Michigan Cavalry that had barely escaped capture earlier that morning near the Duck River. After they alerted Hoefling about Rebel units on their flanks, he directed them east of town to join the cavalry outposts along the crest of a hill.

Forrest's cavalry struck this Federal line head-on, expecting only moderate resistance. Instead, they encountered sustained fire that stopped them and threw them back. Forrest, who had a much larger force than did the defenders, gradually recovered and gained ground, finally approaching the edge of Spring Hill. When he saw Union wagons still coming into the village, he ordered the Twenty-first Tennessee Cavalry to charge. Then the Second Michigan Cavalry came forward with a heavy barrage from the troopers' deadly Spencer carbines. Across the open field, the Tennesseans were easy targets.

The cavalries skirmished for four hours on the eastern side of Spring Hill as the Confederates continued their attempts to enter the town. They were thwarted by infantry, cavalry, and artillery along the turnpike. Two Federal batteries, including four 12-pounder Napoleons and six 3-inch ordnance rifles, mowed through the Confederate ranks, and the Southerners retreated in confusion.

A Wisconsin infantryman later wrote about the impact of the artillery on Forrest's cavalry: "You could see a Rebel's head falling off his horse on one side, and his body on the other, and the horse running and looking for its rider. . . . Others, the horse would get shot and the rider tumble head over heels, or maybe get caught by the horse falling on him."

Forrest, frustrated and running out of ammunition, wondered why Hood's infantry and artillery hadn't arrived.

During the cavalry engagements, Stanley, who had arrived around noon, strengthened his defensive positions, knowing that Rebel infantry, who had numerical superiority, could attack him. He was determined to keep Schofield's escape route open. From that point, everything went awry for the Confederates.

At Rutherford Creek, two and a half miles from Spring Hill, Hood instructed Maj. Gen. Benjamin F. Cheatham to push forward with three divisions and attack the Yankees at Spring Hill. Alexander P. Stewart's corps was to wait at the creek, ready to move when necessary. Then Hood rode to a hill overlooking the enemy's wagons along the turnpike and concluded that the Federals were too weak to launch an attack. The real danger, he realized, would come from the direction of Columbia, when Schofield's army came up the pike. So, without communicating with Cheatham, who was already in motion, Hood revised his plans. He directed Patrick R. Cleburne, his best division commander, to be in a position to strike for the turnpike and confront Schofield's troops as they approached the town. That would keep Schofield's forces divided and enable Hood to attack and defeat Schofield's column and then overwhelm Stanley at Spring Hill.

Hood went to the rear, to a vintage farm home where he stayed the rest of the day and through the night. During the two remaining daylight hours between 4 p.m. and 6 p.m. he would know little about the crucial, fast-developing circumstances at the front. Thus, Hood and Cleburne had one tactical strategy in mind while Cheatham was operating under earlier orders that were totally different. Hood's failure to communicate new orders to Cheatham was one of the worst mistakes of the war.

Cleburne's infantrymen, while going forward toward the turnpike, unknowingly passed near a concealed line of Federal breastworks and were subjected to intense fire. Rebel brigade commander Brig. Gen. Mark Lowrey swung to attack them and ran into a brigade of new recruits from the Midwest.

Maj. Gen. David Sloane Stanley saved Schofield's command at Spring Hill through effective use of artillery combined with confusion among the Confederate generals.

Lowrey sought help from Cleburne, and the Irishman jerked his fist upward and exclaimed, "I'll charge them!" When he did, he outflanked the midwesterners, and they fled in disorder. Cleburne's two brigades ran after them, shooting some in the back, and yelling, "Halt, you Yankee sons of bitches!" But it was the Rebels who came to an abrupt halt. Stanley's artillery—eighteen guns on a ridge—mauled Cleburne's line and sent them scurrying for cover.

As Cleburne re-formed his brigades for another assault, Cheatham ordered them to stop. Cleburne was to wait and be part of Cheatham's attack on Spring Hill. Cheatham was fulfilling his earlier, never withdrawn, assignment. The rough-and-tumble fighter from Tennessee ordered all troops to concentrate. Nearly nineteen thousand men streamed from all directions to prepare to rout Stanley's meager Federal force of six thousand. Stanley's situation appeared hopeless.

Cheatham, who had been waiting for Maj. Gen. William B. Bate's division, decided to look for it himself. Cheatham also made a hasty visit to Hood at the farmhouse to tell him about Cleburne's stalled advance and the renewed attack in preparation. Hood apparently asked few questions and assumed the attack would be in Cleburne's sector. Cheatham, however, assumed Hood knew he was talking about the assault on Spring Hill.

At 5:30 p.m. Maj. Gen. John C. Brown sent Rebel skirmishers forward on the extreme right. He was to lead the assault against the ridge on the town's outskirts. The sound of his small-arms fire would be the signal for other troops to attack in their sectors.

More time than necessary passed, and Cleburne grew impatient. Cheatham, nearing Bate's position, asked his staff: "Why don't we hear Brown's guns?"

Brown had just started his advance when veteran brigade commander Otto F. Strahl rode up and told Brown his line was outflanked to the east by Federal infantry and that, if he continued, his men would be caught in a crossfire from both flank and front. Brown looked and saw the Union troops. On the advice of his brigade commanders, Brown decided not to advance farther until he had conferred with Cheatham, who was looking for Bate. One of Cheatham's staff officers found him and reported the suspended attack. Cheatham met with Brown at 6:15 p.m., and Brown told him it would be "inevitable disaster" to make an attack without protection on his right flank. Brown wondered where Forrest was; Forrest had disappeared.

Night set in. Brown's men were exhausted. A force of unknown size was in their front. Cheatham was not a risk taker. He rubber-stamped Brown's action and called off the attack. Cheatham then rode to Hood's farmhouse to brief him.

Earlier that afternoon Hood brought up Alexander P. Stewart from Rutherford Creek with instructions to take his corps north of Spring Hill to cut off a Federal retreat.

When Cheatham showed up at Hood's headquarters, Hood demanded, "Why in the name of God have you not attacked the enemy and taken possession of that pike?" Cheatham explained that an enemy force had outflanked his exposed right, and he needed Stewart's help. Hood quickly dispatched a staffer to tell Stewart to join with Cheatham's right flank.

The order surprised Stewart, but he redirected the march of his eight-thousand-man corps and then went with the staff officer to find Cheatham. Instead they met with Brown, and he asked Stewart to extend the line to Brown's east, away from the turnpike. He obeyed.

Hood also had ordered Bate's twenty-one-hundred-man division to join Cleburne's division in protecting the pike south of Spring Hill. Bate couldn't find Cleburne, because Cheatham had already deployed him to the "concentration." Shortly, one of Cheatham's staff officers who was looking for Bate ordered him to move up on Cheatham's left flank. Bate didn't want to leave the pike uncovered, but he had no choice.

Col. Emerson Opdycke's disobedience at Franklin enabled him to lead his Union brigade in a countercharge that stopped the initial penetration of a frontal assault. His success determined the outcome of the battle—and aided his promotion to general.

Because of the poor communication between Hood and Cheatham, the turnpike was left open. Cheatham, after canceling the attack on Spring Hill, apparently gave no further thought to the pike. Regardless of orders, his one-dimensional thinking was inexcusable. He had become another Confederate goat.

Stymied by stupidity and narrow-mindedness, Cheatham ordered his men to bivouac until morning. Stewart's corps also went into camp, next to Cheatham. Forrest, who wasn't around for Cheatham's expected assault, had pulled back at 4:30 with his exhausted troopers. Nearly out of ammunition, and with Hood's supply wagons far to the rear, he and his troopers bedded down for the night.

Back at the farm home, Hood unstrapped his artificial leg around 9 p.m., swallowed a tincture of opium for his pain from falling off his horse that day, and went to sleep. He assumed Schofield's main force was still at Columbia since he had received no report to the contrary. If the Federals were anywhere south of Spring Hill, they were trapped, Hood assured himself; they were at his mercy. He was convinced they could not possibly march through Spring Hill past the arrayed Confederate troops in the middle of the night. He expected to fight them in the morning and destroy them.

Actually, Schofield had marched out of Columbia many hours earlier and was on the edge of Spring Hill. Everything was quiet; no one was in his path. The Federal army continued up the pike and right through the town. Seeing Confederate campfires east of the road, they marched quietly, passing sleeping Confederates within a hundred yards of them. By daybreak the Federals were gone. Schofield later wrote in his memoirs, "Since the Confederates were all asleep and the Union troops were all awake, there was no reason not to continue the march to Franklin."

When Hood awakened that morning and learned that Schofield had escaped, he was furious; "wrathy as a rattlesnake . . . striking at everything," reported a staff officer. Hood especially blamed Cheatham for "this grave misfortune" and strongly criticized Cheatham's division commanders Brown and Cleburne.

But Hood's horrendous communications, careless attitude, and bad military management made him the primary goat, with Cheatham a close second. They had missed their best chance to get between Schofield and Thomas and defeat Schofield's army. Hood later said this "best move in my career I was thus destined to behold come to naught." He called it the greatest lost opportunity "to utterly rout and destroy the Federal army." Corps commander Stephen D. Lee referred to it as "one of the most disgraceful and lamentable occurrences of the war, one that is in my opinion unpardonable." A Texas lieutenant commented, "The most charitable explanation is that the gods of war injected confusion into the heads of our leaders."

Having lost his prey, Hood would not be deterred. He took up the chase. He would make one final effort to overtake and rout Schofield's army before it reached the Union stronghold at Nashville. "I will drive them into the Harpeth River at Franklin," he boasted.

Schofield made it safely to Franklin at dawn on November 30 with his two lead divisions and seven-mile wagon train. Then he faced another problem. To get to Nashville—twenty miles north of Franklin—he had to move his wagons across the Harpeth, but its turnpike bridge had been wrecked by the rising river. Since he didn't have any pontoons, he put his engineers to work flooring the railroad bridge with planks removed from nearby houses.

After they found a fordable section of the river near the town, Schofield, Wilson's cavalry, and Stanley and most of his artillery crossed to the northern side. By midmorning the railroad bridge was usable, and the eight hundred wagons began crossing over.

Schofield placed three divisions—about seventeen thousand troops—on the south side of the river, about a half mile from the town. Their fortifications stretched in a mile-and-a-half semicircle, touching the river on the north and south while straddling the Columbia Pike, the main route into Franklin.

Brig. Gen. George D. Wagner commanded the rear guard of Schofield's forces. Three of his brigades stayed a half mile in front of the entrenchments on the crest of Winstead Hill. If Hood came up and "showed a disposition to advance in force," the brigades were to retire within the main lines as a reserve force.

One brigade commander, however, chose to disobey orders and retire earlier. Col. Emerson Opdycke's men had been standing rear guard for hours. They were exhausted and hungry, and Opdycke didn't like being in an exposed position. After an angry exchange with Wagner, Opdycke marched his brigade back to the lines around Franklin and allowed them to eat and rest. (His disobedience, as will be seen later, may have saved Schofield's army.) Schofield issued orders that, if Hood's army didn't attack before sunset, all troops on the south side of the Harpeth should cross the railroad bridge and rejoin the rest of the army, which would then proceed to Nashville.

On the north side of the river, Brig. Gen. Thomas J. Wood's division took positions on the high bank overlooking the town and the fields south of the entrenchments. Wood was well situated to protect the Nashville Pike and to move quickly to assist Wilson's horsemen in dealing with Rebel flankers on that side of the river.

Sixty powerful guns protected the front and the flanks. They faced the unobstructed, two-mile-deep plain south of the entrenchments.

Schofield was ready for whatever Hood chose to throw at him. Each side would have about twenty thousand infantry up for the battle.

By midafternoon Hood was within three miles of Franklin with two corps. He had moved in "light marching order," that is, without the encumbrances of his wagons and artillery—a huge mistake. He dismounted with the help of an orderly who handed him his crutches. Looking through his field glasses, he studied the Yankee position. When he lowered his glasses, he said, "We will make the fight."

Hood's generals couldn't believe their ears. "Make the fight?" They saw the flat plain and the cannon and the fortifications as a killing ground that would favor the defending Yankees.

"Yes, make the fight," Hood repeated. He called for an all-out frontal assault within the hour.

Cheatham and Cleburne opposed the plan. It made no sense to them. They didn't have adequate artillery to soften up the Federal defenses; the enemy was dug in with strong artillery support.

Cleburne borrowed a telescopic sight. "They have three lines of works," he said aloud, "and they are all completed. . . . I don't like the looks of the fight."

Maj. Gen. Benjamin Cheatham was Hood's scapegoat at Spring Hill. Hood had ordered Cheatham to attack the Yankees there but then changed his mind—without telling Cheatham. The confusion led to a concentration of forces in the wrong place and helped to squander one of the best tactical battlefield opportunities of the war.

Cavalry commander Nathan Bedford Forrest told Hood he lacked good sense. Forrest argued, "Give me one strong division of infantry with my cavalry and within two hours I can flank the Federals from their works."

Hood wouldn't listen. His subordinates had, after all, failed him at Spring Hill. "No! No!" he exclaimed. "Charge them out!" He apparently believed the charge would purge his commanders of their timidity and improve his army's morale after its bitter disappointment at Spring Hill.

Earlier, Hood's critics had complained in Richmond that he had "the heart of a lion and a head of wood." Biographer John P. Dyer wrote that the general's concept of battle was a long line of men "charging to glory across an open field." On the plains before Franklin he again would execute that concept.

At four o'clock, the charge was launched with the wave of a flag. Regimental bands played "Dixie" and "The Bonnie Blue Flag." It was a grand spectacle. With battle flags fluttering in the late afternoon sun, twenty-two thousand soldiers swept forward across the plain to attack the three Union divisions behind their works. The tramp of marching feet rolled across the ground like the "low, hollow rumble of distant thunder," said one onlooker.

After observing the advancing Rebels, Wagner's two brigades of four thousand men were supposed to return to the main lines, but their officers made them stay put. They even fired a couple of short-range volleys. Soon, eight thousand Confederates charged against the front and flanks of these hapless brigades, and the midwesterners ran for the main Federal entrenchments. With a bone-chilling Rebel Yell, the graybacks charged after them and captured more than seven hundred. The Federals in the main line didn't fire into the clashing lines for fear of shooting their comrades.

The Rebels kept coming. They penetrated the earthworks and opened a two-hundred-yard gap in Schofield's line. Soldiers from Wagner's brigades dropped exhausted into the ditches. The battled raged above their heads.

From Fort Granger across the river, Schofield watched in shock. "For a moment, my heart sank within me," he recalled in his memoirs. Then two dozen guns along the Federal line opened up, and Opdycke's rested brigade followed with a strong charge into the oncoming Confederates. It was a full-scale melee. The Rebels fell back to the front of the works. Both sides exchanged point-blank fire across the entrenchment and then engaged in hand-to-hand combat. The Rebels got the worst of it and withdrew. Opdycke's troops prevailed. They took nearly four hundred prisoners. Had

Opdycke obeyed orders and remained with the isolated brigades far to the front, Schofield's army might have been defeated.

Meanwhile, the Rebel divisions attacking on the Union left were stalled by a thick four-foot-high hedge of thorny Osage orange trees. Unable to get through, they came under heavy fire from the big guns at Fort Granger. When the divisions changed their position to avoid these guns, they were struck by other batteries on their flank. Brig. Gen. John Adams tried to rally and guide his men by leaping a parapet, but both horse and rider were struck. Adams was hit by seven to nine bullets and fell into the inner ditch.

Elsewhere along the line, Rebels were hit by flanking fire from both sides as they confronted Yankees with repeating rifles. An onlooker said that the weapons "blazed out a continuous sheet of destruction."

Hood's divisions hurled themselves at Schofield's lines time after time with no success. "They came up to the very works," a Union colonel said later, "but they never [again] crossed them except as prisoners."

The outcome of the battle had been determined when Opdycke stopped the initial penetration. But the killing raged well into the night before ending in silence.

"I never seen men fight . . . more determined than the Rebs did," an Illinois sergeant later noted. "And I never seen enemy men fall so fast."

Confederate losses were heavy everywhere. One Confederate officer said later, "It seemed to me that hell itself had exploded in our faces."

Nearly seven thousand fell, about a quarter of Hood's army. Eighteen hundred died. Among the Confederate dead or mortally wounded were fifty-four regimental commanders and five generals, including the irreplaceable Stonewall of the West, Patrick R. Cleburne, regarded as one of the South's best fighting generals. While trying to swing the weight of his brigade toward the cotton gin at the center of the Union line, he disappeared into a cloud of powder smoke. He was struck by a single bullet through the heart. The loss of general officers in the Confederate army was more than that suffered by either side in any other battle of the war. Hood had wrecked his army, top to bottom. Confederate Gen. Joseph E. Johnston referred to the battle of Franklin as "useless butchery."

Union casualties totaled 2,326, of whom about 700 were killed. More than half of the casualties were from Wagner's division. Except for Maj. Gen. David Sloane Stanley, who took a bullet in the back of his neck, no Federal above the rank of colonel was among the casualties.

When Confederates approached Nashville, they saw the Union flag atop the Tennessee State Capitol and heard military music. The new capitol building, completed in 1859, was situated on a high hill, dominating the city landscape.

Early the next morning, Hood finally had his artillery on the field, and he began to bombard the Union entrenchments with a hundred guns. That's what he should have done the previous day if he had had the foresight to wait for his artillery until launching his grand assault. This time, the bombardment proved embarrassing. Shortly after it began, word came back that there was nothing in the earthworks except the dead and wounded. During the previous night, Schofield had withdrawn his army across the river under the "strictest silence." He had wrapped the wheels of his cannon with blankets and spread blankets across the planks of the railroad bridge. Then he burned the bridge behind him. By noon, Schofield and his army were in Nashville. He talked to Thomas, then went to bed and slept until sunset the next day.

Back at Franklin, Hood lamented his heavy loss of officers and soldiers but said, "We have shown to our countrymen that we can carry any position occupied by our enemy." A Missouri captain noted, "Two such victories will wipe out any army the power of man can organize."

Surprisingly, one of Hood's staunchest defenders was his opponent, Schofield. Describing the situation at Franklin, he later wrote:

> Hood must have been aware of our relative weakness of numbers at Franklin, and of the probable, if not certain, concentrations of large reinforcements at Nashville. He could not hope to have at any future time anything like so great an advantage in that respect. The army at Franklin and the troops at Nashville were within one day's march of each other; Hood must therefore attack on November 30 or lose the advantage of greatly superior numbers. It was impossible, after the pursuit from Spring Hill, in a short day to turn our position or make any other attack but a direct one in front. Besides our position with the river on our rear, gave him the chance of vastly greater results, if his assault were successful, than could be hoped for by any attack he could make after we had crossed the Harpeth.
>
> The Confederate cause had reached a condition closely verging on desperation, and Hood's commander in chief had called upon him to undertake operations that he thought appropriate to such an emergency. Franklin was the last opportunity he could expect to have to reap the results hoped for in his aggressive movement. He must strike there, as best he could, or give up his cause as lost.

The next day Hood marched for Nashville. Thomas then had sixty thousand men to defend the city. Not wanting to attack entrenched troops again, Hood placed his twenty-three thousand men in a defensive position and waited for Thomas to attack him. Two weeks passed. Hood then made a tactical error. He sent his cavalry and two infantry brigades away from Nashville on a mission to cut Thomas's supply line and harass the Union garrison at Murfreesboro. His timing proved fatal.

During these two weeks Thomas went about his preparations methodically and unhurried. "Old Pap," as his men called him, was not one to be rushed. Not only was he completing defensive lines around Nashville and the three pikes coming in from the south, he also was preparing to take Hood and his army out of the war for good. No one could deliver combat power like the Rock of Chickamauga. But he required time to do it. Thomas had adequate infantry for the job, but he was short on cavalry. Before mounting an attack, he needed more cavalrymen and more horses.

Newspapers reported the presence of Hood's army outside of Nashville.

That caused anxiety in Washington and throughout the North. Thomas's slowness annoyed the War Department and congressmen. Telegrams rocketed back and forth. Thomas was no longer worried about Hood. But he resented the pressure from the capital to act quickly. With his strong fortifications he believed he could safely remain on the defensive until he felt his force was potent enough to attack.

Secretary of War Edwin M. Stanton, trying to micromanage the battle from Washington without seeing the situation, believed Thomas's potency was already adequate. He directed Thomas to attack Hood "before he fortifies" or gets away. Grant, now the commanding general of all Union armies, added, "After the repulse of Hood at Franklin it looks to me that instead of falling back to Nashville, we should have taken the offensive against the enemy where he was."

Thomas patiently responded that, after Franklin, his force wasn't sufficient to take the offensive, but that it would be in a few days. He urgently needed more cavalry, he said, and especially more horses for the unmounted cavalrymen in Nashville. He was in the process of impressing every horse in the city.

On December 6, Grant fired back with a direct order to attack at once. Old Pap said he would, but then two days later wired Washington that he needed more time to perfect his arrangements. "There is no better man to repel an attack," Grant said of Old Pap, "but I fear he is too cautious ever to take the initiative."

Grant, overly impatient and not taking into account Thomas's remarkable record of never having failed in any operation, asked chief of staff Henry W. Halleck to replace Thomas with Schofield. Halleck drew up the order, but before sending it, he wired Thomas that Grant was furious about the delay.

Thomas replied that "a terrible storm of freezing rain" made an attack impossible, but if they wanted to replace him, they should do so. Thomas said he regretted Grant's "dissatisfaction," and added, "I have done everything in my power. . . . If he should order me to be relieved, I will submit without a murmur." Grant relented and suspended the order.

Thomas could not comprehend how Grant could conclude what was practicable for a hastily assembled army. But Thomas's chief of staff, Brig. Gen. William D. Whipple, suggested that someone was "using the wires to undermine" him in Washington or City Point (where Grant was based).

Nashville's strong fortifications, such as this ironclad casemate at Fort Negley, helped persuade Hood not to attack the city. A series of shots from this artillery battery initiated the two-day battle of Nashville.

Whipple believed that the Judas in their midst was Schofield, and this was confirmed when a staffer found at the telegraph office the original copy of a recent message from Schofield to Grant. In Schofield's handwriting, it read: "Many officers here are of the opinion that General Thomas is certainly slow in his movements."

"Why does he send such telegrams?" Thomas asked Maj. Gen. James Blair Steedman, a hero of Chickamauga who was in the room.

Steedman responded, "Who is next in command to you in case of removal?"

Thomas paused for a moment. "Oh, I see." He shook his head in disgust.

On December 11, Grant continued the telegraphic goading. Fearing that the Rebel army might move for the Ohio River and then east to Virginia, he asserted, "Delay no longer!" Grant demanded that Thomas attack, ice or no ice, with or without reinforcements.

Thomas replied: "I will obey the order as promptly as possible, however . . . the attack will have to be made under every disadvantage. The whole country is covered with a perfect sheet of ice and sleet." He sent a similar message to Halleck.

Finally, on December 14, warmer weather returned, the ice melted, and Thomas finalized his plans to attack Hood. He wired Halleck, "The enemy will be attacked tomorrow."

Grant meanwhile had ordered Maj. Gen. John A. Logan to Nashville to assume command if the army had not attacked by the time he arrived. And Grant himself prepared to go to Nashville.

While a heavy fog covered most of Nashville on December 15, fifty thousand bluecoats moved into position to attack Hood's twenty-five thousand. As an added bonus for the Federals, most of the Rebel cavalry was still thirty miles away, obeying orders to watch a small Union force at Murfreesboro.

The Federals made strong demonstrations along Hood's entire front to keep the enemy's infantry in place. Then they struck at both flanks. One division, including two brigades of African American soldiers, attacked Hood's right before sunrise. The major blow came shortly after noon on Hood's left from two infantry corps and a division under Schofield. The constant jabs on the right and fierce blows on the left forced Hood to retreat two miles to a shorter line anchored by hills.

Although Hood's army was in mortal danger of being destroyed, Hood decided to continue fighting for another day. Had he scampered south on the night of December 15, he might have saved most of his army. But strangled by his stubbornness, he didn't.

Thomas, meanwhile, wired Grant of his progress, and Grant responded, "Push the enemy now, and give him no rest until he is entirely destroyed."

On December 16, Thomas punched even more fiercely at the Rebels than he had the day before. He hit them with nonstop artillery bombardment all along their line. Adding to the pounding, two infantry corps smashed into the left flank head-on, and Wilson's cavalrymen dismounted with rapid-fire carbines, moved around the enemy's left flank, and delivered an enfilading fire into the rear of the line. Hit on three sides, and with envelopment almost completed, panic spread along the line. Rebel divisions vanished, more than four thousand surrendered, and others fled southward "in the wildest disorder and confusion."

Only two determined stands saved the Army of Tennessee from destruction. One brigade's rear-guard action held a position just long enough for Cheatham to get what was left of his corps to an escape route—the Franklin Pike. And Hood's remaining cavalry prevented Wilson's horsemen from cutting off all routes of escape. Otherwise, Hood's army would have been trapped.

Thomas's cavalry pursued the fleeing Rebels. He used every fresh horse he had acquired during those two weeks Grant and Stanton kept pushing him to attack.

Rebel cavalry fought a continuing rear-guard battle as the hungry infantry trudged along for 120 miles in the bitter cold. Many of them left bloody footprints on the crust of ice along the trail. All were close to exhaustion. Still, they were able to sing. And they did. To the tune of "Yellow Rose of Texas," they added new words:

> My feet are torn and bloody,
> My heart is full of woe;
> I'm going back to Georgia
> To see my Uncle Joe.
>
> You may talk about your Beauregard
> You may sing of Bobby Lee,
> But the gallant Hood of Texas,
> He played hell in Tennessee.

The chase continued for two weeks until the Confederates were across the Tennessee River and in Alabama. The remnants of the Army of Tennessee staggered into Tupelo, Mississippi, in January 1865. Of the forty thousand who had marched northward seven weeks earlier, only about fifteen thousand returned. Hood, depressed, relinquished his command and his temporary commission as a full general. By early spring, no significant Confederate forces existed in the western theater. The Army of Tennessee was reconstituted under Joseph E. Johnston. Less than four months later, it surrendered to Sherman in North Carolina.

At Nashville, Hood lost an estimated 40 percent of his army. More than 5,500 men were killed or wounded, another 4,500 were captured. Thomas lost about 3,000 of his 50,000 engaged. These included 387 killed, 2,562 wounded, and 112 missing.

When news of Hood's "irretrievable disaster" reached Richmond, ordnance chief Josiah Gorgas said, "This is one of the gloomiest [days] in our struggle." In Washington, Lincoln told the Congress, "We are gaining strength, and may, if need be, maintain the contest indefinitely. . . . [Our resources] are unexhausted and, we believe, inexhaustible."

Thomas's Nashville offensive was one of the best-planned attacks of the war. He shattered a splendid Southern army in stunning fashion. His success ended major combat in the western theater.

Hood is, of course, the goat of Spring Hill, Franklin, and Nashville. He led the brave and dedicated soldiers of the Army of Tennessee to defeat and to a rout as complete as any in the war. Lacking tactical skills and committing the military sins of mismanagement, poor communication, and bad judgment and timing, he wasted and wrecked the Confederacy's second most formidable army. It was an army the South could not afford to lose.

ANDERSONVILLE

17

ANDERSONVILLE: 1864–65

MISDIRECTED POPULAR CLAMOR

FOUR COMPANIES OF UNION solders surrounded the gallows in the court-yard of the Old Capitol Prison in Washington, D.C. The date was November 10, 1865, seven months after Robert E. Lee's surrender at Appomattox Court House. At about 10:15 a.m., forty-two-year-old Henry Wirz appeared in the yard, flanked by two Catholic priests. The soldiers snapped to attention. As Wirz walked up the thirteen steps to the platform, they chanted in unison, "Wirz, remember Andersonville! Wirz, remember Andersonville!" The 250 spectators clustered in the yard joined in the chanting. The sound was deafening. Clenched fists punched the air.

The major in charge apologized to Wirz for the crowd's behavior. "I deplore this duty," he said.

Wirz replied: "I know what orders are, Major. And I am being hanged for obeying them."

One of the priests asked Wirz if he had anything to confess. "No," he said. "I haven't done anything wrong to confess."

After the reading of the court's execution order, Wirz responded loudly: "I go before . . . Almighty God who will judge between us. I am innocent, and I will die like a man." He stood straight, his head slightly bowed, his shoulders back.

As the crowd continued its chanting, a black hood was placed over the condemned man's head and a noose around his neck. Then the trap was sprung. Wirz dropped through the opening. He squirmed for what seemed an eternity, dying slowly. The drop had failed to break his neck. It took an excruciating two minutes for Wirz to strangle to death. When it was over, the crowd cheered and yelled. Their voices finally subsided as they sensed that Wirz was getting his just reward in hell.

And so this Swiss immigrant who came to America for a better life found instead a short, bitter one. Wanting to be a physician—a healer—he ended up being hated so much that he became the first person legally executed in the United States for atrocities committed during a time of war—committed at a prison in southwest Georgia called Andersonville. It was officially known as Camp Sumter. Wirz was the prison's commandant.

The prison—actually a stockade—opened in February 1864 and closed in May 1865. During these fifteen months it quickly evolved into the worst "death camp" ever to exist on American soil. Why? The answer is complex.

Prisoner exchanges between North and South were an on-again-off-again practice during the war. In the first year, the Union government refused to negotiate prisoner exchanges, because it didn't recognize the Confederacy as a nation. But starting in July 1862 with an agreement between two generals—John Dix of the Union and Daniel Harvey Hill of the Confederacy—exchanges were widely practiced until Ulysses S. Grant abruptly ended them in the western theater in July 1863. Union Gen. Benjamin F. Butler reported what Grant said to him: "By the exchange of prisoners we get no men fit to go into our army, and every soldier we [give] the Confederates [goes] immediately into theirs, so that the exchange was of much aid to them and none to us."

Since the Confederacy was running out of manpower, Grant's decision had an adverse affect on the South's ability to replenish its armies. That meant fewer men to fight Grant in the coming campaigns. It also meant a death sentence for a large number of Union prisoners who would otherwise have been exchanged.

Grant's order was immediately followed by a directive from Secretary of War Edwin M. Stanton. Furious over the South's refusal to exchange captured African American soldiers, he halted all prisoner exchanges. The South soon realized it could not care for the rapidly growing number of Union prisoners. It offered to exchange prisoners regardless of race or rank. Stanton refused.

With thousands of prisoners jammed into existing prisons, and tens of thousands being added, the Confederacy had to find places to put them. In late November 1863 Brig. Gen. John H. Winder, the chief prison keeper and

Regarding Capt. Henry Wirz, Georgia writer Eliza Frances Andrews wrote, "Had he been an angel from heaven, he could not have changed the pitiful fate of privation and hunger [at Andersonville] unless he had possessed the power to repeat the miracle of the loaves and fishes."

provost marshal for Richmond, was ordered to find a site in Georgia near Americus or Fort Valley, on the Southwestern Railroad—a site isolated from the fighting and out of danger of Union cavalry raids. Winder assigned the task to his thirty-year-old son, Capt. Sidney Winder, a lawyer who had served on his father's staff since 1861.

The young Winder settled on a site near the village of Andersonville Station, which consisted of a post office, two general stores, a blacksmith shop, a Methodist church, a one-room schoolhouse, and about a dozen houses. The Macon train rattled through town twice daily, once each way. The town's leading merchant and land speculator, Ben Dykes, assured Winder that the area residents supported the prison and would gladly hire out their slaves and provide tools and wagons to help build it. He lied. Dykes looked out for himself and no one else. He steered Winder to one of his heavily forested parcels east of the railroad tracks and tried to persuade him to rent it for the stockade. Dykes expected to get rich from the rent and from his sales to prison guards and captives.

There was no water source on the property, so Winder explored a few hundred yards to the south and found a branch of Sweetwater Creek and a large clearing. That land was part of the plantation of the deputy sheriff. Winder leased both properties, believing the combined areas would provide plenty of drinkable water and timber for the stockade.

The *Sumter Republican*, published in nearby Americus, reported a week later that six thousand Yankees were coming. "Trot out your 'Home Guards,'" the paper wrote facetiously.

Winder staked out the stockade's square perimeter, with 750 feet on each side. That should be adequate, he thought, for the anticipated six thousand prisoners. What Winder didn't know was that the prison population would grow to more than thirty thousand.

In what was becoming a Winder family project, General Winder sent one

Brig. Gen. John H. Winder (right) assigned his son, Capt. Sidney Winder, the task of finding a site in Georgia to construct a Confederate prison. General Winder later took command of all prisons east of the Mississippi and established his headquarters at Andersonville. Had he not died from a massive heart attack, he—not Wirz—would probably have been hanged.

of his cousins, Capt. Richard B. Winder, to help construct the outdoor prison. Although subordinate to Sidney, Richard took charge of the operation in December 1863. With his first-hand knowledge of the growing prisoner popu-lation in Richmond, he expanded the layout to an enclosure of seventeen acres—large enough he thought to accommodate ten thousand prisoners.

To build the stockade, Winder needed a labor force, horses, lumber, and other materials. When he received no help from the area residents, he took what he needed by force. Confederate Secretary of War James Seddon author-ized such action. Impressed slave gangs began work on January 10, 1864.

One-man sentry towers were spaced at ninety-foot intervals. Crude la-trines, called sinks, were established near the prison wall and the creek. On the opposite side, the creek was dammed to create a small pool of water for drinking and cooking.

Richard Winder also had to find and store food. But there were no major sources nearby. The Confederate quartermaster general advised him to bake his own bread and round up beef cattle from southern Georgia and northern Florida. Unfortunately, Winder couldn't find more than a handful of men will-ing to make the long cattle drive. Pork was an available alternative, thanks to the herds of wild hogs in south Georgia and the large number of pigs raised by Southern farmers. But these farmers were able to get better prices else-where for their choicest animals. They sold only the poorest sowbelly to Winder. Sowbelly was the fatty underbelly of the hog; it was often rancid.

Corn was another logical food source, but it was hard to come by. Farm-ers who planted corn preferred to boost their profits by converting it to whiskey instead of selling it for food. Cotton took precedence over corn on many farms because of its high demand by blockade-runners and others.

Winder finally found a mill south of Americus that produced cornmeal for animal feed. Not only was it made from the poorest quality of corn, but the corn was combined with the cob and shucks to give it more bulk. At Andersonville it would be baked into cornbread that would torture the intestines of all who ate it.

Back in Richmond, the adjutant general of the Confederate army wanted a Georgian of higher rank than Sidney Winder to be the prison's permanent commander. Col. Alexander W. Persons, a twenty-seven-year-old lawyer from Fort Valley, Georgia, received the nod. He and a hundred soldiers from the Fifty-fifth Georgia arrived in mid-February just ahead of ten thousand prisoners en route to Andersonville.

The first five hundred prisoners shuffled into the half-finished prison stockade on February 24, 1864. It had no barracks, shelters, or sanitary facilities. Rations consisted of raw food. Prisoners literally had to make their own beds, find wood to build fires, and figure out how to cook without pots and pans. The lucky ones brought their own pup tents and utensils; the others had to make them or steal them. Some made small ovens out of the red Georgia clay, spoons from pieces of wood, and dinnerware from old shingles and pieces of tin. Many prisoners ate out of their shoes and caps. For shelter, some made flimsy huts and lean-tos from the logs, branches, and brush left within the prison. Others dug gravelike holes in the flat ground or burrowed out communal caves in the side of creek banks. Richard Winder requested tents, but the quartermaster general didn't have any. Savannah had a stockpile, but officials would not release them to prisons.

Having no facilities for recreation and exercise, prisoners devised their own diversions. Some used their idle time to count and kill lice and fleas. Others assembled for prayer meetings.

Persons panicked at the perilous problems he inherited. Giving himself the easier role, he took responsibility for commanding the troops and courting local citizens. He assigned to Richard Winder the insurmountable challenges of figuring out how to feed, clothe, and shelter the prisoners, while also preventing them from escaping and rioting.

The first death, from pneumonia, occurred on February 27. He was buried in a quickly created cemetery north of the stockade. Within a month, 19 more graves were added. Within fourteen months, 12,920 Union prisoners of war would be buried there, naked, shoulder to shoulder, under less than three feet of dirt.

To handle health problems, General Winder assigned a twenty-five-year-old army surgeon, Isaiah White, to Andersonville. His initial hospital was a single tent with a bed of pine straw. When the first case of smallpox was discovered on March 3, White added an isolated "hospital" of several tents outside the stockade.

White attributed the prison's high mortality rate to "the debilitated condition of many prisoners admitted into the prison, having been confined for a long time in other prisons." He said that "smallpox was introduced by prisoners sent from Richmond." White also cited the horrible position of the hospital inside the stockade, with drainage from the latrines passing through the hospital grounds. Other contributing factors, he wrote, were exposure to the elements, absence of sanitary regulations, overcrowding, and limited and defective rations.

General Winder realized his cousin Richard was overworked at Andersonville and sent another officer to command the "inner" prison—the stockade. That man was Henry Wirz.

Forty-one-year-old Wirz was no Southerner, but he loved the South. Born and educated in Switzerland, he grew up in a German-speaking, middle-class family. Rebellious against his family's Protestant faith, he embraced Catholicism, incurring the wrath of his parents. His personal problems continued with his failed marriage at age twenty-one to a woman several years older. Deeply in debt, the couple argued frequently. After four years of marriage, his pregnant wife left him and took their son and returned to her parents. A year later, Wirz immigrated to America.

Always wanting to be a physician, he became an assistant to German-speaking doctors in Hopkinsville and Louisville, Kentucky, before setting up his own practice in Cadiz, Kentucky. With no licensing required, he became a homeopathic physician—one who cures others by giving them minute doses of substances that cause similar symptoms in healthy persons. Regular physicians resented him because patients preferred his pain-free treatments to their painful practices of drawing blood and applying hot plasters.

Wirz courted a young Methodist widow, Elizabeth Wolfe, who had two daughters by her first marriage. Soon Henry and Elizabeth married and produced a daughter, Cora. Catholics weren't widely accepted in this rough river town, and a mixed marriage between a Kentucky Protestant and a Swiss Catholic with a heavy German accent didn't help Wirz's popularity. Nor did his brusque personality. The couple shortly relocated to Louisiana, a haven for Catholics. Near Milliken's Bend he became a physician to slaves on a plantation, earning about three hundred dollars a year, which was a comfortable income at the time.

When the war began, Wirz enlisted as a Louisiana infantry private. While his unit was guarding Yankee prisoners after First Manassas, he first came into contact with General Winder and apparently made a good impression.

At the battle of Seven Pines on June 1, 1862, Wirz was wounded in the right arm and shoulder, causing permanent painful damage. His wounds never healed. His right arm remained nearly paralyzed for the rest of his life, and he suffered long bouts of depression and frequent fits of violent temper. His wounds and hospitalization brought him back into contact with Winder, who commissioned him as a captain. After a brief assignment in Winder's Richmond office, Wirz was placed in command of a prison in Alabama. His success there, with no charges of mistreatment of prisoners, led to a new assignment—a yearlong secret mission to Europe starting in December 1862. After returning to Richmond in February 1864, he received orders to report to Andersonville. He and his family arrived on March 27, 1864.

Wirz was actually the third officer to command at Andersonville, following Colonel Persons and Capt. Sidney Winder. With a shift in responsi-

The four-foot-high fence on the right side of this photograph of Andersonville prison was called the deadline. Anyone who crossed it was shot. Such deadlines were common in prisons both North and South.

bilities, Wirz was placed in charge of enforcing discipline, preventing escapes, capturing escapees, and maintaining good order. He had nothing to do with food, clothing, shelter, or medical care. Persons, the Winders, and Dr. White handled those tasks.

Wirz's personality suited his role as a disciplinarian. He was harsh, rancorous, and ill natured. Cursing came natural to him. The tormenting pain from his wound probably worsened his disposition. He could be gentle, kind, and compassionate, but few prisoners saw that side of him.

Wirz immediately strengthened security by building a four-foot-high fence inside the stockade. It was ten feet from the exterior wall. This fence—a plank board atop pine posts—was called the "deadline." Wirz ordered sentries to shoot anyone who crossed it. Such deadlines were common in both Southern and Northern prisons.

Wirz also implemented efficient record keeping, including daily roll calls each morning to calculate the day's rations. In addition he supervised two Union prisoners who kept a daily record of men who died in the stockade. These records included their name, regiment, grave number, and cause of death. This record keeping was significant. Although Andersonville had the most deaths of any Confederate prison, it had the lowest percentage of graves marked with "Unknown Union Soldier."

Wirz stopped the practice of prisoners playing "roots." To acquire extra rations, they caused disorder in the chow lines so that others could slip into a different line and respond to the roll call with a sick or dead person's name. Wirz withheld rations until the game ceased.

Prisoners were supposed to receive the same daily rations given to Confederate soldiers. That included either a one-third-pound piece of pork or a one-pound serving of beef and a one-and-a-quarter-pound serving of ground cornmeal. When available, the rations also included sweet potatoes, onions, peas, beans, molasses, and salt. On rare days they actually received such rations. More typical were the daily diets described in diaries of prisoners.

"[Today I got] one-third of a loaf of bread and a piece of bacon about the size of a penny spongecake and one tablespoon of mush."—Eugene Forbes, Fourth New Jersey

"Our ration was a half pint of boiled rice, no meat or bread or meal to go with it. The rice is sour enough to kill the Devil or any other tough cuss."—a Vermont private

"The beans were so wormy and weavel-eaten that it took one of us to skim off the maggots and insects all the time it was boiling."—Pvt. Bjorn Aslaksan, Ninth Minnesota Cavalry

"[Today] we drew rations for the first time in three days. A mixture of coarse cornmeal and swamp water, half cooked, good to give a hog the colic."—David Kennedy, Ohio cavalryman

The cornmeal, which continued to include the cob and shucks, was indigestible and caused severe diarrhea and dysentery, a painful intestinal affliction. So did the bread, which was made partly from husks. Affected prisoners who couldn't make it to the latrines scraped out shallow latrines for immediate use. Heavy rains filled these small latrines, washing the human waste into the creek and the swamp. The stench was so strong that farmers miles away complained about the smell.

Prisoners with money could supplement their meager rations with food purchased from the post's sutler. On some days vegetables, condiments, cakes, and pies were available. Black beans cost forty cents a pint; eggs, fifty cents each; dried peas, a dollar a quart; pork or bacon, six dollars a pound.

While prisoners complained about the shortages of food, clothing, and other basic necessities, the problem wasn't limited to them. Rebel armies didn't fare much better. Thus, prisoners of war were the government's least concern. The South had no textile mills to turn cotton into cloth, and the Union blockade prevented the shipping of cotton to mills outside of the South. Blankets, clothing, and bandages had to be made from existing furnishings, such as tablecloths, bed sheets, rugs, and draperies. Basic building implements—such as hammers, saws, and crowbars—were all imported and could not be replaced because of the blockade.

Texas beef had supplied the army with food and shoes, but the Union's victory at Vicksburg and control of the Mississippi cut off those shipments. Infantries desperately needed shoes, and they fashioned them from old harnesses and rugs. The shipment of food and materials from places where they did exist was complicated by the South's railroad system—five-foot-wide track gauge in some states, four-feet-eight-inches in other states, and a mixture of both in Virginia.

Hoarding and speculation were widespread. Warehouses controlled by war profiteers and cartels of speculators held plenty of leather, soap, coffee, medicines, nails, and salt, the last item badly needed to preserve meat. Making money was more important that winning a war. The problem was aggravated by the failure of state legislatures to do anything about it. They were

Some thirteen thousand prisoners died at Andersonville during the fifteen months it existed. Corpses were placed side by side, naked, in trenches six feet wide.

controlled by the wealthy gentry—people allied with or involved in the scheme of hoarding products to force prices up.

In May 1864—two months after Wirz's arrival—the Confederacy's adjutant and inspector general directed Capt. Walter Bowie to inspect Andersonville. He reported one-fourth of the stockade "altogether unfit" for an encampment, "extremely dirty" clothing and persons, and a "terribly overcrowded hospital." But he did not find fault with Wirz, Dr. White, or the food. "Captain Wirz," he wrote, "is very firm and rigid in regard to the discipline of the prisoners, and at the same time exercised toward them all proper acts of kindness." He praised Wirz's "ability and efficiency" and added: "His activity and zeal in the discharge of his arduous duties is highly commendable."

Another inspector, Maj. Thomas P. Turner, came later that month. He also praised the commandant: "Captain Wirz deserves great credit for the good sense and energy he has displayed in the management of the prison. He is the only man who seems to fully comprehend his important duties. He does the work of commandant, adjutant, clerk, and warden, and without his presence . . . everything would be chaos and confusion; in my opinion, at least two commissioned officers should be assigned to duty to assist him."

Turner recommended Wirz's promotion not only because he deserved it but also because officials who held his present rank refused to obey his orders. Wirz had long complained that his rank hampered him in working with Confederate agencies. Clerks and officials in Richmond and Columbus showed him no respect. They often ignored his requisitions. Wirz had to beg. The system was badly stifled by bureaucratic snafus.

Soon, both of Wirz's superiors were transferred, and General Winder was given command of all Confederate prisons east of the Mississippi, with his headquarters at Andersonville. On June 17, 1864, he assumed command of that post too.

The sixty-five-year-old general was the son of a socially prominent and politically powerful Maryland family. He could be a Southern gentlemen or a relentless despot, depending upon the situation. As supervisor of military police in Richmond he had exercised unbridled authority over prisoners, citizens, and dignitaries. His secret police were drawn from disreputable ruffians. They issued signed passes freely to friends but charged a thousand dollars or more to someone who looked prosperous. The general had many enemies, and they were quick to tell others that he was the son of the general responsible for allowing the British to burn Washington in 1814.

Captain Wirz welcomed Winder, hoping that a general would have enough power and influence to acquire food and supplies. General Winder did all he could—probably more than anyone else—to improve life at Andersonville. He rebuilt the latrines, instilled tighter discipline on the guards, punished those he found guilty of brutality, and improved rations for a while by procuring fresh vegetables from area farmers and cornmeal and meat from Columbus.

Adding to the prisoners' woes were the thieves and marauders among their fellow captives. These rowdy thugs—about five hundred in number—formed gangs consisting of twenty to fifty men. Known as "Raiders," the gangs were named after the men who led them. They targeted newly arrived prisoners who looked prosperous. Gang members befriended them and then, after dark, beat them and robbed them of their jewelry, blankets, and other items of interest.

Pvt. S. O. Lord of the Eleventh Connecticut Infantry wrote: "Thieving was the order of the day. When we lay down at night we would tie our cup and spoon to our arms, and I often felt a pull at my string. None but an old prisoner can realize the value of a cup and spoon."

The prisoners—that is, healthy prisoners with a conscience and moral values—formed self-defense groups for their own safety. One such group, called the "Regulators," sent a delegation to Wirz and requested pistols to arrest the Raiders. Wirz knew better than to give firearms to prisoners, so he concocted a plan to detail his best guards to arrest the Raiders after the Regulators pointed out the rowdies. The Raiders, unfortunately, learned of the plan and prepared to fight. A confrontation turned into a huge brawl, but by the end of the day, more than a hundred Raiders were removed from the stockade and tied to trees near the guards' camp.

Wirz, feeling compelled to punish everyone involved, did not feed them that day. Ironically, the brawl occurred on July 4, 1864. At Wirz's trial a year and a half later, prosecutors argued that Wirz refused to provide meals on July 4 in order to keep the prisoners from celebrating Independence Day—an illustration of the prosecution's deceit in building its case against Wirz.

To punish the Raiders, Wirz created a court-martial board made up of prisoners. He selected another group of prisoners to act as jurors. He allowed the Raiders to choose defense attorneys from the prison population. They chose prison ministers.

All of the accused Raiders were found guilty. Six were sentenced to hang. Wirz turned over the execution to the prisoners. He didn't want his soldiers or himself to be held responsible. The hangings occurred on July 11, 1864.

Pvt. John Warren of a Wisconsin artillery unit wrote that the plan "to overthrow the murderous Raiders" was Wirz's, and "it is certain that the efforts of the [Regulators and the guards] all of whom deserve great credit . . . would have been fruitless but for [Wirz's] cooperation."

Wirz meanwhile acquired captured Federal artillery as his strongest weapons to prevent a mass escape or riot. He used them only twice—to fire blank shots as a warning and to fire an artillery round over the stockade to restore order after part of one wall collapsed during a storm.

Meanwhile, the prison population continued to grow. On July 25, General Winder wrote Adj. Gen. Samuel Cooper: "There are 29,400 prisoners, 2,650 troops, 500 Negroes and other laborers, and not a ration on the post."

A week later the small stockade held more than thirty-two thousand men. Clean water for drinking and washing was scarce, and soap was nonexistent. Wirz reported, "Vinegar and soap, both very important articles, are very seldom issued, as the commissary says he cannot get them."

The small creek provided adequate water for up to six thousand men but could not meet the needs of thirty-two thousand. It also flooded, which turned one-fourth of the grounds within the stockade into a swamp. The location of the guards' camp upstream from the prison contributed to more filth. Ashes, grease, and sewage from the camp ended up in the stream and flowed into the stockade. Those who drank it said their faces swelled to a point where they couldn't see.

One new arrival wrote: "There isn't a hog sty in the North any nastier than this camp. Us boys [shoveled] off the top of the ground, and it was alive with maggots where we lay, and boys say the ground is [like that] all around here."

Wirz hoped to eliminate the swamp by digging drainage ditches, but he was unable to obtain the necessary tools. The poor food and sanitation, the lack of shelter and health care, and the hot Georgia sun all took their toll. Dysentery, scurvy, malaria, and diarrhea reached epidemic levels. By the first of August a prisoner died every five minutes.

"We look about us, and we see skeleton-like faces, drawn lips, and burning eyes of famine and disease," wrote Pvt. J. N. Daniels of New York.

The Confederate government kept a watchful eye on conditions at Andersonville while doing very little for the prison. They sent another inspector in early August, Col. Daniel T. Chandler, who was assisted by Maj. W. Carvel Hall. At the time, prisoners were shoveling dry clay on a portion of the swamp and reconstructing and cleaning out the latrines. Chandler praised Wirz's energy and efforts while calling General Winder, three surgeons, and one staff officer inefficient and incompetent. He criticized nearly everything about the prison—its inadequate size, the lack of barracks, the stream polluted with cookhouse waste, a layout that inhibited attempts to control filth, incompetent doctors, a wholly inadequate hospital with no medicines, insufficient rations and the lack of fresh fruits and vegetables to prevent the deadly scourge of scurvy (which rotted gums, weakened blood, and produced large sores on the body), and an inefficient garrison, of whom 452 had no weapons and 45 percent were sick, absent without leave, under arrest, or detailed for other duty.

To help counter scurvy, Wirz allowed some prisoners to plant small vegetable gardens outside the stockade. While complicating security, the gardening saved lives.

Just when the prisoners thought life couldn't get any worse, the hot, humid summer weather typical of southern Georgia reached temperatures in triple digits. "On the 7th, 8th, and 9th [of August] the weather was so awfully hot [110 in the shade] that it really appeared as if the heat would kill us all," one prisoner wrote in his diary. On August 9, 175 prisoners died, and the mortality in the three days was nearly 500.

When someone died, those around him stripped him of his clothes and possessions. His body was carried to the "dead house" outside the stockade, where stacks of corpses awaited burial in six-foot-wide trenches. Many prisoners were so depressed that they intentionally crossed the deadline, hoping that the guards would shoot them and end their suffering.

Nearly everyone bad-mouthed Wirz and General Winder for the misery. But some blamed the Union government. One prisoner wrote in his diary, "What can the Government be thinking to let their soldiers die in this filthy place!"

Wirz also became ill in August, suffering from high fever and weakness. Others contracted similar illnesses—probably spread by mosquitoes—and many died. Wirz continued to work until his legs failed him, and he required help to mount his horse. Finally General Winder placed him on a train to Augusta for hospital treatment. Wirz returned at the end of the month but was so weak he had to work from a bed in his office.

During Wirz's illness, Winder acquired enough nails and lumber to build three barracks with a roof and floor but no walls. They provided cover for eight hundred men, lying shoulder to shoulder. Thousands still lacked any shelter when the year's worst storm struck late in the afternoon of August 9 and continued for three days. Most prisoners removed their ragged clothing and stood naked to cool off after the intense heat wave and enjoy their first bath in weeks.

On August 12 "we had a chance to look around and see what the storm had done for us," wrote one incarcerated infantryman. "The entire prison, including the swamp, was swept in such a manner as to be quite clean. Almost all the filth and vermin was flushed away." The surge of water and waste also washed out part of the prison wall, and militiamen loped around to fill the gaps and to man the guns around the prison. Winder feared a mass rush to escape, but most prisoners were too weak to attempt it. Some sick prisoners drowned while lying on their beds of straw.

When the sunshine returned, a group of prisoners noticed a trickle of water emerging from the ground. It was a spring. But it was inside the deadline. By tying tin cups to the end of tent poles, prisoners were able to catch cool, pure water for drinking. With Winder's approval, they nailed a couple of boards together and made a trough. It conducted the water into the camp. A guard was posted to prevent a rush on it and to make the prisoners take turns. "It was rightly called Providence Springs," one prisoner wrote, "for it was truly a divine gift." It had appeared out of nowhere at the height of the prison's population—about thirty-three thousand—and it had brought relief when it was most needed.

* * *

With Yankee cavalry raids striking in Alabama and north Florida, and with one-third of Georgia in Union hands, Andersonville-area citizens realized a raid on the prison might release thirty-three thousand Yankee prisoners on their countryside. Quickly, they provided shovels, axes, wagons, and hundreds of slaves to build defensive structures around the prison.

The old general, however, viewed Andersonville as hopeless. Too many prisoners, too little food, too much filth, not enough shelter. The best solution, he said, was to move the prisoners to better locations. Richmond officials approved his suggestion.

This illustration shows Union prisoners of war assembling for rations of bread at Andersonville in August 1864. Such rations were rare. The prison bakery was wholly inadequate for the thirty-two thousand prisoners.

BATTLES AND LEADERS

By the end of November 1864 only 1,359 prisoners remained at Andersonville. But on Christmas Eve 3,500 prisoners were transferred to Andersonville, bringing the total to almost 5,000. Nearly 900 of them died during the winter.

A young woman who arrived by train on January 15 warmed up the camp a bit. Ann Williams claimed to be a refugee from Savannah. She mingled freely with the prisoners, most of whom hadn't seen a woman in months. She had sex with seven of them in one day. One wonders why she would want to be intimate with dirty, stinking, diseased men who were infested with lice, or how these men had the energy to participate or where they could find privacy. When Wirz discovered what was going on, he ordered the woman brought to his office. She said she wasn't a prostitute and took no money for her trysts. Yet her purse was stuffed with considerable cash. The Yankees "are as good as [Southerners]," she boasted as Wirz bristled. He had her escorted to a military base in Florida.

General Winder, as part of his responsibilities for all prisons east of the Mississippi, traveled to Florence, South Carolina, in February. Firmly against cruel and inhumane acts, he wanted to personally discipline three officers charged with mistreating prisoners. Unfortunately for Wirz's future, Winder suffered a massive heart attack and died while walking from the train station to the depot. If Winder had lived, he—not Wirz—probably would have been tried for the horrors at Andersonville. With his death, Wirz became the scapegoat.

After Winder died, Mary Boykin Chesnut, wife of a prominent Confederate leader, wrote: "Well, Winder is safe from the wrath to come. General Mansfield Lovell said that if the Yankees had ever caught Winder, it would have gone hard with him."

Prisoner exchanges resumed in March 1865. By early May, the stockade at Andersonville was deserted, except for 250 prisoners in the hospital. From March to May, the Andersonville prisoners were jammed into boxcars and carried to exchange points, with many of them going to Vicksburg. One large contingent from Andersonville was joined in Vicksburg by a smaller group of prisoners from Cahaba, Alabama. They boarded the river steamer *Sultana* en route to Cairo, Illinois. The boat, carrying more than two thousand men, was considerably overloaded and set at maximum speed. The *Sultana*'s three boilers exploded around two o'clock in the morning, throwing bodies and wreckage into the river. More than fourteen hundred died. It was the greatest maritime disaster in American history, even exceeding the number who would die years later on the *Titanic*. The tragedy may have been an act of terrorism. A strong case has been made that a "coal bomb" was loaded on board the ship and subsequently used to stoke the fires for the boilers.

On May 4, 1865, a small U.S. army detachment commanded by Capt. N. E. Noyes stepped off the train at the Andersonville depot. They found Henry Wirz at his home with his wife and daughters. One of them, ten-year-old Cora, later said that Noyes was warmly received and that he joined the family for dinner. After the meal, Noyes told Wirz that he must return with him to Macon, Georgia. Wirz's wife, Elizabeth, became hysterical, suspecting she would never see her husband again. She was right.

As the detachment boarded a train for Macon the next morning, Wirz handed a letter to Noyes for delivery to Maj. Gen. James H. Wilson, the commanding officer of the Union garrison at Macon. Wirz's letter explained that he was a citizen of Switzerland who wanted to return to Europe as soon as possible. He asserted: "Men who were prisoners [at Andersonville] seem disposed to wreck their vengeance upon me for what they have suffered. . . . [I] was only . . . the tool in the hands of my superiors. . . . The duties I had to perform were arduous and unpleasant, and I am satisfied that no man can or will justly blame me for things that happened here, and which were beyond my power to control." Europe, Wirz surmised, would be his only refuge from the released Andersonville prisoners and other Yankees.

Wilson, uncertain what to do with Wirz, kept him under guard at Macon until May 20. Wilson also was responsible for finding Jefferson Davis, and on May 10, Wilson's troopers cornered the Confederate president near Irwinville, Georgia. Davis and his family were taken to Macon under heavy guard on May 13. Thus, both Wirz and Davis were in Macon at the same time, but there was no communication between them. Wilson then received orders to transport Wirz to Washington. Noyes and a guard detachment escorted him. They took with them all the records found at Andersonville.

Along the way, unruly crowds and drunken mobs frequently harassed Wirz at train stops. At Chattanooga, while in the hands of the U.S. Army provost marshal, he was badly beaten, and his uniform was ripped and soiled. At Nashville, Noyes and his men risked their lives to keep Wirz from being attacked by a mob.

This anger was fueled by articles and illustrations in *Harper's Weekly* about Confederate prisons and Union prisoners. Illustrations of the recently

HARPER'S WEEKLY

This illustration shows the courtroom during Wirz's trial. Wirz, who became ill during the trial, is lying on the couch. He was brought into court on a stretcher.

released prisoners showed emaciated men with swollen limbs or none at all. Former prisoners eagerly told horror stories—sometimes exaggerated—about their lives at Andersonville. Some would say anything to ensure their captors were punished. One escaped prisoner called Wirz a "madman" who maintained discipline by riding around the outside of the stockade each morning followed by a pack of vicious dogs.

Actually, when prisoners escaped (usually by tunneling under the stockade), Wirz asked a local hunter, Benjamin Harris, to put his dogs on the scent. The dogs frequently found their prey, and the escapees were brought staggering back to the prison.

Sgt. Eugene Forbes of the Fourth New Jersey Infantry said that when he walked around the camp, the sight was deplorable: "Some [prisoners] without clothing, some in last agonies of death; others writhing under the pangs of disease or wounds; some as black as mulattos with smoke and dirt."

Another soldier recalled, "Men were literally rotting alive, limbs dropping off with scurvy and other diseases, until death came to their relief."

Northerners were outraged. They demanded revenge. To them, Wirz was "the fiend of Andersonville." He had to die for his alleged sins.

In Washington, Wirz was taken to the Old Capitol Prison, a block from the U.S. Capitol. He would be tried before a military commission three months later.

* * *

Abraham Lincoln had been assassinated on April 15, 1865. Secretary of War Edwin M. Stanton did not share the martyred president's position of "malice toward none." Nor was he interested in binding up the nation's wounds. Stanton wanted Southern leaders punished. He was under pressure to free Jefferson Davis, whom he had kept under heavy guard in a cell so hot and humid that mildew grew on the prisoner's shoes. Stanton hoped that Wirz's defense would be that he was obeying orders from Davis to deliberately murder Union prisoners of war. Then Stanton could use that evidence to prosecute Davis. Instead, Wirz's attorneys, Otis H. Baker and Louis Schade (from the respected Washington law firm of Hughes, Denver, and Peck), chose to argue that Wirz did the best he could with the resources he had; he did not violate any rules of war.

Stanton chose as the chief prosecutor Col. Norton P. Chipman, a twenty-six-year-old Iowa attorney. Maj. Gen. Lew Wallace headed the military commission that would hear the case against Wirz; a few months earlier Wallace had served on the military court that had tried the Lincoln assassination conspirators. The rest of the commission consisted of six generals and three colonels. Several of them had political ambitions in their home states. They knew what Stanton wanted and what their future constituents expected. Politics would take precedence over evidence. Three of them would eventually become governors.

The trial began on August 21, 1865. Wirz was charged with (1) "Maliciously, willfully, and traitorously, combining, confederating, and conspiring" with Gen. John H. Winder, R. R. Stevenson (chief surgeon at Andersonville), Joseph White (the head of the prison hospital), Capt. Sidney Winder (who chose the prison site and laid out the stockade), and "others unknown" to "injure the health and destroy the lives of soldiers . . . then held as prisoners of war . . . so that the armies of the United States might be weakened and impaired; in violation of the laws and customs of war" and with (2) "Murder in violation of the laws and customs of war."

The commission allowed the most absurd hearsay evidence imaginable while rejecting testimony that contradicted the official charges. Prosecutor

Chipman's witnesses from among former prisoners portrayed Wirz as a vulgar and uncaring maniac who was obsessed with strict discipline. Prisoners who held an opposite view were not allowed to testify. One of them, James Madison Page of the Sixth Michigan Cavalry, was so offended by the one-sided testimony that he published a book defending Wirz.

The charge that Wirz brutalized prisoners was ludicrous. All tactics he used were standard procedures in both military and civilian prisons. For example, he punished offenders and escapees by fitting them with a ball and chain, by putting them in stocks under shade trees for several hours, or by placing iron shackles around each leg, with an iron bar between them. Yet witnesses swore that they saw Wirz strike and shoot prisoners in August 1864. That was the month he was away from Andersonville on sick leave.

Dr. C. M. Ford, in charge of the hospital at the Old Capitol Prison, testified that his examination of Wirz's swollen and inflamed arm convinced him that Wirz was "incapable of knocking a man [down] or lifting a very heavy instrument of any kind without doing great injury to his arm."

The real issue before the court was whether Wirz personally murdered Union prisoners of war. He was charged with thirteen counts. Prosecutors said he stomped and jumped on them, beat and shot them with a pistol, released ferocious dogs to attack and kill them, and ordered guards to shoot them.

While a few witnesses named one or two men shot by guards, most witnesses could not name any alleged victim killed by Wirz or the date of the alleged murder. Some said they were repeating camp gossip. Wirz had ordered sentries to shoot anyone who crossed the deadline, and one witness said he saw Wirz order a sentry to fire on a prisoner who was close to the deadline. But no one saw Wirz shoot anybody. They couldn't have because Wirz carried broken revolvers; he used them only to look intimidating.

One witness accused Wirz and/or General Winder of promising guards a thirty-day furlough for killing a Yankee prisoner. But no evidence supported the charge, which, if true, would have produced mass killings.

Of all the charges against Wirz, the most asinine was "conspiracy to murder prisoners of war by allowing the conditions to exist." In a written statement, Wirz pointed out that when he reported for duty on March 27, 1864, the conditions that caused so much death and misery were already in place. He had no hand in creating them and had no power to change them.

Wirz's lawyers produced thirty-two witnesses. One of the most impressive was Father Peter Whelan, a sixty-year-old Catholic priest. He was at the prison from June 16 to early October 1864. Ministering to the men's spiritual needs, he said that no one spoke to him about any personal violence, and he never saw any. The only complaint he heard against Wirz was his use of profanity.

When the prosecution tried to blame Wirz for the gruesome medical problems, they neglected to note that he was not placed in command of the prison hospital until it was too late to do anything about the problem. If the Andersonville authorities couldn't get medical supplies, the problem lay more with the Union than with the Confederacy. The naval blockade of the South had effectively impeded needed supplies from reaching anyone in the South—the Confederate army, civilian noncombatants, *and* Union prisoners.

The prosecution attempted to prove that food, lumber, and other supplies were readily available in the Andersonville area and that Wirz failed to obtain them. If Maj. Gen. William T. Sherman could feed an army of sixty-five thousand during his famous March to the Sea, why couldn't Wirz feed thirty-two thousand prisoners, they asked rhetorically. The simple answer was that Wirz, as a junior officer, didn't have the authority to seize anything from private citizens, and furthermore, he wasn't responsible for securing food, clothing, and shelter. All Wirz could do was complain about the shortages, and his attorneys presented a letter from Wirz to prove he had done so.

The prosecution's primary effort early in the trial was to convince the commission that Jefferson Davis was responsible for the conditions at Andersonville. Prosecutor Chipman presented two reports from Colonel Chandler's inspection of the prison—reports strongly critical of General Winder (but not Wirz) and the conditions inside the stockade. Chandler quoted Winder as saying, "It was better to let half of [the prisoners] die than to take care of them." Chipman was unable to prove that the Confederate president had seen the reports, but he wondered why they were not acted upon quickly. It was probably because of con-

Col. Norton P. Chipman, an Iowa attorney, was named the chief prosecutor at Wirz's military trial by Secretary of War Edwin M. Stanton. Stanton did not share the martyred president's position of "malice toward none" and hoped Wirz's defense would be that he was obeying orders from Jefferson Davis.

fusion in Richmond. General Winder, a close personal friend of Davis, had submitted a counterreport that raised questions about Chandler's motives.

The prosecutors seemed to be finding more evidence against the deceased general than against Wirz. Yet their position was that evidence against one was evidence against both. The general, according to plantation owner Ambrose Spencer, even prohibited a group of local women from delivering several wagons of food, blankets, and clothing they had collected for the prisoners. Spencer said General Winder uttered profanities about Georgia becoming "Yankee" and said he would be damned if he didn't stop it.

Although Wirz became ill during the trial, he was forced to attend each session. He was brought into court on a stretcher.

On October 24, 1865, with twenty-nine defense witnesses waiting to be heard, the Wirz trial came to a sudden end. Wallace ordered the proceedings closed and declared the court had heard enough testimony and would now deliberate.

Nine days later, on November 3, Wallace read the verdict: guilty of one count of conspiracy to commit murder by allowing the conditions at Andersonville to exist and guilty of eleven of thirteen specifications of actual mur-

The execution of Henry Wirz was carried out on November 10, 1865, in the courtyard of the Old Capitol Prison in Washington, D.C. His last words were, "I am innocent, and I will die like a man."

der. He was found not guilty of beating or shooting prisoners with his pistol. The sentence was death by hanging on November 10.

Stanton was obviously pleased. So was the entire North.

During the week between the sentencing and the hanging, Wirz was reportedly approached by War Department officials who offered him a deal. President Andrew Johnson would pardon him if he would testify that Jefferson Davis had ordered the atrocities at Andersonville. Wirz said that there were no such orders, and he wouldn't lie about it. This alleged conversation was reported by the Catholic priest who accompanied Wirz.

In 1901, the U.S. government concluded a massive work (128 volumes) titled the *Official Records of the Union and Confederate Armies in the War of the Rebellion*, commonly referred to as the *Official Records* (OR). Documents contained with the *Official Records* vindicate Wirz and the Winders. Their strongly worded letters to superiors and to Richmond authorities clearly described the horrendous situation at Andersonville and the need for better food and shelters. For example, in a letter to the acting adjutant at Andersonville, Wirz complained bitterly that the cornmeal was unfit to eat and more buckets were an absolute necessity. Without them, he said, the rations of vinegar, rice, beans, and molasses could not be issued to the prisoners.

The *Official Records* also show conclusively that Wirz and Winder were hampered in their efforts to get more and better food by the lack of support from Georgia officials and by the Confederacy's flawed transportation and bureaucracy. There is no evidence in the *Official Records* of any brutality committed by Wirz or other officers. Undisciplined guards did shoot prisoners unnecessarily and were severely reprimanded. Wirz wrote in one report: "The worthlessness of the guard force is on the increase day by day."

Gross mismanagement, the Union blockade, the North's refusal to exchange prisoners, severe shortages of food, medicines, clothing, and tools, transportation problems, local politics, and a poorly trained and undisciplined Confederate guard force were more to blame for the horrors of Andersonville than any deliberate attempt to mistreat prisoners. But these problems did not relieve the South of its obligation to treat prisoners properly. No government, unless degraded and degenerate, should permit the hellish conditions found at Andersonville. "It was horrible," wrote Southerner Eliza Frances Andrews, "and a blot on the fair name of the Confederacy."

If the paucity of resources and the dwindling fortunes of the Confederacy made civilized treatment impossible, then the government should have paroled the prisoners of war held under such conditions. In fact, Wirz proposed such in July 1864. General Winder and the commander of Georgia's reserve corps, Maj. Gen. Howell Cobb, also proposed paroling prisoners in September 1864. The buck stopped with Jefferson Davis. While Stanton and Chipman tried unsuccessfully to prove that the Confederate president ordered the mistreatment of prisoners, they perhaps should have made a case that, by doing nothing, Davis prolonged the suffering and agony at Andersonville.

In 1909, the Georgia Division of the United Daughters of the Confederacy erected a monument to Henry Wirz at Andersonville "to rescue his name from the stigma attached to it by embittered prejudice." It was officially dedicated on May 12 with Wirz's daughter Cora (then Mrs. J. S. Perrin) present. One inscription on the monument states: "Discharging his duty with such humanity as the harsh circumstances of the times, and the policy of the foe permitted, Captain Wirz became at last the victim of a misdirected popular clamor."

Another panel on the monument quotes Ulysses S. Grant, taken from a letter in the *Official Records*: "It is hard on our men held in Southern prisons not to exchange them, but it is humanity to those left in the ranks to fight our battles. At this particular time to release all rebel prisoners . . . would ensure Sherman's defeat and would compromise our safety here. August 18, 1864."

Many historians agree that while Wirz was ill tempered and in some respects incompetent, he was not guilty of the charges against him. They also agree that the testimony presented by the prosecution was in several instances exaggerated or wholly fabricated, and that the trial itself was conducted in an irregular and highly prejudicial manner. But it gave Stanton the results he wanted, and it gave the North the vengeance it demanded. It also made Henry Wirz the scapegoat of Andersonville.

EPILOGUE

THE GOAT AND SCAPEGOAT AWARDS

The Goat Award
For the Worst Performance by a General in a Single Battle or Campaign

Top Ten Nominees (in random order):

1. ***Stonewall Jackson***, CS, Seven Days' campaign (chapter 4): for failure to show up five times, thereby jeopardizing the fate of the Confederate army.
2. ***John Pope***, US, Second Bull Run (chapter 5): for being unprepared and surprised by Robert E. Lee's all-out assault that routed the Union army and for mismanagement of a battle that resulted in 16,054 Union casualties—21 percent of the number engaged.
3. ***Ambrose E. Burnside***, US, Fredericksburg (chapter 6): for poor generalship in losing a battle in which he outnumbered the enemy 106,000 to 75,000 but suffered 12,653 casualties compared to 5,300 for the Confederates.
4. ***Robert E. Lee***, CS, Gettysburg (chapter 8): for disorganized and poorly coordinated troop movements, vague and discretionary directives, and ordering Pickett's Charge, all of which produced a total of 28,063 Confederate casualties.
5. ***Daniel E. Sickles***, US, Gettysburg (chapter 9): for disobeying George Gordon Meade's orders, creating a huge gap in the main Union line by isolating his corps in front of it, and coming perilously close to causing a spectacular disaster, while losing nearly half his own corps (4,200 casualties).
6. ***George Gordon Meade*** and ***Ambrose E. Burnside***, US, the Crater (chapter 11): Meade, for interfering with Burnside's plan at the last minute and not providing supplies and assistance in the mine's excavation.

Burnside, for deciding by lot which division would lead the assault after the explosion, resulting in the army's most incompetent divisional commander being selected and the attack morphing into a fiasco with 5,300 Union casualties.

7. ***Ulysses S. Grant***, US, Cold Harbor (chapter 11): for incredibly poor generalship in ordering a massive assault in which the Confederates, outnumbered nearly two to one, stopped the Yankees cold and inflicted more than 7,000 casualties in a battle that lasted only one hour.

8. ***Gideon Pillow***, CS, Fort Donelson (chapter 12): for ordering a retreat after his Rebel army had broken the Union line and was in a position to escape from the Fort Donelson trap and even to destroy Grant's army, resulting instead in Grant's capturing an entire army of 13,000 men—the largest capture ever made on the continent.

9. ***Braxton Bragg***, CS, Chickamauga and Chattanooga (chapters 14 and 15): for not taking advantage of opportunities to destroy the Army of the Cumberland at Chickamauga after winning decisively and for severely weakening his command at Chattanooga by sending away two large forces—his ablest corps commander with 15,000 troops and an entire division of eleven thousand troops on the eve of battle, resulting in the loss of a major rail center and Grant's capture of more than 6,100 prisoners.

10. ***John Bell Hood***, CS, Spring Hill, Franklin, Nashville (chapter 16): for wasting and wrecking the Confederacy's second most formidable army through foolish frontal assaults on well-entrenched Union troops, mismanagement, tactical incompetence, poor communication, and bad judgment and timing.

My choice for the worst goat of the Civil War is GIDEON PILLOW for his pitiful performance at Fort Donelson.

The Scapegoat Award
For the Worst Injustice to a General in a Single Battle or Campaign

The Four Finalists (in random order):

1. ***Fitz John Porter***, US, Second Bull Run (chapter 5). A victim of the "reign of terror" launched by Radical Republicans to destroy Democratic generals, he was the first army officer to be convicted by general

court-martial since the War of 1812. It took him twenty-three years to clear the record and his name.

2. ***Charles P. Stone***, US, Ball's Bluff and alleged Southern sympathies (chapter 2). He was the victim of shady dealings and dirty politics practiced by Secretary of War Edwin M. Stanton and the Joint Committee on the Conduct of the War. Although never officially charged with any crime, he was placed in solitary confinement in a dungeon for fifty days and then, after protests by a physician, transferred to a prison where he was allowed to exercise under guard. Stone probably would have remained in prison throughout the war had it not been for legislation requiring notification of charges and a trial within a specified time. Officially cleared of any wrongdoing after eighteen months in prison, Stone was later stripped of his commission. With his career destroyed, he left the country for thirteen years.

3. ***Jeb Stuart***, CS, Gettysburg (chapter 8). Southerners and military officials blamed him for the Confederacy's defeat in Pennsylvania. They falsely accused him of depriving Lee of cavalry to do the main army's reconnaissance by taking a joyride around the Union army that made him late for the battle. However, he was following Lee's orders, and he provided Lee with substantial cavalry assistance, which Lee misused. Killed in May 1864 during the Wilderness campaign, Stuart never had much of a chance to defend himself against the charges.

4. ***Henry Wirz***, CS, Andersonville (chapter 17). After Lincoln's assassination, Stanton and the Radical Republicans abandoned the martyred president's "malice toward none" policy and looked for scapegoats. Wirz, who was not responsible for many of the prison's problems and lacked resources to improve conditions, was singled out. He was tried and convicted by a military commission after exaggerated and fabricated testimony in a trial conducted in a highly prejudicial manner. Wirz was hanged.

My choice is CHARLES P. STONE. He suffered what the *New York Times* called "the worst blot on the National side in the history of the war."

Two other awards could be given. The best turnaround from a goat in one battle to a hero in another goes to Joseph Hooker (chapters 7 and 15), who messed up at Chancellorsville but scored a stunning victory at Chattanooga.

And to the general for conducting the best retreat when he could have advanced and won the war, the award goes to GEORGE B. McCLELLAN for the Seven Days' campaign (chapter 4).

The fact that Lee, Jackson, Grant, and Sherman had rare bad days should not detract from their overall magnificence. Their names are forever etched on the tablets listing the great military leaders in the history of the world. To a large extent, their greatness was due to the heroism of subordinates and the valor of men willing to make the ultimate sacrifice. Grant's military career might have ended at Shiloh had it not been for the incredible stand made by Benjamin Prentiss, Stephen Hurlbut, and William H. L. Wallace. At Gettysburg, victory for the Union probably would have been impossible without the alertness of Gouverneur K. Warren and the heroism of John Buford, Winfield Scott Hancock, and Joshua Chamberlain, among others. At Chattanooga, Joseph Hooker carried the supposedly impregnable Rebel fortress at Lookout Mountain, and the remnants of the Army of the Cumberland acted on its own initiative, without orders, and charged up the steep, rocky ridge at Missionary Ridge to clinch the battle and rout the Confederates. Grant received the credit. They were the real heroes.

For the Confederacy, Nathan Bedford Forrest, James Longstreet, Jeb Stuart, and Patrick R. Cleburne made a major difference. Such acts of heroism are covered in this book because goats are best identified in the context of the battles in which they surfaced. Weakness emerges in the midst of greatness.

Goats are present in every war. There will always be plenty of blame to go around . . . unless we follow the advice of Robert Burns: "Oh, would some power the giftie give us / to see ourselves as others see us! It would from many a blunder free us."

President Lincoln put it in perspective when he said: "Neither let us be slandered from our duty by false accusations against us, nor frightened from it by menaces of destruction to the government, nor of dungeons to ourselves. Let us have faith that right makes might; and in that faith let us to the end dare to do our duty as we understand it."

SELECTED SOURCES

Arnold, James R. *Shiloh 1862: The Death of Innocence*. Osprey Military Campaign Series, no. 54. Oxford, England: Osprey, 1998.

Ballard, Ted. *Staff Ride Guide: Battle of Ball's Bluff*. Washington, DC: Center of Military History, 2001.

Banfield, Susan. *The Andersonville Prison Civil War Crimes Trial*. Berkeley Heights, NJ: Enslow Publishers, 2000.

Bigelow, John, Jr. *The Campaign of Chancellorsville*. New Haven: Yale University Press, 1910.

Blackford, W. W. *War Years with Jeb Stuart*. New York: Scribner's, 1945.

Bohannon, Keith S. "One Solid Unbroken Roar of Thunder: Union and Confederate Artillery at the Battle of Malvern Hill." In *The Richmond Campaign of 1862: The Peninsula and the Seven Days*, ed. Gary W. Gallagher, pp. 217–49. Military Campaigns of the Civil War. Chapel Hill: University of North Carolina Press, 2000.

Botkin, B. A., ed. *A Civil War Treasury of Tales, Legends and Folklore*. 1960. Reprint, New York: Promontory Press, 1981.

Bowman, John S., ed. *Who Was Who in the Civil War*. New York: Crescent Books, 1994.

Brooks, Victor. *The Fredericksburg Campaign: October 1862–January 1863*. Great Campaigns of the Civil War Series. Cambridge, MA: Da Capo Press, 2000.

Brooks, William E. *Lee of Virginia: A Biography*. Indianapolis: Bobbs-Merrill, 1932.

Brown, Kent Masterson. *Retreat from Gettysburg*. Chapel Hill: University of North Carolina Press, 2005.

Carpenter, John A. "General O. O. Howard at Gettysburg." *Civil War History*. September 1963.

Cartmell, Donald. *The Civil War Up Close: Thousands of Curious, Obscure, and Fascinating Facts About the War America Could Never Win*. Franklin Lakes, NJ: New Page Books, 2005.

Casdorph, Paul D. *Prince John Magruder: His Life and Campaigns*. New York: Wiley, 1996.

Castel, Albert. *Decision in the West: The Atlanta Campaign of 1864.* Lawrence: University Press of Kansas, 1992.

Chamberlain, Joshua L. *Bayonet Forward: My Civil War Reminiscences.* Gettysburg: Stan Clark Military Books, 1994.

—— and Mark Nesbitt, ed. *Through Blood and Fire: Selected Civil War Papers of Major General Joshua Chamberlain.* Harrisburg, PA: Stackpole, 1996.

Clark, Jacquelyn. "The Vilification of Henry Wirz: Two Creative Nonfiction Approaches to a Controversial Question." Senior Seminar Paper and Thesis. Saratoga Springs, NY: American Studies Program, Skidmore College, 2005–6.

Coddington, Edwin B. *The Gettysburg Campaign: A Study in Command.* New York: Scribner's, 1968.

Connelly, Thomas L. *The Marble Man: Robert E. Lee and His Image in American Society.* 1977. Reprint, Baton Rouge: Louisiana State University Press, 1978.

Cooling, Benjamin Franklin. *Forts Henry and Donelson: The Key to the Confederate Heartland.* Knoxville: University of Tennessee Press, 1987.

Cowley, Robert, ed. *With My Face to the Enemy: Perspectives on the Civil War.* New York: Putnam, 2001.

Cozzens, Peter. *The Battles for Chattanooga.* National Park Civil War Series. Conshohocken, PA: Eastern National, 1996.

——. *General John Pope: A Life for the Nation.* Urbana: University of Illinois Press, 1994.

——. *No Better Place to Die: The Battle of Stones River.* Urbana: University of Illinois Press, 1990.

——. *The Shipwreck of Their Hopes: The Battle for Chattanooga.* Urbana: University of Illinois Press, 1994.

Daniel, Larry J. *Shiloh: The Battle That Changed the Civil War.* New York: Simon and Schuster, 1997.

Davis, William C. *The Battlefields of the Civil War.* London: Salamander Books, 1999.

——. *Breckinridge: Statesman, Soldier, Symbol.* Baton Rouge: Louisiana State University Press, 1974.

Dickson, Keith D. *The Civil War for Dummies.* Hoboken, NJ: Wiley, 2001.

Dowdey, Clifford, and Louise H. Manarin, eds. *The Wartime Papers of R. E. Lee.* New York: Brambal House, 1961.

Dyer, John P. *The Gallant Hood.* Indianapolis: Bobbs-Merrill, 1950.

Eicher, John H., and David J. Eicher. *Civil War High Commands.* Stanford, CA: Stanford University Press, 2001.

Eisenschiml, Otto, and Ralph Newman. *The American Iliad: The Epic Story of the Civil War as Narrated by Eyewitnesses and Contemporaries.* Indianapolis: Bobbs-Merrill, 1947.

Fishel, Edwin C. "Pinkerton and McClellan: Who Deceived Whom?" *Civil War History,* June 1988, 115–42.

Foote, Shelby. *The Civil War: A Narrative.* 3 vols. New York: Random House, 1958–74.

Freeman, Douglas Southall. *Lee's Lieutenants.* New York: Scribner's, 1946.

———. *R. E. Lee: A Biography.* 4 vols. New York: Scribner's, 1934–35.

Furguson, Ernest B. *Chancellorsville 1863: The Souls of the Brave.* New York: Random House, 1993.

Futch, Ovid L. *History of Andersonville Prison.* Gainesville: University of Florida Press, 1968.

Gallagher, Gary W., ed. *The Fredericksburg Campaign: Decision on the Rappahannock.* Chapel Hill: University of North Carolina Press, 1995.

Garrison, Webb. *The Encyclopedia of Civil War Usage.* Nashville: Cumberland House, 2001.

Garrison, Webb, Jr. *Strange Battles of the Civil War.* Nashville: Cumberland House, 2001.

Gibbon, John. *Personal Recollections of the Civil War.* 1928. Reprint, Dayton, OH: Morningside Press, 1978.

Hallock, Judith Lee. *Braxton Bragg and Confederate Defeat,* vol. 2. Tuscaloosa: University of Alabama Press, 1991.

Hassler, Warren W., Jr. *General George G. McClellan: Shield of the Union.* Baton Rouge: Louisiana State University Press, 1957.

Hattaway, Herman. *Reflections of a Civil War Historian: Essays on Leadership, Society, and the Art of War.* Columbia: University of Missouri Press, 2004.

Hillard, G. S. *Life and Campaigns of George B. McClellan, Major-General U.S. Army.* Philadelphia: Lippincott, 1864.

Hoke, Jacob. *The Great Invasion of 1863, or General Lee in Pennsylvania.* Reprint, Gettysburg: Stan Clark Military Books, 1992.

Hooker, Joseph. Testimony. *Report of the Joint Committee on the Conduct of the War, at the Second Session, Thirty-eighth Congress.* Vol. 1. Washington, DC: Government Printing Office, 1865.

Jackson, Thomas J. *Report of Maj. Gen. Thomas J. Jackson, C.S. Army, Peninsular Campaign—Seven Days' Battles.* Richmond: Official Reports, ser. 1, vol. 11/2 [S#13], February 20, 1863.

Johnson, Curt, and Mark McLaughlin. *Civil War Battles.* New York: Fairfax Press, 1981.

Johnson, Robert U., and Clarence C. Buel, eds. *Battles and Leaders of the Civil War.* 4 vols. Reprint, New York: Castle Books, 1956.

Johnson, Swafford. *Great Battles of the Confederacy.* New York: W. H. Smith, 1985.

Keneally, Thomas. *American Scoundrel: The Life of the Notorious Civil War General Dan Sickles*. New York: Doubleday, 2002.

Lee, Robert E. *Report of General Robert E. Lee, C.S. Army, Commanding Army of Northern Virginia, Peninsular Campaign—Seven Days' Battles*. Richmond: Official Reports, ser. 1, vol. 11/2 [S#13], March 6, 1863.

Long, Armistead L. *Memoirs of Robert E. Lee*. 1886. Reprint, Secaucus, NJ: Blue and Grey Press, 1983.

Long, E. B., and Barbara Long. *The Civil War Day by Day: An Almanac*. Garden City, NY: Doubleday, 1971.

Longacre, Edward G. *General Ulysses S. Grant: The Soldier and the Man*. Cambridge, MA: Da Capo Press, 2006.

Longstreet, James. *From Manassas to Appomattox: Memoirs of the Civil War in America*. 1896. Reprint, New York: Mallard Press, 1991.

McDonough, James Lee. *Chattanooga—A Death Grip on the Confederacy*. Knoxville: University of Tennessee Press, 1984.

———. *Shiloh: In Hell Before Night*. Knoxville: University of Tennessee Press, 1977.

McLaws, Lafayette. "The Battle of Gettysburg." *Philadelphia Weekly Press*, April 21, 1886.

———. "The Second Day at Gettysburg: General Sickles Answered by the Commander of the Opposing Force: The Federal Disaster on the Left." *Philadelphia Weekly Press*, August 4, 1886.

McClellan, George B. *McClellan's Own Story*. New York: Webster, 1887.

McPherson, James M. *Battle Cry of Freedom*. New York: Oxford University Press, 2003.

McWhiney, Grady. *Braxton Bragg and Confederate Defeat, vol. 1—Field Command*. New York: Columbia University Press, 1969.

Macartney, Clarence E. *Little Mac: The Life of General George B. McClellan*. Philadelphia: Dorrance, 1940.

Martinez, J. Michael. *Life and Death in Civil War Prisons*. Nashville: Rutledge Hill Press, 2004.

Marvel, William. *Andersonville: The Last Depot*. Chapel Hill: University of North Carolina Press, 1994.

———. *Burnside*. Chapel Hill: University of North Carolina Press, 1991.

Meade, George. *Did General Meade Desire to Retreat at the Battle of Gettysburg?* Philadelphia: Porter & Coates, 1883.

———. *The Life and Letters of George Gordon Meade*. Edited by George G. Meade. 2 vols. New York: Scribner's, 1913.

Miller, Francis T., ed. *Photographic History of the Civil War*. 10 vols. 1911. Reprint, Secaucus, NJ: Blue and Grey Press, 1987.

Morgan, James A., III. *A Little Short of Boats: The Fights at Ball's Bluff and Edward's Ferry, October 21–22, 1861.* Fort Mitchell, KY: Ironclad Publishing, 2004.

Mosby, John S. *The Letters of John S. Mosby.* Richmond: Stuart-Mosby Historical Society, 1986.

———. *Mosby's War Reminiscences, Stuart's Cavalry Campaigns.* New York: Dodd, Mead, & Company, 1898.

Nesbitt, Mark. *Saber & Scapegoat: J.E.B. Stuart and the Gettysburg Controversy.* Mechanicsburg, PA: Stackpole Books, 1994.

Nevin, David. *The Road to Shiloh: Early Battles of the Civil War.* The Civil War. Alexandria, VA: Time-Life, 1983.

Nichols, Edward J. *Toward Gettysburg: A Biography of General John Reynolds.* University Park: Pennsylvania State University Press, 1958.

Nofi, Albert A. *The Gettysburg Campaign, June–July 1863.* Conshohocken, PA: Combined Books, 1993.

Phillips, David, and John C. Wideman. *Chronicles of the Civil War.* New York: Metro-Books, 1999.

Pollard, Edward A. *The Lost Cause.* New York: E. B. Treat & Co., 1867.

Roberts, Edward F. *Andersonville Journey: The Civil War's Greatest Tragedy.* Shippensburg, PA: Burd Street Press, 1998.

Robertson, James I., Jr. *Stonewall Jackson: The Man, the Soldier, the Legend.* New York: Macmillan, 1997.

Robertson, William G. *The Battle of Chickamauga.* National Park Civil War Series. Conshohocken, PA: Eastern National, 1995.

Roland, Charles. *Albert Sidney Johnston: Soldier of Three Republics.* Austin: University of Texas Press, 1964.

Ropes, John Codman. *The Army Under Pope.* Campaigns of the Civil War, vol. 4. 1881. Reprint, Harrisburg, PA: Archive Society, 1992.

Sauers, Richard A. *Gettysburg: The Meade-Sickles Controversy.* Washington, DC: Brassey's, 2003.

Sears, Stephen W. *Controversies and Commanders: Dispatches from the Army of the Potomac.* Boston: Houghton Mifflin, 1999.

———. "The Curious Case of McClellan's Memoirs." *Civil War History,* June 1988, 101–14.

———. *To the Gates of Richmond: The Peninsula Campaign.* New York: Ticknor & Fields, 1992.

Shaara, Jeff. *Jeff Shaara's Civil War Battlefields: Discovering America's Hallowed Ground.* New York: Ballantine Books, 2006.

Smith, Timothy B. "Why Lew Was Late." *Civil War Times,* January 2008, 30–37.

Stackpole, Edward J. *The Battle of Fredericksburg.* 1965. Reprint, Harrisburg, PA: Eastern Acorn Press, 1981.

———. *The Fredericksburg Campaign: Drama on the Rappahannock.* 2nd ed. Harrisburg, PA: Stackpole Books, 1991.

Stone, Charles P. *The Battle of Ball's Bluff: The Report of Brig. Gen. Charles P. Stone.* In OR, ser. 1, vol. 5, 330–32.

———. Letters: Brig. Gen. Charles P. Stone to the Hon. Benjamin F. Wade, March 6, 1863; Brig Gen. Andrew Porter, February 8, 1862; Commanding Officer, Fort Lafayette, February 8, 1862; Brig. Gen. S. Williams, assistant adjutant general, Army of the Potomac, February 9, 1862; Lt. Col. Martin Burke, Fort Hamilton, April 5, 1862; Hon. E. M. Stanton, September 7, 1862; Brig. Gen. L. Thomas, adjutant general, U.S. Army, September 25, 1862; Maj. Gen. George B. McClellan, December 1, 1862.

Sutherland, Daniel E. *The Emergence of Total War.* Civil War Campaigns and Commanders Series. Edited by Grady McWhiney. Forth Worth: Ryan Place Publishers, 1996.

———. *Fredericksburg and Chancellorsville: The Dare Mark Campaign.* Lincoln: University of Nebraska Press, 1998.

Sword, Wiley. *Shiloh: Bloody April.* Dayton, OH: Morningside Press, 1974.

———. *The Confederacy's Last Hurrah: Spring Hill, Franklin, and Nashville.* Modern War Studies. Lawrence: University Press of Kansas, 1992.

Taylor, Walter H. *Four Years with General Lee: Being a Summary of the Most Important Events Touching the Career of General Robert E. Lee in the War Between the States.* New York: Appleton, 1877.

———, and James I. Robertson. *Four Years with General Lee.* Bloomington: Indiana University Press, 1996.

"The Battle of Ball's Bluff." Northern Virginia Regional Park Authority. www.nvrpa .org/ballsbluffbattle.html.

Trial of Henry Wirz, 40th Congress, 2nd Session, House Document 23, Washington, DC, 1868.

Tucker, Glenn. *Chickamauga: Bloody Battle in the West.* Indianapolis: Bobbs-Merrill, 1961.

———. *High Tide at Gettysburg: The Campaign in Pennsylvania.* 1958. Reprint, Dayton, OH: Morningside Press, 1973.

———. *Lee and Longstreet at Gettysburg.* Indianapolis: Bobbs-Merrill, 1968.

Tyler, Dennett, ed. *Lincoln and the Civil War in the Diaries and Letters of John Hay.* New York: Dodd, Mead & Co., 1939.

U.S. Congress. Joint Committee on the Conduct of the War. *The Battle of Ball's Bluff.* 1863. Reprint, Millwood, NY: Kraus, 1977.

U.S. Navy Department. *Official Records of the Union and Confederate Navies in the War of the Rebellion.* 30 vols. Washington, DC: Government Printing Office, 1894–1927.

U.S. War Department. *The War of the Rebellion: A Compilation of the Official Records of the Union and Confederate Armies.* 128 vols. Washington, DC: Government Printing Office, 1880–1901.

Wallace, Lew. *Smoke, Sound, and Fury: The Civil War Memoirs of Major-General Lew Wallace, U.S. Volunteers.* Edited by Jim Leeke. Philadelphia: Polyglot, 2004.

Warner, Ezra. *Generals in Blue.* Baton Rouge: Louisiana State University Press, 1964.

Wiley, Bell I. *The Life of Billy Yank: The Common Soldier of the Union.* Indianapolis: Bobbs-Merrill, 1952.

———. *The Life of Johnny Reb: The Common Soldier of the Confederacy.* Indianapolis: Bobbs-Merrill,1962.

Williams, T. Harry. *Lincoln and His Generals.* New York: Knopf, 1952.

———. *Lincoln and the Radicals.* Madison: University of Wisconsin Press, 1941.

Woodworth, Steven E. *Jefferson Davis and His Generals: The Failure of Confederate Command in the West.* Lawrence: University Press of Kansas, 1990.

———. *Nothing but Victory: The Army of the Tennessee.* New York: Knopf, 2005.

INDEX